String Music
of
Black Composers

STRING MUSIC
OF
BLACK COMPOSERS

A BIBLIOGRAPHY

Compiled by
AARON HORNE

Foreword by Dominique-René de Lerma

Music Reference Collection, Number 33

GREENWOOD PRESS
New York • Westport, Connecticut • London

Library of Congress Cataloging-in-Publication Data

Horne, Aaron.
　　String music of Black composers : a bibliography / compiled by Aaron Horne.
　　　　p.　cm.—(Music reference collection, ISSN 0736-7740 ; no.
　33)
　　Includes index and discography.
　　ISBN 0-313-27938-1 (alk. paper)
　　1. Composers, Black—Bibliography.　2. Composers, Black—
Biography.　3. Music—Bibliography.　　I. Title.　　II. Series.
　ML128.B45H7　1991
　016.787'08996—dc20　　　91-26742

British Library Cataloguing in Publication Data is available.

Library of Congress Catalog Card Number: 91-26742
ISBN: 0-313-27938-1
ISSN: 0736-7740

First published in 1991

Greenwood Press, 88 Post Road West, Westport, CT 06881
An imprint of Greenwood Publishing Group, Inc.

Printed in the United States of America

The paper used in this book complies with the
Permanent Paper Standard issued by the National
Information Standards Organization (Z39.48-1984).

10 9 8 7 6 5 4 3 2 1

Dedicated to
my wife, Myrtle,
and my children, Ericka and Aaron, Jr.

Contents

x   Contents

Foreword

Information on Black musical culture has increasingly become an international priority during the second half of the twentieth century, sometimes as a remedial gesture, sometimes as the goal of a liberated intellect. The search has been a dynamic one, obscured by a popular image advanced by the media which see no conflict between culture and sociology, and which has often attempted to glamorize the ghetto and trivialize the culture, quite ignorant of the heritage.

Against this is the objective historical research conducted by such scholars as Eileen Southern and Samuel A. Floyd, Jr., which has uncovered a past concealed by layers ranging from relatively innocent myopia to overt avoidance, but there is no longer any justification for the alert to remain innocent, even if the missionary task is not completed.

Stringed instruments, for example, are not generally regarded as of any substantial importance in this history. The implicit message of popular media, enhanced by cooperative peer pressures, inhibits interests of embryonic musical talents who might have been stimulated to explore the viola or cello. While a guest speaker in the Caribbean, I saw young adults reject William Dawson's Negro folk symphony only because its performance forces included violins. For ten years, I produced a weekly radio show in Baltimore, addressing a wide variety of topics from Black music history. Shortly after a program on the violin was aired, I received a phone call from a lady who said her son had been ashamed to walk through his neighborhood, violin under his arm, on the way to his lessons. After hearing the broadcast, she said, he knew more about his heritage than did his taunting contemporaries, and he went to those lessons better informed and with pride. The roots of freedom rest not only in a priori philosophical stances, but in history.

And that past includes figures such as the eighteenth-century Chevalier de Saint-Georges (whose works for violin challenge contemporary performers), George Bridgetower (who at age 11 sat in the first violin section of Haydn's London orchestra), José White (who substituted for his professor at the Paris Conservatory), Joseph Douglass (whose grandfather, Frederick, was also a violinist), José Jiménez-Berra and Claudio Brindis de Salas (whose social status permitted concert careers), Clarence Cameron White (one of many from his generation who replaced performance plans with pedagogical activities), Will Marion Cook (who studied with Joseph Joachim). There remain yet the contributions for plectral instruments, ranging from the "historically significant" works of Justin Holland to the compositions of Leo Brouwer.

There have been many violinists whose careers have had a focus on performance, rather than composition. Examples include Sanford Allen (whose award-winning recording of Roque Cordero's violin concerto was issued while he was the only Black musician of the New York Philharmonic) and those violinists whose presence represents at best a duo or trio of Black members in American orchestras or are principally active in education: Joseph Striplin, Booker Rowe, Winterton Garvey, Sylvia Morris, Darwyn Apple, Charlene Clark, Sandra Billingslea, Ron Clark, Roland Isaacs, Gayle Dixon, or Elwyn Adams, as samples.

And we have not even begun to cite those who distinguish themselves outside of "concert music" (not a felicitous term), such as Ray Nance, or those for whom traditional categories are distinctly artificial, such as Leroy Jenkins.

Were our exemplars to include other string artists, we would need to give serious attention to violists Marcus Thompson and Maxine Roach, cellists Anthony Elliott, Kermit Moore, and Eugene Moye, and double bassists Arthur Cunningham, Arthur Davis, George Willington, and Bill Lee.

It is a world which was quite unknown and unsuspected by the professional and lay public alike, who can not much longer excuse their innocence. Explorations into the literature can revive the encore repertoire of Jascha Heifetz with the folkloric settings of Harry Burleigh and Clarence Cameron White, but they can also provide innovations for recitals which include the sonatas and quartets of Saint-Georges, the crossover essays of David Baker, the spiritual settings of Lawrence Brown, and their search might locate works of William Dawson and José Mauricio Nunes-Garcia.

The liberation from stereotypes in other areas gave us Olly Wilson, Kathleen Battle, Ben Holt, Charlie Parker, Talib Hakim, Natalie Hinderas, Anthony Davis, James DePriest, Louise Parker, Antoinette Handy, James Furman, Wynton Marsalis . . . On these shoulders already stand a new generation aspiring for opportunities to evolve their gifts, and there is no reason why we should hesitate to accept this enrichment. The message is certainly eligible for high priority by the pre-college teacher, all of whose students need to be introduced to these composers and performers, rather than figures and idioms ubiquitously encountered.

In a virtuosic flourish of research, initiated with his <u>Woodwind Music of Black Composers</u> (New York: Greenwood Press, 1990), Aaron Horne is providing answers to questions posed with intensifying frequency by performers, educators, and other curious souls who have validly suspected the genius of the race has not been as restricted as we have been led to believe. In any of these volumes appears literature which ranges from the ephemeral to the masterwork, pieces suitable for February excursions as well as subscription series, compositions which reflect the unfettered spectrum of idioms, creations which offer a cultural perspective from four continents and three centuries. The guidelines are now registered for a new dimension of contributions, not just as political gestures or for condescending compromises, but for the invigoration of repertoires and the liberal expansion of audience sensibilities.

Dominique-René de Lerma

Acknowledgments

Included amongst the numerous persons deserving my sincere gratitude for their inspiration and contributions are: Professor Frank T. Greer, retired Director of Bands, Tennessee State University, Dr. Thomas Jefferson Anderson, Tufts University, and Professor Benjamin Butler, Director of Bands at Texas Southern University for their nurturing, advising, and support during my early academic years; Dr. Sam Floyd, Academic Dean and Director of the Center for Black Music Research, Columbia College-Chicago, for suggesting this book, complete use of resources at the Center for Black Music Research, and continued advice and support; Dr. Dominique-Rene de Lerma, Associate Director of the Center for Black Music Research, Columbia College-Chicago, for his advice and use of his unlimited resources about Black Composers; Professor Himie Voxman, Professor and Director Emeritus of the School of Music, University of Iowa for suggesting and advising my initial research of Music by Black Composers; Professor Leon Forrest, Chairperson, African-American Studies, Northwestern University, for his timely advice; Ms. Kathleen E. Bethel, African-American Studies Librarian, Northwestern University, for her advice and assistance concerning available related scholarly materials at Northwestern University and other resource centers throughout the country; Dr. Vincent Oddo, Professor of Music, Northeastern Illinois University, for reading and editing; and Ms. Judith Hardin, Secretary, Department of English, Western Illinois University, for her numerous contributions that made this work possible.

Key to Publishers, Collections, and Manuscripts

AAMOA Press, Minneapolis, MN

Anton J. Benjamin, Werderstrasse 44, Hamburg 13, Germany (AMP)

Alnur Music, P. O. Box 343, Teaneck, NJ

American Composers Alliance, 170 West 74th Street, New York, NY 10023
(212/362-8900)

American Music Center, Inc., 2109 Broadway, Suite 15-79, New York, NY
10023

Associated Music Publishers, Inc., 866 Third Avenue, New York, NY 10023

Atsoc Music Co., c/o Noel DaCosta, 95 West 9th Street, New York, NY

Belwin-Mills, CPP Belwin & Inc., 15800 NW 48th Avenue, Miami, FL 33014

Black Productions, 4500 Lee Road, Suite 227, Cleveland, OH 44128
(212/587-2270)

Bnte-Block Publisher, c/o Associated Music Publishers, Inc.

Boosey & Hawkes. Lawson Blvd., P. O. Box 130, Oceanside, NY 11572

Bourne Co., 1212 Sixth Avenue, New York, NY 10036

Breitkopf & Härtel, Walkmühlstrasse 52, D 6200 Wiesbaden 1, Germany (AMP)

Broadcast Music, Inc., 589 Fifth Avenue, New York, NY 10017

Center for Black Music Research, Columbia College, Chicago, IL

Center for Ethnic Music, Department of Music, Howard University, Washington, DC   20059

Chappell & Co., Inc., 810 7th Avenue, New York, NY   10019

Chester Ltd., J & W, Eagle Court, London ECL, England (M-B)

Church, John, Co. - See Theodore Presser Co.

Composers' Facsimile Edition, 170 West 74th Street, New York, NY   10023

Cunningham Music, Nyack, NY

Ditson, Oliver, Co. - See Theodore Presser Co.

Doorway Music (BMI), 2509 Buchanan Street, Nashville, TN   37208

Edition Fazer, Postbox 260, 00101 Helsinki 10, Finland

Elkan-Vogel Co., 1716 Samson Street, Philadelphia, PA

European American Music Corp., P. O. Box 850, Valley Forge, PA   19482 (215/648-0506)

The Executive Editor, University of Ife Press, University of Ife, Ile-Ife, Nigeria

Fana Music, Box 393, Amherst, ME   01002

Fischer, Carl, Inc., 62 Cooper Square, New York, NY   10003

Fleisher, Edwin A., Music Collection, Free Library of Philadelphia, Philadelphia, PA

Fox, Sam, Publishing Co., RCA Building, Radio City, New York, NY

Frangipani Press, P. O. Box 669, Bloomington, IN   47402 (800/367-4002)

Galaxy Music Corp., 2121 Broadway, New York, NY   10023

General Music Publishing Co., Inc., P. O. Box 67, Hastings-on-Hudson, NY 10706

Harkie-Coovey Music Co., P. O. Box 374, Oxford, OH   45056

Hema Music Corp., 35 Palo Alto Pl., Mt. Vernon, NY

Institute of African Studies, University of Ghana, Legon, Ghana, West Africa

Indiana University Music Library, Bloomington, IN (manuscript)

Lawson-Gould Music Publishers, Inc., 866 Third Avenue, New York, NY   10222

Leeds Music Co., 445 Park Avenue, New York, NY   10019 (MCA)

Library of Congress, Washington, D.C.

Marks Music Corp., 1790 Broadway, New York, NY 10019

MCA Music, 445 Park Avenue, New York, NY 10022

McKinley Publishers, Inc., 797 8th Avenue, New York, NY

Mercury Music Corp. (Theodore Presser, agent)

Mills (see Belwin-Mills)

MJQ Music Inc., 200 West 57th Street, New York, NY 10019

Music Press of Tuskeegee Institute, Tuskeegee, AL

Music Workshop Publications, Chicago, IL

Musica Rara, 2 Great Marlborough Street, London W.1, England

Mutual Music Society (Chappell & Co., agent)

New Music Company (Division of Son-Key, Inc.), P. O. Box 31757, Aurora, CO 80041

New York Public Library, New York, NY

Novello & Co., Ltd., Borough Green, Sevenoaks, Kent, England, OR Box 1811, Trenton, NJ 08607

Oxford University Press, Inc., 200 Madison Avenue, New York, NY 10016

Peer International Corporation, 1740 Broadway, New York, NY 10019

Peer-Southern Concert Music, 810 Seventh Avenue, New York, NY 10019

Peters (C.F.) Corporation, 373 Park Avenue South, New York, NY 10016

Presser, Theodore, Presser Place, Bryn Mawr, PA 19010

Ragtime Society, Weston, Ontario, Canada

Richmond (Ken) Music, 42 Winterset Drive, Rochester, NY 14625

Ricordi, G., & Co., Via Salomone 77, Rome, Italy (B-M) - changed to Franco Colombo Publications, 25 Deshon Drive, Melville, NY 11746 (B-M)

Rodeheaver Hall-Mack Co., 124 North 15th Street, Philadelphia, PA, OR 28 East Jackson Boulevard, Chicago, IL

Rudnor Pub., 33 Riverside Drive, New York, NY

Schirmer, G., Inc., 609 5th Avenue, New York, NY 10017

Schott & Co., Ltd., 48 Great Marlborough Street, London W.1, England (B-M)

Schott's, B., Sohne, Weihergarten 1-9, 65 Mainz, Germany (B-M)

Seesaw Music Co., 2067 Broadway, New York, NY 10023

(SELF) - available from composer

Shawnee Press, Inc., Delaware Water Gap, PA 18327

Sibley Music Library, Eastman School of Music, Rochester, NY

Soper Library, Morgan State University, Baltimore, MD

Southern Music Co., 1100 Broadway, Box 329, San Antonio, TX 78292

Southern Music Publishing Co., Inc., 1740 Broadway, New York, NY 10019

Spratt Music Co., 17 West 60th Street, New York, NY 10023

Summy-Birchard Co. or Clayton F. Summy Co., Evanston, IL 60204

Sweet Jams Music Co., c/o Howard Beldock Javits & Javits, 1340 Avenue of the Americas, New York, NY 10019

Tacoma Public Library, Tacoma, WA

University of Iowa Music Library, Iowa City, IA (manuscript)

Unknown (no information concerning the availability or location of the music)

Verlag Neue Musik, Berlin, Germany

Volkwein Bros., Inc., 117 Sandusky Street, Pittsburgh, PA 15212

WGS Music, 1262 Victoria Avenue, Los Angeles, CA 90019

Walton Music Publishers/Music 70, 170 NE 33rd Street, Fort Lauderdale, FL 33334

Weintraub Music Co., c/o Music Sales Corp., 33 West 60th Street, New York, NY 10023

Witmark & Sons, c/o Warner Bros. Publications, 75 Rockefeller Plaza, New York, NY 10019

World Library of Sacred Music, 2145 Central Parkway, Cincinnati, OH 45214

Biographical Background
and a Bibliography of Composers
of African Ancestry
and Their String Music

African Composers

AKINWOLE, OBATAIYE (n.d.)

Works

    THE ROAD TO FREEDOM - Chorus, soli, narrator, dancers, piano, and orchestra.

Sources

    De Lerma, Dominique-René, ed. AAMOA Reports, 7.2,3 (May/June 1975).

AKPABOT, SAMUEL (1931 -)

    Samuel Akpabot was born October 3, 1931, in Uyo, Southeastern State, Nigeria.

    He attended King's College in Lagos (diploma, 1954); the Royal College of Music in London (Associate, 1959); Trinity College of Music in London (Fellow, 1967); University of Chicago (M.A., 1967); and Michigan State University (Ph.D., 1975).

    Besides lecturing on African music in the United States during the 1970s, he also contributed articles to such scholarly journals as African Music, African Arts, Presence Africaine, and The Black Perspective in Music, wrote an essay for Reflections on Afro-American Music (Kent State UP, 1973), and had a book, Ibibio Music in Nigerian Culture, published by Michigan State UP in 1975.

    At the 1956 Cannes Film Festival, Akpabot received first prize for a commercial jingle for Barclay's Bank of London. He has also won prizes in composition competition.

    His best-known works include Cynthia's Lament (1972); Three Nigerian Dances (1975); Verba Christi (1975); Festival Fanfare (1975); Ofala Festival (1975); Jaja of Opobo (1972); and Three Roads to Tomorrow (1959).

    Akpabot was Senior Music Producer with the Nigerian Broadcasting Corporation in Lagos from 1959-62. Thereafter he taught at the University of Nigeria in Nsukka (1962-64, 1967-70), the University of Ife (1970-73), Michigan State University (1973-75), and the University of Calabar (1975-).

Works

CYNTHIA'S LAMENT - Orchestra. Duration: 7 minutes.

JAJA OF OPOBO (1972) - Operetta with English and Nigerian text.

NIGERIA IN CONFLICT - Orchestra.

OVERTURE FOR A NIGERIAN BALLET, Op. 2 (1960) - Orchestra. Duration: 6 minutes. Publisher: New York, Oxford University Press, 1973 (rental only).

SCENES FROM A NIGERIAN BALLET - Orchestra. Publisher: Oxford Press, 1972.

THREE NIGERIAN DANCES (1975) - String orchestra and percussion. Duration: 9 minutes. Publisher: Oxford University Press.

VERBA CHRISTI (1975) - Cantata for soloist, chorus, narrator, and orchestra. Note: Texts based on Synoptic Gospels and congregational hymns.

Sources

Information submitted by the composer.

Roach, Hildred. Black American Music: Past and Present Vol. II. Miami: Krieger Publishing Company, 1985, pp. 157-58.

Southern, Eileen. Biographical Dictionary of Afro-American and African Musicians. Westport, CT: Greenwood Press, 1982, p. 7.

BALLANTA-TAYLOR, NICHOLAS GEORGE JULIUS (1893 - 19??)

Nicholas George Julius Ballanta-Taylor was born March 14, 1893, in Kissy, near Freetown, Sierra Leone; his date of death is undetermined.

After studying organ as a child, in 1917 he passed the first examination for the B.A. degree in music at the Fourah Bay College in Freetown, an affiliate of Durham College in London. He was unable to travel to London for the final exam, however, so did not obtain his degree. In 1921 an American, Mrs. Caseley-Hayford, arranged for him to study at the Institute of Musical Art in New York City (now Juilliard School of Music), where he received his diploma in 1924. Other patrons included George Foster Peabody, Frank Damrosch (head of the Institute), and Walter Damrosch, conductor of the New York Symphony.

Ballanta-Taylor produced pageants and published articles about African music, and was the first African to stage African pageants in the United States. He received a Guggenheim fellowship which enabled him to collect folksongs in Africa.

Among his works are The Music of Africa, a symphonic work based on African themes which he wrote for his thesis, and the choral composition "Belshazzar's Feast" (1919). He also published Negro Spirituals of St. Helena's Island (New York, 1925).

Works

CANTATA - Chorus and orchestra.

THE MUSIC OF AFRICA - Symphony. NOTE: Thesis project at the Institute of Musical Art in New York (now the Juilliard School of Music).

OVERTURE ON AFRICAN THEMES - Orchestra.

Sources

Carter, Madison H. An Annotated Catalogue of Composers of African Ancestry. New York: Vantage Press, 1986.

Southern, Eileen. Biographical Dictionary of Afro-American and African Musicians. Westport, CT: Greenwood Press, 1982, p. 25.

BEBEY, FRANCIS (1929 -)

Francis Bebey was born in Douala, Cameroon.
He was educated at the Sorbonne in musicology and French literature.
He has written several books and articles, including African Music: A People's Art (Lawrence Hill).
Among his compositions for guitar are The Chant of Ibadan: Black Tears, Black Woman, Christ Was Born in Bomba; other compositions are The Ashanti Doll Is Sleeping, Tingrela, The Meaning of Africa, Fali Orison, Breaths, E Titi Bu (in Duala), and Idira.

Works

BLACK WOMAN - Guitar. Recording: Ocora in France; Compositions for Solo Guitar.

CHRIST WAS BORN IN BOMBA - Guitar. Recording: Ocora in France; Compositions for Solo Guitar.

CONCERT POUR UN VIEUX MASQUE - Guitar. Recording: Philips, France.

GUITARE D'UNE AUTRE RIME - Guitar. Publisher: EMI, France.

THE CHANT OF IBADAN: BLACK TEARS - Guitar. Recording: Ocora in France; Compositions for Solo Guitar.

Sources

Roach, Hildred. Black American Music: Past and Present, Vol. II. Miami: Krieger Publishing Company, 1985, pp. 155-56.

DAFORA HORTON, ASADATA (1889-1965)

Asadata Horton Dafora was born in 1889 in Freetown, Sierra Leone, West Africa, and died in New York City March 4, 1965.
Dafora studied music in Europe. At the same time he taught dance in Germany, sang at La Scala, and toured with a group of African drummers and German female dancers he had trained.

He went to the United States in 1929 and began organizing a troupe of singers, dancers, and drummers. This resulted in the 1934 debut of his folk opera Kykuntor (The Witch Woman), with a mixed cast of Africans and African Americans.

He regularly presented African dance festivals and folk operas in New York over the next thirty years. Among his other well-known works are the dance opera Zunguru and the tribal opera Africa.

Works

AFRICA (1944) - Tribal opera.

KYKUNTOR (THE WITCH WOMAN) - Folk opera.

ZUNGURU (1940) - Dance opera.

Sources

Southern, Eileen. Biographical Dictionary of Afro-American and African Musicians. Westport, CT: Greenwood Press, 1982, p. 92.

EKWUEME, LAZARUS EDWARD NNANYELU (1936 -)

Lazarus Edward Nnanyelu Ekwueme was born January 27, 1936, in Oko, Nigeria.

He studied in Nigeria at the St. John's Anglican School in Oko, the Church Missionary Society Central School in Ekwulawbia (1943-48), and Government College at Umuahia (1948-54); in Great Britain at the University of Durham (B.Mus., 1964), the Royal College of Music in London (M.Mus., 1965); and in the United States at Yale (M.A., Ph.D., 1970). He also earned the Licentiate of Music of degree from Trinity College in London.

His teaching career included tenures at the University of Nigeria at Nsukka (1964-66), the State University of New York at Stony Brook (1970-73), the State University of New York at Oneonta (1973-74), and the University of Nigeria at Lagos (1974-).

He published widely in professional journals such as African Music, Journal of African Studies, and The Black Perspective in Music. He toured as a lecturer and guest choral conductor in Africa and the United States, and in 1977 he was a member of the music committee for the Second World Festival of Black and African Arts held in Lagos, Nigeria.

Among his compositions are Nigerian Rhapsody for strings, Dance for the Black Witches for quintet, and Two Igbo Introits for choir.

Works

FLOW GENTLY SWEET NIGER (1962) - Tone poem for chamber orchestra.

NEGRO RHAPSODY - Strings.

NIGERIAN RHAPSODY - Strings.

A NIGHT IN BETHLEHEM (1963) - A Christmas chamber opera.

PIANO CONCERTINO IN RE (1963) - Piano and chamber orchestra.

PSALM 23 FOR CONTRALTO (OR BARITONE) AND CHAMBER ORCHESTRA (1962)

Sources

Information submitted by the composer.

Roach, Eileen. Black American Music: Past and Present. Miami: Krieger Publishing Company, 1985, p. 163.

Southern, Eileen. Biographical Dictionary of Afro-American and African Musicians. Westport, CT: Greenwood Press, 1982, p. 123.

EL-DABH, HALIM (1921 -)

Halim el-Dabh was born March 4, 1921, in Cairo, Egypt.
El-Dabh attended Sulez Conservatory in Cairo, but went on to Cairo University to earn a degree in agricutural engineering (1945). However, after the critical acceptance of "It is dark and damp on the front" in 1949, he devoted his energies to music. He went to the United States the next year, where he studied with Aaron Copeland and Irving Fine at the Berkshire Festival Center, the New England Conservatory of Music (M.Mus., 1953), Brandeis (MFA, 1954), and the University of New Mexico. Other influences were Allen Barker, Hussein Helmy, Kamal Iskander, Piere Nouri, and Henry Shlala.
Among his best-known works are the opera trilogy Ptah-mose and the Magic Spell: The Osiris Ritual, Anton and the Word, and The Twelve Hours Trip; Unity at the Cross Road; the ballets Clytemnestra, Cleopatra, Black Epic, and Lucifer; and electronic music such as Symphonies in Sonic Vibrations and Leiyla and the Poet.
El-Dabh taught at Haile Selassie University in Ethiopia, Howard University, and Kent State.

Works

AGAMEMNON - Orchestra. Publisher: C. F. Peters.

ANTON AND THE WORLD (1973)

BACCHANALIA - Orchestra. Duration: 5 minutes. Publisher: C. F. Peters.

BLACK EPIC (1968) - Voice, dancers, actors, orchestra.

CITADELLE - Orchestra. 21 movements. Publisher: New York, C.F. Peters Corp., for rental only (Peters Edition, 6348).

CLYTEMNESTRA; BALLET SUITE - Orchestra. Duration: 20 minutes. Publisher: New York, C.F. Peters Corp., for rental only (Peters Edition, 6180).

CONCERTO - Derabucca or timpani and string orchestra.

FANTASIA-TAHMEEL - Timpani and strings. Duration: 6 minutes and 30 seconds. Publisher: New York, C.F. Peters Corp., for rental only (Peters Edition, 6181).

FURIES IN HADES - ballet. Publisher: C. F. Peters.

IPHIGENIA; BALLET SUITE - Orchestra. Duration: 12 minutes. Publisher: New York, C.F. Peters Corp., for rental only (Peters Edition, 6182).

LUCIFER - Ballet. Choreography: Martha Graham. Premiere: 1975, by Rudolf Nureyev and Margot Fonteyn.

ONE MORE GAUDY NIGHT - Ballet. Duration: 20 minutes. Publisher: New York, C.F. Peters Corp., for rental only (Peters Edition, 6349).

OPERA FLIES (1971) - opera.

PIERRE JUSQU' AU CIEL - male voice and orchestra.

PTAH-MOSE AND THE MAGIC SPELL: THE OSIRIS RITUAL (1972) - Trilogy.

SYMPHONIC EPILOGUE - Orchestra.

SYMPHONY NO. 1 - Orchestra.

SYMPHONY NO. 2 - Orchestra.

SYMPHONY NO. 3 - Orchestra. Duration: 25 minutes. Publisher: New York, C.F. Peters Corp., for rental only (Peters Edition, 6235).

TAHMEELA - Soprano, flute, oboe, clarinet, bassoon, horn, viola. Publisher: C.F. Peters.

TAHMEELA FOR DERABUCCA AND STRINGS (1959) - Premiere: 1959, New York Metropolitan Museum, Leopold Stokowski, Conductor.

THE TWELVE HOURS TRIP (1973) - Opera.

THULATHIYA - Viola, oboe, and piano.

TONOGRAPHY (a series of chamber works) (1980) - Orchestra.

UNITY AT THE CROSS ROADS (1978) - Orchestra.

USH KA MASRIYA - Harpsichord and tape.

Sources

Baker's Biographical Dictionary of Musicians, 6th ed. Revised edition by Nicholas Slonimsky. New York: Schirmer Books, 1984.

De Lerma, Dominique-René. AAMOA Reports 7.2,3 (March/June 1975).

De Lerma, Dominique-René. Black Concert and Recital Music: Provisional List. Bloomington, IN: Afro-American Music Opportunities, 1975.

New Grove Dictionary of American Music. New York: Grove's Dictionaries of Music, 1986.

Roach, Hildred. Black American Music: Past and Present. Miami: Krieger Publishing Company, Inc., 1985.

Southern, Eileen. <u>Biographical</u> <u>Dictionary</u> <u>of</u> <u>Afro-American</u> <u>and</u> <u>Afri-</u><u>can</u> <u>Musicians</u>. Westport, CT: Greenwood Press, 1982, pp. 123-24.

EUBA, AKIN (1935 -)

Akin Euba was born April 28, 1935, in Lagos, Nigeria.
He received his musical education at Trinity College of Music in Lon-
don (1952-57), UCLA (BA, 1964; MA 1966), and University of Ghana at Legon
(Ph.D., 1974).
He published widely, including articles in <u>The Journal of the Interna-</u>
<u>tional Folk Music Council</u> and <u>Essays on Music and History in Africa</u>.
He served as organist-choirmaster at the Church of St. James-the-Less
while he was in London. In 1972, <u>Dirges</u>, African poems arranged for sing-
ers, speakers, instrumentalists, and dancers, was premiered at the Munich
Olympics. In 1977 he was chairman of the music committee for the Second
World Festival of Black and African Arts at Lagos, Nigeria, where his <u>Fes-</u>
<u>tac 77 Anthem</u> (text by Margaret Walker) was premiered.
Among his other well-known works are <u>Four Pieces for African Orches-</u>
<u>tra</u>, <u>Scenes from Traditional Life</u>, <u>Six Yoruba Songs</u>, <u>Two Tortoise Folk</u>
<u>Tales in Yoruba</u>, and <u>Black Bethlehem</u>.
Euba was a fellow at Trinity College and a senior lecturer at the
University of Nigeria-Ife.

Works

ABIKU - Orchestra.

ALATANGANA - Ballet.

AMICI - String quartet.

CHAKA (1970) - Soloists, chorus, and orchestra. Text: Leopold Sedar
Senghor.

FOUR PIECES FOR AFRICAN ORCHESTRA (1966)

ICE CUBES - String orchestra.

LEGEND OF OLUROUNBI - Orchestra. Premiere: in the U.S. during the
1966-67 season.

MUSIC - Violin, horn, piano, and percussion.

OLUROUNBI (1967) - symphony orchestra. Premiere: by the Portland
(Maine) Symphony Orchestra, Arthur Bennett Lipkin, Conductor.

STRING QUARTET (1957) - Held by Indiana University Music Library
(M452.E86).

THE WANDERER - Violoncello and piano. Held by Indiana University
(M233.E86 W2).

Sources

Information submitted by the composer.

De Lerma, Dominique-René. Black Concert and Recital Music: Provisional List. Bloomington, IN: Afro-American Music Opportunities,
1975.

Roach, Hildred. Black American Music: Past and Present Vol. II.
Miami: Krieger Publishing Company, 1985.

Southern, Eileen. Biographical Dicstionary of Afro-American and African Musicians. Westport, CT: Greenwood Press, 1982, p. 128.

Uzoigwe, Josua. "Akin Euba, An Introduction to the Life and Music of
a Nigerian Composer." M.A. Thesis, Queen's University at Belfast,
Ireland, 1978.

FIBERESIMA, ADAM (1926 -)

Adam Fiberesima was born in Okrika, Rivers State, Nigeria, in 1926.
He studied at Trinity College of Music in London, where he received a
fellowship in composition.
He served as head of the music department of the Voice of Nigeria in
Lagos.
Among his works are Concertos Nos. 1 and 2 for trumpet, Fantasia Ori-
gin, the opera Opu Jaja and the musical Buluwayo, Music for Brass Band,
four symphonies, Concert Overtunes for orchestra, and Three Ballads.

Works

CONCERTO OVERTUNES - Orchestra.

OPU JAJA - Opera.

SYMPHONY NO. 1 - Orchestra.

SYMPHONY NO. 2 - Orchestra.

SYMPHONY NO. 3 - Orchestra.

SYMPHONY NO. 4 - Orchestra.

Sources

Roach, Hildred. Black American Music: Past and Present, Vol. II.
Miami: Krieger Publishing Co., 1985, p. 157.

KEBEDE, ASHENAFI (1938 -)

Ashenafi Kebede was born in Ethiopia in 1938.
He attended Teacher's Training Institute in Ethiopia, then received
his B.A. from the University of Rochester in 1962, and his M.A. (1969) and
Ph.D. (1971) from Wesleyan University.
His honors include the Diploma of Distinction from the International
Biographical Center, the designation as National Composer of Ethiopia, and
the 1958 nomination for Most Outstanding Ethiopian, which awarded him a
four-year college grant to the United States. He also received the Haile

Selassie I Foundation Grant for Outstanding Achievement in Musical Composition (1967), the Wesleyan Graduate Fellowship (1968), a UNSECO grant, Cana-
dian Music Council Grant, American Council of Learned Societies Travel
Grant (to Germany), a National Endowment for the Humanities grant, and a
Florida Fine Arts Council Grant (1981-82). He has been protocol guest of
governments in Hungary, Bulgaria, and Iran.

He has taught at the graduate school of the City University of New
York, at the New England Conservatory of Music, at Brandeis School of
Music, and at Florida State University School of Music.

He serves as director of the Black Studies Center for Black Culture at
FSU and as executive director of the Florida Arts Council for Afro-American
Affairs. In 1963 he served as founder and administrator of the National
School of Music in Ethiopia; in 1970, he coordinated Programs of World
Music at Queens College in New York; in 1978 he worked as UNESCO Consultant
in Khartoum, Sudan; and he wrote the syllabi of the Institute of Music,
Dance, and Drama for the government of Sudan.

He has written for such journals as Black Perspective in Music, Ethnomusicology, The Musical Quarterly, African Music, Cahiers D'Histoire Mon-
diale, The Ethiopian Observer, and others. He is the author of Roots of
Black Music (Prentice Hall, 1982), and co-author of Ethiopie: Musique De
L'Eglise Copte.

He edited, produced, and recorded the Anthology of the World's Music
(Society of Ethnomusicology, Ethiopia, 1969), and edited and composed the
text for Music of Ethiopia (from the Laura Boulton Collection of Columbia
University, RCA Victor, Canada, 1966). He recorded several of his works on
Pentatonism and Microtonality (International Music, Newton, MA, 1979).

Among his compositions are Soliloquy for Soprano, Japanese Koto, and
Flute; Mot for Two Sopranos; and Koturasia: Pentamelodic Exposition for
Japanese Koto, Clarinet, and Violin.

Works

KOTURASIA: PENTAMELODIC EXPOSITION - Japanese koto, clarinet, and
violin. Written especially for Fusako Yoshida, Master of Koto, who
helped popularize Japanese koto music in New York City and Washington,
D.C. Premiere: 3 March 1974, Colden Auditorium, Queens College, by
Master Yoshida.

Sources

Roach, Hildred. Black American Music: Past and Present Vol. II.
Miami: Krieger Publishing Co., 1985, pp. 159-63.

LADIPO, DURO (1931 -)

Duro Ladipo was born in Oshogbo, Western State, Nigeria, on December
18, 1931.

Born into a musical family, he sang in school choir as a child, and
wrote his first play at the age of 15. Under the influence of Ulli Beier,
who advised him to use historical themes, traditional drumming, and classical Yoruba poetry in his work, he became a pioneer in Nigerian modern theatre.

In 1962 he co-founded the Mbari Mbayo Club for actors and playwrights.
A year later he founded the Duro Ladipo Players, which in time became the
National Theatre of Nigeria.

His best-known folk operas are <u>Oba Kosa</u>, <u>Oba Moro</u>, <u>Oba Waja</u>, <u>Eda</u>, and <u>Moremi</u>.

Works

EDA (1965) - Folk opera.

MOREMI - Folk opera.

OBA KOSA - Folk opera.

OBA MORO - Folk opera.

OBA WAJA - Folk opera.

Sources

Southern, Eileen. <u>Biographical Dictionary of Afro-American and African Musicians</u>. Westport, CT: Greenwood Press, 1982, pp. 235-36.

NKETIA, JOSEPH HANSON KWABENA (1921 -)

Joseph Hanson Kwabena Nketia was born June 22, 1921, in Mampong, Ashanti Region, Ghana.
He received his musical education at the Teaching Training College in Akropong (teacher's certificate, 1940); the School of Oriental and African Studies of London [England] University (certificate in phonetics, 1946); Birkbeck College and Trinity College of Music, London (B.A., 1949); Columbia University and Juilliard School of Music, New York City (1958-59); and Northwestern University, Evanston, Illinois (Ph.D.).
Nketia served as director of the musical ensemble for the Ghana Dance Troupe, and began writing music during his college years at Akropong. He toured widely as a lecturer and workshop consultant, and delivered papers at international gatherings of professional societies. He served as director for the International Society for Music Education (1967-), and was an executive member of the International Music Society (1968-) and a council member of the Society for Ethnomusicology (1968-).
His honors include fellowships from the Rockefeller Foundation (1958-59) and the Ford Foundation (1961), the Cowell Award from the African Music Society (1958), the Grand Medal of Ghana (1968), the Ghana Arts Award (1972), and election to the Ghana Academy of Arts and Sciences and to the Royal Anthropological Institute of Great Britain as an honorary fellow.
He contributed numerous articles to such scholarly journals as <u>African Arts</u>, <u>Africa Reports</u>, <u>Yearbook of the International Folk Music Council</u>, <u>Ethnomusicology</u>, and <u>The Black Perspective in Music</u>. His book-length publications include <u>Funeral Dirges of the Akan People</u> (1955), <u>Folk Songs of Ghana</u> (1962), <u>African Music in Ghana</u> (1962), <u>Drumming in Akan Communities</u> (1963), and <u>The Music of Africa</u> (1974).
Among his best-known compositions are <u>Suite for Flute and Piano</u>; <u>Four Akan Songs</u>; <u>Canzona</u> for flute, oboe, and piano; and <u>Chamber Music in the African Idiom</u>.

Works

CHAMBER MUSIC IN THE AFRICAN IDIOM - Violin and piano with partos.

Sources

Information submitted by the composer.

Roach, Hildred. Black American Music: Past and Present, Vol. II.
Miami: Krieger Publishing Co., 1985, pp. 133-35.

Southern, Eileen. Biographical Dictionary of Afro-American and African Musicians. Westport, CT: Greenwood Press, 1982.

NZEWI, EMEKA MEKI (1938 -)

Emeka Meki Nzewi was born October 21, 1938, at Nnewi, Nigeria.
He studied at the University of Nigeria in Nsukka (B.A., 1965), and at
Queen's University in Belfast, Ireland (Ph.D., 1977), and was influenced
especially by Edna Smith Edet, head of the music department at University
of Nigeria.
He contributed articles to professional journals such as Ibadan,
Conch, African Music, Africa Arts, and The Black Perspective in Music, and
published books, including Two Fists in One Mouth and Drama Scene in
Nigeria. In November 1980 he was one of two Nigerian professors sent to
China on a cultural exchange tour.
He serves on the faculty of the University of Nigeria at Nsukka
(1970-), where he organized an Institute of Theatre Arts called Productions 4-D.
His best-known works are the opera-dramas Ogbunigwe, The Lost Finger
and The Ordeal for Regeneration; the operetta Mystery is Illusion; and a
musical, A Drop of Honey.

Works

THE LOST FINGER (1970) - Opera-drama.

MYSTERY IS ILLUSION (1974) - Operetta.

OGBUNIGWE (1968) - Opera-drama.

THE ORDEAL FOR REGENERATION (1980) - Opera-drama.

SYMPHONIC POEM (1966) - Orchestra.

Sources

African Arts 5 (Winter 1972): 36-68; 5 (Summer 1974): 5.

Southern, Eileen. Biographical Dictionary of Afro-American and African Musicians. Westport, CT: Greenwood Press, 1982.

SOWANDE, OLUFELA ("FELA") (1905 - 1987)

Fela Sowande was born May 29, 1905, in Oyo, Nigeria, and died in 1987.
When he was 7, he began to study music with T.K. Phillips, organist
and choirmaster at the Christ Church in Lagos. He attended the Mission
School and King's College in Lagos, and London University (B. Mus., 1956)

and Trinity College, where he studied with George Oldroyd, George Cunningham, and Edmund Rubbra.

He also studied jazz with Jerry Moore, who had him listen to and learn
the solo styles of Art Tatum, Earl Hines, and Teddy Wilson. During the
mid- to late '30s, he played jazz in London nightclubs, and came into
contact with Fats Waller, Paul Robeson, J. Rosamond Johnson, and Adelaide
Hall, with whom he played from 1938 until the outbreak of World War II.

Among his honors are the MBE (1956); the Member of the Federation of
Nigeria (1964); the Traditional Chieftaincy Award, the Bagbile of Lagos
(1968); a Rockefeller Foundation grant, and an honorary doctorate from the
University of Nigeria at Ife (1972).

Sowande was an active performer during the pre-war years. He toured
the vaudeville circuit as a soloist and performed with The Blackbirds of
1937, conducted a regular radio-broadcast series, recorded, and organized a
jazz group composed of West Indians living in London. He continued active
during the war, beginning a radio series, "West African Music and the Pos-
sibilities of Its Development," in 1940, and serving as Musical Advisor to
the Colonial Film Unit. He began playing his own music in the West London
Mission of the Methodist Church at Kingsway Hall, where he was organist-
choirmaster (1941-50). In 1944 the BBC Symphony Orchestra performed his
Africana.

In 1953 he served as musical director of the Nigerian Broadcasting
Service in Lagos. In 1962 he established the Sowande School of Music at
Nsukka, Nigeria.

Sowande taught at Ibadan University, Nigeria; Howard University (Washington, D.C.); and the University of Pittsburgh.

Among his best-known works are African Suite (1952), A Folk Symphony
(1960), organ settings of African folk songs and Negro spirituals, and art-
song settings of poems by Anthony Granville-Gascoigne.

Works

AFRICAN SUITE (AFRICAN THEMES) - String orchestra. Duration: 14
minutes 17 seconds. Publisher: Chappell, 1950. Recording: London
Symphony Orchestra; Paul Freeman, Conductor; Black Composers Series,
Vol. 7, Columbia M-33433, 1975.

AFRICANA - Orchestra.

FOLK SYMPHONY (NIGERIAN THEMES) - Orchestra. Publisher: Leeds.

NIGERIAN MINIATURES (AN ORCHESTRAL SUITE) - Orchestra. Publisher:
PRS.

Sources

Abdul, Raoul. "Fela Sowande's Seventieth Birthday." In Blacks in
Classical Music. New York: Dodd, Mead & Co., 1977, pp. 32-33.

De Lerma, Dominique-René. "A Concordance of Scores and Recordings of
Music by Black Composers." Black Music Research Journal, December
1984.

Roach, Hildred. Black American Music: Past and Present Vol. II.
Miami: Krieger Publishing Co., 1985.

Southern, Eileen. Biographical Dictionary of Afro-American and African Musicians. Westport, CT: Greenwood Press, 1982.

"Sowande, Fela." The New Grove Dictionary of Music and Musicians, Vol. 17, p. 780.

African American Composers

ADAMS, ALTON AUGUSTUS (1889 -)

Alton Augustus Adams was born November 4, 1889, in St. Thomas, the Virgin Islands.

He took correspondence courses from several universities and received a BMus degree from the University Extension Conservatory of Music, Chicago.

He formed Adams' Juvenile Band in 1910, and from 1918 to 1931 he supervised the music program for the Virgin Islands public schools. He also produced musical radio programs.

He was the editor of the band department of Jacobs' Band Monthly from 1913 to 1917, the Virgin Islands correspondent for the Associated Press, and the author of articles for various music journals, newspapers, and magazines.

His works include the Virgin Islands March, the islands' national anthem.

Works

THE GOVERNOR'S OWN - March. Small orchestra and piano or full orchestra and piano or band. Score at the Library of Congress and in photocopy format at the Center for Black Music Research, Columbia College-Chicago.

Sources

Farr, K. R. "Adams, Alton Augustus." Historical Dictionary of Puerto Rico and the U.S. Virgin Islands. Metuchen, NJ: Latin American Historical Dictionaries No. 9, 1973.

Floyd, Samuel A., Jr. "Alton Augustus Adams." BPIM 1977: 173.

Schlesinger, T. "Alton Adams: A Point of View." All-Ah-Wee 1.3 (1977): 28.

Scores at the Center for Black Music Research, Columbia College, Chicago, Illinois.

Phillipp, Margot Lieth. Die Musikkultur der Jungferninseln. Dissertation in preparation, University of Cologne, Germany.

ADAMS, LESLIE (1932 -)

Leslie Adams was born in Cleveland, Ohio, in 1932.
He received his B.M. from Oberlin Conservatory of Music in 1955 where
he studied with Herbert Elwell and Joseph Woods. He received the M.M. from
California State University in 1967 and the Ph.D. from Ohio State Universi-
ty in 1973. His teachers included Robert Starer, Vittorio Giannini, Leon
Dallin, Marshall Barnes, Edward Mattila, and Marcel Dick.
He has received grants and awards from the Cleveland Foundation, the
Rockefeller Foundation, and the National Endowment for the Arts, and resi-
dencies at Karamu House (Cleveland), Villa Serebelloni (Italy), and Yaddo
Arts Colony (summer 1980 and winter 1983).
Some of his best known works are the opera Blake (1984), The Righteous
Man (cantata in memory of Martin Luther King, Jr.), First Symphony, Cello
Sonata, Organ Prelude and Fugue, Psalm 121, and Dunbar Songs.

Works

ALL THE WAY (1965) - Chamber orchestra. Incidental music to the play
by Tad Mosel, in form of "cues," with improvisation sections. Duration: 25 minutes. Commissioned by Karamu House Theatre, Cleveland,
Ohio. Premiere: 6 April 1965, Arena Theatre, Karamu House, Cleveland, Ohio; Ad hoc Chamber Orchestra, Leslie Adams, Conductor. Reviewed 7 April 1965 by Stan Anderson in Cleveland Press in Cleveland
Plain Dealer.

BLAKE (1984) - Opera. Libretto by Daniel Mayers.

CONCERTO FOR PIANO AND ORCHESTRA (1965) - In three movements. Duration: 23 minutes. Publisher: New York, American Composers Alliance
(1981). Premiere: 7 March 1976, Special Bicentennial Celebration
Concert, Swarthout Recital Hall, University of Kansas, Lawrence, Kansas; Kansas University Symphony Orchestra, George Lawner, Conductor;
Richard Reber, piano.

DUNBAR SONGS (1981) - High soprano or tenor voice and chamber orchestra. Three songs on a text by Paul Lawrence Dunbar. Titles: "The
Lark," "He/She Gave Me a Rose," and "The Valse." Duration: 15
minutes. Commissioned by the Ohio Chamber Orchestra on the occasion
of its Tenth Anniversary. Publisher: New York, American Composers
Alliance (1983). Premiere: 22 November 1981.

FIVE SONGS (on Texts of Edna St.-Vincent Millay) (a.k.a. FIVE MILLAY
SONGS) (1960) - Solo voice--medium--mezzo soprano or baritone, orches-
tra. Titles: "Wild Swans," "Branch by Branch," "For You There Is No
Song," "The Return from Town," "Gone Again Is Summer the Lovely" (or-
chestrated in 1987). Commissioned by Accord Associates, Inc., of
Cleveland, Ohio. Premiere (orchestra version): 24 January 1988,
Accord Community Orchestra, Dwight Oltman, Conductor; Hilda Harris,
mezzo soprano. Reviewed by Robert Finn, 25 January 1988, The Plain
Dealer.

HYMN TO FREEDOM (1989) - In two parts for soprano, tenor, baritone,
and chamber orchestra. Text by Paul Lawrence Dunbar. Title of movements: "When storms arise. . . ." and "Lead, gentle Lord . . ."
Duration: 12 minutes. Commissioned by the Borg-Warner Foundation
through a grant to the Center for Black Music Research, Columbia

College, Chicago, for its 15 member Black Music Repertory Ensemble, Chicago, Illinois. Publisher: New York, American Composers Alliance (1990). Premiere: 13 October 1989, Sheldon Concert Hall, St. Louis Missouri; Bernadine Oliphint, soprano; William Brown, tenor; Donnie Ray Albert, baritone; the Black Music Repertory Ensemble, Michael Morgan, Conductor. Reviewed by John Huxhold in the St. Louis Post-Dispatch, 15 October 1989.

INTERMEZZO (1953) - Violin and piano. In one movement. Duration: 4 minutes. Publisher: New York, American Composers Alliance (1953).

A KISS IN XANADU (1954; orchestration revised, 1973) - Chamber orchestra. Ballet in three scenes. Also performed in concert version. Duration: 40 minutes. Premier: 4 April 1954, Hall Auditorium, Oberlin College, Oberlin, Ohio; with instrumental ensemble, David Daniels, Conductor; Marilyn Adams, choreographer; Richard McPhee, story adapter. Reviewed by William Kennick in The Oberlin Review, 2 April 1954.

THE MEADOWLARK (from DUNBAR SONGS) (1980) - Solo high voice and orchestra. Duration: 5 minutes. Premiere: 28 February 1982, Church of the Intercession, New York, New York; Opera Ebony Orchestra, Margaret Harris, Conductor; Alpha Floyd, soprano. Reviewed by Raoul Abdul in New York Amsterdam News, 13 March 1982. NOTE: This work later became part of Dunbar Songs, for voice and chamber orchestra, and voice and piano.

NIGHT SONG, a.k.a. NIGHT MUSIC (1983) - Flute and harp. In one movement. Duration: 4 minutes. Publisher: New York, American Composers Alliance (1986). Premiere: 22 April 1989, Brooklyn Philharmonic Concert, Brooklyn Academy of Music, Brooklyn, New York; Paula Bing, flute; Stacey G. Shames, harp. Reviewed by Judy Antell in The Newspaper (Brooklyn, NY), 2 June 1989.

ODE TO LIFE (1979; revised 1982) - Orchestra. In one movement. Duration: 12 minutes. Commissioned by the Cuyahoga Community College of Cleveland, Ohio, on the occasion of its 15th Anniversary. Publisher: New York, American Composers Alliance (1986). Premier: 13 April 1979, CCC Metro Campus Auditorium, Cuyahoga Community College, Cleveland, Ohio; Cleveland Civic Orchestra, John Ross, Conductor. Premiere, revised orchestrated version: 23 January 1983, Kleinhaus Music Hall, Buffalo, New York; Buffalo Philharmonic Orchestra, Julius Rudel, Conductor. Reviewed by Herman Trotter in The Buffalo News Publisher, 24 January 1983.

PASTORAL FOR VIOLIN AND PIANO (1952) - In one movement. Duration: 5 minutes. Publisher: New York, American Composers Alliance (1990). Premiere: 2 May 1954, Warner Hall, Oberlin Conservatory of Music, Oberlin, Ohio; Larrie Moore, violin; Richard Fiske, piano. Reviewed by Bill Selmier in The Oberlin Review, 4 May 1953.

THE RIGHTEOUS MAN (CANTATA NO. 1) (CANTATA TO THE MEMORY OF DR. MARTIN LUTHER KING) (1985) - Chorus and orchestra. In four movements, performed individually. Text by Daniel Mayers. Duration: 25 minutes. Commissioned by the Paul Kaye Singers, University of Minnesota. Publisher: Cleveland, Blake Productions (1986). Premiere: 19 January 1986, Northrup Memorial Auditorium, University of Minnesota, Minneapolis, Minnesota; The Paul Kaye Singers and Orchestra, Paul Kaatrud,

Conductor. Reviewed by Michael Anthony in the Star Tribune, 21 January 1986.

ROMANCE (from CONTRASTS FOR PIANO) (1961) - Orchestra. Duration: 3 minutes. Unpublished work.

SIX SONGS (ON TEXTS OF AFRO-AMERICAN POETS) (a.k.a. AFRO-AMERICAN SONGS) (1961) - medium--mezzo soprano or baritone--solo voice and strings. Titles: "Prayer" (Langston Hughes); "Drums of Tragedy" (Langston Hughes); "The Heart of a Woman" (Georgia Douglas Johnson); "Night Song" (Clarissa Scott Delany); "Since You Went Away" (James Weldon Johnson); and "Creole Girle" (L. Morgan Collins). Orchestrated in 1987. Commissioned by Orchestration of Afro-American Songs by Accord Associates, Inc., of Cleveland, Ohio. Publisher: New York, American Composers Alliance (1988). Premiere (orchestrated version): 24 January 1988, Accord Community Orchestra, Dwight Oltman, Conductor; Hilda Harris, mezzo soprano. Reviewed by Robert Finn in The Plain Dealer, 25 January 1988.

SKETCH: "SARABANDE" (1951) - Composition draft for string ensemble; unpublished. Duration: 3 minutes.

SONATA FOR CELLO AND PIANO (1964; completed in 1975) - In three movements. Duration: 23 minutes. Publisher: New York, American Composers Alliance (1981). Premiere of complete version: 8 January 1978, Swarthout Recital Hall, University of Kansas, Lawrence, Kansas; Edward Laut, cello; Leslie Adams, piano.

SONATA FOR VIOLIN AND PIANO (1961) - In three movements. Duration: 15 minutes. Publisher: New York, American Composers Alliance (1982). Premiere: 1 December 1981; Steinway Hall, New York, New York; Hiam Shtrum, violin; Leslie Adams, piano.

SYMPHONY NO. 1 (1979) - Orchestra. In four movements. Duration: 43 minutes. Commissioned by the Graduate Faculty Research Grant, University of Kansas, Lawrence, Kansas. Also supported through a grant from the Cleveland Foundation to Karamu House, Cleveland, Ohio, and in-kind contribution from the Rockefeller Foundation Study and Conference center, Bellagio, Italy. Copying costs of instrumental parts funded through a grant from the National Endowment of the Arts. Publisher: New York, American Composers Alliance (1983).

Sources

Information submitted by the composer.

Fain, Kenneth. "Artists and Their Art: Composers." Cultural Post/ National Endowment for the Arts (May-June 1979).

Finn, Robert. "Slave Rebellion Before Civil War Stirs Work on Opera." Cleveland Plain Dealer (January 1, 1983).

Green-Crocheron, Karen. "Meet Composer Leslie Adams." Galore Magazine [Cleveland, OH] (May 1982).

Holly, Ellistine Perkins, Ed. Biographies of Black Composers and Songwriters. Dubuque, IA: Wm. C. Brown Publishers, 1990.

ALLEN, GILBERT (1907 -)

Gilbert Allen was born in Indianapolis, Indiana, in 1907.
He received his B.A. from University of California at Los Angeles. He
also attended the University of Virginia, the University of Indiana,
Virginia State College, and Juilliard.
He served as conductor, composer and arranger for the Gilbert Allen
Singers, the Wiley College Choir, the Samuel Huston Choir and the Wings
Over Jordan Choir.
He taught at Samuel Huston College (now Huston-Tillotson) in Austin,
Texas, at the Hayden High School in Franklin, Virginia, and at Wiley Col-
lege, were he also served as chairman of music.
He published a book of poetry, Prelude, and contributed regularly to
the Journal and Guide, the Suffolk Herald newspaper, and others.

Works

STEAL AWAY - Opera. Unpublished.

Source

Roach, Hildred. Black American Music: Past and Present, Vol. I.
Miami: Krieger Publishing Co., 1985, p. 175.

ANDERSON, T[HOMAS] J[EFFERSON] (1928 -)

Thomas Jefferson (TJ) Anderson was born August 17, 1928, in Coates-
ville, Pennsylvania.
His mother, a professional musician, began giving him piano lessons
when he was five. More formally, he received a B.Mus. from West Virginia
State College in 1950; the M. Mus. Ed., from Pennsylvania State University
in 1951; and the Ph.D. from University of Iowa in 1958. He also attended
the Cincinnati Conservatory of Music during the summer of 1954, and at the
Aspen School of Music during the summer of 1964.
He has received fellowships and grants from the McDowell Colony (summers 1960-63, 1968), the Copley Foundation (1964), the Fromm Foundation
(1964), the Rockefeller Foundation (1968), the Yaddo Foundation (summers
1970-71), and the National Endowment for the Arts (1976). In 1978, to mark
his fiftieth birthday, "Retrospective Concerts" of his music were held in
Chicago, Illinois, and Cambridge, Massachusetts.
He produced a wide variety of work, including: Classical Symphony
(1961), Squares (1965), Intervals (1970), and Messages, a Creole Fantasy
(1979), all for orchestra; In Memoriam Zach Walker (1968) for band; chamber
works such as Chamber Symphony (1961), Fanfare for Solo Trumpet and Four
Mini Bands (1976), Transitions (1971), Swing Set (1972), and Variations on
a Theme by Alban Berg (1978); a piano solo, "Watermelon," (1971); and vocal
works such as Variations on a Theme by M. B. Tolson (1969), In Memoriam
Malcolm X (1974), Block Songs (1972), Horizon '76 (1976), and Re-Creation
(1978). In 1972 he orchestrated Scott Joplin's score for the opera Tree-
monisha, and 1979 he was commissioned by Indiana University's School of
Music and Office of Afro-American Affairs to write an opera, Soldier Boy,
Soldier (libretto by Leon Forrest).
Anderson spent the years 1969-71 as composer-in-residence with the
Atlanta Symphony. Prior to that he had been a teacher in High Point, North
Carolina (1951-54), and at West Virginia State College (1955-56), Langston
University (1958-63), Tennessee State University (1963-69), and Tufts

University (1972-).   From 1971-72 he was Danforth Visiting Professor at Morehouse College in Atlanta. Currently Anderson is Fletcher Professor of Music, after serving eight years as Chairman of the Department of Music at Tufts University in Medford, Massachusetts.

Works

CHAMBER CONCERTO (REMEMBRANCES)(1988) - Orchestra. Duration: 14 minutes. Commissioned by Cleveland State University. Publisher: American Composers Alliance. Premiere: 15 January 1989, Cleveland, Ohio; Cleveland Chamber Symphony, Edwin London, Music Director.

CHAMBER SYMPHONY (1968) - Orchestra. (one movement) Duration: 12 minutes, 30 seconds. Commissioned by Thor Johnson. Publisher: American Composers Alliance (1969). Premiere: 1969, by the Nashville Symphony, Thor Johnson, Conductor. Recording: Composers Recordings, Inc., SD-258, ca. 1970.

CLASSICAL SYMPHONY (1961) - Orchestra. (three movements) Duration: 14 minutes. Commissioned by Oklahoma City Junior Symphony. Publisher: American Composers Alliance, rental. Premiere: 1961, by the Oklahoma City Junior Symphony, T. Burns Westman, Conductor.

CONCERTO FOR TWO VIOLINS AND CHAMBER ORCHESTRA (1988) - Duration: 13 minutes, 30 seconds. Commissioned by Richard Hunt for Elliott Golub, Nisanne Graff, and Music of the Baroque. Publisher: American Composers Alliance (1988). Premiere: 29 May 1988, studio of Richard Hunt, Chicago, Illinois; Elliot Golub and Nissane Graff, violins, Music of the Baroque, Thomas Wikman, Conductor.

BRIDGING AND BRANCHING - Flute and double bass. Commissioned by Richard Hunt in celebration of his 50th birthday for Joseph Guastafeste. Publisher: German, Bote & Bock, 1987. Premiere: May 1986, studio of Richard Hunt; Lyon Leifer, flute, and Joseph Guastafeste, double bass.

HORIZON '76 (1975) - Soprano and orchestra. Text: Milton Kessler. Duration: 50 minutes. Publisher: American Composers Alliance (1975).

IN MEMORIAM MALCOLM X (1974) - Soprano and orchestra. Text: Robert Hayden. Duration: 10 minutes. Commissioned by Symphony of the New World for Betty Allen. Publisher: American Composers Alliance (1974). Premiere: 1974, Lincoln Center, New York City; by Betty Allen, soprano, Symphony of the New World, Leon Thompson, Conductor.

INTERVALS (1970-71) - Orchestra. Duration: 1 hour. Publisher: American Composers Alliance (1972). Premiere: 1972-73 season, Atlanta Symphony Orchestra, Robert Shaw, Conductor.

INTRODUCTION AND ALLEGRO (1959) - Orchestra. Duration: 8 minutes. Publisher: New York Composers Facsimile Edition. Premiere: 1959, Oklahoma City Symphony Orchestra, Guy Fraser Harrison, Conductor.

IVESIANNA - Violin, cello, and piano. Duration: 13 minutes. Commissioned by The Music School at Rivers. Publisher: New York, American Composers Edition, Inc. Premiere: Weston, Massachusetts, 10 April

1988; Jeana Lee, violin, Dana Feder, violoncello, Jonathan Jao, piano-forte.

MESSAGES, A CREOLE FANTASY (1979) - Orchestra. Duration: 14 minutes. dedication: To the Family of Ila Marshall and David DeWitt Turpeau. Publisher: Carl Fischer, Inc.; rental. Premiere: 3 May 1980, by the Atlanta Symphony Orchestra, Robert Shaw, Conductor.

NEW DANCES (1960) - Orchestra. Duration: 17 minutes. Publisher: American Composers Alliance (1967). Premiere: 1960, by the Oklahoma City Symphony Orchestra, Guy Fraser Harrison, Conductor.

PYKNON OVERTURE (1958) - Orchestra. Note: This work was a part of the composer's Ph.D. dissertation.

SIX PIECES FOR CLARINET AND CHAMBER ORCHESTRA (1962) - Duration: 13 minutes. Publisher: American Composers Alliance (1966). Premiere: 1962, by Earl Thomas, clarinet, Oklahoma City Symphony Orchestra, Guy Fraser Harrison, Conductor.

SOLDIER BOY, SOLDIER (1979) - Opera. Libretto by Leon Forrest.

SPIRITUALS (1979) - Orchestra, jazz quartet, chorus, children's choir, tenor, and narrator. Text: Robert Hayden, Stanley Madeja. Commissioned by Union United Methodist Church, Boston, Massachusetts. Publisher: American Composers Alliance (1979). Premiere: 1982, dedication of the Martin Luther King, Jr., Center for Social Change, Atlanta, Georgia; William Brown, tenor. Atlanta Symphony Orchestra, Robert Shaw, Conductor.

SQUARES: AN ESSAY FOR ORCHESTRA (1965). Duration: 7 minutes, 29 seconds. Commissioned by West Virginia State College in celebration of its 75th anniversary. Publisher: American Composers Alliance (1966). Premiere: 1966, Third Annual Inter-American Festival of the Arts, Chickasha, Oklahoma, by the Oklahoma City Symphony Orchestra, Guy Fraser Harrison, Conductor. Recording: Black Composers Series, vol. 8, Columbia M-33434 (1975).

SYMPHONY IN THREE MOVEMENTS (1963) - Orchestra. Dedication: To the memory of John F. Kennedy. Publisher: American Composers Alliance (1966). Premiere: 1964, Festival of Twentieth-Century Music, by the Oklahoma City Symphony Orchestra, Guy Fraser Harrison, Conductor.

THOMAS JEFFERSON'S ORBITING MINSTRELS AND CONTRABAND (A 21st CENTURY CELEBRATION OF 19th CENTURY FORM) - String quartet, woodwind quintet, jazz sextet, dancer, soprano, computer, visuals, and keyboard synthesizer. Text: Stephen Soreff. Poem: T. J. Anderson III. Spoken Text and Scientific Advisor: Herbert Freeman. Visuals: Stanley Madeja. Sculptures: Richard Hunt. Duration: 1 hour 35 minutes. Publisher: New York, Composers' Facsimile Edition (1984). Premiere: 12 February 1986, Northern Illinois University, DeKalb, Illinois; Steven Squires, Conductor; Lee Cloud, musical coordinator; Diane Ragains, soprano; Danielle Jay, dancer; Geoffrey Madeja, technical director; Herbert Nelson, media consultant; Dennis De Lap, graphic design; Donna Flanagan, production assistant; The Shanghai String Quartet; 12 musicians, 3 technicians.

VARIATIONS ON A THEME BY ALBAN BERG (1977) - Viola and piano. Duration: 12 minutes. Publisher: New York, Composers' Facsimile Edition (1977). premiere: 1977, Cambridge, Massachusetts, Longy School of Music; Marcus Thompson, viola; Seth Carlin, piano.

VARIATIONS ON A THEME BY M. B. TOLSON (1969) - Mezzo-soprano, alto saxophone, trumpet, trombone, violin, violoncello, and piano. Text: after Melvin Beaunorus Tolson (1900-1966). Publisher: New York, Composers' Facsimile Edition (1969). Recording: Nonesuch H-71303 (1974).

VOCALISE (1980) - Violin and harp. Duration: 8 minutes. Commissioned by Richard Hunt for Jacques and Gail Israelivitch. Publisher: New York, Composers' Facsimile Edition (1980). Premiere: 23 November 1980, Jacques Israelivitch, violin; Gail Israelivitch, harp.

WHAT TIME IS IT? - Boys choir and jazz orchestra. Text: T. J. Anderson. Duration: 15 minutes, 30 seconds. Commissioned by ASCAP Foundation and Meet the Composer, Inc. to honor a great American--Harold Arlen. Publisher: New York, American Composers' Edition. Premiere: 1 December 1986, Cooper Union, New York, New York; Harlem Boys Choir and the American Jazz Orchestra, T.J. Anderson, Conductor.

Sources

Information submitted by the composer.

Baker, David N., Lida M. Belt and Horwan C. Hudson. The Black Composer Speaks. Metuchen, NJ: The Scarecrow Press, Inc., 1978.

De Lerma, Dominique-René. Black Music in Our Culture. Kent, OH: The Kent State University Press, 1970, p. 171.

Holly, Ellistine.   Biographies of Black Composers and Songwriters. Dubuque, IA: Wm. C. Brown Publishers, 1990.

Hunt, J. "Conversation with Thomas J. Anderson: Blacks and the Classics." The Black Perspective in Music 1.2 (Fall 1973): 156-65.

Southern, Eileen. "Anderson, T(homas) J(efferson)." In The New Grove Dictionary of Music and Musicians Vol. I, pp. 49-50.

Southern, Eileen. Biographical Dictionary of Afro-American and African Musicians. Westport, CT: Greenwood Press, 1982, pp. 14-15.

Thompson, Bruce A. "Musical Style and Compositional Techniques in Selected Works of T. J. Anderson." Ph.D. dissertation, Indiana University, 1979.

Trythall, Gilbert. "T.J. Anderson." BMI: The Many Worlds of Music (April 1969): 17.

Who's Who Among Black Americans (1975-76).

ANDERSON, WALTER F. (1915 -)

    Walter Anderson was born in Zanesville, Ohio.
    He received his B. Mus. from Oberlin College. He studied with William
Bailey at Capital University, and earned the Fellow's Degree from the American Guild of Organists (AAGO and FAGO).
    His honors include a Bartol Scholarship and an honorary Doctor of
Musical (1979) from the Cleveland Institute of Music.
    He taught at Kentucky State (1939-42) and Western Reserve (1944-46),
then became head of the music department at Antioch College (1946-68).
    He served as project director of the music programs of the National
Endowment for the Arts (1967-78), director of the Karamu House in Cleveland, director of Wilberforce's Concert Artists Series, founder of the
talent contest for the Metropolitan Opera in Cleveland, and advisor and
organizer of the First National Symposium on the Performing and Fine Arts
for Historically Black Colleges and Universities. Most recently he was
appointed Special Assistant to the Deputy Chairman for Public Partnership
at the National Endowment for the Arts.
    In 1950 he composed the D-Day Symphony based on President Roosevelt's
D-Day prayer. Among his other works are Symphonic Variations (Lord, Lord,
Lord); Settings of Spanish Christmas Carols; Concerto for Harmonica and
Orchestra; String Quartet; Carols from Different Countries; and African
Folk Tunes.

Works

    CONCERTO FOR HARMONICA AND ORCHESTRA

    D-DAY SYMPHONY (1950) - Cantata.   Note: Based on President Roose-
    velt's D-Day Prayer.

    STRING QUARTET

    SYMPHONIC VARIATIONS (LORD, LORD, LORD) - Orchestra.

Sources

    Claghorn, Charles Eugene. Biographical Dictionary of American Music.
    New York: Parker Publishing Co., 1973.

    Roach, Hildred. Black American Music: Past and Present, Vol. II.
    Miami: Krieger Publishing Co., 1985, p. 48.

ATKINS, RUSSELL (1926 -)

    Russell Atkins was born February 25, 1926, in Cleveland, Ohio.
    He attended the Cleveland Music School Settlement and the Cleveland
Institute of Music. Among his musical influences were his piano teachers,
beginning at the age of seven with his mother and later including Murray
Adams, J. Harold Brown, Russell and Rowena Jelliffe, and Walter Anderson,
among others.
    He received an honorary doctorate from Cleveland State University in
1976 and a Creative Artists Fellowship from the Ohio Arts Council in 1978.
    He published articles in periodicals such as The Music Review and The
Saturday Review, and specifically discussed his music theory in 1958 in a
pair of articles in Free Lance titled "A Psychovisual Perspective for

'Musical' Composition." His theory of "psychovisualism" exerted wide influence upon avant-garde composers.
    Among his best-known works were four Object-Forms: for violin and
piano (1953), cello and piano (1958), piano (1969), and concerto for piano
and orchestra (1977). Other works included Incidental Music for Riders to
the Sea (1950) and Twenty Spirituals for Piano (1979).

Works

    OBJECT-FORMS (1953) - Violin and piano.

    OBJECT-FORMS (1958) - Violoncello and piano.

    OBJECT-FORM (1977) - Concerto for piano and orchestra.

Sources

    Free Lance 14 (1970). Special Russell Atkins issue.

    Stuckenschmidt, H. H. "Contemporary Techniques in Twentieth-Century
    Music." The Musical Quarterly 49 (1963).

    Southern, Eileen. Biographical Dictionary of Afro-American and Afri-
    can Musicians (Westport, CT: Greenwood Press, 1982), p. 21.

BAIOCCHI, REGINA A. HARRIS (n.d.)

    Regina Baiocchi received her B.M. from Roosevelt University, Chicago,
Illinois. She is an arranger and singer and a member of the Chicago Area
American Women Composers Society. Her unpublished works include: Chase,
Two Piano Etudes, Send Your Gifts, and Father, We Thank Thee.

Works

    STRING QUARTET (1979) - One movement; unpublished.

    TWO ZORA NEALE HURSTON SONGS (1990) - Mezzo-soprano, violoncello, and
    piano. Based on 1928 Hurston essay. Dedicated to Barbara Jean Polk.
    Unpublished.

Sources

    Information submitted by the composer.

    Holly, Ellistine Perkins, ed. Biographies of Black Composers and
    Songwriters. Dubuque, IA: Wm. C. Brown Publishers, 1990.

BAKER, DAVID NATHANIEL (1931 -)

    David Baker was born December 21, 1931, in Indianapolis, Indiana.
    He studied tuba and trombone at Jordan Conservatory in Indianapolis
and attended Indiana University (B. Mus. Ed. 1953; M. Mus. Ed., 1954), the
Berklee School of (Jazz) Music in Boston, and the School of Jazz at Lenox,
Massachusetts. He also studied privately with George Russell and John
Lewis, among others.

In 1959 Baker won the Down Beat Hall of Fame Scholarship Award, in 1962 the Down Beat New Star Award in Trombone, and in 1968 The National Association of Negro Musicians Outstanding Musician Award.   Other honors include nomination for the Pulizter Prize in Music (1973) and a Grammy nomination in 1979.

He contributed articles to Down Beat, Orchestra News, and others, and published several books, including four manuals on Jazz Improvisation (1969-76), four volumes on Techniques of Improvisation (1971), Jazz Styles and Analysis: Trombone (1973), and two volumes on Jazz Improvisation for Stringed Instruments. He is co-author of The Black Composer Speaks and The Humanities Through the Black Experience and a contributor to the 6th edition of Grove's Dictionary of Music and Musicians.

Some of his best known works are Black America: To the Memory of Martin Luther King (1968); The Beatitudes (1968); Levels (nominated for the 1973 Pulizer Prize); Le Chat Qui Perche (1974); Two Improvisations for Orchestra and Jazz Combo (1974); Concerto for Cello and Chamber Orchestra (1975); and Ethnic Variations on a Theme of Paganini (1976).

He has been Professor of Jazz at the Indiana University School of Music since 1966. He also taught at Lincoln University (1956-57) and at Indiana Central College (1963-64); and at Tanglewood, University of Wisconsin, University of Oklahoma, University of Nebraska, University of Pittsburgh, Brigham Young University, Elmhurst College, Rutgers, and Atlanta University.

Works

BAKER'S SHUFFLE (1970) - String orchestra.   Duration: 4 minutes. Publisher: ˙Creative Jazz Composers (1976).

BALLAD (1967) - F horn, alto saxophone, and violoncello. Duration: 7 minutes. Commissioned by and dedicated to Peter Gordon. Premiere: 1967, Indiana University, Bloomington, Indiana; Peter Gordon, horn; James Green, alto saxophone; and Nella Hunkins, violoncello.

BIRDSONG (1984) - Orchestra.

BLACK AMERICA: TO THE MEMORY OF MARTIN LUTHER KING, JR. (1968; has undergone several revisions) - Cantata in four movements for jazz ensemble, narrators, chorus (SATB), soloists, and string orchestra. Texts utilized include: Black Man: White World (Stanley Warren); The Burying Ground (traditional); I Dream a World (Langston Hughes); Sorrow Is the Only Faithful One (Pauli Murray); Now That He Is Safely Dead (Carl Hines); Thou Dost Lay Me in the Dust of Death (Biblical); If We Must Die (Claude McKay). Duration: 45 minutes. Premiere: 1968, Indiana University, Bloomington, Indiana. Note: Broadcast yearly on the anniversary of Dr. King's death by Voice of America.

BLACK-EYED PEAS AND CORNBREAD (1970) - String orchestra. Duration: 4 minutes. Publisher: Creative Jazz Composers, 1976.

BLUE STRINGS (1970) - String orchestra. Duration: 4 minutes. Publisher: Creative Jazz Composers, 1976.

BLUES (1966) - String orchestra. Duration: 5 minutes. Publisher: Creative Jazz Composers, 1976. Note: Adaptation of "Deliver My Soul" from PSALM 22.

BLUES WALTZ (1976) - Violin, violoncello, and piano.

CALYPSO - NOVA NO. 1 (1970) - String orchestra. Duration: 4 minutes. Publisher: Creative Jazz Composer, 1976.

CALYPSO - NOVA NO. 2 (1971) - String orchestra. Duration: 10 minutes. Publisher: Creative Jazz Composers, 1976.

CONCERTO (1986) - Clarinet and orchestra. Three movements. Duration: 35 minutes. Commissioned by: Michael Limoli.

CONCERTO (1987) - Tenor saxophone and chamber orchestra. Commissioned by the Ohio Chamber Orchestra. Premiere; 15 January 1988, Ohio Chamber Orchestra, Ernie Krivda.

CONCERTO (1988) - Alto saxophone and orchestra. Duration: 35-40 minutes. Commissioned by Lee Konitz. Premiere: Spring 1990, Leningrad and Moscow Symphony.

CONCERTO FOR BASS VIOL AND JAZZ BAND (1972) - Bass viol, jazz ensemble, string quartet, and solo violin. Four movements. Duration: 35 minutes. Commissioned by and dedicated to Gary Karr. Premiere: 1973, Indiana University, Bloomington, Indiana; Indiana University Jazz Ensemble, David N. Baker, Conductor; Gary Karr, bass viol.

CONCERTO FOR BRASS QUINTET AND ORCHESTRA (1987)

CONCERTO FOR CELLO AND CHAMBER ORCHESTRA (1975) - Three movements. Duration: 15 minutes. Commissioned by and dedicated to Janos Starker. Publisher: G. Schirmer, rental. Premiere: 1975, Minneapolis, Minnesota; St. Paul Chamber Orchestra, Dennis Russell Davies, Conductor; Janos Starker, cello.

CONCERTO FOR CELLO AND JAZZ BAND (1987)

CONCERTO FOR FLUTE AND JAZZ BAND (1971) - Flute/alto flute, jazz ensemble, and string quartet. Three movements. Duration; 25 minutes. Commissioned by and dedicated to James Pellerite. Premiere: 1971, Indiana University, Bloomington, Indiana; Indiana University Jazz Ensemble, David N. Baker, Conductor; James Pellerite, flute.

CONCERTO FOR FOURS (1980) - Solo quartet (flute, cello, tuba, contrabass), tuba quartet, contrabass quartet, percussion quartet.

CONCERTO FOR SAXOPHONE AND CHAMBER ORCHESTRA (1987)

CONCERTO FOR TROMBONE, JAZZ BAND, AND CHAMBER ORCHESTRA (1972) - Four movements. Duration: 35 minutes. Commissioned by and dedicated to Thomas Beversdorf. Premiere: 1973, Indiana University, Bloomington, Indiana; Indiana University Jazz Ensemble, David N. Baker, Conductor; Thomas Beversdorf, trombone.

CONCERTO FOR TRUMPET, ORCHESTRA, AND JAZZ BAND - Commissioned by and dedicated to Dominic Spera.

CONCERTO FOR TRUMPET, STRING ORCHESTRA, AND JAZZ BAND

CONCERTO FOR TWO PIANOS, JAZZ BAND, CHAMBER ORCHESTRA, AND PERCUSSION (1976) - Four movements. Duration: 13 minutes. Commissioned by and dedicated to: Charles Webb and Wallace Hornibrook. Premiere: Fall 1977, Indiana University, Bloomington, Indiana; Indiana University Jazz Ensemble, David N. Baker, Conductor; Charles Webb and Wallace Hornibrook, pianists.

CONCERTO FOR VIOLIN AND JAZZ BAND (1969)

CONTRASTS (1976) - Violin, violoncello, and piano. Four movements: 1. Passacaglia; 2. A Song; 3. Episodes (CEI/CCP); 4. Kaleidoscope. Duration: 32 minutes. Commissioned by the Western Arts Trio. Premiere: 1976, University of Wyoming, Laramie, Wyoming; the Western Arts Trio.

DELIVER MY SOUL (1966) - Chorus (SATB), narrators, jazz ensemble, string orchestra, and dancers.

DELIVER MY SOUL (1968) - Violin and piano. Duration: 5 minutes. Premiere: 1968, Indianapolis Museum of Art; David Collins, violin; John Gates, piano. Note: Adaptation of "Deliver My Soul" from PSALM 22.

THE DUDE (1962) - Violin and piano.

DUO (1988) - Clarinet and violoncello. Three movements. Commissioned by Ronen Chamber Ensemble. Premiere: 25 October 1988; David Bellman and Ingrid Fischer-Bellman.

ELECTRIC STERE-OPTICON (1975)- Violoncello and electronic instruments. Duration: 30 minutes. Commissioned by and dedicated to J. B. Floyd.

ELLINGTONES: A FANTASY FOR SAXOPHONE AND ORCHESTRA (1987) - Commissioned by the New York Philharmonic. Premiere: 4, 5, and 6 June 1987, Avery Fischer Hall, New York City; New York Philharmonic and Dexter Gordon.

ELLINGTONES (extended version, 1988) - Premiere: 1988, Tokoyo Symphony and Dexter Gordon. Recording; Released in spring 1990.

ETHINC VARIATIONS ON A THEME OF PAGANINI (1976) - Violin and piano. Theme and nine variations. Duration: 9 minutes. Commissioned by and dedicated to Ruggerio Ricci. Recording: By Ruggerio Ricci for Vox, 1976. Note: Based on Paganini's 24th Caprice.

EVENING SONG (1970) - String orchestra. Duration: 4 minutes. Publisher: Creative Jazz Composers, 1976.

AN EVENING THOUGHT - String orchestra.

FANTASY (1954) - Soprano, brass ensemble, and harp. Text by Albert Cobine. Duration: 5 minutes.

FIRST DAY OF SPRING (1969) - String orchestra. Duration: 5 minutes. Publisher: Creative Jazz Composers, 1976.

GIVE AND TAKE (1975) - Soprano and chamber ensemble (flute/alto flute, oboe/English horn. viola, violoncello, and percussion). Six movements: 1. The Branch of a Green Tree; 2. The Gift; 3. The Funeral Is All; 4. They Will Not Tell; 5. An Almost Death; 6. Canonization II. Text by Terence Diggory. Duration: 15 minutes. Commissioned by and dedicated to Edith Diggory. Premiere: 1975, Bloomington, Indiana; Edith Diggory, soprano; David N. Baker, conductor.

GUADELOUPE-CALYPSO (1974) - Orchestra, soprano, and jazz quartet.

HARLEM PIPES (1973) - Orchestra and jazz trio.

I WILL TELL THY NAME (1966) - Chorus (SATB), narrators, jazz ensemble, string orcehstra, and dancers. See PSALM 22.

IMPROVISATION #1 FOR UNACCOMPANIED VIOLIN (1975) - Duration: 4 minutes. Commissioned by and dedicated to Ruggiero Ricci.

IMPROVISATION #2 FOR UNACCOMPANIED VIOLIN (1975) - Duration: 5 minutes. Commissioned by and dedicated to Ruggiero Rucci.

THE JAMAICAN STRUT - String orchestra.

JAZZ SUITE FOR VIOLIN AND PIANO (1979)

JEANNE MARIE AT THE PICTURE SHOW (1982) - Orchestra.

KALEIDOSCOPE (1968) - Jazz ensemble, narrators, chorus (SATB), soloist, and string orchestra. See BLACK AMERICA.

KOSBRO (1973; revised 1975) - Orchestra. Duration: 13 minutes. Commissioned by and dedicated to Paul Freeman. Publisher: Associated Music, 1975. Premiere: 1974; Houston Symphony, Paul Freeman, Conductor.

LEVELS: A CONCERTO FOR SOLO CONTRABASS, JAZZ BAND, FLUTE QUARTET, HORN QUARTET, AND STRING QUARTET (1973) - Three Movements. Commissioned by and dedicated to Bertram Turetzky. Premiere: 1973, Claremont Music Festival, Claremont, California; David N. Baker, Conductor; Bertram Turetzky, contrabass. Note: This work was nominated for the Pulizter Prize in 1973.

LIMA BEBA SAMBA - Orchestra.

LITTLE PRICE WALTZ (1959) - String orchestra. Duration: 3 minutes 30 seconds. Publisher: Creative Jazz Composer, 1976.

MALCOLM - Opera. Libretto by Mari Evans. Based on the life of Malcolm X.

MOD WALTZ (1970) - String orchestra. Duration: 4 minutes. Publisher: Creative Jazz Composers, 1976.

PASTORALE (1959) - String quartet. Duration: 5 minutes. Publisher: Fema Music Publications (Interlochen Series), 1975.

PIECE FOR VIOLONCELLO AND PIANO (1966) - Duration: 10 minutes.

PSALM 22 (1966) - A modern jazz oratorio for chorus (SATB), narrators, jazz ensemble, string orchestra, and dancers.   Biblical text.   17 parts: 1. Prelude; 2. My God, My God; 3. Yet Thou Art Holy; 4. But I Am a Worm; 5. Narration; 6. I Am Poured Out Like Water; 7. Thou Dost Lay Me in the Dust of Death; 8. Narration; 9. Deliver My Soul; 10. Pastorale; 11. I Will Tell of Thy Name; 12. Yea, to Him Shall All the Proud of the Earth Bow Down; 13. All the Ends of the Earth Shall Remember; 14. Narration; 15. Praise Him, Praise Him; 16. Men Shall Tell of the Lord; 17. Finale.   Duration: 60 minutes.   Commissioned by Christian Theological Seminary.   Premiere: 1966, Christian Theological Seminar, Indianapolis, Indiana.

QUINTET FOR JAZZ VIOLIN AND STRING ORCHESTRA (1987)

REFLECTION ON A SUMMER - Cello choir.

REFLECTIONS (1969) - Jazz ensemble and orchestra.   Duration: 20 minutes.   Comissioned by the Indianapolis Arts Council for the Indianapolis Summer Symphony.   Premiere: 1969; Indianapolist Summer Symphony.   Note: A.k.a. MY INDIANAPOLIS.

RELIGION (1972) - Soprano and string quartet.   See SONG OF THE NIGHT.

ROOTS (1976) - Violin, cello, and piano.

SANGRE NEGRO (1974) - Orchestra and jazz trio.   See TWO IMPROVISATIONS FOR ORCHESTRA AND JAZZ COMBO.

SINGER OF SONGS, WEAVER OF DREAMS (1980) - Violoncello and solo percussion.

SLOW GROVE (1970) - String orchestra. Duration: 4 minutes. Publisher: Creative Jazz Composers, 1976.

SOMBER TIME (1970) - String orchestra.   Duration: 3 minutes.   Publisher: Creative Jazz Composers, 1976.

SOME NOT SO PLAIN OL' BLUES (1990) - String quartet.

SONATA FOR FRENCH HORN AND STRING QUARTET

SONATA FOR JAZZ VIOLIN AND STRING QUARTET

SONATA FOR PIANO AND STRING QUINTET (1971) - Four movements. Duration: 38 minutes. Commisioned by and dedicated to Helen Freire. Publisher: AAMOA Press. Premiere: 1972, Indiana University, Bloomington, Indiana; Helena Freire, piano. Recording: Helena Freire, pianist (AAMOA NS-7401).

SONATA FOR TUBA AND STRING QUARTET (1971) - Four movements. Duration: 20 minutes. Commissioned by and dedicated to Harvey Phillips. Recording: Harvey Phillips, tuba, and the Composers String Quartet (Golden Crest CRS-4122).

SONTATA FOR VIOLA AND PIANO (1966) - Three movements. Duration: 15 minutes. Commissioned by Hugh Patridge.

SONATA FOR VIOLA, GUITAR, AND CONTRABASS (1973) - Four movements. Duration: 25 minutes. Commissioned by and dedicated to Hugh Patridge.

SONATA FOR VIOLIN AND CELLO (1974) - One movement. Duration: 7 minutes.

SONATA FOR VIOLIN AND PIANO (1967) - Duration: 12 minutes. Commissioned by and dedicated to David Collins. Premiere: 1967, Indianapolis Museum of Art; David Collins, violin. Note: a.k.a. SONATA IN ONE MOVEMENT.

SONATA FOR VIOLIN, VIOLONCELLO, AND FOUR FLUTES (1980)

SONATA FOR VIOLONCELLO AND PIANO (1973) - Three movements. Duration: 19 minutes. Publisher: Associated Music, 1975. Recording: Janos Starker, violoncello; Alain Planes, piano (Columbia M-33432: Vol. 6, Black Composer Series).

SONATA IN ONE MOVEMENT (1967) - see SONATA FOR VIOLIN AND PIANO.

A SONG (1976) - Violin, violoncello, and piano. See CONTRASTS.

A SONG OF MANKIND (1970) - Chorus (SATB), orchestra, jazz ensemble, rock band, vocal soloists, lights, and sound effects. Commissioned by Faith for a City, Inc., for the Indiana Sesquicentennial. Premiere: 1971, Indiana War Memorial, Indianapolis, Indiana. Note: Each part of this seven-part cantata was written by a different composer; David Baker wrote one part.

SONGS OF THE NIGHT (1972) - Soprano, string quartet, and piano. 12 parts: 1. Reve; 2. Night: Four Songs (text by Langston Hughes); 3. Fragments (text by Langston Hughes); 4. Kid Stuff (text by Frank Horne); 5. Poppy Flower (text by Langston Hughes); 6. Borderline (text by Langston Hughes); 7. Where Have You Gone? (text by Mari Evans); 8. Gethesmane (text by Arna Bontemps); 9. Religion (text by Conrad Kent Rivers); 10. Now That He Is Safely Dead (text by Carl Wendell Hines, Jr.); 11. End (text by Langston Hughes); 12. Evening Song. Duration: 14 minutes 30 seconds. Commissioned by and dedicated to Rita Sansone. Premiere: 1972, Indiana University, Bloomington, Indiana; Rita Sansone, soprano. Note: REVE and EVENING SONG are for solo piano; all other parts of this work are for soprano and string quartet.

STRING QUARTET NO. 1 (1962) - One movement. Duration: 9 minutes. Commissioned by and dedicated to the Meredian String Quartet.

SUITE FOR FRENCH HORN, STRING QUARTET, AND CONTRABASS (1985)

SUITE FOR UNACCOMPANIED VIOLIN (1975) - Five movements. Duration: 25 minutes. Commissioned by and dedicated to Ruggiero Ricci.

SUITE OF LITTLE ETHNIC PIECES (1983) - String orchestra and jazz quartet.

THE SUNSHINE BOOGALOO (1970) - String orchestra. Duration: 4 minutes. Publisher: Creative Jazz Composers. 1976.

THOU DOST LAY ME IN THE DUST OF DEATH (1966) - Chorus (SATB) and string orchestra. See PSALM 22.

THREE SHORT PIECES FOR SOLO BASS

THROUGH THIS VALE OF TEARS - Tenor and string quartet.

TRIPLET BLUES (1970) - String orchestra. Duration: 4 minutes. Publisher: Creative Jazz Composers, 1976.

TWO CELLO STRING QUINTET (1987)

TWO IMPROVISATIONS FOR ORCHESTRA AND JAZZ COMBO (1974) - Orchestra and jazz trio (piano, bass, and drums). Two movements: Harlem Pipes (8 minutes); Sangre Negro (7-10 minutes). Publisher: Associated Music, 1975. Premiere: 1975, Louisville Symphony Orchestra, Jorge Mester, Conductor; Dan Haerle, piano; Rufus Reed, bass; Jack Gilfoy, drums.

A WALK WITH A CHILD (1968) - Voice and guitar.

WALPURGISNACHT (1976) - Violin, cello, and piano.

Sources

Information submitted by the composer.

Baker, David N., Lida M. Belt and Herman C. Hudson. The Black Composer Speaks. Metuchen, NJ: The Scarecrow Press, 1978, pp. 15-69.

Claghorn, Charles E. Biographical Dictionary of American Music. West Nyack, NY: Parker Publishing Co., 1973.

De Lerma, Dominique-René, ed. Black Music in Our Culture: Curricular Ideas on the Subjects, Materials, and Problems. Kent, OH: Kent State University Press, 1973.

De Lerma, Dominique-René. Reflections on Afro-American Music. Kent, OH: Kent State University Press, 1973.

Southern, Eileen. Biographical Dictionary of Afro-American and African Musicians. Westport, CT: Greenwood Press, 1982.

BATISTE, ALVIN (1932 -)

Alvin Batiste was born in New Orleans, Louisiana, in 1932.
He attended Southern University in Baton Rouge (BME) and Louisiana State University (MA). Jazz saxophonist Charlie Parker was an early influence.
He taught in the New Orleans public school system and at Southern University.
After retiring from Southern University, he embarked on a full-time performing career. He has played with Henry Butler, Ron Carter, Jack De Johnette; and with Ellis Marsalis on National Public Radio's "Jazz Alive" program. He is an original member of "Clarinet Summit," and has a number of record albums to his credit, including Venus Flow Batiste.
Honors include being voted "Top Clarinetist" by International Jazz Magazine in 1986.

Works

THE AYJALA SUITE - Clarinet, piano, and double bass (improvisation required). Publisher: SELF.

ETUDE ONE - Solo clarinet and/or piano or bass. Publisher: SELF.

THE KHERI HEBS - Clarinet and string orchestra. Publisher: SELF.

MUSIQUE D'AFRIQUE NOUVELLE ORLEANS - Clarinet and orchestra. Publisher: SELF.

NORTH AMERICAN IDIOSYNCRASIES - Clarinet, piano, double bass, drums, and orchestra. Publisher: SELF.

PICOU - Clarinet and violoncello. Publisher: SELF.

PLANETARY PERSPECTIVE FOR GRASS-ROOTS PLAYERS AND ORCHESTRA - Clarinet and/or various ethnic instruments and orchestra. Publisher: SELF.

Sources

Information submitted by the composer.

BARNETT, WILLIS L.

Works

PERSPECTIVES (1981) - string orchestra.

SYMPHONY NO. 1 (1982) - orchestra. Dedicated to the memory of a great American.

Sources

Scores at the center for Black Music Research

BECKON, LETTIE M. (nee LETTIE BECKON ALSTON) (1953 -)

Lettie M. Beckon was born in Detroit, Michigan, April 13, 1953.
She attended the Bailey Temple School of Music, and studied under William Wise, Al Green, and Lesley Fishwick. She received her BA (1976) and her MA (1978) from Wayne State University.

Works

HEAD A WOE (1975) - 2 violins and cello.

HEAD A WOE (1978) - String orchestra.

HELP (1976) - Women's choir and string quartet.

INTEGRATED CONCERTO (1978) - Piano and orchestra.

PIECE (1977) - Chamber orchestra.

PULSATIONS (1975) - Violin.

SYMPHONIC ESSAY (1977) - String orchestra and percussion.

Sources

Anderson, E. Ruth. Contemporary American Composers: A Biographical Dictionary. Boston: G.K. Hall, 1982, p. 36.

Cohen, Aaron I. International Encyclopedia of Women Composers. New York: R.R. Bowker Co., 1981, p. 45.

De Lerma, Dominique-René. Black Concert and Recital Music: Provisional List. Bloomington, IN: Afro-American Music Opportunities, 1975.

BELAFONTE, HARRY (1927 -)

Harold George Belafonte was born March 1, 1927, in New York.
He lived in Kingston, Jamaica, from 1935-40, then returned to New York, where he studied in Erwin Piscator's drama workshop at the New School of Social Research.
He began working as an actor in 1945 and singing in 1949. In 1950 he began to sing traditional melodies from Africa, Asia, America, and the Caribbean collected in folk-music archives, and secured a recording contract with RCA in 1952.

Works

RECOGNITION (1968) - voice and guitar. Publisher: New York, Marks (1968) (in Ballad of Ira Hayes and Other New Folk Songs; pl. No. 14812).

Sources

De Lerma, Dominique-René. Black Music in Our Culture. Kent, OH: Kent State University Press, 1970, p. 171.

BELAKA, O'SAI TUTU (a.k.a. CHARLES HENDERSON BELL, SR.) (1935 -)

Works

BROTHER MALCOLM - Piano, double bass, electric bass, flute, percussion, and violoncello.

CONCERTO - Piano, drums, and orchestra. Held by Indiana University (M1040 .B42 C6).

Sources

De Lerma, Dominique-René. Black Concert and Recital Music: Provisional List. Bloomington, IN: Afro-American Music Opportunities Association, 1975.

De Lerma, Dominique-Rene. Black Music in Culture. Kent, OH: Kent
State University Press, 1970, p. 171.

BILLUPS, KENNETH BROWN (1918-1985)

Kenneth Brown Billups was born April 15, 1918, in St. Louis, Missouri;
he died October 10, 1985, in St. Louis.

From an early age, he sang in choirs at the Antioch Baptist Church and
organized his own little groups which performed in the community. He graduated from Lincoln University (Missouri), where he conducted the college
Kappa-Delta Choir. He obtained the M.Mus degree at Northwestern University
and studied further at Washington University in St. Louis.

He served as Minister of Music and director of the Chancel Choir at
Antioch Baptist Church for over forty years, and was a music teacher and
administrator in the St. Louis public schools for more than thirty-five
years.

Works

AMERICA IN THE 40s - Suite for orchestra.

SPIRITUALS - String orchestra and chorus.

Sources

De Lerma, Dominique-Rene. Black Concert and Recital Music: Provisional List.   Bloomington, IN: Afro-American Music Opportunities,
1975.

BLAND, EDWARD OSMUND ("ED") (n.d.)

Ed Bland was born in Chicago and received his musical education from
the American Conservatory of Music, University of Chicago, Wilson Jr. College, and the New School for Social Research. He studied composition with
John Becker and attributes influences on his music to Ellington, Tatum,
Stravinsky, Black gospel, West African tribal drumming, and other musical
events.

He has written for orchestra, chamber groups, solo instruments, and
mixed groups of electronic, amplified, and acoustic instruments. He was
composer and orchestrator for two movies, House of Dies Drear and A Soldier's Story, and has served as producer, composer, and arranger for Dizzy
Gillespie, Al Hurt, Lionel Hampton, and George Benson, and as executive
producer for Vangard Records.

Works

ATALANTA'S CHALLENGE (1988) - Solo soprano saxophone, chamber orchestra, percussion, and electric piano.

CONCERTO FOR ELECTRIC VIOLIN AND CHAMBER ORCHESTRA - Commissioned by
The New Cal Arts Twentieth Century Players and Janos Negyesy.

FOR VIOLIN (1980) - Recording: Cambria Records #1026, 1986.

LET PEACE BE FREE (1984) (manuscript) - Orchestra.   Note: Instrumentation includes electric guitar and Fender bass.

MAGNETIC VARIATIONS (1982) - Solo clarinet, flute, clarinet, oboe/ English horn, 2 percussion, electric piano, violoncello, electric bass, violin (amplified).   Dedicated to William Power.

PAEAN FOR AN ENDANGERED PLANET (1989) - Flute, oboe, clarinet, bassoon, 2 percussion, guitar, harp, piano/electric piano, violin (amplified), viola (amplified), violoncello. Commissioned by the California Institute of the Art of Contemporary Music Festival (1989). Dedicated to Charles Schlein.

PASSA IN BLUE (1987) - Flute, oboe, clarinet, bassoon, 2 percussion, electric guitar, harp, electric piano, violin (amplified), viola (amplified), and violoncello.

PIECE FOR CHAMBER ORCHESTRA (1979) - Duration: 15 minutes.   Recording: Cambria Records #1026, 1986.

PRIMO COUNTERPOINT (1981) - Flute, clarinet, trumpet, trombone, 2 percussion, electric piano, violoncello, electric bass.

ROMANTIC SYNERGY (1987) - Solo flute and chamber orchestra.

SKETCHES SET I (1965) - Clarinet, trumpet, two cellos, and timpani. Recording: Cambria Records #1026, 1986.

SKETCHES SET II (1964) - Clarinet, trumpet, trombone, and violoncello.

Sources

Information submitted by the composer.

Holly, Ellistine Perkins, ed. Biographies of Black Composers. Dubuque, IA: Wm. C. Brown Publishers, 1990, pp. 5-6.

BLEDSOE, JULES (1898-1943)

Jules Bledsoe was born December 29, 1898, in Waco, Texas, and died July 14, 1943, in Hollywood, California.
He received his BA from Chicago Musical College in 1919, then studied voice in Paris and Rome.
He sang the central role in Show Boat in 1927, and Gruenberg's Emperor Jones in 1933.

Works

AFRICAN SUITE - Violin and orchestra.

BONDAGE - Opera.   NOTE: Based on Harriet Beecher Stowe's Uncle Tom's Cabin.

Sources

Anderson, E. Ruth. Contemporary American Composers: A Biographical Dictionary. Boston: G.K. Hall, 1982.

Carter, Madison H.   An Annotated Catalogue of Composers of African Ancestry. New York: Vantage Press, 1986.

BOATNER, EDWARD HAMMOND (1897-1981)

Edward Hammond Boatner was born November 13, 1897, in New Orleans, Louisana.

Boatner studied at Western University in Quindara, Kansas, and later won a scholarship at the Boston Conservatory. Later he attended the Longy School of Music in Boston, where he met Robert Nathaniel Dett. In 1932, Boatner graduated from the Chicago College of Music.

He has won awards from the National Federation of Music Clubs, the National Association of Negro Musicians, the Brooklyn Lyceum, the Detroit Association of Musicians, and the New York Uptown Musicians, among others. In February 1979 he was honored by the Chicago branch of the National Association of Negro Musicians.

He has written twenty textbooks on harmony, theory, and composition, pedagogical works, plays, music for stage works, and novels, a piano self-study course, and several books of his arrangements of spirituals. Titles include Great Achievements Black and White, The Damaging Results of Racism, Black Humor, and One Drop of Blood, a novel.

His most notable contributions have been his arrangements of spirituals, including Thirty Afro-American Choral Spirituals and Spirituals Triumphand Old and New.

Boatner has also served as Music Director of the National Baptist Convention (1925-1933), and taught at Wiley College (where he was Dean of Music) and at Sam Houston College, before opening the Edward Boatner Studio. His pupils have included Josephine Baker, Libby Holman George Shirley, and Clifton Webb.

Works

JULIUS SEES HER IN ROME, GEORGIA (1935; revised 1975) - Musical comedy for chorus, solosit, and orchestra; 2 acts. Text based on a book by Edward Boatner, unpublished (LC). Duration: 2 hours. Note: Story of Julius Caesar made into a musical.

TROUBLE IN MIND (1975-78) - opera in 3 acts.

Sources

Hare, Maud Cuney. Negro Musicians and Their Music. Washington, DC: Associated Press, 1936, p. 347.

Obituary. The Black Perspective in Music 9.2 (Fall 1981): 239.

Southern, Eileen. Biographical Dictionary of Afro-American and African Musicians. Westport, CT: Greenwood Press, 1982.

Tischler, Alice. Fifteen Black American Composers, A Bibliography of Their Works. Detroit Studies in Music Bibliography. Detroit: Information Coordinators, 1981.

BOND, CURTIS HORACE (1954 -)

Curtis Horace Bond was born March 20, 1954, in Forrest City, Arkansas.
His works include Rainbow and Moon Circles (tone poems), Flowers for chamber orchestra, and numerous choral compositions.

Works

FLOWERS - chamber orchestra. In three movements. Duration: 15 minutes. Manuscript.

MOON CIRCLES (TONE POEM) - piano and string quartet. Duration: 5 minutes. Manuscript.

RAINBOW (A CONCERTINA) - piano, string quartet, flute. A tone poem in four connected movements. Duration: 12 minutes. Manuscript.

Source

Information submitted by the composer.

BONDS, MARGARET ALLISON (1913-1972)

Margaret Allison Bonds was born March 3, 1913, in Chicago, Illinois, and died April 26, 1972, in Los Angeles.
She began to study piano at the age of 5 with her mother, a music teacher. She obtained her music education at Northwestern University (B. Music, M. Music) and at Juilliard, studying with Martha Anderson, T. Theodore Taylor, Emily Boettcher Bogue, Roy Harris, and Robert Starer, among others. Her style of composition was influenced by Harry T. Burleigh and by Will Marion Cook.
In 1932 her song "Sea Ghost" received a prize in the Wanamaker competition. She received a Rosenwald Fellowship and awards from the National Council of Negro Women, ASCAP, and the National Association of Negro Musicians. Northwestern awarded her the Alumni Award in Arts and Letters in 1967.
Of her more than 70 compositions, best known are Ballad of the Brown King, Three Dream Portraits, and "The Negro speaks of rivers," all with texts by Langston Hughes; the arrangements Five Spirituals ; the ballet Migration; and musicals Romey and Julie and Shakespeare in Harlem, USA. She also was commissioned to arrange a group of spirituals for Leontyne Price and for the Los Angeles Jubilee Singers.

Works

CREDO (1972) - Chorus (SATB), baritone solo, and orchestra. Text by W.E.B. DuBois. Unpublished. Premiere: May 1972, Los Angeles, California; Los Angeles Philharmonic, Zubin Mehta, Conductor. Contents: 1. I believe in the devil and his angels, 2. I believe in Liberty, 3. I believe in Patience.

EZEKIEL SAW THE WHEEL (1959) - Voice and piano; voice and orchestra. Publisher: New York, Beekman Music.

FIVE SPIRITUALS (1946) - "Dry Bones," "Sit Down Servant," "Lord I Just Can't Keep from Crying," "You Can Tell the World," also for voice and orchestra. Publisher: New York, Mutual Music Society.

GEORGIA (c. 1939) - Voice and piano or orchestra. Text by Andy Razaf, Margaret Bonds, and Joe Davis. Unpublished. Notes: Co-composed with Andy Razaf and Joe Davis. Also arranged as a fox trot for orchestra (c. 1939), not by Bonds.

HE'S GOT THE WHOLE WORLD IN HIS HANDS (1963) - Voice and piano; voice and orchestra. Publisher: New York, Beekman Music.

HOLD ON - Chorus (SATB) and orchestra. Publisher: New York, Presser, 1968.

I GOT A HOME IN THAT ROCK (1959) - Voice and piano; voice and orchestra. Publisher: New York, Beekman Music (1962; re-issued 1968).

I WANT JESUS TO WALK WITH ME - Spiritual for cello and piano. Unpublished. Premiere: 10 September 1964, Maryland; Kermit Moore, cello.

I WISH I KNEW HOW IT WOULD FEEL TO BE FREE - Voice, chorus, and orchestra. Text: spiritual. Unpublished. Recording: RCA Victor LSC-3183. Note: Arranged for Leontyne Price.

JOSHUA FIT DA BATTLE OF JERICHO - Voice (medium) and piano or orchestra. Text: spiritual. Publication: Brywn Mawr, Pennsylvania, Mercury (1967). (IU) Orchestral material available from Presser, New York.

JOY - Chorus (SAT), string quartet, and piano. Text by Langston Hughes. Unpublished. Premiere: McClain Chorale, George McClain, Conductor.

MASS IN D MINOR (Latin Text) - Chorus and orchestra.

MONTGOMERY VARIATIONS (1965) - Orchestra. Dedicated to Martin Luther King, Jr. Unpublished. Contents: 1. Jesus Walk with Me, 2. Prayer Meeting, 3. March, 4. One Sunday in the South, 5. Dawn in Dixie. Note: Written for the March on Montgomery, Alabama, in 1965.

THE NILES FANTASY - Piano and orchestra. Manuscript.

PETER GO RING DEM BELLS - Chorus and string quartet. Text: spiritual. Unpublished. Premiere: 9 September 1956, Town Hall, New York City; Uptown Men's Chorale.

QUINTET IN F MAJOR (1933) - Piano quintet in one movement. Unpublished.

SCRIPTURE READING - Chamber orchestra. Commissioned by Nichlauss Wyss, Conductor of the Little Symphony of San Francisco Symphony Orchestra.

SINNER PLEASE DON'T LET THIS HARVEST PASS - Voice, chorus (SATB), and orchestra. Text: spiritual. Unpublished. Recording: RCA Victor LSC-3183. Note: Arranged for Leontyne Price.

SPIRITUALS FIVE (1942) - Voice (high) and orchestra. Text: spiritual. Commissioned by Hortense Love. Published: New York, Mutual Music, 1946; orchestra parts on rental from Chappell, New York. Premiere: Town Hall New York City; Hortense Love, Soprano. Contents: 1. Dry Bones, 2. Sit Down Servant, 3. Lord I Just Can't Keep from Cryin', 4. You Can Tell the World, 5. I'll Reach to Heaven.

STANDIN' IN THE NEED OF PRAYER - Voice, chorus (SATB), and orchestra. Text: spiritual. Unpublished. Recording: RCA Victor LSC 3183. Note: Arranged for Leontyne Price.

THIS LITTLE LIGHT OF MINE - Voice, chorus (SATB), and orchestra. Text: spiritual. Unpublished. Recording: RCA Victor LSC-3183. Note: Arranged for Leontyne Price.

TROUBLE WATER: Cello and piano.

Sources

Abdul, Raoul. "Black Women in Music." In Blacks in Classical Music. New York: Dodd, Mead and Co., 1977, pp. 53-55.

Ammer, Christine. Unsung: A History of Women in American Music. Westport, CT: Greenwood Press, 1980, pp. 153-56.

Bonds, Margaret. "A Reminiscence." In The Negro in Music and Art, ed. Lindsay Patterson. New York: Publishers Company, Inc., 1968, pp. 190-93.

Green, Mildred Denby. Black Women Composers: A Genesis. Boston: Twayne Publishers, 1983.

Jackson, Barbara Garvey. "Bonds, Margaret (Allison)." In The New Grove Dictionary of American Music, Vol. 1 pp. 255-56.

Southern, Eileen. Biographical Dictionary of Afro-American and African Musicians. Westport, CT: Greenwood Press, 1982.

Tischler, Alice. Fifteen Black American Composers: A Bibliography of Their Works. Detroit Studies in Music Bibliography. Detroit: Information Coordinators, 1981.

BROOKS, HARRY (1895-1970)

Harry Brooks was born in Homestead, Pennsylvania, in 1895, and died in Teaneck, New Jersey, in 1970.
He studied with Walter Spriggs and played in dance orchestras. He also worked as a composer and arranger for various publishing companies.
With Fats Waller and Andy Razaf, he wrote the score for the 1929 musical Hot Chocolates, which included the song "Ain't Misbehavin'."

Works

CONNIE'S HOT CHOCOLATES (1929) - Opera. Publisher: Mills (1929).

Sources

De Lerma, Dominique-René. Black Music in Our Culture. Kent, OH: The Kent State University Press, 1970, p. 172.

BROUWER, LEO (1939 -)

Works

APUNTES (1959) - Guitar. Contents: 1. Del homenaje a falla; 2. De un fragmento instrumental; 3. Sobre un canto de Bulgaria. Duration: 4 minutes 20 seconds. Recording: Inter-American Musical Editions, OAS-012 (1981); Everton Gloeden, guitar.

CONCERTO FOR GUITAR - Recording: CBS M-36680; Williams, Howart, London Sinf.

DANZA CARACTERISTICA (1957) - Guitar. Duration: 1 minute 56 seconds. Publisher: Mainz, Scotts Söhne. Recording: Musical Heritage Society MHS-3777 (1973); Oscar Cáceres, guitar.

DANZAS CONCERTANTES (1958) - Guitar and orchestra. Contents: 1. Allegro (3:32); 2. Andantino quasi allegreto (4:43); 3. Toccata (5:11). Publisher: Berlin, Verlag Neue Musik. Recording: Musical Heritage Society MHS-3777 (1973); Oscar Cáceres, guitar; instrumental ensemble; Leo Brouwer, conductor.

ELOGIA DE LA DANZA (1964) - Guitar. Contents: 1. Lento; 2. Obstinato. Publisher: Mainz, Schotts Söhne. Recordings: 1. Musical Heritage MHS-1445 (1972); Turbio Santos, guitar; 2. Musical Heritage Society MHS-3603 (1972); Alberto Ponce, guitar; 3. Musical Heritage Society MHS-3777 (1973); Oscar Cáceres, guitar.

LA ESPIRAL ETERNA (1971) - Guitar. Duration: 7 minutes 24 seconds. Publisher: Mainz, Schotts Söhne. Recordings: 1. Musical Heritage Society MHS-3839 (1972); Leo Brouwer, guitar; 2. Musical Heritage Society MHS-3777 (1973); Oscar Cáceres, guitar.

MICROPIEZAS (ca. 1955) - 2 guitars. Contents: 1. Tranquillo; 2. Allegro vivace; 3. Vivacicimo; 4. Andantino. Publisher: Max Eschig. Recording: Musical Heritage Society MHS-3777 (1973); Oscar Cáceres and Leo Brouwer, guitars.

PARABOLA - Guitar. Recording: DG/Japan MG-1077 PSI; Narciso Yepes, guitar.

PIEZE SIN TITULO (1956) - Guitar. Duration: 1 minute 14 seconds. Publisher: Max Eschig. Recording: Musical Heritage Society MHS-3777 (1973); Oscar Cáceres, guitar.

Sources

De Lerma, Dominique-René. "A Condordance of Scores and Recordings of Music by Black Composers." Black Music Research Journal (1984): 22-59.

BROWN, JOHN HAROLD (1909 -)

John Harold Brown was born September 28, 1909, in Shellman, Georgia. He studied at Fisk University (BM) and Indiana University (MM). His honors include 6 Wanamaker awards.
Brown was director of music at Florida A&M University, then at Southern University in Baton Rouge. In the 1950s he was director at Karamu House and Huntington Playhouse, Florida.

Works

A MINOR - String quartet.

Sources

Anderson, E. Ruth. Contemporary American Composers: A Biographical Dictionary. Boston: G.K. Hall, 1982.

Carter, Madison H. An Annotated Catalogue of Composers of African Ancestry. New York: Vantage Press, 1986.

Southern, Eileen. Biographical Dictionary of Afro-American and African Musicians. Westport, CT: Greenwood Press, 1982, p. 51.

BROWN, LAWRENCE (1893-1972)

Works

FIVE NEGRO FOLK SONGS - Cello and piano. Publisher: London, Schott & Co. Ltd., ca. 1923.

SPIRITUALS: FIVE NEGRO FOLK SONGS FOR VIOLONCELLO AND PIANO - Dedicated to Beatrice Harrison. Publisher: London, Schott (1923). Held by Indiana University (M235 .B87 S7).

Sources

Carter, Madison H. An Annotated Catalogue of Composers of African Ancestry. New York: Vantage Press, 1986.

De Lerma, Dominique-René. Black Concert and Recital Music: Provisional List. Bloomington, IN: Afro-American Music Opportunities, 1975.

BROWN, OSCAR, JR. (1926 -)

   Oscar Brown, Jr., was born in 1926 in Chicago, Illinois.
   Among his works are "Brown Baby" (recorded by Mahalia Jackson), "New
Freedom Suite" (by Max Roach); and lyrics for the following works: "Work
Song" (by Nat Adderley), "Dat Dere" (by Bobby Timmons), "All Blues" (by
Miles Davis), "So Help Me" (by Les McCann), and "One Foot in the Gutter"
(by Clark Terry).
   He was MC of the 1962 TV show "Jazz Scene USA."

Works

   KIRK AND CO. - Opera. Publisher: New York, Marks.

Source

   De Lerma, Dominique-René. Black Music in Our Culture.   Kent, OH:
   Kent State University Press, 1970, p. 172.

BROWN, UZEE (1951 -)

   Uzee Brown was born November 14, 1951, in Spartanburg County, South
Carolina.
   He received his formal music training at Morehouse College (BA, 1972),
Bowling University (Master's in Theory and Composition, 1974), and the
University of Michigan (Master's in Voice Performance, 1977, and DMA in
Voice, 1980).
   He received fellowships to study in Graz, Austria, in 1985, and in
Italy in 1987 (Sessione Senese per Musica e Parte).
   He is the co-founder of Onyx Opera, Atlanta, and a professor of music
at Morehouse College.

Works

   EBONY PERSPECTIVE - Bass voice, clarinet, trumpet, trombone, tuba,
   banjo, and percussion. Publisher: SELF.

Source

   Information submitted by the composer.

BURLEIGH, HENRY THACKER ("HARRY") - (1866-1949)

   Henry Thacker Burleigh was born December 2, 1866, in Erie, Pennsylvania, and died September 12, in Stamford, Connecticut.
   Though he had no formal music education as a child, odd jobs provided
him with opportunities to hear performances of visiting artists and inspired him to become a singer. He found work in Erie singing in local
churches and synagogues. At the age of 26 he competed for a scholarship at
the National Conservatory of Music in New York City and won a scholarship.
When Antonin Dvořák came to New York, Burleigh studied with him and also
spent time outside the classroom singing spirituals and copying manu-
scripts. From Dvořák Burleigh learned to regard African American and In-
dian folk music as a basis from which to develop a nationalistic school of
music in the United States.

Burleigh held two prestigious church positions in New York, that of church soloist at the aristocratic St. George's Protestant Episcopal Church, which he won over 49 other applications and held for fifty-two years, and that of soloist at Temple Emanu-El, where he was the first African American soloist, and remained for 25 years.

He was the first African American composer to win critical acclaim for composing art songs and received numerous honors, including the Spingarn Medal (1917), a Harmon Foundation Award (1929), and honorary degress from Atlanta University (MA, 1918) and Howard University (Doctorate, 1920). He was a charter member of ASCAP.

Best known of his art songs are "I love my Jean" (Robert Burns poem), "Little mother of mine," "Dear old pal of mine," "In the great somewhere," and "Lovely, dark and lonely one" (a Langston Hughes poem). He also arranged spirituals in the style of art songs for solo voice, the first of which was "Deep River" (1916). Other works include Six Plantation Melodies for Violin and Piano, From the Southland, and Southland Sketches.

Works

EV'RY TIME I FEEL THE SPIRIT - Orchestra and chorus. Publisher: New York: G. Ricordi, n.d. Recording: RCA LSC-2600 (1962); Leontyne Price, soprano; orchestra and chorus; Leonard De Paur, Conductor (and arranger).

SIX PLANTATION MELODIES FOR VIOLIN AND PIANO (1901).

SOUTHLAND SKETCHES (1916) - Violin and piano.

Sources

Adams, Russell L. Great Negros, Past and Present, 3rd. ed. Chicago: Afro-Am Publishing Co., 1969, p. 176.

Allison, Roland. "Burleigh, Harry [Henry] T(hacker)." In The New Grove Dictionary of American Music, Vol. 1, p. 327.

"Burleigh, Harry Thacker." Dictionary Catalogue of the Schomburg Collection, Vol. 2, pp. 1121-24. Contains an extensive list of Burleigh scores held by the Schomburg.

Fax, Elton C. "Burleigh, Harry T[hacker]." In Dictionary of American Negro Biography, eds. Rayford W. Logan and Michael T. Winston. New York: W.W. Norton, 1982, pp. 79-80.

Lovingood, Penman. Famous Modern Negro Musicians. New York: Da Capo Press, 1978. (Reprint of 1921 ed.)

Roach, Hildred. Black American Music: Past and Present. Miami: Kreiger Publishing, 1985.

Slonimsky, Nicolas, ed. Bakers Biographical Dictionary of Musicians (6th ed.). New York: Schirmer Books, 1978.

Southern, Eileen. Biographical Dictionary of Afro-American and African Musicians. Westport, CT: Greenwood Press, 1982, pp. 55-57.

Southern, Eileen. "Burleigh, Harry [Henry] T(hacker)." In The New
Grove Dictionary of Music and Musicians, Vol. 3, pp. 421-22.

BURRS, LESLIE (1952 -)

Leslie Burrs was born in Philadelphia, Pennsylvania, in 1952.
He is a graduate of the Philadelphia College of Performing Artists
Workshop.
He has been guest soloist with Grover Washington Jr., the Duke Elling-
ton Orchestra, and the Pennsylvania School Districts (as Artist-in-Resi-
dence).
His works include Precarious, She Stands in Quiet Darkness, Elegance,
and A Woman's Song.

Works

SONG FOR WINNIE - string quartet. Commissioned by Max Roach for the
Uptown String Quartet in Philadelphia. Dedicated to Winnie Mandela.
Recording: Phillip Records, August 1989.

Sources

Holly, Ellistine P. "Composers' Notes." CBMR Digest, Vol. 2, No. 2,
Fall 1989.

Roach, Hildred. Black American Music: Past and Present, Vol. II.
Miami: Krieger Publishing Co., 1985, p. 105.

CAPERS, VALERIE (1937 -)

Works

SOJOURNER - Opera.

Source

Holly, Ellistine Perkins. Biographies of Black Composers and Songwriters. Dubuque, IA: Wm. C. Brown Publishers, 1990, p. 80.

CARTER, JOHN (1937 -)

John Carter was born in St. Louis, Missouri, in 1937.
He received his education at Oberlin College, and received grants from
the Rockefeller Foundation, the American Music Center, and the ASCAP organization. He was Composer-in-Residence in 1968 with the Washington National
Symphony Orchestra. He taught at the new Federal City College in Washington. Among his works are Cantata, Requiem Seditiosam, In Memoriam: Medgar
Evers and Japanese Poems.

Works

CANTATA (1964) - Voice and orchestra or piano.

EMBLEMES - Violin.

EPIGRAMS - Ballet.

IN MEMORIAM, MEDGAR EVERS - Orchestra.

PIANO CONCERTO

REQUIEM SEDITIOSAM: IN MEMORY OF MEDGAR EVERS (ca. 1967) - Baritone/
bass with orchestra (piano reduction available). Publisher: New
York, American Music Center.

Sources

De Lerma, Dominique-René. Black Music in Our Culture. Kent, OH:
Kent State University Press, 1970, p. 172.

Holly, Ellistine Perkins, ed. Biographies of Black Composers and
Songwriters. Dubuque, IA: Wm. C. Brown Publishers, 1990, p. 10.

Roach, Hildred. Black American Music: Past and Present, Vol. I.
Miami: Krieger Publishing Co., 1985, pp. 171-173.

CARTER, WARRICK L. (1942 -)

Warrick Carter was born in 1942 in Charlottesville, Virginia.
He obtained his B.S. from Tennessee State University (1964), and his
Master of Music and Ph.D. from Michigan State University. He also studied
at the Blair Academy of Music.
He received the Best Drummer Award from the Collegiate Jazz Festival
at Notre Dame in 1970. He also received a Graduate Fellow award from
Michigan State University's Center for Urban Affairs.
Carter taught in the Chattanooga public schools and at the University
of Maryland, Eastern Shore (1966-68) and Governors State University, Chicago, Illinois (1972-83), where he served as Chairman of the Division of
Fine and Performing Arts. Presently he serves as Dean of Faculty at Ber-
keley in Boston. During the summers of 1970 and 1971 he served as director
of Music Eduation for Urban Schools Symposium at Michigan State University.
He has contributed a number of articles on jazz education.
Among his compositions are Concerto for Bassoon and Nose Flute (1966)
and Life Part I (1963); First Love, ICC, Little People, Memo, and Clay for
jazz ensemble; Two Tunes (jazz quartet); Questions and Music to be Sounded
for jazz octet and electronic tape; and Eight Quartets for Percussion, Poco
a Poco and Rondo for percussion ensemble.

Works

ERIC (1977) - Soprano saxophone or clarinet, 2 violins, viola, and
violoncello (may be played by string orchestra). Duration: 11
minutes. Dedicated to Eric Wick, Chicago Symphony. Publisher: SELF.

THE HAMPTON THOUGHT (1977) - Jazz ensemble with strings. Commissioned
by NEA.

KEISHA Z (1972) - Jazz ensemble with strings.

LIFE PART I (1963) - Orchestra.

LOVE ALL LIVING THINGS (1976) - Jazz ensemble with strings. Commissioned by NEA.

MAGNOLIA THUNDERPUSSY (1973) - Jazz ensemble with strings.

MONIQUE (1976) - Jazz ensemble with strings.

PONTA DE AREIA (1976) - Jazz ensemble with strings. Commissioned by NEA.

THURSDAY'S LOVE (1974) - Jazz ensemble with strings. Commissioned by Chicago Chamber Orchestra.

Sources

Information submitted by the composer.

Roach, Hildred. Black American Music: Past and Present, Vol. II. Miami: Krieger Publishing Co., 1985, pp. 96-99.

CASSEUS, FRANTZ GABRIEL (1921 -)

Works

DANCE OF THE HOUNSIES - Guitar. Publisher: Belwin Mills Corp.

Sources

Carter, Madison H. An Annotated Catalogue of Composers of African Ancestry. New York: Vantage Press, 1986.

CHANDLER, LEN H., JR. (1935 -)

Len Chandler was born in Akron, Ohio, in 1935.
He studied at the University of Akron and at Columbia University in New York.
He wrote more than fifty folk songs, including The Wicked Weirs, commemorating Medgar Evers.

Works

THE LOVIN' PEOPLE (1967) - Voice and guitar. Publisher: New York, Marks (1967).

Source

De Lerma, Dominique-René. Black Music in Our Culture. Kent, OH: Kent State University Press, 1970, p. 172.

CHEATHAM, WALLACE McCLAIN (1945 -)

Wallace Cheatham was born in Cleveland. Tennessee, in 1945.
He received his B.S. from Knoxville College, his M.S. from the University of Wisconsin (Milwaukee), and his Ph.D. from Columbia Pacific

University. He also studied at Northwestern University and the University
of Wisconsin-Madison.   His teachers included Ernesto Pellegrini, Nathan
Carter, and Robert McFerrin.
     Among his compositions are: Three Songs (1982), Missa (1983), Por-
traits (1983), Ebenezer (1985), Symphony (1986), and String Quartet (1987).
His choral works include Dese Bones Gonna Rise Again, My Hope is Built, and
My Soul is a Witness.

Works

     PORTRAITS (1982) - orchestra.   Premiere: 15 May 1988, The Racine
     Symphony, Stephen Colburn, Conductor.

     STRING QUARTET NO. 1 (1987-88)

     SYMPHONY (1986) - orchestra.

Sources

     Information submitted by the composer.

     Holly, Ellistine Perkins, ed.   Biographies of Black Composers and
     Songwriters.   Dubuque, IA: Wm. C. Brown Publishers, 1990.

CLARK, EDGAR ROGIE (1913-1978)

     Edgar Rogie Clark was born April 3, 1913, in Atlanta, Georgia, and
died February 15, 1978, in Detroit, Michigan.
     He received his B.A. in 1935 from Clark College, and the M.A. in 1942
from Columbia University Teachers College.   He also studied at Chicago
Musical College, Juilliard, and the Berkshire Music Center in Tanglewood,
Massachusetts.
     Clark received fellowships from the Ford Foundation, John Hay Whitney
Foundation, and the National Endowment for the Arts, and an award from the
National Association of Negro Musicians.
     He contributed to such journals as Journal of American Folklore, Musi-
cal America, Music Journal, Journal of Negro Education, and Phylon.
     Well-known compositions include the opera Ti Yette, Fete Creole, John
Henry Fantasy, and the collections Six Afro-American Carols for Christmas
and Six Afro-American Carols for Easter.
     He taught at Fort Valley (Georgia) State College (1936), in the New
York City public schools, at Jackson State College, Wayne County Community
College (Detroit), Central State College (Ohio), and in the public schools
of Warren Woods, Michigan (1966-78).

Works

     DIVERTIMENTO (1969) - String quartet.   Duration: 13 minutes.   Pre
     miere: 1970, Detroit. Unpublished.

     ELEGIA (1968) - String orchestra. Duration: 10 minutes. Dedicated
     to Martin Luther King, Jr.   Premiere: 1970, Detroit, Michigan; De-
     troit Metropolitan Orchestra, Charles Sumner, Conductor. Unpublished.

ETUDE (1974) - Violin and piano. Duration: 10 minutes. Premiere: 1976. Detroit, Michigan; Detroit Symphony Orchestra; Joseph Striplin, violin. Unpublished.

FETE CREOLE (1970) - Orchestra. Duration: 8 minutes. Premiere: 27 October 1970. Community Arts Auditorium, Detroit, Michigan; Detroit Metropolitan Orchestra, Charles Sumner, Conductor. Note: Based on Creole themes. Unpublished.

FIGURINE (1965) - Cello and piano. Duration: 15 minutes. Unpublished.

KAFFIR DRINKING SONG (1976) - Voice (baritone) and orchestra. Text: traditional African. Duration: 4 minutes. Premiere: 11 February 1976, Detroit, Michigan; Detroit Symphony Orchestra, Paul Freeman, Conductor; Willis Patterson, baritone. Unpublished.

LARGHETTO (1970) - String orchestra. Duration: 15 minutes. Unpublished.

THE STRANGER (1967) - Opera in one act for 4 characters and chamber orchestra (13 players). Text based on Rupert Brook's Play. Duration: 1 hour 45 minutes. Unpublished.

THIS WICKED RACE (1976) - Voice (baritone) and orchestra. Text: spiritual adapted and arranged by the composer. Duration: 5 minutes. Premiere: 11 February 1976, Detroit, Michigan; Detroit Symphony Orchestra, Paul Freeman, Conductor; Willis Patterson, baritone. Unpublished.

TI YETTE (1940) - Opera for 4 characters, chorus, and chamber orchestra. Text adapted from the play by John Matthews. Duration: 1 hour 20 minutes. Premiere: 21 June 1959, Detroit, Michigan. Unpublished.

Sources

Holly, Ellistine Perkins, ed. Biographies of Black Composers and Songwriters. Dubuque, IA: Wm. C. Brown Publishers, 1990.

Southern, Eileen. Biographical Dictionary of Afro-American and African Musicians. Westport, CT: Greenwood Press, 1982.

Tischler, Alice. Fifteen Black American Composers, A Bibliography of Their Works. Detroit Studies in Music Bibliography. Detroit: Information Coordinators, 1981.

CLAY, OMAR (n.d.)

Works

CHUN DYNASTY - Marimba and violin.

Source

Abdul, Raoul. Blacks in Classical Music. New York: Dodd Mead and Company, 1977, p. 68.

CLOUD, LEE VERNELL (1950 -)

Lee Vernell Cloud was born in Winston-Salem, North Carolina, in 1950.
He received his BA from Morehouse College in 1972, his MM from Bowling Green State University in 1973, and his PhD from the University of Iowa.
He has performed in Scott Joplin's Treemonisha with the Atlanta Symphony (Robert Shaw, conductor), and is a former member of the Winston-Salem Chorale.
He has taught at Winston-Salem State University and Bowling Green State University, and is currently Professor of Music at Northern Illinois University.

Works

7 FOR 5 IN 4 - Flute, clarinet, vibes, viola, and double bass.

SURVIVAL - Flute, string quartet, double bass, 8 voices, and perrcussion.

Source

Information submitted by the composer.

COLEMAN, CHARLES DeWITT (1926 -)

Charles Coleman was born in 1926 in Detroit, Michigan.
He attended Wayne State University, where he received his B. Mus. (1952) and M. Mus (1955), graduating with honors (AAGO). His teachers included Mildred Clumas, August Mackelberghe, Robert Cato, and Virgil Fox. He also studied organ and piano with Van Dessel and conducting with Walter Poole.
Among his compositions are Sonata in F for organ, Sonatine for piano, Fantasia for flute, Suite for two violins, and the choral works John Kennedy, Blest Be the Tie, Be Thou Faithful Unto Death, Let Us Break Bread Together, Live-a Umble, Let All Those That Seek Thee Rejoice, Before the Throne of God, O Perfect Love, and Alleluia.

Works

SUITE - 2 violins.

Sources

Anderson, E. Ruth. Contemporary American Composers: A Biographical Dictionary. Boston: G.K. Hall & Co., 1982, p. 101.

Roach, Hildred. Black American Music: Past and Present, Vol. II. Miami: Krieger Publishing Co., 1985, p. 39.

COLEMAN, ORNETTE (1930 -)

Ornette Coleman was born March 29, 1930, in Fort Worth, Texas.
Though he studied saxophone and played in the school band during high school, Coleman's musical education was largely informal, and gathered

while he played rhythm and blues with local groups before and after gradu-
ation.   He also attended the School of Jazz at Lenox, Massachusetts, in
1959.
Coleman received two Guggenheim fellowships for composition (1967 and
1974), as well as numerous awards from the music industry.
He published a book, Harmolodic Theory, which explained his special
approach to theory.
His best known orchestral work is Skies of America.

Works

SKIES OF AMERICA (1972) - Jazz quartet and orchestra. Premiere: July
1972, Philharmonic Hall, Lincoln Center, New York City; the American
Symphony Orchestra, Leon Thompson, Conductor.

Sources

Feather, Leonard. The New Edition of the Encyclopedia of Jazz.   New
York: Horizon Press, 1960.

Southern, Eileen. Biographical Dictionary of Afro-American and African Musicians. Westport, CT: Greenwood Press, 1982, pp. 77-78.

Spellman, A. B. Black Music: Four Lives. 1966; reprint, New York,
1970.

COOK, WILL MARION (1869-1944)

Will Marion Cook was born January 27, 1869, in Washington, D.C., and
died in New York on July 19, 1944.
He studied at Oberlin Conservatory in Ohio when he was 15. He also
studied violin with Josef Joachim in Berlin and attended the National Conservatory of Music in New York, where he studied with Antonin Dvořak.
At first a concert violinist, in the mid-1890s he encountered vaudeville, and in 1898 he collaborated with Paul Laurence Dunbar on a musical
comedy sketch, "Clorindy, or The Origin of the Cakewalk."   He served as
musical director/composer for the George Walker/Bert Williams company,
producing The Sons of Ham, In Dahomey, In Abyssinia and In Bandanna Land.
His musical The Southerners was produced on Broadway in 1904. He collaborated on other musicals, including The Traitors, In Darkeydom, and The
Cannibal King; with Will Vodery he wrote and produced Swing Along. Besides
musicals, he also wrote songs such as "Swing along," "Exhortation," "Red,
red rose," and "The rain song."

Works

CLORINDY, THE ORIGIN OF THE CAKEWALK (1898) - Operetta.

IN DAHOMEY (1902) - Orchestral overture. Edited by Paul Steg. Duration: 10 minutes. Performance: 18 February 1984; Baltimore, Maryland; Peabody/Morgan Black Music Symposium; Peabody Chamber Orchestra,
Edward Polochick, Conductor.

ST. LOUIS WOMAN (1929) - Folk opera. Libretto by Mercer Cooke.

Sources

BPIM 6 (Spring 1978): 71-88.

Holly, Ellistine Perkins, ed. Biographies of Black Composers and Songwriters. Dubuque, IA: Wm. C. Brown Publishers, 1990.

Southern, Eileen. Biographical Dictionary of Afro-American and African Musicians. Westport, CT: Greenwood Press, 1982, pp. 81-82.

COOKE, CHARLES L. (1891-1958)

Works

PRO ARTE. AN OVERTURE - Orchestra.

Source

Carter, Madison H.   An Annotated Catalogue of Composers of African Ancestry. New York: Vantage Press, 1986.

COOPER, WILLIAM BENJAMIN (1920 -)

William Benjamin Cooper was born February 14, 1920, in Philadelphia, Pennsylvania.
He received his BM (1951) and MM (1952) from Philadelphia Musical Academy, where he studied with Stefan Wolpe and Julius Hijman. Later he studied with Harold Friedell at the Union Theological Seminary School of Sacred Music.
He taught at Bennett College (1951-53) and in the public schools of New York (1958 -). He served as Minister of Music at St. Philip's Church (New York, 1953-74) and St. Martin's Episcopal Church (New York, 1974 -).

Works

CANTATA (1975) - Soprano and orchestra.

CHRONIKOS (1977) - Chamber ensemble.   NOTE: Received Atwater-Kent Award.

DISTILLATIONS (1977) - Solo cello.

FANTASY - Organ and cello. Manuscript.

SOLO VIOLIN

Sources

Information submitted by the composer.

Anderson, E. Ruth.   Contemporary American Composers: A Biographical Dictionary. Boston: G.K. Hall, 1982.

Carter, Madison H.   An Annotated Catalogue of Composers of African Ancestry. New York: Vantage Press, 1986.

CUNNINGHAM, ARTHUR (1928 -)

Arthur Cunningham was born November 11, 1928, in Nyack, New York.
He began to study piano when he was six, and obtained his musical
education at Fisk University in Nashville (BA, 1951), the Metropolitan
Music School in New York, Juilliard, and Columbia University Teachers College (M.A., 1957).
Honors include grants from ASCAP and the National Endowment for the
Arts; in 1968 his piece Concentrics received a nomination for the Pulitzer
Prize.
He began writing music as a child, and over the years wrote in a wide
variety of forms, including three symphonies, two concertos, two ballets,
five operas, four hundred jazz/rock ballads, art songs, and special material for singers in musical shows, revues, and television. Some of his best
known works are Lullabye for a Jazz Baby, Harlem Suite Ballet, and the
stage works House By the Sea, Shango, and Ostrich Feathers.

Works

ADAGIO (1954) - Oboe and string orchestra. Duration: 6 minutes.
Commissioned by the Suburban Symphony of Rockland County, Suffern, New
York. Unpublished. Premiere: 1954, Suffern, New York; Suburban
Symphony of Rockland County.

BALLET (1968) - String quartet with jazz quartet. Duration: 30
minutes. Commissioned by French shoe manufacturers. Unpublished.
Premiere: February 1968, New York City, Circle in the Square; composer at the piano and conducting.

BASIS (1968) - 4 double basses. In 5 units. Duration: 9 minutes.
Unpublished. Premiere: 1971, Montclair, New Jersey; members of the
New Jersey State Orchestra. Note: Excerpted from CONCENTRICS.

CONCENTRICS (1968) - Orchestra. Duration: 19 minutes. Commissioned
by Benjamin Steinberg. Unpublished; score and orchestral material
available on rental from Theodore Presser, New York. Premiere: 2
February 1969, Avery Fischer Hall, New York City; Symphony of the New
World, Benjamin Steinberg, Conductor. Reviewed: New York Times, 3
February 1969, p. 30. Note: Nominated for a Pulitzer Prize in 1969.

CONCERTO FOR DOUBLE BASS (1971) - Double bass and orchestra. Duration: 16 minutes. Unpublished; score and orchestral material
available on rental from Theodore Presser, New York. Note: Originally titled The Walton Statement and dedicated to Ortiz Walton.

DIALOGUE FOR PIANO AND ORCHESTRA (1966) - Piano and chamber orchestra.
Duration: 10 minutes. Publisher: Bryn Mawr, Pennsylvania, Theodore
Presser (1967) (available on rental).

DIM DU MIM (TWILIGHT) (1968-69) - English horn or oboe and chamber
orchestra. Duration: 8 minutes. Dedicated to "The donkey who walked
to Bethlehem." Unpublished. Premiere: 1971, Montclair, New Jersey;
New Jersey State Orchestra.

ECLATETTE (1969) - Violoncello. Commissioned by Earl Madison for the
1970 Tchaikovsky Competition in Moscow. Dedicated to William Grant

Still. Publisher: Nyack, New York, Cunningham Music (1975). In The Black Perspective in Music, 3.2 (May 1975): 226-34.

HARLEM SUITE (1969) - Ballet for chorus (SATB), solo voices, piano, electric bass, drums, orchestra, and dancers. Text by Arthur Cunningham. Commissioned by Dr. Robert Jones for the Laurentian Singers of St. Lawrence University, Canton, New York.

HOUSE BY THE SEA (1966) - Opera.

INVENTIONS, TWO (1952) - 2 double basses. Duration: 3 minutes. Unpublished.

JILL ELLEN (1975) - Violin, viola, violoncello, and guitar. Duration: 5 minutes. Unpublished. Premiere: 1975, Nyack College, Nyack, New York.

JILL ELLEN (1977) - Guitar. Duration: 5 minutes. Dedicated to Jill Abrams. Unpublished. Premiere: March 1977, Pardington Hall, Nyack College, Nyack, New York; Terry Staub, guitar.

LIGHTS ACROSS THE HUDSON (1956) - Orchestra. Duration: 4 minutes 30 seconds. Unpublished. Premiere: 1957, Columbia University, New York City. NOTE: Tone poem.

LITANY (1972) - Chorus (SATB) and orchestra. Text by Arthur Cunningham. Commissioned by Dr. Robert Jones for the Summer Chorus of Stanford University. Dedicated "To the flower children."

LULLABYE FOR A JAZZ BABY (1969) - Orchestra. Duration: 6 minutes 30 seconds. Recording: Desta 7107 (1970). Reviewed in The Black Perspective in Music, Vol. 4, No. 3 (Fall 1976), p. 343. NOTE: Written for Andre Kostelanetz.

MINAKESH (1969) - a. oboe and piano; b. violoncello and strings; c. voice and piano (1970) vocalise. Duration: 5 minutes. Unpublished. Premiere (voice and piano): 15 December 1970, National Gallery of Art, Washington, D.C.; Louise Parker, contralto. NOTE: Title means conjurer for good or evil.

MUNDY MAN (1970) - Chorus (SATB), orchestra, and harmonica. Duration: 3 minutes 30 seconds. NOTE: Blues composition; has received numerous performances.

NIGHT BIRD (1978) - Jazz quintet, solo voice, and chamber orchestra. Text by Arthur Cunningham. Duration: 12 minutes. Commissioned by James Frazier for the A.M.E. Zion Church, Philadelphia, Pennsylvania. Dedicated to Benjamin Breggin. Unpublished. Premiere: 12 November 1978, California State University, Carson City, California; Bill Renee Jazz Ensemble; Sue Harmon, soprano; Francis Steiner Conductor.

NIGHT LIGHTS (1955) - Orchestra. Duration: 4 minutes. Unpublished.

NIGHT SONG (1973) - Theatre piece for chorus (SATB), soloist, and orchestra. Text: Swahili/Gulla from Sea Islands; and English. Duration: 1 hour 30 minutes. Commissioned by Cheyney State College, Cheyney, Pennsylvania. Publisher: New York, Theodore Presser, 1974.

Contents: 1. Utumbrizo (Lullabye), 2. Kai (Truth), 3. Toa (Producer of Tomorrow).

OMNUS (1968) - String orchestra. Duration: 6 minutes. Three movements. Unpublished. NOTE: Excerpted from CONCENTRICS.

PATADITOS (1970) - Piano and orchestra. Duration: 5 minutes. Note: Title means "Little Kicks."

PERIMETERS (1965) - Flute, clarinet, vibraphone, and double bass. Duration: 11 minutes. Unpublished. Contents (four movements): 1. Arc, 2. Radius, 3. Circumference, 4. Diameter.

ROOSTER RHAPSODY (1975) - Orchestra and narrator. Text by Barbara Brenner. Duration: 17 minutes. Publisher: Bryn Mawr, Pennsylvania, Theodore Presser. NOTE: Work is for children.

SERENADE (1950) - Violoncello and piano. Duration: 4 minutes. Unpublished.   Premiere: 1950, Fisk University, Nashville, Tennessee; Bessye Atkins, cello.

SUN BIRD (1974-75) - Voice, chamber orchestra, and guitar. Text by Arthur Cunningham. Duration: 17 minutes. Commissioned by Cary McMurran. Unpublished. Premiere: March 1975, Hampton Roads Coliseum, Hampton, Virginia. NOTE: Written for Charlie Byrd and Louise Parker.

THEATRE PIECE (1966) - Orchestra. Duration: 10 minutes. Premiere: Festival of Contemporary Music, Spelman College, Atlanta, Georgia; Atlanta Symphony Orchestra.

THISBY DYING (1968) - Flute and violoncello or violoncello alone. Duration: 5 minutes. Unpublished. Premiere: Virginia State College Norfolk, Virginia; Antoinette Handy, flute. Recording: Eastern ERS-513 (1972). NOTE: This work is an arrangement of Asleep My Love from Four Songs. Later arranged for flute and viola (1975) and performed in spring 1976.

TRINITIES (1969) - Violoncello and 2 double basses.   Duration: 15 minutes. Commissioned by Arthur Davis. Unpublished. Contents: 1. Statement, 2. Hymn, 3. Strut (Jubilee).

TRIO FOR FLUTE, VIOLA AND BASSOON (1952) - Duration: 3 minutes. Unpublished.   Premiere: 1952, Juilliard School of Music, New York City; student ensemble.

TRIO FOR VIOLIN, VIOLA, AND VIOLONCELLO (1968) - Three movements. Duration: 10 minutes. Unpublished. NOTE: Excerpted from CONCENTRICS.

TWO WORLD SUITE (1971) - 6 double basses. Duration: 4 minutes. Unpublished. NOTE: a.k.a. STRUT.

VIOLETTA (1963) - Musical for soprano, tenor, baritone, and bass, with string quartet and string octet. Text by Odiberti; adaptation of his play "Le Mal Coeur." Duration: 2 hours. Unpublished (lc: piano-vocal score). NOTE: a.k.a. VIOLETS AND PHOSPHER.

Sources

Holly, Ellistine Perkins. Biographies of Black Composers and Songwriters. Dubuque, IA: Wm. C. Brown Publishers, 1990.

Southern, Eileen. Biographical Dictionary of Afro-American and African Musicians. Westport, CT: Greenwood Press, 1982.

Southern, Eileen. "Cunningham, Arthur." In The New Grove Dictionary of American Music, Vol. 1, p. 555.

Southern, EIleen. "Cunningham, Arthur." In The New Grove Dictionary of Music and Musicians, Vol. 5, p. 97.

Tishler, Alice. Fifteen Black American Composers: A Bibliography of Their Works. Detroit Studies in Music Bibliography. Detroit: Information Coordinators, 1981.

DABNEY, WENDELL PHILLIPS (1865-1952)

Works

MOMENTS OF PLEASURE WALTZ - Guitar. Dedicated to Jas A. Allen Esq. Publisher: Cincinnati, James F. Roach. Score: Library of Congress and in photocopy format at the Center for Black Music Research, Columbia College-Chicago.

THE MYSTIC SHRINE - Guitar. Dedicated to Jno D. Potts Esq. Score: Library of Congress and in photocopy format at the Center for Black Music Research, Columbia College-Chicago.

ONLY A DREAM - Guitar. Score: Library of Congress and in photocopy format at the Center for Black Music Research, Columbia College-Chicago.

PLANTATION CLASSIC - 2 guitars. Dedicated to Dr. Dvořák. Score: Library of Congress and in photocopy format at the Center for Black Music Research, Columbia College-Chicago.

Source

Scores at the Center for Black Music Research Columbia College-Chicago.

DA COSTA, NOEL (1929 -)

Noel Da Costa was born December 24, 1929, in Lagos, Nigeria.
Da Costa received his musical education at Queens College, CUNY (B.A., 1952) and Columbia University (M.A., 1956).
He received a Seidle Fellowship in composition at Columbia and a Fulbright Fellowship to study composition with Luigi Dallapiccola in Italy.
His first published composition was Tambourines (a Langston Hughes poem). Among his best known works are the song cycle The Confession Stone (text by Owen Dodson), "Jes Grew," Spiritual Set, and The Singing Tortoise, a theatre piece for children.

Da Costa has taught at Queens and Hunter College-CUNY, Hampton Institute in Virginia, and in 1970 was appointed to the music faculty of Rutgers.

Works

BLUE MIX: A COMPOSITION IN THE FORM OF A CHART (1970)- Solo contrabass/Fender bass, violoncello, contrabass, and percussion (1 player). Duration: 17 minutes. Written for and dedicated to Ron Carter. Publisher: Atsoc Music.

THE BLUE MOUNTAINS (1962) - Mezzo-soprano, flute, oboe, clarinet, bass clarinet, F horn, trumpet, viola, violoncello, contrabass, and percussion. See IN THE LANDSCAPE OF SPRING.

CEREMONY OF SPIRITUALS (1976) - Soprano, soprano/tenor saxophone, orchestra, and chorus. Commissioned by the New York State Arts Council in conjunction with the Symphony of the New World.

THE CONFESSION STONE (1969) - Soprano, trio (SSA), and instrumental ensemble (flute, oboe, clarinet, bassoon, F horn, trumpet, viola, violoncello, contrabass, and piano). Text by Owen Dodson. Duration: 20 minutes. Publisher: Atsoc Music. Premiere: 1969, Society of Black Composers, New York City.

EPIGRAMS (1965) - Solo violin and flute, clarinet, bass clarinet, bassoon, vibraphone, and piano. Duration: 10 minutes. Publisher: Atsoc Music.

FIVE EPITAPHS (1956) - Soprano and string quartet. Text by Cuntee Cullen. Duration: 12 minutes. Publisher: Atsoc Music. Premiere: ca. 1956, Queens College, Flushing, New York; Charlotte Holloman, soprano. Contents: 1. For a Poet, 2. For My Grandmother, 3. For Paul Laurence Dunbar, 4. For a Lady I Know, 5. If You Should Go.

FIVE VERSES WITH VAMPS (1968) - Violoncello and piano in five movements. Duration: 9 minutes. Publisher: Kings Crown Music Press (Galaxy Music), 1976. Premiere: 1970, Alice Tully Hall; Evalyn Steinbock, violoncello.

IN SPACE (1972) - Solo contrabass. Duration: 12 minutes. Publisher: Atsoc Music. Premiere: 1973, at the Space for Innovative Development in New York City; Ron Carter, contrabass.

IN THE CIRCLE (1970) - 4 electric guitars, Fender bass, and percussion (1 player). Duration: 2 minutes. Publisher: Atsoc Music. Note: The composer describes this work as an interpolation on a Haitian folk tale.

IN THE LANDSCAPE OF SPRING (1962) - Mezzo-soprano, flute, oboe, clarinet, bass clarinet, F horn, trumpet, viola, violoncello, contrabass, and percussion. Text based on three Zenrin poems. Duration: 10 minutes. Publisher: Atsoc Music. Premiere: 1964, University of Illinois; David Garvey Ensemble. Three movements with interludes after movements one and two: In the Landscape of Spring; Sitting Quietly, Doing Nothing; The Blue Mountains.

JES' GREW #1 CHANT VARIATIONS FOR VIOLIN (1973) - Violin and electric piano. Duration: 12 minutes. Publisher: Atsoc Music. Premiere: 1973, the Gallery of Music in Our Time, New York City; Max Pollikoff, violin; Paul Griffin, electric piano.

MAGNOLIA BLUE (1975) - Violin and piano. Duration: 10 minutes. Publisher: Atsoc Music.

NOVEMBER SONG (1974) - Concert scene for soprano, violin, saxophone, and piano (with improvisation). Text by Gwendolyn brooks. Duration: 7-15 minutes. Publisher: Atsoc Music.

OCCURRENCE FOR SIX (1965) - Flute, clarinet, bass clarinet, tenor saxophone, trumpet, and contrabass. Duration: 11 minutes. Publisher: Atsoc Music.

QUIETLY . . . VAMP IT AND TAG IT (1971) - Orchestra. Duration: 8 minutes. Publisher: Atsoc Music. Note: An educational piece in the form of a chart (especially for a younger audience).

RIFF TIME (1972) - Violin, violoncello, piano, and percussion (5 players). Duration: 10-15 minutes. Publisher: Atsoc Music. Note: Written especially for a younger audience, who will participate in the percussion parts.

SITTING QUIETLY, DOING NOTHING (1962) - Mezzo-soprano, flute, oboe, clarinet, bass clarinet, F horn, trumpet, viola, violoncello, contrabass, and percussion. See IN THE LANDSCAPE OF SPRING.

SPACES (1966) - Trumpet and contrabass. Duration: 12 minutes. Publisher: Atsoc Music.

STATEMENT AND RESPONSE (1966) - Flute, oboe, bass clarinet, trumpet, trombone, tuba, viola, violoncello, and contrabass. Duration: 15 minutes. Publisher: Atsoc Music.

"STILL MUSIC" No. 1 (1965) - 2 violins. Duration: 10 minutes. Publisher: Atsoc Music.

TIME . . . ON AND ON (1971) - Violin, tenor saxophone, and pre-recorded electronic sounds. Duration: 40 minutes. Publisher: Atsoc Music.

TWO PIECES FOR UNACCOMPANIED CELLO (1973) - Duration: 1 minute. Publisher: Atsoc Music. Premiere: 1973, Alice Tully Hall; Ronald Lipscomb, violoncello. Note: Based on Ewe chant rhythms.

Sources

Abdul, Raoul. "Folk Music in Symphonic Garb." In Blacks in Classical Music. New York: Dodd, Mead & Co., 1977, pp. 44-47.

Baker, David N., Lida M. Belt, and Herman C. Hudson. The Black Composer Speaks. Metuchen, NJ: The Scarecrow Press, 1978.

Claghorn, Charles E. Biographical Dictionary of American Music. West Nyack, NY: Parker Publishing Co., 1973.

McDaniel, L. "Out of the Black Church." American Organist 13.5 (1979): 34-38.

Moore, Carman. "Da Costa, Noel (George)." In The New Grove Dictionary of American Music, Vol. 1, p. 560.

Southern, Eileen. Biographical Dictionary of Afro-American and African Musicians. Westport, CT: Greenwood Press, 1982.

DAVIS, ANTHONY (1951 -)

Anthony Davis was born February 20, 1951, in Paterson, New Jersey.
He studied music at Yale (BA, 1975).
In 1973 he co-founded Advent, a free-jazz group. From 1974 to 1977 he was a member of the New Dalta Ahkri band led by Leo Smith. He played with Leroy Jenkin's trio (1977-79) in New York, and has worked in a duo and a quartet with James Newton. He also worked with Lewis and Abdul Wadud.

Works

MAPS (198?) - Concerto for violin and symphony orchestra. Recording: Gramavision 18-8807; Kansas City Symphony Orchestra, William McGlaughlin, Conductor; Shem Guibbory, violin.

NOTES FROM THE UNDERGROUND (1988) - Orchestra. Duration: 9 minutes.
Publisher: Oxford University Press.

STILL WATERS (1982) - Orchestra. Duration: 17 minutes. Publisher: Oxford University Press.

UNDER THE DOUBLE MOON (1989) - Opera. Premiere: Summer 1989; Opera Theatre of St. Louis.

VIOLIN CONCERTO (1988) - Duration: 25 minutes. Publisher: Oxford University Press.

WAYGANG NO. 5 (1988) - Concerto for piano and orchestra. Recording: Grammavision 18-8807; Kansas City Orchestra, William McGlaughlin, conductor; Anthony Davis, piano; Pheeron Aklaff, percussion.

WYANG V (1985) - Piano and orchestra. Duration: 25 minutes. Publisher: Oxford University Press.

X, THE LIFE AND TIMES OF MALCOLM X (1985) - Opera.

XCERPTS (1986) - Concert presentation of arias and highlights from the opera X, The Life and Times of Malcolm X. Duration: 105 minutes.
Publisher: Oxford University Press.

Sources

Blair, Gwenda. "Evening the Score." Daily News Magazine (28 September 1986): 20-24.

Interviews with Christopher Anthony and Thulani Davis on their operatic collaboration "X," about the late civil rights leader Malcolm X.

Kerner, Leighton. "Malcolm X, His Opera." Village Voice 29 October 1985: 82.

Kerner, Leighton. "The Overhaul of X." Village Voice 21 October 1986: 78.

Malitz, Nancy. "The Black Classical Musician Moving into the Mainstream." Ovation Magazine February 1989.

Mandel, Howard. "Caught: X (The Life and Times of Malcolm X) New York City Opera/New York." Down Beat (January 1987): 50.

Piccarella, John. "Malcolm in Midtown: The Terrain of Recent Black American History Shifts Beneath X's Operatic Convention." Village Voice 21 October 1986: 77-78.

Rockwell, John. "Malcolm X--Hero to Some, Racist to Others--Is Now the Stuff of Opera." New York Times 28 September 1986: 2.1, 21.

Rowes, B. "For Composer Anthony Davis, X Marks the Premiere of What May Be the First Major Black Opera." People (6 October 1986): 129-130.

Schneider, Steve. "Cable TV Notes--Series Explores Contemporary Composers and Choreographers." New York Times 21 September 1986 Sec. 2. Short notice on video profile of Anthony Davis' opera "X" (The Life and Times of Malcolm X).

Seligman, G. "The Road to X." Opera News (September 1986): 28-30.

DAVIS, NATHAN (1937 -)

Nathan Davis was born February 15, 1937, in Kansas City, Kansas.
He studied at the University of Kansas, Wesleyan University (Ph.D., 1974), and the Sorbonne in Paris (where he studied with Andre Hodeir).
He has received the WAMO Distinguished Musician award and was selected by Ebony magazine for its success series of Who's Who in Black America.
Davis is vice-president of Segue Records.
He is director and founder of the jazz studies program at Paris American Academy, and director and founder of the jazz studies program at the University of Pittsburgh.
Among his best known works are The United Spirited, Makatura, Rules of Freedom, Happy Girl, and To Ursula with Love.

Work

THE UNITED SPIRITED - Jazz orchestra, string quartet, choir.

Source

Jacobi, Hugh William. Contemporary American Composers Based at American Colleges and Universities. Paradise, CA: Paradise Arts, 1975, p. 125.

DAWSON, WILLIAM LEVI (1899-1990)

William Levi Dawson was born September 26, 1899, in Anniston, Alabama. He entered Tuskegee Institute at the age of 13, where he studied music under Frank L. Drye and Alice Carter Simmons, played in the band and orchestra, and served as music librarian. He later attended Washburn College, the Horner Institute of Fine Arts (B. Mus., 1925), the American Conservatory of Music-Chicago (M.Mus., 1927). After receiving his Master's degree he remained in Chicago to study with Thorvald Otterstrom and Felix Borowski, and did additional graduate work at the Eastman School of Music. He also studied privately with Carl Busch and Regina Hall.

He received Wanamaker Awards in 1930 and 1931 for the Scherzo for orchestra and Lovers Plighted. Other honors included an honorary doctorate from Tuskegee in 1955, an Alumni Achievement Award from the University of Missouri-Kansas City in 1963, and an American Choral Directors Association Award in 1975. In 1975 he was elected to the Alabama Arts Hall of Fame.

He was best-known for his arrangements of numerous spirituals. Among his other works are Negro Folk Symphony (revised to reflect African rhythms and idioms after a sabbatical spent studying native music in West Africa), Negro Worksong for Orchestra, Sonata in A for violin and piano, and Trio in A for violin, cello, and piano.

Dawson taught at Kansas Vocational College-Topeka (where he served as director of music), Lincoln High School in Kansas City, and at Tuskegee Institute from 1931-56, when the Tuskegee Choir gained international renown under his leadership.

Works

BREAK, BREAK, BREAK - Chorus and orchestra.

NEGRO FOLK SYMPHONY (1931; revised 1952) - Orchestra. Duration: 35 minutes. Three movements: 1. The Bond of Africa, 2. Hope in the Night, 3. O Le' Me Shine, Shine Like a Morning Star. Publisher: Delaware Water Gap, Pennsylvania, Shawnee Music (1965). Premiere: 14 November 1934, Philadelphlia, Pennsylvania; Philadelphia Orchestra, Leopold Stokowski, Conductor. Recording: Decca DL 710077 (revised version) 1963. Reviewed: Philadelphia newspaper, 24 November 1934; Music Journal, October 1964, Vol. 22, pp. 64-65; Kansas City Star, 30 January 1966; Nashville Tennessean, 2 May 1966. Notes: Manuscript in Moreland Collection, Howard University.

A NEGRO WORKSONG FOR ORCHESTRA (1941) - Commissioned by Columbia Broadcasting System, 1940, for American School of the Air. Publisher: New York, 194 (NYPL). NOTE: Based on the folksong "Stewball."

OUT IN THE FIELDS - Voice and piano (orchestra). Text by Louise Imogen Guiney. Duration: 2 minutes 35 seconds. Publisher: Chicago, Camble Hinged Music (1929); Distributer: KJOS Music Co. Recording: Desto DC-7107 (1972), orchestral version.

OUT IN THE FIELDS - Chorus (SATB) and piano (orchestra); women's chorus (SSA) and piano (orchestra). Dedication: "In memory of my beloved wife, Cornella." Publisher: Music Press of Tuskegee Institute (1957); orchestral accompaniment available on rental from KJOS Music Co.

SCHERZO (1920) - Orchestra. Note: Won the Wanamaker Prize in 1930.

SONATA IN A - Violin and piano.

SONATA IN A MINOR FOR VIOLIN AND PIANO (1927)

TRIO IN A MAJOR FOR VIOLIN, VIOLONCELLO, AND PIANO (1925)

Sources

Abdul, Raoul. "Spotlight on Black Composers." In Blacks in Classical Music. New York: Dodd, Mead & Co., 1977, pp. 58-59.

Braithwaite, Coleridge Alexander. "A Survey of the Lives and Creative Activities of Some Negro Composers." Dissertation, New York Teachers' College, Columbia University, 1952.

Howard, John Tasker. Our Contemporary Composers. New York: Corwell, 1941.

Malone, M.H. "William Levi Dawson: American Music Educator." Dissertation (Ph.D.), Florida State University, 1981.

Reis, Claire R. Composers in America. New York: McMillan, 1947.

Southern, Eileen. Biographical Dictionary of Afro-American and African Musicians. Westport, CT: Greenwood Press, 1982, pp. 79-99.

Southern, Eileen. "Dawson, William Levi." In The New Grove Dictionary of Music and Musicians, Vol. 5, p. 286.

Southern, Eileen. "Dawson, William Levi." In The New Grove Dictionary of American Music, Vol. 1, p. 590.

Spady, James G., ed. William Dawson: A UMUM Tribute and a Marvelous Journey. Philadelphia, PA: Creative Artists' Workshop, 1981, 60 pp.

Tischler, Alice. Fifteen Black American Composers: A Bibliography of Their Works. Detroit Studies in Music Bibliography. Detroit: Information Coordinators, 1981.

DEDÉ, EDMOND (1827-1903)

Edmond Dedé was born in New Orleans, Louisiana, November 20, 1827, and died in 1903 in France.

His parents, migrants from the French West Indies, encouraged him when he began to show musical talent. He studied with Constantin Deburque, director of the Philharmonic Society, and L. Gabici, director of the St. Charles Theater orchestra. In 1848 he studied in Mexico, and in 1857 he entered the Conservatory in Paris, where he studied composition with Jacque-François Halévy and Jean-Delphin Alard.

Around 1868 he became director of the L'Alcazar Theater orchestra in Bordeaux, where he remained for twenty-five years.

Some of his best-known compositions were "Les faux mandarins," "La sensitive," "Emilie," "Le palmier overture," and the opera Sultan d'Ispahan.

Works

L'ANNEAU DU DIABLE (1880) - Dramatic piece in three acts.

L'ANTROPOHAGE (1880) - Operetta in one act.

APRÈS LE MIEL (1880) - Opéra comique.

ARCADIA OVERTURE - Orchestra.

UNE AVENTURE DE TÉLÉMAQUE - Opera.

LES CANOTIERS DE LORMENT (1880) - Ballet-divertissement.

CARYATIS - Ballet-divertissement.

CHANT DRAMATIQUE - Orchestra.

CHICAGO: GRANDE VALSE À L'AMÉRICAINE - Orchestra. Publisher: Paris, E Fromont, 1891. Score: Bibliotèque Nationale, Paris, France.

CHIK-KING-FO (1878) - Operetta in one act.

EN CHASSE; MAZURKA ELEGANTE - Orchestra. (by Eugène Dédé) Edited by Edmond Dédé. Paris: n.p., 1891. Score: Bibliotèque Nationale, Paris, France.

DIANA ET ACTÉON - Ballet-divertissement.

ELLIS - Ballet.

LES FAUX MANDARINS - Ballet.

MÉPHISTO MASQUE: POLKA FANTASTIQUE - Orchestra. Publisher: Paris, L. Bathlot et Héraud (1889). Score: Bibliotèque Nationale, Paris, France.

MIRLITON FIN DE SIÈCLE: POLKA ORIGINALE - Orchestra. Publisher: Paris, E. Fromont (1891). Score: Bibliotèque Nationale, Paris, France.

MON SOUS OFF'CIER: QUADRILLE BRILLIANT - Orchestra. Publisher: Bordeaux, E. Philibert (1877). Score: Bibliotèque Nationale, Paris, France.

NÉHANA, REINE DES FÉES (1862) - Ballet in one act.

LE NOYE - Opera comique.

LES NYMPHES ET CHASSEURS (1880) - Ballet in one act.

LE PALMIER OUVERTURE - Orchestra.

RÊVERIE CHAMPÊTRE: FANTAISIE - Duet for violin and violoncello or flute and bassoon, with piano accompaniment. Publisher: Author, 1891. Score: Bibliotèque Nationale, Paris, France.

LA SENSITIVE (1877) - Ballet in two acts.

SPAHIS ET GRISETTES (1880) - Ballet-divertissement.

SULTAN D'ISPAHAN - Opera in four acts.

SYMPHONY ("QUASIMODO," by 1865)

LE TRIOMPHE DE BACCHUS (1880) - Ballet-divertissement.

Sources

Christian, Marcus B. "Dedé, Edmund." In Dictionary of American Negro Biography, eds. Rayford W. Logan and MIchael R. Winston. New York: W.W. Norton, 1982, pp. 168-69.

Desdunes, Rodolphe. Our People and Our History. Trans. Dorothea Olga McCants. Baton Rouge: Louisiana State University Press, 1973. (Originally published as Nos Hommes et Notre Histoire. Montreal, 1911.)

Southern, Eileen. Biographical Dictionary of Afro-American and African Musicians. Westport, CT: Greenwood Press, 1982.

Trotter, James M. Music and Some Highly Musical People. 1878. Rpt. Chicago: Afro-Am Press, 1969, pp. 340-41.

Wyatt, Lucius. "Composers Corner." BMR Newsletter, Vol. 9, No. 1.

Wyatt, Lucius. "Updated Music List--Six Composers of Nineteenth-Century New Orleans." BMR Newsletter 9.1.

DENNIS, MARK ANDREW, JR. (1949 -)

Mark Andrew Dennis was born in Atlanta, Georgia, in 1949.
He received his BS from Morehouse College in 1971 and his MM from Bowling Green State University in 1973.
In 1967 he won a piano soloist competition for performance with the Atlanta Symphony Orchestra. In 1973 he received a commission for a harp composition from Archola E. Clark of the Frysk Orchestra, Leeuwarden, in the Netherlands.
He is currently teaching at Bowling Green State University.

Works

BLACK MIRRORS (1972-73) - Instrumental ensemble and choir. Publisher: SELF.

SERENE (1973) - Harp, electronic tape, and voice.

A SET OF THREE (1972) - Clarinet and violin. Publisher: SELF

Source

Information submitted by the composer.

DETT, R[OBERT] NATHANIEL (1882-1943)

Robert Nathaniel Dett was born October 11, 1882, in Drummondsville, Ontario, Canada, and died October 2, 1943, in Battle Creek, Michigan.
He came from a musical family, and first played piano by ear.   In 1893, when his family moved to the US side of Niagara Falls, he began piano study with a local teacher.   Later he studied with Oliver Willis Halsted, then enrolled at Oberlin Conservatory in Ohio (B. Mus., 1908), where he studied with Howard Handel Carter, Arthur E. Heacos, and George Carl Hastings, and in 1913 he spent the summer studying with Karl Gehrkens at Oberlin.   He studied at Harvard in 1919-20.   In 1929 he studied with Nadia Boulanger at the American Conservatory in Fontainebleau, France.   He received his M. Mus. in 1932 from The Eastman School of Music in Rochester, New York.
He received numerous awards and honors, including an award from the Harmon Foundation, honorary doctorates from Howard University and Oberlin, and the Palm and Ribbon Award from the Royal Belgian Band.   While at Harvard he won the Francis Boott Prize for his choral composition "Don't be weary, traveler," and the Bowdoin Prize for his essay, "The Emancipation of Negro Music."   He was one of the founders of the National Association for Negro Musicians in 1919, and served as its president from 1924-26.
Dett was one of the most celebrated African American composers of his time and, like contemporaries Harry T. Burleigh and Will Marion Cook, placed considerable emphasis on African American folk idioms in his work. He was influenced in this by Azalia Hackley and his appreciate of her work. He published two sets of spiritual arrangements: Religious Folksongs of the Negro and The Dett Collection of Negro Spirituals.   Other well-known compositions are the choral motets and oratorios such as "Don't be weary, traveler" and "I'll never turn back no more."   He also wrote Music in the Mine, The Chariot Jubilee, The Ordering of Moses, and the piano suites Magnolia, In the Bottoms, Enchantment, Tropic Winter, and Eight Bible Vignettes.
Dett was widely known during his lifetime as a concert pianist, choral conductor, and teacher.   He performed in the All-Colored Composers' Concerts produced by William Hackney during 1914-16.   He began teaching at Lane College in Jackson, Tennessee.   Later he taught at Lincoln University-Missouri, Hampton Institute in Virgina, and Sam Huston College.   From 1937-42 he taught at Bennett College, Greensboro, North Carolina.

Works

THE CHARIOT JUBILEE (1921) - Tenor, chorus and orchestra.

ENCHANTMENT SUITE - Orchestra.   Arr.   Publisher: John Church, n.d. Held by Fleisher Collection (No. 3627).

IN THE BOTTOMS: JUBA DANCE - Orchestra.   Arr.   Publisher: Detroit, Luck's Music Library, n.d.

MUSIC IN THE MINE (1916) - Chorus and orchestra.

THE ORDERING OF MOSES - Oratorio (chorus and orchestra).   Publisher: New York, J. Fischer & Bro., 1937 (Fischer edition 7230).

QUARTET - Strings.   Publisher: New York, Southern Music Publishing Co. (after 1974).

Sources

Abdul, Raoul. "Recordings: Black Piano Music." In Blacks in Classical Music. New York: Dodd, Mead & Co., 1977, pp. 61-62.

Adams, Russell L. Great Negroes, Past and Present. Chicago: Afro-Am Publishing Co., 1969, p. 177.

BPIMI, Spring 1973.

De Lerma, Dominique-Rene. Black Concert and Recital Music: Provisional. Bloomington, IN: Afro-American Music Opportunities Association, 1975.

Dett, R. Nathaniel. The Collected Piano Works, with introductions by Dominique-Rene de Lerma and Vivian McBrier. Evanston, IL, 1973.

Fisher, Walter. "Dett, Robert Nathaniel." In Dictionary of American Biography, Supplement 3, pp. 224-26.

Hare, Maud Cuney. Negro Musicians and Their Music. Washington, D.C.: Associated Publishers, 1936, pp. 249, 262, 336-39.

McBrier, Vivian Flagg. R. Nathaniel Dett: His Life and Works. Washington, D.C., 1977.

Southern, Eileen. Biographical Dictionary of Afro-American and African Musicians. Westport, CT: Greenwood Press, 1982, pp. 104-05.

Southern, Eileen. "Dett, R(obert) Nathaniel." In The New Grove Dictionary of American Music, Vol. 1, pp. 610-11.

Southern, Eileen. "Dett, R(obert) Nathaniel." In The New Grove Dictionary of Music and Musicians, Vol. 5, pp. 404-05.

DICKERSON, ROGER DONALD (1934 -)

Roger Donald Dickerson was born in New Orleans on August 24, 1934.
He began to study piano at the age of 8 and began playing brass instruments in high school in New Orleans. He earned his B.A. at Dillard University in New Orleans and his M. Mus. at Indiana University-Bloomington. He also studied with Karl Schiske at the Akademie fur Music and Darstellende Kunst in Vienna between 1959 and 1962.
He received Fulbright and John Hay Whitney Fellowships and the Louis Armstrong Memorial Award, and in 1978 was the subject of a PBS documentary film, "New Orleans Concerto."
Some of his best known works are Essay for Band, A Musical Service for Louis (with reference to Louis Armstrong), Orpheus an' His Slide Trombone, and New Orleans Concerto.
Dickerson co-founded the Creative Artists Alliance in 1975. He serves as a consultant in music to the Humanities Section of the Institute for Services to Education, where he also served as music editor for three books published by the Institute.

Works

CONCERT OVERTURE FOR ORCHESTRA (1957) - Duration: 15 minutes. Unpublished; on rental from Southern Music Publishing Co., New York. Premiere: 1965, Tulane University, New Orleans, Louisiana; New Orleans Philharmonic, Werner Torkanowsky, Conductor. Recorded: Voice of American in South America. Reviewed in Saturday Review, 172 Paril 1965, p. 30. Notes: Written for Master's thesis.

CONCERT PIECES FOR BEGINNING STRING PLAYERS TEN (1973) - Duration: 19 minutes. Contents: 1. Cathedral Bells; 2. Jubilee; 3. Angelic Chorus; 4. Dance; 5. Mysteries; 6. Song; 7. Parade of the Dragons; 8. An American Village; 9. Figures in Space; 10. The Machine Age. Commissioned by the Youth String Program of the New Orleans Philharmonic through a Rockefeller Foundation Grant. Publisher: New York, Southern Music Publishing Co. (1977). Premiere: (pieces 1, 5, 7, and 9): 1973, Ursuline Academy, New Orleans, Louisiana; Youth String Orchestra, Carter Nice, Conductor.

MUSIC FOR STRING TRIO (1957) - Duration: 3 minutes 30 seconds. Unpublished.

A MUSICAL SERVICE FOR LOUIS (A REQUIEM FOR LOUIS ARMSTRONG) (1972) - Orchestra with optional mixed chorus (no text). Duration: 15 minutes. Commissioned by the New Orleans Philharmonic through a National Endowment for the Arts grant. Dedicated to Louis Armstrong. Publisher: New York, Southern Music Publishing Co. (1973). Premiere: 17 March 1972, New Orleans, Louisiana; New Orleans Philharmonic, Werner Torkanowsky, Conductor. Notes: Brief description in: Second Line, 24 (Spring 1972), 10. Reviewed: States-Item (New Orleans) 8 March 1972; Times-Picayune (New Orleans) 9 March 1972; Mobile Register (Alabama) 9 March 1972; Clarion Herald (New Orleans) 16 March 1972; New York Times 6 February 1973; Greensboro Record (North Carolina) 14 July 1974; Greensboro Daily News 14 July 1975.

NEW ORLEANS CONCERTO (1976) - Piano, orchestra, with soprano solo. Three movements. Duration: 25 minutes. Commissioned by Werner Torkanowsky and Alexis Weissenberg for the Bicentennial. Publisher: New York, Southern Music Publishing Company. Premiere: 14 January 1977, New Orleans, Louisiana; New Orleans Philharmonic, Werner Torkanowsky, Conductor; Leon Bates, piano. Notes: Reviewed: Clairon Herald (New Orleans) January 1977; Times-Picayune (New Orleans) 20 January 1977; Washington Post   28 February 1978. The Institute for Services to Education (Washington, D.C.O has released a film about the creation of this work; presented twice on national networks.

ORPHEUS AN' HIS SLIDE TROMBONE (1974-75) - Orchestra and narrator. Text based on Jeanne Greenberg's "Orpheus an' Eurydice" in Rites of Passage. Duration: 22 minutes. Dedicated to Werner Torkanowsky. Publisher: New York, Southern Music Publishing Co. Premiere: 18 March 1975, New Orleans, Louisiana; New Orleans Philharmonic, Werner Torkanowsky, Conductor; Roscoe Lee Brown, narrator. Notes: Text and brief description in New Orleans Philharmonic Symphony Orchestra Program Notes, 18-19 March 1975. Reviewed: Clarion Herald (New Orleans) 3 April 1975; St. Paul Pioneer Press (Minnesota) 21 February 1977.

STRING QUARTET (1956) - Three movements. Duration: 15 minutes.
Dedicated to Mr. and Mrs. Melville Bryant. Publisher: New York,
Southern Music Publishing Co. Premiere: 1957, Indiana University,
Bloomington, Indiana; Berkshire Quartet.

Sources

McGinty, Doris Evans. "Dickerson, Roger." In The New Grove Dictionary of American Music, Vol. 1, p. 615.

Southern, Eileen. Biographical Dictionary of Afro-American and African Musicians. Westport, CT: Greenwood Press, 1982, p. 106.

Tischler, Alice. Fifteen Black American Composers: A Bibliography of
Their Works. Detroit Studies in Music Bibliography. Detroit: Information Coordinators, 1981.

DITON, CARL ROSSINI (1886-1962)

Carl Rossini Diton was born October 30, 1886, in Philadelphia, and
died there January 25, 1962.
He first studied music with his father, Samuel James Diton, a professional musician. He received his BS from the University of Pennsylvania in
1909, and was encouraged in his music study by E. Azalia Hackley, who
raised funds for a scholarship that enabled him to study in Munich, Germany, during 1910-11.
Diton taught at Paine College in Augusta, Georgia, at Wiley College in
Marshall, Texas, and at Talladega College, Alabama.
He was the first African American pianist to make a transcontinental
tour 1909-10), and continued to give piano recitals until the mid-20s. He
made his debut as a concert baritone in 1926, and went to New York to study
further at Juilliard (diploma, 1930).
As a composer, he won first prize in 1914 in a New York contest for
his arrangement of four Negro spirituals, and in 1930 received the Harmon
Award for composition.
Diton conducted music studios in Philadelphia and in New York City,
became organist/choirmaster at St. Martin's Church, and was active as an
accompanist with such singers as Marian Anderson, Jules Bledsoe, Caterina
Jarboro, and Enzio Pinza.
In 1919 he became a charter member of the National Association of
Negro Musicians, and served as national president from 1926 to 1928.

Works

SYMPHONY IN C MINOR - Orchestra

Sources

Carter, Madison H. An Annotated Catalogue of Composers of African
Ancestry. New York: Vantage Press, 1986.

Roach, Hildred. Black American Composers: Past and Present, Vol. 1.
Miami: Krieger Publishing Co., 1985, p. 36.

Southern, Eileen. The Music of Black Americans. New York: W.W.
Norton & Co., 1983, pp. 279-80.

DORSEY, JAMES ELMO (1905 -)

Works

AN AMERICAN VIGNETTE - Full choral symphony in four movements. Cho-
rus, contralto solo, and orchestra. Contents: 1. The Mother; 2. The
Romance of Jake and Sue; 3. Pic-a-nic, Barndance, Brawl; 4. Epilogue:
The Mother's Lament, The Mother's Faith. Dissertation (Ph.D.) Univer-
sity of Pennsylvania (1949). Held by Indiana University (msM 1539
.D71 A5).

Source

De Lerma, Dominique-René. Black Concert and Recital Music: Provisional List. Bloomington, IN: Afro-American Music Opportunities,
1975.

DREW, JAMES M. (1929 -)

James M. Drew was born in St. Paul, Minnesota, February 9, 1929.
He attended the New York School of Music, and received his MA from
Tulane University. He studied composition with Wallingford Rieger ˋand
Edgard Varèse.
Drew received a Guggenheim Fellowship in 1972/73 and the Pan American
Prize in 1974.
He has been a faculty member at Northwestern University (1965-67),
Yale University (1957-73), Louisiana State University (1973-75), and
Tanglewood (1973), and has been visiting composer at California State
University at Fullerton (1976-77) and at University of California at Los
Angeles (1977-78).
He served as director of the American Music Theatre in 1977.

Works

STRING QUARTET NO. 1 (LUX INCOGNITUS) - Publisher: Theodore Presser.

SYMPHONY NO. 2 - Orchestra. Publisher: Theodore Presser.

WEST INDIANS LIGHTS (1973) - Orchestra. Publisher: Theodore Presser,
1973. Score: Center for Black Music Research, Columbia College,
Chicago, IL.

Source

Horne, Aaron. "Orchestral Works by Black Composers: A Compilation
from Selected Sources." Black Composers, Black Performers, and the
American Symphony Orchestra. Chicago: Center for Black Music Research, 1988, pp. 8-23.

DUBOIS, SHIRLEY GRAHAM (Graham, Shirley Lola) (Mrs. McCanns, Mrs. W.E.B.
Dubois) (1904? - 1978)

Shirley Graham DuBois was born November 11, 1904(?) in Indiana, and
died September 6, 1978.

She studied at Oberlin College, Howard University, the Institute of Musical Art in New York City, and the Sorbonne in Paris.

She served as musical director at Morgan College, Baltimore, MD.

She was also active as an author, and wrote books, plays, and articles. Among her publications are the biographies Booker T. Washington (1955), George Washington Carver (1944), His Day Is Marching On: A Memoir of W.E.B. DuBois (1971), and The Story of Phyllis Wheatley: Poetess of the American Revolution (1949); plays, Cool Dust, Elija's Raven, and It's Morning; and articles including "Spirituals to Symphonies" (Etude, November 1936, pp 691-2) and "Tribute to Paul Robeson" (Freedomways, first quarter 1971, pp. 6-7).

Works

LITTLE BLACK SAMBO (1938) - Opera.

TOM-TOM (1932) - Opera. Libretto by the composer.

Sources

Abdul, Raoul. "Operas by Black Composers." In Blacks in Classical Music. New York: Dodd, Mead & Co., 1977, pp. 123-24.

Carter, Madison H. An Annotated Catalogue of Composers of African Ancestry. New York: Vantage Press, 1986.

Cohen, Aaron I. International Encyclopedia of Women Composers. New York: R.R. Bowker Co., 1981.

Davis, Russell H. Blacks in Cleveland. Washington, D.C.: Associated Publishers, 1972, p. 301.

"Graham, Shirley." Current Biography 1946, pp. 221-22.

Hare, Maud Cuny. Negro Musicians and Their Music. Washington, D.C.: Associated Publishers, 1936, p. 345.

Peterson, B.L. "Shirley Graham DuBois: Composer and Playwright." The Crisis (May 1977): 177-79.

Southern, Eileen. Biographical Dictionary of Afro-American and African Musicians. Westport, CT: Greenwood Press, 1982, p. 152.

DUCANDER, STEN (1923 -)

Works

FIVE NEGRO SPIRITUALS FOR MALE CHOIR, FLUTE, AND GUITAR. Publisher: Helsinki, Edition Fazer, 1967, 1962. Held by Indiana University (M 1671 .D82 N3).

Source

De Lerma, Dominique-Rene. Black Concert and Recital Music: Provisional List. Bloomington, IN: Afro-American Music Opportunities, 1975.

DUNCAN, JOHN (1913-1975)

John Duncan was born November 25, 1913, in Lee County, Alabama. He died in Montgomery, Alabama, September 15, 1975.

He earned both his bachelor's and master's degrees at Temple University, and studied further at New York University.

Few of his compositions were published, but they were extensively performed. His best known works were the Concerto for Trombone and Orchestra, An Easter Canticle, the opera Gideon and Eliza, and Black Bards for flute, cello, and piano.

He taught at Sam Huston College in Texas, then moved in 1939 to Alabama State University, where he taught until his death. In 1947 he received an honorary degree from the university.

Works

ATAVISTIC - String quartet.

BLACK BARBS - Flute, cello and piano.

CONCERTO FOR TROMBONE AND ORCHESTRA

DIVERSIONS, NO. 1 - Flute, horn, and strings.

DIVERTIMENTO - Trombone and string quartet.

GIDEON AND ELIZA - Opera.

QUINTET (1967) - Clarinet, 2 violins, viola, and violoncello. Score: Indiana University Music Library; Center for Black Music Research, Columbia College, Chicago, IL.

ROMANTIC SUITE - Voice, flute, and string quartet.

THREE PROCLAMATIONS FOR TROMBONE AND STRING QUARTET

THE HELLISH BANDIT BANDITI (1974) - Opera.

Sources

Anderson, E. Ruth. Contemporary American Composers: A Biographical Dictionary. Boston: G. K. Hall & Co., 1982, p. 146.

De Lerma, Dominique-Rene. black Music in Our Culture. Kent, OH: Kent State University Press, 1970, p. 174.

Southern, Eileen. Biographical Dictionary of Afro-American and African Musicians. Westport, CT: Greenwood Press, 1982, pp. 117-18.

EDWARDS, LEO (1937 -)

Leo Edwards was born January 31, 1937, in Cincinnati, Ohio.

He studied with Scott Huston in Cincinnati, Norman Dello Joio at Mannes College of Music, and Robert Starer at the City University of New York.

He was a faculty member at Mannes College (1968-74) and at Brooklyn College-CUNY (1970-74).

Among his works are Fantasy Overture, Etude for Brass and Psalm 150.

Works

FANTASY OVERTURE (1972) - Orchestra. Premiere: May 1972; Philharmonic Hall, Lincoln Center, New York City; Cosmopolitan Young People Symphony, S. Simon, Conductor.

PSALM 150 - Soprano and orchestra. Premiere: 10 December 1972; New York.

STRING QUARTET (1968; revised 1970)

Sources

Carter, Madison H.   An Annotated Catalogue of Composers of African Ancestry. New York: Vantage Press, 1986.

Horne, Aaron. "Orchestral Works by Black Composers: A Compilation from Selected Sources." Black Composers, Black Performers, and the American Symphony Orchestra. Chicago: Center for Black Music Research, 1988, pp. 8-23.

Roach, Hildred. Black American Music: Past and Present, Vol. 1. Miami: Krieger Publishing Co., 1985.

ELLINGTON, EDWARD KENNEDY ("DUKE") (1899-1974)

Edward Kennedy Ellington, popularly known as Duke, was born April 29, 1899, in Washington, D.C. He died in New York City, May 24, 1974.

He began to study piano when he was six, and studied with Henry Grant at Armstrong High School and privately. He also studied with Will Marion Cook and Will Vodery. He was influenced by Louis Brown, Louis Thomas, and Doc Perry, among others.

He began playing professionally in high school, and had his own small band by the time he was 20. In late 1927 he took his expanded 10-piece band into Harlem's Cotton Club. He first toured Europe and Britain in 1933. During the 1930s, the band made four feature-length movies, and between 1943 and 1950 gave annual Carnegie Hall recitals.

He was honored many times and in many ways: sixteen honorary doctorates (including Columbia, Howard, Brown, and Yale), the President's Gold Medal (1966, from Lyndon B. Johnson), the Presidential Medal of Freedom (1969, from Richard M. Nixon), the Springarn Medal (1959), the French Legion of Honor, and awards from professional societies, councils, associations, institutes, music festivals, the music and recording industries, and individuals, including Pope Paul VI. A Duke Ellington Fellowship Program was established at Yale in 1972.

Ellington was a prolific composer of more than 2000 pieces of varying form and length. Among the best known are the songs "Sophisticated Lady," "Mood Indigo", "Solitude," "In a Sentimental Mood", and "I Got It Bad"; works for theatre including Jump for Joy, Beggar's Holiday (adapted from John Gay's Beggar's Opera, 1947), and The River (written for Alvin Ailey and the American Ballet Theatre, 1970); works for orchestra Deep South Suite, Liberian Suite, New World A-Comin, and Black, Brown, and Beige (all written for the Carnegie concerts); film scores Anatomy of a Murder, Paris Blues, and Assault on A Queen; a pageant, My People (1963); television shows A Drum is a Woman (CBS, 1957) and the series "Asphalt Jungle."

Works

BLACK BROWN & BEIGE - Orchestra.

BOOLA - Opera.

CELEBRATION - Orchestra. Premiere: 16 May 1972 by the Jacksonville Symphony Orchestra, Willis Page, Conductor.

DEEP SOUTH SUITE - Orchestra.

IN THE BEGINNING GOD (1965) - Orchestra, chorus, two soloists, and dancer.

LIBERIAN SUITE - Orchestra.

NEW ORLEANS SUITE (1971)

NEW WORLD A-COMIN - Orchestra

THE RIVER - Ballet suite.

Sources

Anderson, E. Ruth. Contemporary American Composers: A Biographical Dictionary. Boston: G.K. Hall, 1982.

Roach, Hildred. Black American Music: Past and Present Vol. I. Miami: Krieger Publishing Co., 1985, pp. 85-86.

ELIE, JUSTIN (1883 - 1931)

Justin Elie was born September 1, 1883, in Cap-Haitien, Haiti. He died December 2, 1931, in New York City.
After showing early musical talent, he was sent to France where he studied with de Beriot, Marmontel, Vital, and Pessart at the Paris Conservatory of Music.
He toured the Americas as a concert pianist, often with his daughter, Lily, also a pianist; and conducted a music studio in Port-au-Prince.
Among his best-known works are Quisqueye, two piano concertos, Legende Creole for piano and violin, and the songs "Chant des Houssis" and "Hymne a Dambala."

Works

ABORIGINAL SUITE - Orchestra.

GRANDE VALSE DE CONCERT - Orchestra.

HAITIAN LEGEND - Violin and piano. Publisher: New York, G. Schirmer, n.d.

LEGENDE CREOLE - Piano and violin.

MELINDA; A CREOLE TROPICAL DANCE - Orchestra.   Arr. by Charles J. Roberts. Publisher: New York, Carl Fischer, 1927.

QUISQUEYE - Symphonic suite.

VOUDOU - Ballet.

Sources

De Lerma, Dominique-Rene. Black Concert and Recital Music: Provisional List. Bloomington, IN: Afro-American Music Opportunities, 1975.

New York Age, 27 November 1920.

Southern, Eileen. Biographical Dictionary of Afro-American and African Musicians. Westport, CT: Greenwood Press, 1982, p. 124.

FAX, MARK OAKLAND (1911-1974)

Mark Fax was born June 15, 1911, in Baltimore, and died January 2, 1974, in Washington, D.C.
Fax studied music as a child, and was influenced by his high school teacher, W. Llewellyn Wilson. He received his B.Mus. from Syracuse University, and studied at the Eastman School of Music (M. Mus., 1945) and at New York University.
Among his best known works are Three Piano Pieces and Toccatina, and the operas A Christmas Miracle and Till Victory is Won.
He taught at Paine College, Augusta, Georgia, from 1934-42, where he organized the first curriculum in music, and at Howard University in Washington, D.C., from 1947-73, where he served as Director of the School of Music from 1972 until his death.

Works

A CHRISTMAS MIRACLE (1958) - Opera. Libretto by Owen Dodson.

THE LOST ZOO - Opera.

MERRY GO ROUND - Opera.

MUSIC (1947) - Piano and orchestra.

SHORT PIECE (ca. 1946) - Orchestra.

TILL VICTORY IS WON (1967) - Opera. Libretto by Owen Dobson.

Sources

Anderson, E. Ruth. Contemporary American Composers: A Biographical Dictionary. Boston: G. K. Hall & Co., 1982.

De Lerma, Dominique-René. Black Concert and Recital Music: Provisional List. Bloomington, IN: Afro-American Music Opportunities, 1975.

Jones, Velma. "The Life and Works of Mark Oakland Fax." Thesis (M.A.), Morgan State University, 1978.

Southern, Eileen. Biographical Dictionary of Afro-American and African Musicians. Westport, CT: Greenwood Press, 1982, p. 131.

FISCHER, WILLIAM S. (1935 -)

William S. Fischer was born March 5, 1935, in Shelby, Mississippi.
He began to study piano at the age of 7 and saxophone at the age of 13. He received his musical education at Xavier University in New Orleans (B.S., 1956) and at Colorado College-Colorado Springs (M.A., 1962). He also studied with Gottfried von Einem at the Akademie fur Musik and Darstellende in Vienna.
He received a Fullbright Fellowship in 1965-66, grants from Austria (1965) and West Germany (1964), and from the New York State Council on the Arts (1971).
In 1962, he published Analysis of Arnold Schoenberg's Fourth String Quartet.
He began playing professionally in jazz groups during the 1950s. During the 1960s and 70s he became increasingly active as a composer, arranger, record producer, musical director, and publisher. His best known recording was The Rise and Fall of the Third Stream; his best known compositions include Experience in E, Quiet Movement for Orchestra, Electronic Music, and the opera Jesse.
Fischer taught at Xavier University (1962-66), in the New York public schools (1967-75), and at Newport and Cardiff Colleges in Wales, as artist-in-residence (1966-67). He also served as visiting lecturer at colleges such as University of Michigan-Ann Arbor (1970) and Norfolk State University (1971).

Works

CONCERTO GROSSO - Jazz quintet and orchestra.

CONCERTO GROSSO, NO. 1 (1968) - Jazz ensemble with orchestra.

CONCERTO GROSSO, NO. 2 ("BLUES") - Jazz ensemble with orchestra. Premiere: 3 December 1969; Austin, Texas, by the Austin Symphony Pops; William S. Fischer, conductor.

EXPERIENCE IN E - Jazz quintet and orchestra.

GIFT OF LESBOS (1968) - Cello, piano, and tape.

INTRODUCTION AND SONG (1959) - Orchestra.

JACK-JACK (1968) - Opera. Text: Megan Terry. Premiere: New York, 1970.

JESSE (1966) - Opera.

MOVEMENT FOR '65 (1965) - Flute and harp.

MUSIC FOR FLUTE AND HARP (1964)

PIECE (1955) - Viola and piano.

PREDILECTIONS (1963) - Viola.

QUARTET, NO. 1 (1954) - Strings.

QUARTET, NO. 2 (1962) - Strings.

QUIET MOVEMENTS (1966) - Orchestra. Duration: 12 minutes. Publisher: Associated Music Publishers. Recording: Desto DC-7107, ca.
1971; Oakland Youth Orchestra.

SHORT PIECE (1962) - Violin and harpsichord.

SONATA (1962) - Violin and piano. Premiere: Xavier University, New
Orleans.

STATEMENT (1964) - For speaking chorus with orchestra.

STRING QUARTET (1957)

SUITE FOR THREE - Piano, flute, and violin. Premiere: Xavier University, New Orleans.

TIME I (1966) - Saxophone, viola, cello, percussion, and electronic
sounds.

TIME II (1967) - Saxophone, viola, violoncello, percussion, and electronic sounds.

TRILOGY (1964) - Women's chorus (three part) and orchestra. Premiere:
1965; Xavier University, New Orleans.

TRIO - Piano, clarinet, timpani, violin [sic].

VARIATIONS (1961) - Orchestra.

VARIATIONS, NO. 2 (1964) - Orchestra.

Sources

Anderson, E. Ruth. Contemporary American Composers: A Biography
Dictionary. Boston: G. K. Hall & Co., 1982, pp. 168-69.

De Lerma, Dominique-René. Black Concert and Recital Music: Provisional List. Bloomington, IN: Afro-American Music Opportunities,
1975.

De Lerma, Dominique-René. Black Music in Our Culture. Kent, OH:
Kent State University Press, 1970, p. 174.

Feather, Leonard. The New Edition of the Encyclopedia of Jazz. New
York: Horizon Press, 1960.

Southern, Eileen. Biographical Dictionary of Afro-American and African Musicians. Westport, CT: Greenwood Press, 1982, p. 132.

FLETCHER, JOHN (n.d.)

Works

SUITE (1973) - Organ, flute, clarinet, bassoon, violin, cello, and brass quartet.

Sources

Carter, Madison H. An Annotated Catalogue of Composers of African Ancestry. New York: Vantage Press, 1986.

Hancock, Eugene. "A Partial Listing of Organ Music by Black Composers." Unpublished paper.

FOUNTAIN, PRIMOUS, III (1949 -)

Primous Fountain III was born August 1, 1949, in St. Petersburg, Florida.

He received his musical education in high school, where he studied trumpet and string bass, and at Kennedy-King Junior College and DePaul University. He was influenced by Stravinsky and Miles Davis.

In 1968 he won an award for composition from BMI, and in 1969 he became the youngest person ever to receive a Guggenheim fellowship. He also received an ASCAP grant, a second Guggenheim, and commissions from music foundations and organizations.

His Manifestation became a ballet for the Arthur Mitchell Dance Theater of Harlem. Other compositions included Ritual Dance of the Amaks, Duet for Flute and Bassoon, and Concerto for Cello and Orchestra.

Works

THE ART OF FRUSTRATION - Orchestra.

AUXILIARY 2 - Orchestra.

CADENCES - Chamber ensemble. Premiere: 25 January 1969; members of the Chicago Symphony Orchestra.

CONCERTO FOR CELLO AND ORCHESTRA

EVOLUTIO QUAESTIONIS - Orchestra. Premiere: 3 August 1970; Berkshire Music Center Orchestra; Gunther Schuller, conductor.

INCOHERENT - Orchestra.

IRRELEVANCE - Orchestra.

HUH - Orchestra. Premiere: 10 March 1972; Chicago Civic Orchestra; Gordon Peters, conductor.

MANIFESTATION (1969) - Orchestra. Publisher: New York, Belwin-Mills (ca. 1975). Premiere: 13 March 1970; Chicago Symphony Orchestra; Richard Duffalo, conductor. NOTE: transformed into a ballet for the Arthur Mitchell Dance Theater of Harlem.

MOVEMENT - Orchestra, piano, flute, and double bass.

RICIA (1977) - Piano trio. Commissioned by the American Dance Festival for Arthur Mitchell's Dance Theatre of Harlem.

RICIA FOR TRIO - Violin, cello, and piano.

RITUAL DANCE OF THE AMAKS (1973) - Orchestra. Commissioned by the Fromm Foundation. Premiere: Festival of Contemporary Music at Tanglewood; Gunther Schuller, conductor.

SATURN - Orchestra.

SYMPHONY NO. 1 ("EPITOME OF THE OPPRESSED") - Orchestra.

THREE PIECES - Chamber ensemble. Premiere: 25 January 1969; members of the Chicago Symphony Orchestra.

TRANSITION AND/OR REFORMATION - Orchestra.

TRIPTYCH - Orchestra. Premiere: 6, 8 August 1970; Berkshire Music Center Orchestra; Gunther Schuller, conductor.

VARIATIONS ON TITLES - Chamber ensemble.

Sources

Abdul, Raoul. "Primous Fountain and the Amaks." In Blacks in Classical Music. New York: Dodd, Mead & Co., 1977, pp. 48-49.

Clemons, J.G. "Classical Composer Primous Fountain, 3d." Black Enterprise (July 1980):24

De Lerma, Dominique-Rene. Black Concert and Recital Music: Provisional List. Bloomington, IN: Afro-American Music Opportunities, 1975.

McGinty, Doris Evans. "Fountain, Primous, III." In The New Grove Dictionary of American Music, Vol. 2, p. 159.

Holly, Ellistine. "Composers Notes." CBMR Digest 1.1 (Summer 1988).

Southern, Eileen. Biographical Dictionary of Afro-American and African Musicians. Westport, CT: Greenwood Press, 1982, p. 137.

FOX, JAMES INGRAM (1916 -)

Works

(4) AFRICAN SUITES - Violin and piano.

AFRICAN CEREMONIAL DANCE SUITE - Orchestra.

ANDANTE CON MOTO - String orchestra.

BORNU FAREWELL - Orchestra.

QUARTET - Strings.

SYMPHONY NO. 1 - Orchestra.

SYMPHONY NO. 2 - Orchestra.

SYMPHONY NO. 3 - Orchestra.

SYMPHONY NO. 4 ("EMANCIPATION") - Orchestra.

Source

De Lerma, Dominique-René. Black Concert and Recital Music: Provisional List. Bloomington, IN: Afro-American Music Opportunities, 1975.

FREEMAN, HARRY LAWRENCE (1869 - 1954)

Harry Lawrence Freeman was born October 9, 1869, in Cleveland, and died March 21, 1954, in New York City.

Musically precocious, he played piano and was serving as an assistant church organist by the time he was 10.   He studied piano with Edwin Schonert and Carlos Sobrino, and theory, composition, and orchestration with Johann Beck.

He worked as a church organist, first in Cleveland, then in Denver, Colorado, where his first opera, The Martyr, was first produced. He served as musical director for Ernest Hogan's Rufus Rastus company in 1905, and for the Pekin Theater Stock Company in Chicago. In New York he worked with the Bob Cole/Johnson brothers The Red Moon company. When that show closed in 1910 Freeman established the Freeman School of Music in New York.   In 1920 he organized the Negro Grand Opera Company, which produced two of his operas, Vendetta and Voodoo.   In 1923 he founded the Freeman School of Grand Opera.

In 1930, Freeman received a first-place award from the Harmon Foundation.   In 1947, The Martyr was presented as a concert in Carnegie Hall.

Besides a total of 14 operas, he wrote two ballets (Slave Ballet from Salome and Zulu King), a symphonic poem, The Slave, two cantatas, and many songs and instrumental pieces.   He is cited as being the first African American composer in the United States to conduct a symphony orchestra in a rendition of his own work (O Sing a New Song, Minnesota, 1907).

Works

AFRICAN KRAAL (1903; revised in 1934) - Opera in one act. Text: Harry L. Freeman. Never performed.

AFRICAN ROMANCE (1927) - Opera.

AMERICAN ROMANCE - Jazz opera.

ATHALIA (1916) - Opera in Prologue and three acts. Text: Harry L. Freeman.

THE FLAPPER (1929) - Opera in four acts.

LEAH KLESCHNA (1931) - Opera. Text: Harry L. Freeman, after C.M.S. McClellan.

THE MARTYR (1893) - Opera. Premiere: September, 1893, Deutsches Theatre, Denver, Colorado; Freeman Grand Opera Company. NOTE: Originally PLATONUS. NOTE: Reportedly the first opera composed by an African American and first opera to be totally Black produced.

THE OCTOROON (1904) - Opera. Text: Harry L. Freeman, after M.E. Braddon. Never performed.

THE PLANTATION (1915) - Opera in three acts. Text: Harry L. Freeman. Never performed.

THE PROPHECY (1911) - Opera in one act. Text: Harry L. Freeman. Never performed.

THE SLAVE (1925) - Orchestra. Symphonic poem. Never performed.

SLAVE BALLET FROM SALOME (1932) - Chorus and orchestra. Premiere: 22 September 1932; Harlem Academy; Hemsley Winfield Negro Ballet; sponsored by the Friends' Amusement Guild.

SLAYING OF THE LION - Opera.

THE TRYST (1909) - Opera in one act. Text: Harry L. Freeman. Premiere: May 1911; Crescent Theatre, New York City; Freeman Operatic Duo (Carlotta Freeman and Hugo Williams); conducted by the composer.

UZZIAH (1934) - Opera. Text: Florence Lewis Speare.

VALDO (1905) - Opera. Text: Harry L. Freeman. Premiere: May 1906; Weisgerber's Hall, Cleveland, Ohio; Freeman Grand Opera Company (Katherine Skeene Mitchell, Dazalia Underwood, Walter Revels, Walter Randolph); conducted by the composer.

VENDETTA (1923) - Opera in three acts. Text: Harry L. Freeman. Premiere: 12 November 1923; Lafayette Theatre, Harlem; Negro Grand Opera Company (Carlotta Freeman, Cecil De Silva, Louise Mallory, Marie Woodby, E. Taylor Gordon, Voldo Freeman); conducted by the composer.

VOODOO (1914) - Opera in three acts. Text: Harry L. Freeman. Premiere: 20 May 1928 on WCBS Radio (abridged version). First staged performance: 10 September 1928; Palm Garden; Carlotta Freeman, Doris Trutman, Ray Yates; conducted by the composer. Photostat at Howard University. NOTE: Reportedly the first black-composed and black-written opera to have been staged on Broadway.

ZULU KING (WITCH HUNT) (1934) - Ballet, for orchestra. Photostat at Howard University.

ZULUKI (1898) (unfinished) - Opera. Text: Harry L. Freeman. Original title NADA.

ZULUKI - Orchestra. Contents: Prayer, Intermezzo, and Romance. Premiere: March 1900; Cleveland Symphony Orchestra; Johann Beck, conductor. NOTE: Might be orchestral extracts of ZULUKI.

ZULULAND (1947) - Opera. Contents: 1. Nada, the Lily (composed 1944);   2. Allah (1947); 3. The Zulu King (1934); 4. The Slave (1932).

Sources

Abdul, Raoul. "Operas by Black Composers." In Blacks in Classical Music. New York: Dodd, Mead & Co., 1977, p. 123.

Davidson, Celia Elizabeth. "Operas by Afro-American Composers: A Critical Survey and Analysis of Selected Works." Dissertation. The Catholic University of America, 1980.

De Lerma, Dominique-René. Black Concert and Recital Music: Provisional List. Bloomington, IN: Afro-American Music Opportunities, 1975.

De Lerma, Dominique-René. "Freeman, Harry Lawrence." In Dictionary of American Negro Biography, eds. Rayford W. Logan and Michael R. Winston. New York: Norton, 1982, pp. 244-245.

Hipsher, Edward E. "Harry Lawrence Freeman." In American Opera and Its Composers. New York: Da Capo Press, 1978, pp. 189-194.

Holly, Ellistine Perkins, ed. Biographies of Black Composers and Songwriters. Dubuque, IA: Wm. C. Brown Publisher, 1990, p. 20.

Roach, Hildred. Black American Music: Past and Present, Vol. I. Miami: Krieger Publishing Co., 1985, p. 98.

Southern, Eileen. Biographical Dictionary of Afro-American and African Musicians. Westport, CT: Greenwood Press, 1982, p. 138.

Southern, Eileen. "Freeman, Harry Lawrence." In The New Grove Dictionary of American Music, Vol. 2, p. 167.

Southern, Eileen. "Freeman, Harry Lawrence." In The New Grove Dictionary of Music and Musicians, Vol 6, p. 815.

FREEMAN, PAUL (DOUGLAS) (1936 -)

Works

GEISTERLIED (1960) - String orchestra with percussion. Held by Sibley Music Library at the Eastman School of Music.

Sources

Ardoin, J. "A Black Composers Concert." American Musical Digest 1.5 (1970): 5-6. [Reprinted from The Dallas Morning News, 31 January 1970.]

De Lerma, Dominique-René. Black Concert and Recital Music: Provisional List. Bloomington, IN: Afro-American Music Opportunities, 1975.

De Lerma, Dominique-René. "Freeman, Paul (Douglas)." In The New Grove Dictionary of American Music, Vol. 2, p. 167.

"Dr. Paul Freeman Is to Symphony Music What Jackie Robinson Was to Baseball." Sepia April 1968: 37.

Freeman, Paul. "Black Symphonic Music Will Now Be Heard." Symphony News 24.6 (1973-74): 7-10.

Henahan, Donal. "Conductor Brings to Light Blacks' Symphonic Works." New York Times 8 May 1974: 39.

Southern, Eileen. Biographical Dictionary of Afro-American and African Musicians. Westport, CT: Greenwood Press, 1982, pp. 138-89.

FURMAN, JAMES B. (1937-1989)

James B. Furman was born January 23, 1937, in Louisville, Kentucky.
He studied piano as a child, and received degrees from University of Louisville (B. Mus. Ed., 1958; M. Mus., 1965). He also studied at Brandeis (1962-64) and Harvard (summer 1966).
In 1953, he won first place in the Louisville Philharmonic Society's Young Artist Contest and appeared as a soloist with the Louisville Symphony.
Among his compositions are the symphonic oratoria I Have A Dream, the trio Variants, the choral suite Four Little Foxes, and Declaration of Independence for orchestra and narrator.
He taught in the public schools of Louisville and Mamaroneck, New York, and at Western Connecticut State College in Danbury (1965 -).

Works

CANTILENA FOR STRINGS (1976) - Duration: 3 minutes 50 seconds. From DECLARATION OF INDEPENDENCE.

CONCERTO FOR CHAMBER ORCHESTRA (1964) - Duration: 9 minutes. Unpublished (piano score only available).

DECLARATION OF INDEPENDENCE (1977) - Orchestra and narrator. Duration: 15 minutes. Unpublished. Premiere: 28 April 1977, Ives Concert Hall, Danbury, Connecticut; Western Connecticut State College Orchestra, composer conducting; Governor Ella Grasso, narrator. NOTES: Orchestration includes bagpipes and optional organ. Premiere broadcast over Voice of America, May 1977. Reviewed in News-Time (Danbury, CT) 21 April 1977.

FANTASIA AND CHORALE FOR STRINGS (1971) - Duration: 5 minutes 20 seconds. From I HAVE A DREAM.

I HAVE A DREAM (1970; revised 1971) - Oratorio for chorus (SATB), gospel chorus, baritone, folk and gospel solos, orchestra, gospel piano, organ, guitar, banjo, combo organ, electric bass, electric guitar, and drum set. Text: Writings and statements of Martin Luther King, Jr. Duration: 40 minutes. Commissioned by the Greenwich Choral Society. Dedication: "To the beloved memory of my friend, Martin Luther King, Jr." Unpublished. Contents: Part I - In the River of Life; Part II - I Have a Dream; Part III - Let Freedom Ring. Premiere (original version): 19 April 1970, Greenwich, Connecticut; Greenwich Choral Society; composer conducting; (revised version): 22, 23, and 24 January 1971, Cincinnati, Ohio; Cincinnati Symphony Orchestra; Baroque Choral Ensemble; Central State University Choir; Kentucky State College Chapel Choir; Wilberforce University Choir; Erich Kunzel, Conductor.

MOMENTS IN GOSPEL (1985) - Orchestra. Contents: 1. Walk to the Altar; 2. Invitation and Prayer; 3. Holy Dance. Duration: 17 minutes. Premiere: 5 May 1985; Ives Concert Hall, Danbury, Connecticut; the Danbury Little Symphony, Richard Brooks, conductor.

STRING QUARTET (1986) - Duration: 18 minutes. Premiere: 9 August 1987; Falls Village, Connecticut; Manhattan String Quartet.

Sources

Information submitted by composer.

Southern, Eileen. Biographical Dictionary of Afro-American and African Musicians. Westport, CT: Greenwood Press, 1982, p. 141.

Tischler, Alice. Fifteen Black American Composers: A Bibliography of Their Works. Detroit: Information Coordinators, 1981. pp. 135-47.

GRIDER, JOSEPH WILLIAM (n.d.)

Works

SUITE - Orchestra.

Sources

Carter, Madison H.   An Annotated Catalogue of Composers of African Ancestry. New York: Vantage Press, 1986.

HAGAN, HELEN EUGENIA (1891-1964)

Helen Eugenia Hagan was born in 1891 and died in 1964.
She graduated from the School of Music at Yale University, and won the Lockwood and the Samuels Simmons Sanford Fellowship awards for study abroad.
She made her debut as a pianist in Aeolian Hall, New York City.

Works

CONCERTO IN C MINOR - Piano and orchestra.

Sources

Carter, Madison H.   An Annotated Catalogue of Composers of African Ancestry. New York: Vantage Press, 1986.

Hare, Maud Cuney. Negro Musicians and Their Music. Washington, D.C.: Associated Publishers, 1936, pp. 276.

Lovingood, Penman. Famous Modern Negro Musicians 2nd ed. New York: Da Capo Press, 1978. (Reprint of 1921 ed.)

Southern, Eileen. Biographical Dictionary of Afro-American and Afri- can Musicians. Westport, CT: Greenwood Press, 1982.

HAILSTORK, ADOLPHUS CUNNINGHAM, III (1941 -)

Adolphus Cunningham Hailstork III was born in Albany, New York, on April 17, 1941.

After studying piano as a child, he attended Howard University (B. Mus., 1963), the Manhattan School of Music (B. Mus. in composition, 1965; M. Mus. in composition, 1966), and Michigan State University (Ph.D., 1971). He also attended the American Institute at Fontainebleu, France, where he studied with Nadia Boulanger, the Electronic Music Institution at Dartmouth College, and at SUNY-Buffalo. He studied under Mark Fax, Ludmila Ulehla, Nicholas Flagello, Vittorio Giannini, David Diamond, John Appleton, and H. Howe.

In 1963, Hailstork received the Lucy E. Moten Travel Fellowship. He was co-winner of the 1970-71 Ernest Block Award for choral composition, and in 1977 received the Belwin-Mills/Max Winkler Award for a band composition.

Among his best-known works are "Mourn Not the Dead", Bellevue and Celebration for orchestra, Bagatelles for Brass, "Spritual" for brass en- semble, Suite for Organ, Sonatina for Flute and Piano, and two songs, "A charm at parting" and "I loved you."

He taught at Michigan State University (1969-71), Youngstown State University in Ohio (1971-76), and Norfolk State University in Virginia (1976 -).

Works

AN AMERICAN FANFARE (1985) - Orchestra. NOTE: An "opener."

AMERICAN LANDSCAPE NO. 2 (1978) - Violin and cello. Duration: 20 minutes. Premiere: April 1978, Unitarian Church, Norfolk, Virginia. Note: Tape available from the composer.

AN AMERICAN PORT OF CALL (1984) - Orchestra. Duration: 8 minutes 30 seconds.

BELLEVUE (1974) - Orchestra. Duration: 4 minutes. Commissioned by the Southern Baptists Convention. Premiere: March 1975, Nashville, Tennessee; Nashville Symphony. Note: A prelude on the hymn tune "Bellevue"; tape of first performance available from the composer.

CAPRICCIO FOR A DEPARTED BROTHER: SCOTT JOPLIN (1869-1917) (1969) -
String orchestra. Duration: 6 minutes. Dedicated to Scott Joplin.
Manuscript (IU).

CANTO CARCELERA (1978) - Oboe and guitar. Duration: 4 minutes.

CELEBRATION (1974) - Orchestra.   Duration: 3 minutes 30 seconds.
Commissioned by J. C. Penny for a bicentennial composition for orches-
tra.   Printed in New York under the auspices of J.C. Penny, 1975.
Premiere: May 1975, Minneapolis, Minnesota; Minnesota Orchestra, Paul
Freeman, Conductor.   Recording;   Columbia M-34556 (1978).   Notes:
Band transcription available from composer. Reviewed: New York Times
3 September 1977 (New York Philharmonic performance).

CONCERTO FOR VIOLIN, HORN, AND ORCHESTRA (1975) - Duration: 15
minutes. Dedicated to Carol Clark.   Premiere: Youngston, Ohio; the
Youngstown High School Orchestra, Adolphus Hailstork, conductor.
NOTE: Tape recording of the first performance available from the
composer.

DONE MADE MY VOW: A CEREMONY (1985) - Chorus, soloists, and orchestra. Manuscript.

EPITAPH (1979) - Orchestra. Duration: 8 minutes.

ESSAY FOR STRINGS (1986) - Dedication: To The Memory of Glen Hull, a
Colleague in Music.

FROM THE DARK SIDE OF THE SUN (1971) - Flutes, alto flute, soprano
saxophone, marimbas, vibraphones, glockenspiel, celeste, triangles,
bongo drums, and strings. Duration: 12 minutes. Note: Ph.D. dissertation; abstract in Dissertation Abstracts, Section A, 32:3350,
December 1971.

PHAEDRA (1966) - Tone poem for orchestra. Duration: 10 minutes.

SERENADE (1971) - Women's chorus (SSA), soprano solo violin solo, and
piano.   Texts: Elizabeth Barrett Browning and Walt Whitman.   Duration: 10 minutes. Premiere: Spring 1971, Lansing, Michigan; Eastern
High School Girls Chorus. Note: Tape available from composer.

SEXTET FOR STRINGS (1971) - Duration: 15 minutes.   Note: Ph.D. dissertation; abstract in Dissertation Abstracts, Section A, 32:3350,
December 1971.

SONATA FOR VIOLIN AND PIANO (1972) - Duration: 10 minutes. Two movements.

SONGS OF THE MAGI (1987) - Oboe and strings. Manuscript. Premiere:
Norfolk State University.

SPORT FOR STRINGS

STATEMENT, VARIATION, AND FUGUE (1966) - Orchestra.   Duration: 15
minutes.   Premiere: 1966, Baltimore, Maryland; Baltimore Symphony.
Note: Master's Thesis.

SUITE (1979) - Violin and piano. Duration: 10 minutes. Contents:
1. Prelude; 2. Tango; 3. Meditation; 4. Demonic Dance. Premiere: 8
April 1979, Norfolk State University.

SYMPHONY NO. 1 (1988) - Orchestra. Manuscript. Premiere: 1 August
1988; Festival of the Classics; Ocean View, New York.

THREE ROMANCES FOR VIOLA AND CHAMBER ORCHESTRA (1988) - Manuscript.

TRAPEZIUM (1974) - Viola. Duration: 3 minutes. Dedicated to Cindy
Evans.

TRIO FOR VIOLIN, CELLO, AND PIANO (1985) - Duration: 23 minutes.
Premiere: 31 March 1985; Nova Trio.

TWO STRUTS WITH BLUES (1985) - String orchestra, flute, horn, and jazz
quartet. Duration: 45 minutes. Manuscript. Commissioned by the
Massachusetts Council of the Arts and Swedish Radio Company. Pre-
miere: 18 June 1985; Emmanuel Church, Boston, Massachusetts; The
Living Time Orchestra, George Russell, conductor. Recording: Blue
Note, 1985.

Sources

McGinty, Doris Evans. "Hailstork, Adolphus." In The New Grove Dictionary of American Music, Vol. 2, p. 307.

Southern, Eileen. Biographical Dictionary of Afro-American and African Musicians. Westport, CT: Greenwood Press, 1982, pp. 158-59.

Tischler, Alice. Fifteen Black American Composers: A Bibliography of
Their Works. Detroit Studies in Music Bibliography. Detroit: Information Coordinators, 1981.

HAKIM, TALIB RASUL (1940 - 1988)

Talib Rasul Hakim was born Stephen Alexander Chambers in Asheville,
North Carolina, on February 8, 1940. He died in 1988.
He was musically active as a child, and received his formal musical
education from the Manhattan School of Music (1958-59), the New York Col-
lege of Music (1959-63), and the New School for Social Research in New York
(1963-65). He also studied at Adelphi University and the Mannes College of
Music in New York. His teachers included Margaret Bonds, Robert Starer,
Hall Overton, Chou Wen-Chung, and Ornette Coleman, and his style as a composer was influenced by the music of Miles Davis, John Coltrane, Mozart,
and Debussy.
Between 1965 and 1969 his works were performed on the "Music in Our
Time" concert series in New York. He received fellowships from the Ben-
nington Composers Conference (1964-69), composer awards from ASCAP (1967-
73), and grants from the National Endowment for the Arts (1973) and the
Creative Artist Public Service Program (1972).
His best-known works were "Sound Gone" for piano, Placements for five
percussions and piano, Visions of Ishwara, Shapes for chamber orchestra,
and Recurrences for orchestra.
Besides composing and touring as a lecturer, he also taught at Pace
College-New York (1970-72), Adelphi College (where he was an adjunct pro-

fessor), and Nassau Community College/SUNY-Garden City, and was visiting professor at Morgan State University, Maryland, during 1978-79.

Works

ARKAN-5 (1980-81) - Chamber orchestra. Duration: 20 minutes. Manuscript. Premiere: May 1980; the Brooklyn Philharmonic Orchestra.

AZ-ZAAHIR-AL BATIN (THE OUTWARD-THE INWARD) (1985-86) - Orchestra. Manuscript. Duration: 13 minutes 15 seconds.

CONCEPTS (1974) - Orchestra

CONTOURS (1966) - Oboe, bassoon, horn, trumpet, violoncello, and contrabass. Duration: 8 minutes. Premiere: 1967. Town Hall, New York City; part of Max Pollikoff's "Music in Our Time" series.

CURRENTS (1967) - String quartet. Duration: 10 minutes.

ELEMENTS (1967) - Flute/alto flute, clarinet/bass clarinet, violin/viola, violoncello, piano, and glass and bamboo wind and hand chimes. Duration: 8 minutes 12 seconds. Premiere: 1969, on "Inside Bedford-Stuyvesant," WNEW-TV, New York City.

LAILATU'L-QADR ("THE NIGHT OF POWER") (1984) - Bass clarinet, string bass, and percussion. Duration: 15 minutes.

MUTATIONS (1964) - Bass clarinet, horn, trumpet, viola, and violoncello. Duration: 7 minutes.

RECURRENCES (1974) - Orchestra. Duration: 13 minutes. Premiere: 1975, Kennedy Center, Washington, D.C.; Washington D.C. Youth Orchestra, Lyn McLain, Conductor.

REFLECTIONS ON THE 5TH DAY (1972) - Narrator and chamber orchestra. Text by Theresa Schoenacher. Duration: 12 minutes. Commissioned by the Brooklyn Chamber Orchestra. Premiere: 1972; Brooklyn Chamber Orchestra, Stephen Gunzenhauser, Conductor.

ROOTS AND OTHER THINGS (1967) - Flute/alto flute, oboe/English horn, clarinet/bass clarinet, trumpet, horn, trombone, viola, violoncello, and contrabass. Duration: 10 minutes. Premiere: 1968, Boston; Society of Black Composers.

SET-THREE (1970) - Soprano, violoncello, and piano. Text by the composer. Duration: 8 minutes. Premiere: 1970, Saratoga Springs, New York; Summer Convocation on the Arts.

SHAPES (1965) - Chamber orchestra. Duration: 10 minutes. Premiere: 1970; Oakland Youth Chamber Orchestra. Robert Hughes, Conductor. Recording: Oakland Youth Orchestra, Robert Hughes, Conductor; Desto DC-7107: The Black Composer in America.

SIX PLAYERS AND A VOICE (1964) - Soprano, clarinet, trumpet, violoncello, 2 percussion, and piano. Text by the composer. Duration: 10 minutes. Premiere: 1969, New York City YMHA/YWHA; part of Max Pollikoff's "Music in Our Time" series.

SOUND IMAGES (1969) - Brass (2 trumpets, 2 flugelhorns, 4 horns, 3 trombones, tuba), 3 percussion, strings, and female chorus. Text by the composer. Duration: 10 minutes. Premiere: 1969, New York City; Society of Black Composers.

THREE PLAY SHORT FIVE (1965) - Bass clarinet, percussion, contrabass. Duration: 8 minutes. Premiere: 1966; part of Max Pollikoff's "Music in Our Time" series.

TIMELESSNESS (1970) - Flugelhorn, horn, trombone, tuba, 2 percussion, contrabass, and piano. Duration: 15 minutes.

TONE-POEM (1969) - Soprano, percussion, contrabass, and piano. Text by Langston Hughes. Duration: 9 minutes. Premiere: 1969, Bowdoin College.

VISIONS OF ISHWARA (1970) - Orchestra. Duration: 8 minutes 55 seconds. Premiere: 1971, Philharmonic Hall; Symphony of the New World, Benjamin Steinberg, Conductor. Recording: Baltimore Symphony Orchestra, Paul Freeman, Conductor (Columbia M-33434: Vol. 8, Black Composers Series).

Sources

Baker, David N., Lida M. Belt, and Herman C. Hudson. The Black Composer Speaks. Metuchen. NJ: Scarecrow Press, Inc., 1978.

Claghorn, Charles E. Biographical Dictionary of American Music. West Nyack, NY: Parker Publishing Co., 1973.

De Lerma, Dominique-René. Black Music in Our Culture: Curricular Ideas on the Subjects, Materials, and Problems. Kent, OH: Kent State University Press, 1970.

James, Richard S. "Hakim, Talib Rasul." In The New Grove Dictionary of American Music, Vol. 2, p. 307.

Johnson, Tom. "Music: Talib Rasul Hakim Has Found His Music." Village Voice 20 February 1978: 80.

Oliver, Christine E. "Selected Orchestral Works of Thomas J. Anderson, Arthur Cunningham, Talib Rasul Hakim, and Olly Wilson: A Descriptive Study." Dissertation (Ph.D.), Florida State University, 1978.

Southern, Eileen. "America's Black Composers of Classical Music." Music Educators Journal 62 (November 1975): 46-59.

HAMMOND, DOUGLAS (n.d.)

Works

SUITE IN TWO COLORS - Flute, violin, viola, violoncello, piano. Score: Center for Black Music Research (Music Collection).

HAMPTON, RALPH (n.d.)

Works

2 SONGS, NO. 2 - Voice, flute, clarinet, horn, cello, and percussion.

Source

De Lerma, Dominique-Rene. Black Concert and Recital Music: Provisional List. Bloomington, IN: Afro-American Music Opportunities Association, 1975.

HANCOCK, EUGENE WILSON (1929 -)

Eugene Wilson Hancock was born February 17, 1929, in St. Louis.
He received his B. Mus. in 1951 from University of Detroit, his M. Mus in 1956 from University of Michigan-Ann Arbor, and his D. Sac. Mus. from the School of Sacred Music of Union Theological Seminary in New York, in 1967, studying under Robert Baker and Marcel Dupre, among others. In 1966 he passed the examination for the Associate of the American Guild of Organists degree.
He published articles in professional journals such as The Journal of Church Music and Pipeline.
Among his best known compositions are An Organ Book of Spirituals, Spirituals for Young Voices and the songs "Absalom" and "Song of Simeon."
Hancock served as organist and choirmaster at Lutheran churches in Detroit, as assistant organist at the Cathedral Church of St. John the Divine, as organist and choirmaster at the New Calvary Baptist Church in Detroit, and at the St Philip's Episcopal Church in New York. He also toured as a concert organist, and taught at the Manhattan Community College/CUNY (1970 -).

Works

SUITE - Organ, strings, oboe, and timpani. Premiere: February 1979. Duration: 15 minutes.

Sources

Information submitted by the composer.

Southern, Eileen. Biographical Dictionary of Afro-American and African Musicians. Westport, CT: Greenwood Press, 1982, pp. 163-64.

HANDY, JOHN RICHARD (1933 -)

John Richard Handy was born in Dallas, Texas, on February 3, 1933.
He taught himself to play clarinet when he was 13, and attended City College/CUNY and San Francisco State College, where he received his BA in 1963.
He is best known as a jazz saxophonist, playing with such groups as Charles Mingus, Randy Weston, and Kenny Dorham, and leading his own groups. He was also active as a lecturer on the college circuit and educational TV. He has received numerous awards from the music industry.

His best known compositions are "The Spanish Lady" and Concerto for Jazz Soloist and Orchestra.

Besides performing and lecturing, Handy also teaches at San Francisco State College (1968 -) and holds lectureships at the University of California-Berkeley, Stanford University, and the San Francisco Conservatory of Music.

Works

CONCERTO FOR JAZZ SOLOIST AND ORCHESTRA (1970)

Source

Southern, Eileen. Biographical Dictionary of Afro-American and African Musicians. Westport, CT: Greenwood Press, 1982, pp. 164-65.

HANDY, WILLIAM CHRISTOPHER (1873-1958)

Works

BLUE DESTINY SYMPHONY; SCHERZO - Orchestra. Publisher: New York, W.C. Handy (1945).

THEY THAT SOW IN TEARS - SATB, TTBB, and orchestra. Text: from Psalms 126. Publisher: New York, Handy Brothers (1950).

Source

De Lerma, Dominique-René. Black Concert and Recital Music: Provisional List. Bloomington, IN: Afro-American Music Opportunities Association, 1975.

HARRIS, HOWARD C., JR. (1940 -)

Howard Harris Jr. was born in New Orleans, Louisiana, in 1940.

He received his B.S. from Southern University and his M.M. from Louisiana State University. He also attended North Texas State University, Washington University, and Southern University (Jazz Institute), and studied composition with William S. Fischer and trumpet with Bobby Bryant.

In 1974 he received a National Endowment Grant.

Harris taught at Delaware State College, the Southern University Laboratory School, Dawson High School, and Texas Southern University (1971 -), where he served as founder-director of the Peoples' Workshop for Visual and Performing Arts.

He served as contributing editor for Jazz Spotlite News, co-authored with Joseph Schmoll Music in the Humanities (Burgess, MN, 1983), and wrote The Complete Book of Improvisation/Composition and Funk Techniques (Houston: DeMos Music Publishers, 1981).

His song Hell of a Fix, written for Marion Jarvis, became number 25 in Billboard during autumn 1974. He wrote 15 songs for the musical play Solomon Northup. Additional works are Black Roots, Passion Is, Folk Psalm (for orchestra), Jazz Memorabilia, Blues of the New World (jazz ensemble), and An American Music Tree (symphony orchestra).

Works

AN AMERICAN MUSIC TREE - Orchestra. Premiere: Houston Orchestra.

FOLK PSALM (1973) - Orchestra. Publisher: San Antonio, Southern Music Company.

PRO VIVA - Flute, piano, cello, and congas.

Sources

Anderson, E. Ruth. Contemporary American Composers: A Biographical Dictionary. Boston: G. K. Hall & Co., 1982, p. 224.

Roach, Hildred. Black American Music: Past and Present, Vol. II. Miami: Krieger Publishing Co., 1985, pp. 91-93.

HARRIS, MARGARET ROSEZARIAN (1943 -)

Margaret Rosezarian Harris was born in Chicago in 1943.
She graduated summa cum laude from Juilliard (B.S. and M.S.).
She has conducted the musical Hair, Raisin, Two Gentlemen of Verona, Guys and Dolls, Amen Corner, and the Negro Ensemble Company. She is co-founder of Opera Ebony.
Her compositions include two piano concerti, four musical production scores, two ballets, and choral and instrumental works.

Works

CONCERTO NO. 2 - Piano and orchestra

Source

Carter, Madison H. An Annotated Catalogue of Composers of African Ancestry. New York: Vantage Press, 1986.

HARRIS, ROBERT A. (1938 -)

Robert A. Harris was born January 9, 1938, in Detroit, Michigan.
He studied at Wayne State University (B.S., 1962), the Eastman School of Music, and Michigan State University (Ph.D., 1971). His teachers included Bernard Rogers and H. Owen Reed.
He received Rockefeller Grants in 1971 and 1972.
He has taught in the Detroit Public School System, at Wayne State (1964-70), at Michigan State (1970-77), and at Northwestern University in Evanston, Illinois (1977-).

Works

ADAGIO FOR STRING ORCHESTRA (1966) - Duration: 4 minutes 30 seconds. Premiere: August 1966, Rochester, New York; East Chamber Orchestra.

CONCERT PIECE FOR BASSOON AND CHAMBER ORCHESTRA (1965) - Duration: 7 minutes.   Premiere: 3 August 1965, Eastman School of Music, Rochester, New York; Edgar Kirk, bassoon.

CONCERT PIECE FOR HORN AND ORCHESTRA (1964) - Duration: 6 minutes. Premiere: 4 August 1964, Eastman School of Music, Rochester, New York; Verne Reynolds, French horn.

CONTRASTS FOR FOUR WINDS AND STRING ORCHESTRA (1966) - Flute, clarinet, bassoon, and French horn with string orchestra.   Duration: 5 minutes 30 seconds.

MOODS FOR ORCHESTRA (1968-69) - Duration: 7 minutes.   Premiere: 4 march 1969, Detroit, Michigan; Detroit Symphony Orchestra, Valter Poole, Conductor.

PSALM 47 (1960-61) - Women's voices and five instruments: flute, clarinet, violin, viola, and cello.   Duration: 7 minutes 30 seconds.

SONATINE FOR TWO VIOLINS (1959-60) - Duration: 8 minutes 30 seconds. Three movements.   Premiere: 2 June 1960, Wayne State University, Detroit, Michigan; Composers' Forum Concert.

STRING QUARTET NO. 1 (1960-68) - Duration: 13 minutes.   Three movements.   Premiere: June 1968, Wayne State University, Detroit, Michigan; Faculty String Quartet.

TWO MOODS IN MINIATURE - Orchestra.   Manuscript.

Sources

Information submitted by the composer

Tischler, Alice. Fifteen Black American Composers: A Bibliography of Their Works. Detroit Studies in Music Bibliography. Detroit: Information Coordinators, 1981.

HAYES, JOSEPH (1920 -)

Joseph Hayes was born in Marietta, Ohio, in 1920.
He studied at the Boston Conservatory of Music and the New England Conservatory of Music; his composition teachers included Warren S. Smith and Gardner Reed.
He was awarded the Whitney Medal for highest attainment at the Boston Conservatory of Music (1940-41).

Works

HORNOTATIONS, NO. 1 (1970) - Horn and string quartet, double bass. Score: Indiana University Music Library.

ON CONTEMPLATING A FLOWER - Solo oboe, chamber choir, and strings.

QUINTET - Clarinet, bassoon, violin, violoncello, and piano.

Sources

Information submitted by the composer.

De Lerma, Dominique-René. <u>Black Concert and Recital Music: Provi-</u><u>sional List</u>. Bloomington, IN: Afro-American Music Opportunities Association, 1975.

HEARD, HENRY A. (n.d.)

Works

CADENCES (1986) - Chamber orchestra. Premiere: Chicago Chamber Orchestra, Dieter Kober, Conductor.

CONJECTURES (1982) - Orchestra. Written for the Chicago Businessmen's Orchestra, Sylvan Ward, Conductor.

SEXTET (1971) - Alto saxophone, trumpet, trombone, violin, contrabass, and piano.

STREET LEVELS (1981) - Soprano voice, flute, clarinet, horn, trumpet, violin, viola, and piano. Written for Suzanne Scherr and the University of Chicago New Music Ensemble, Barbara Schubert, Conductor.

THREE-PIECE (1977) - Flute, viola, and piano. Written for the MENC Spring Concert, Spring 1978.

Source

Information submitted by the composer.

HEATH, JAMES E. (JIMMY) (1926 -)

James E. Heath was born October 25, 1926, in Philadelphia, Pennsylvania.
He studied at the Theodore Presser School in Philadelphia and with Rudolf Schramm in New York.
His awards include the Jazz Festival award, Harstad, Norway; Jazz at Home Club award, Philadelphia; and the Creative Arts Public Service composer grant.
Heath played saxophone with numerous international jazz groups. He also taught privately and with Jazzmobile, and presented jazz lecture concerts in the New York City schools and colleges.
His works include <u>Jazz Themes with Improvisations, Gemini, Gingerbread Boy, A Time and a Place, Big P, One for Juan, The Gap Sealer,</u> and <u>Love and Understanding.</u>

Works

AFRO-AMERICAN SUITE OF EVOLUTION - Soli voices, 6 (STBB), Orchestra. Duration: 60 minutes. Publisher: New York, MJQ Music, Inc.

Sources

Anderson, E. Ruth. Contemporary American Composers: A Biographical
Dictionary. Boston: G.K. Hall, 1982.

Catalog. New York: MJQ Music, Inc.

De Lerma, Dominique-René. Black Concert and Recital Music: Provisional List. Bloomington, IN: Afro-American Music Opportunities
Association, 1975.

Feather, Leonard. The New Edition of the Encyclopedia of Jazz. New
York: Horizon Press, 1960.

HEBRON, J. HARVEY (1888 -)

Works

SONATA - Violin and piano

Source

De Lerma, Dominique-René. Black Concert and Recital Music: Provisional List. Bloomington, IN: Afro-American Music Opportunities
Association, 1975.

HERBISON, JERALDINE SAUNDERS BUTLER (1941 -)

Jeraldine Herbison was born in Richmond, Virginia, in 1941.
She received her B.S. from Virginia State College in 1963. She also
studied at the University of Michigan at Interlochen, where she was awarded
full scholarships in 1973 and 1979. Her composition teachers included Tom
Clark, George Wilson, and Undine Moore.
She has taught in a number of public schools, and is currently educator, orchestra, and choral director at Hampton and Newport News, Virginia.
Among her approximately 20 compositions are Suite 1 in C for strings;
Suite No. 3 for strings, flute, and oboe; Variations for string orchestra;
Promenade for chamber orchestra; Introspection; I Heard the Trailing Gar-
ments of the Night; String Quartet No. 1978; Fantasy in Three Moods; Inter-
mezzo; Six Duos for violin and cello; Metamorphosis; Trio for guitar, violin, and flute; Sonata No. 2; Sonata No. 1; Five Sketches; Four Sonnets;
Spring.

Works

FANTASY IN THREE MOODS (1971) - Cello and piano. Held by Morgan State
University Library, Soper Library.

GENESIS I (1980) - Orchestra. Tone poem.

GENESIS II (1980) - Orchestra. Tone poem.

I HEARD THE TRAILING GARMENTS OF THE NIGHT (1975) - Flute, violin,
cello, and piano.

INTERMEZZO FOR CELLO AND PIANO (1969; revised 1975)

INTROSPECTION (1973) - Oboe, violin, cello, and piano.

LITTLE BROWN BABY (1967) - SAT, 2 violins, and piano. Text by Langston Hughes. Held by Morgan State University Library, Soper Library.

LITTLE SUITE, Op. 2, C Major - String quartet. Held by Morgan State
University Library, Soper Library.

METAMORPHOSIS (1978) - 2 violins, cello, guitar, and piano.

MINIATURE TRIO (1961) - Oboe, violin, and piano. Held by Morgan State
University Library, Soper Library.

NOCTURNE (1961) - Oboe, violin, and piano.

PROMENADE (1982) - Chamber orchestra.

SIX DUOS (1976) - Cello and piano.

SONATA NO. 1 (1977-78) - Cello.

STRING QUARTET (1977)

SUITE NO. 1 IN C (1960; revised 1977) - String orchestra.

SUITE NO. 2 (1963) - String orchestra.

SUITE NO. 3 (1969) - String orchestra.

THEME AND VARIATIONS (1976) - String orchestra. Held by Morgan State
University Library, Soper Library.

TRIO (1979) - Guitar, violin, and flute.

Sources

Anderson, E. Ruth. Contemporary American Composers: A Biographical
Dictionary. Boston: G. K. Hall & Co., 1982.

De Lerma, Dominique-René. Black Concert and Recital Music: Provisional List. Bloomington, IN: Afro-American Music Opportunities
Association, 1975.

Roach, Hildred. Black American Music: Past and Present, Vol. II.
Miami: Krieger Publishing Co., 1985, pp. 94-95.

HEYWOOD, DONALD (1901-1967)

Works

AFRICANA (1934) - Opera.

Source

De Lerma, Dominique-René. Black Concert and Recital Music: Provisional List. Bloomington, IN: Afro-American Music Opportunities
Association, 1975.

HOLDRIDGE, LEE (n.d.)

Works

FANTASY SONATA (1972) - Cello. Premiere: 13 May 1972; Alice Tully
Hall, New York City; Kermit Moore, cello.

Source

De Lerma, Dominique-René. Black Concert and Recital Music: Provisional List. Bloomington, IN: Afro-American Music Opportunities
Association, 1975.

HOLLAND, JUSTIN MINOR (1819 - 1887)

Justin Minor Holland was born in Norfolk County, Virginia, in 1819.
He died in 1887.
He moved to Chelsea, Massachusetts, when he was 14 years old, where he
met Sr. Mariano Perez, a Spanish guitarist and member of a troup at the Old
Lion Theatre in Boston. It was from this association that he became a
serious guitar student, studying with Simon Knaebel and William Schubert.
He also studied the eight-keyed flute with a Scottish gentleman named Pol-
lock. In 1841 he was a student at Oberlin College.
He moved to Cleveland in 1845 and established himself mainly as a
guitar teacher and composer for that instrument.

Works

AN ANDANTE - Guitar. Score: Trotter, James M., Music and Some Highly
Musical People, Johnson Reprint Corporation, 1969, pp. 26-29.

CARNIVAL OF VENICE FANTAISIE (1866) - Guitar. Manuscript: Library of
Congress.

CHOICE MELODIES FOR THE GUITAR (1867) - Guitar. Manuscript: Library
of Congress.

GEMS FOR THE GUITAR (1856?) - Guitar. Manuscript: Library of Congress.

Sources

Davis, Russell H. Black Americans in Cleveland. Washington, D.C.:
Associated Publishers, 1972, pp. 120-21.

Hare, Maude Cuney. Negro Musicians and Their Music. Washington,
D.C.: Associated Publishers, 1936, pp. 205-7.

Simmons, William J. Men of Mark: Eminent, Progressive, and Rising.
Chicago: Associated Publishers Co., 1970, pp. 251-54.

Southern, Eileen. Biographical Dictionary of Afro-American and African Musicians. Westport, CT: Greenwood Press, 1982, p. 186.

Southern, Eileen. "Holland, Justin." In The New Grove Dictionary of
American Music, Vol. 2, p. 410.

Southern, Eileen. "Holland, Justin." In The New Grove Dictionary of
Music and Musicians, Vol. 8, pp. 646-47.

Trotter, James M. Music and Some Highly Musical People. 1878. Rpt.
Chicago: Afro-American Press, 1969, pp. 114-30.

HOLMES, ROBERT L. (1934 -)

Robert Holmes was born March 28, 1934, in Greenville, Mississippi.
Holmes was encouraged early in his career by Gospel pioneer Lucie
Campbell. He received his formal education at Tennessee State University
in Nashville (B.S. 1956, M.S. 1970); the University of Iowa in Iowa City
(1959); and Brandeis University (1960).
He toured as a lecturer and performed with Duke Ellington, Milt Jackson, Quincy Jones, William "Billy" Taylor, and Clark Terry. He has composed for films, television, and radio commercials.
In 1972, he received a grant from the National Endowment of the Arts.

Works

AMAZING GRACE (1981) - Alto flute, jazz trio, string quartet, orch hp.
Duration: 7 minutes. Publisher: Nashville, Tennessee, Doorway Music
(BMI).Premiere: March 27, 1981; Fisk University.

CONCERTO FOR PRO VIVA (1980) - Flute, cello, piano, chamber orchestra.
Duration: 21 minutes. Premiere: April 1980; Richmond Civic Center;
Richmond, Virginia.

EVOLUTIONS I (1969) - Flute, piano. Duration: 4 minutes 15 seconds.
Publisher: DMC. Premiere: January 11, 1977; Trio Pro Viva; Alle-
gheny College, Meadville, Pennsylvania.

EVOLUTIONS II (1969) - Flute, piano. Publisher: DMC.

FANTASY ON A NEGRO SPIRITUAL: WADE IN THE WATER (1978) - Piano,
flute, cello. Publisher: Nashville, Tennessee, Doorway Music (BMI).
Premiere: April 25-26, 1980; Trio Pro Viva; Richmond, Virginia.

TWO DREAMS IN CONTRARY MOTION (1981) - Alto flute, jazz trio, string
quartet, harp. Dedicated to the Music Faculty of Tennessee State
University.

YESTERDAY'S MANSIONS - Flute, cello, piano. Score: Center for Black
Music Research, Columbia College-Chicago. Publisher: Nashville,
Tennessee, Doorway Music (BMI). Recording: Eastern RS-513 (ca.
1973); Trio Pro Viva.

Sources

Information submitted by the composer.

De Lerma, Dominique-Rene. "A Concordance of Scores and Recordings of Music by Black Composers." Black Music Research Journal, 1984.

HOLT, NORA DOUGLAS (1895-1974)

Works

STRING QUARTET

Source

Carter, Madison H.   An Annotated Catalogue of Composers of African Ancestry. New York: Vantage Press, 1986.

JACKSON, J. CALVIN (1919-1985)

Works

CAKE WALK - Piano and orchestra.

COCA-CABANA - Piano and orchestra.

CARL SANDBURG SUITE - Orchestra.

METROPOLIS PER DIEM - Chorus and orchestra.

PROFILES OF AN AMERICAN - Orchestra.

PROPHET - Orchestra. Dedicated to Martin Luther King.

SYMPHONY NO. 1 - Orchestra.

Source

De Lerma, Dominique-Rene. Black Concert and Recital Music: Provi-sional List. Bloomington, IN: Afro-American Music Opportunities Association, 1975.

JENKINS, EDMUND THORNTON (1894-1926)

Edmund Thornton Jenkins was born April 9, 1894, in Charleston, South Carolina, and died September 12, 1926, in Paris.

He studied music with his father, a minister and founder of an orphanage famous for its boys' bands, and by the time he was 14 could play all the band instruments. He attended Avery Institute in Charleston and Atlanta Baptist College (now Morehouse College) in Atlanta, where he studied with Kemper Harreld. Later he attended the Royal Academy of Music in London.

In 1914, he traveled to London with an orphanage band to play at the Anglo-African Exposition. While at the Royal Academy he won the Charles

Lucas Battison Haines Prize for composition and the Oliveria Prescott Prize. In 1925, his works African War Dance for full orchestra and Sonata in A minor for violoncello won Holstein prizes in New York.
    He taught at the Academy, served as a church organist, and played clarinet in the Savoy Theatre orchestra.
    Others of his works are Charlestonia, a rhapsody for orchestra using Negro themes, and Negro Symphony.

Works

    AFRAM, Opus 15 (1924) - Operetta.

    AFRICAN WAR DANCE, Opus 17 (1925) - Orchestra. Note: Received the Holstein Prize.

    AMERICAN FOLK RHAPSODY: CHARLESTONIA (1925) - Orchestra. Performed at the Kursaal d'Ostend in Belgium, 1926. Manuscript. NOTE: Seems to be a re-scoring of the FOLK RHAPSODY. Held by the law firm of Gitlin, Emmer; Jeffrey Green holds manuscript copies of this work.

    BALLET NO. 1: PROCESSIONAL - Strings and woodwinds. Manuscript. Held by the law firm of Gitlin, Emmer; Jeffrey Green holds manuscript copies of this work.

    BALLET NO. 3 - Charlestonia, Opus 16. Orchestra. Held by the law firm of Gitlin Emmer; Jeffrey Green holds manuscript copies of this work.

    CONCERTO FOR CLARINET AND ORCHESTRA - Manuscript. Held by the law firm of Gitlin, Emmer; Jeffrey Green holds manuscript copies of this work.

    DANCE FOR CELLO AND PIANO - Manuscript. Held by the law firm of Gitlin, Emmer; Jeffrey Green holds manuscript copies of this work.

    FOLK RHAPSODY (1919) (NEGRO FOLK RHAPSODY, NO. 1?) - Orchestra. Manuscript. Held by the law firm of Gitlin, Emmer; Jeffrey Green holds manuscript copies of this work.

    FOLK RHAPSODY (1923?) (RHAPSODIE SPIRITUELLE, NEGRO FOLK RHAPSODY, NO. 27) - Orchestra. Manuscript. Held by the law firm of Gitlin, Emmer; Jeffrey Green holds manuscript copies of this work.

    HOW SWEET IS LIFE (1917) - Medium voice and orchestra. Manuscript. Held by the law firm of Gitlin, Emmer; Jeffrey Green holds manuscript copies of this work.

    MUCH ADO, OVERTURE, Opus 1 (1916) - Orchestra. Held by the law firm of Gitlin, Emmer; Jeffrey Green holds manuscript copies of this work.

    NEGRO SYMPHONY - Orchestra. Note: Performed in London from a manuscript copy in 1926. Accepted for performance in Paris in 1927; Jenkins' unexpected death prevented the performance.

    ORCHESTRA, UNTITLED - Soprano instrument and orchestra. Held by the law firm of Gitlin, Emmer; Jeffrey Green holds manuscript copies of this work.

PRAYER (1925) - Low voice and orchestra. Lyrics by Benjamin Brawley. Publisher: Anglo-Continental American Music Press. Held by the law firm of Gitlin, Emmer; Jeffrey Green holds manuscript copies of this work.

PRELUDE RELIGIEUSE. Opus 4 (1917) - Organ and orchestra. Manuscript. Held by the law firm of Gitlin, Emmer; Jeffrey Green holds manuscript copies of this work.

REVERIE: FANTASIE POUR VIOLIN ET PIANO, Opus 11 (1919) - Manuscript. Held by the law firm of Gitlin, Emmer; Jeffrey Green holds manuscript copies of this work.

RHAPSODY NO. 2 - Orchestra.

ROMANCE, Opus 8 (1915) - Manuscript score for: 1. voice and piano (words from "Lady Lindsay's Lyrics"); 2. violin and orchestra (dated 30 April 1917); 3. violin and piano. Publisher: Anglo-Continental American Music Press. Held by the law firm of Gitlin, Emmer; Jeffrey Green holds manuscript copies of this work.

THE SAXOPHONE STRUT (1926) - Saxophone and piano. Held by the law firm of Gitlin, Emmer; Jeffrey Green holds manuscript copies of this work. NOTE: Score for saxophone and orchestra titled MILANO STRUT.

SONATA IN A MINOR - Violoncello. Note: Won Holstein Prize in New York, 1925.

THAT PLACE CALLED ITALIE (1925) - Voice and piano. Manuscript score for orchestra. Words and music by Edmund T. Jenkins   Publisher: Anglo-Continental Music Press, 1926.

Sources

Green, Jeffry. "Edmund Jenkins." The Black Perspective in Music.

Green, Jeffrey. Edmund Thorton Jenkins: The Life and Times of an American Black Composer, 1894-1926. Westport, CT: Greenwood Press, 1982.

Hillmon, Betty. "In Retrospect: Edmund Thorton Jenkins, American Composer: At Home Abroad." The Black Perspective in Music 4.2 (Spring 1986): 143-80.

Holly, Ellistine Perkins, ed. Biographies of Black Composers and Song Writers. Dubuque, IA; Wm. C. Brown Publishers, 1990, p. 25.

Roach, Hildred. Black American Music: Past and Present, Vol. II. Miami: Krieger Publishing Company, 1985, p. 5.

Southern, Eileen. Biographical Dictionary of Afro-American and African Musicans. Westport, CT: Greenwood Press, 1982, pp. 202-03.

JENKINS, LEROY (1932 -)

Leroy Jenkins was born March 11, 1932, in Chicago, Illinois.
He studied violin as a child and played in a church group. He studied with Walter Dyett in Chicago and obtained his B.S. in 1961 from Florida A&M University. He was influenced by Edward ("Eddie") South, Hezekiah ("Stuff") Smith, and Bruce Hayden.
In 1972 he received a grant from the National Endowment for the Arts.
Jenkins has been active with the Association for the Advancement of Creative Musicians as a teacher and performer, and with the Art Ensemble of Chicago, the Jazz Composers Workshop Orchestra, and the Creative Construction Company. He co-founded the Revoluationary Ensemble with Jerome Cooper and Sirone. In 1970 he established his own publishing company, Outward Visions, Inc.
He taught in the public schools of Mobile, Alabama (1961-65) and Chicago, Illinois (1965-69), and taught strings for the Chicago Urban Poverty Corp (1969).
His works include Background to Life (suite for solo violin) and Shapes, Textures, Rhythms, Moods of Sounds (for violin, flute, clarinet, French horn, and bass clarinet).

Works

BACKGROUND TO LIFE - Violin. Publisher: Outward Visions, Inc.

SHAPES, TEXTURES, RHYTHMS, MOODS, AND SOUNDS - Violin, flute, clarinet, french horn, bass clarinet. Publisher: Outward Visions, Inc.

Sources

Southern, Eileen. Biographical Dictionary of Afro-American and African Musicians. Westport, CT: Greenwood Press, 1982, p. 203.

JOHNSON, BESSIE (1878 -)

Works

ODE TO FAITH - Cantata. Chorus, solos, and orchestra. New York Public Library - Reproduction from manuscript.

Source

Carter, Madison H. An Annotated Catalogue of Composers of African Ancestry. New York: Vantage Press, 1986.

JOHNSON, FRANK (a.k.a. FRANCIS JOHNSON) (1792-1884)

Frank Johnson was born in 1792 in Martinique, in the West Indies.
He and his band played in Philadelphia, where they were employed by the State Fencibles and the Philadelphia Grays (white organizations of the 1820s and 1830s). In 1838 Johnson and his band performed for Queen Victoria at Buckingham Palace.

Works

BINGHAM'S COTILLION - Flute or violin and piano.   Score: CBMR (Music Collection).

COL. S. B. GRANT'S PARADE MARCH - Piano, flute.   Score: CBMR (Music Collection).

JOHNSON'S MARCH - Piano with accompaniment for flute or violin. Score: CBMR (Music Collection).

A NEW SPANISH DANCE - Piano with flute or violin.   Score: CBMR (Music Collection).

PARADE MARCH - Piano with accompaniment for flute or violin, obligato for bugle and trumpet. Score: CBMR (Music Collection).

RECOGNITION MARCH OF THE INDEPENDENCE OF HAYTI [sic] - Score: CBMR (Music Collection).

WILLIG'S POCKET COMPANION (containing a selection of fashionable airs) - 1. Health bannie Scotland to thee; 2. Child's March; 3. Tyrolese Peasants Song; 4. Spanish Dance; 5. Tante Angoscie; 6. Down cheek. Flute or violin. Score: CBMR (Music Collection).

Source

LaBrew, Arthur. Selected Works of Frank Johnson. Detroit.

Southern, Eileen. Biographical Dictionary of Afro-American and African Musicians. Westport, CT: Greenwood Press, pp. 205-207.

Southern, Eileen. The Music of Black Americans: A History.   New York: W.W. Norton and Company, Inc., 1983, pp. 107-110.

JOHNSON, HALL (1888-1970)

Hall Johnson was born March 12, 1888, in Athens, Georgia. He died in New York City April 30, 1970.
He studied at the University of Atlanta and the University of Southern Claifornia, and with Percy Goetschius in New York.
His awards include an honorary D.M. from Philadelphia Musical Academy and a citation by the City of New York.
He formed the Hall Johnson Choir in 1925, and the Negro Chorus of Los Angeles in 1936. He toured Germany and Austria in 1951 under the auspices of the State Department.

Works

FESTIVAL MARCH (TO THE BLACK SOLDIERS OF AMERICA) - Orchestra.

FI-YER - Operetta.

G MAJOR - String quartet. Four movements.

NORFOLK - Orchestra. Five movements.

SONATA IN A MINOR - Violin.

SPIRITUAL MOODS NO. 2

SUITE - String orchestra. Five movements.

Sources

Anderson, E. Ruth. Contemporary American Composers: A Biographical Dictionary. Boston: G.K. Hall, 1982, pp. 263-264.

Carter, Madison H. An Annotated Catalogue of Composers of African Ancestry. New York: Vantage Press, 1986.

Southern, Eileen. Biographical Dictionary of Afro-American and African Musicians. Westport, CT: Greenwood Press, 1982, pp. 207-08.

Southern, Eileen. "Johnson, Hall." In The New Grove Dictionary of American Music, Vol. 2, p. 579.

Southern, Eileen. "Johnson, Hall." In The New Grove Dictionary of Music and Musicians, Vol. 9, p. 677.

JOHNSON, JAMES LOUIS ("J.J.") (1924 -)

J. J. Johnson was born in Indianapolis, Indiana, on January 22, 1924. He began to study piano at eleven and trombone at fourteen. He was influenced by Norman Merrifield, and by LaVerne Newsome at Crispus Attucks High School. Later he studied with Earl Hagen.
He played and arranged for a number of groups during the 40s, 50s and 60s, including Clarence Love, Benny Carter, Count Basie, Illinois Jacquet, and Miles Davis. He also toured with his own groups, the J.J. Johnson Quintet and Sextet.
In the 1970s he focused on composing, particularly for film and television. His scores for television shows included "Barefoot in the Park," "Mod Squad," "The Bold Ones," and "Harry-O," among others; his film scores included Man and Boy (1971), Across 110th Street (1972), Cleopatra Jones (1973), and Willie Dynamite (1973), among others.
His works include El Camino Real and Sketch for Trombone and Orchestra (both performed at the Monterey Jazz Festival in 1959), Scenario for Trombone and Orchestra (1962) and Diversions for Six Trombones, Celeste, Harp, and Percussion (1968).

Works

DIVERSIONS (1968) - Six trombones, celeste, harp, and percussion.

RONDO - Vibraphone, piano, contrabass, drum, chamber orchestra. Publisher: New York, MJQ Music, Inc.

SCENARIO (1962) - Trombone and orchestra. Publisher: New York, MJQ Music, Inc.

SKETCH - Trombone and orchestra. Publisher: New York, MJQ Music, Inc.

Sources

Anderson, E. Ruth. Contemporary American Composers: A Biographical Dictionary. Boston: G.K. Hall, 1982.

Catalog. New York: MJQ Music, Inc.

De Lerma, Dominique-Rene. Black Music in Our Culture. Kent, OH: The Kent State University Press, 1970, p. 175.

JOHNSON, JAMES PRICE (1894 - 1955)

James Price Johnson was born February 1, 1894, in New Brunswick, New Jersey, and died November 17, 1955, in New York City.
He began piano study with his mother, and later studied with Ernest Green and Bruto Giannini. among others. He was influenced by Eubie Blake, Lucky Roberts and Richard ("Abba Labba") McLean.
In 1912 he began playing professionally at summer resorts. Later he played in nighclubs and toured the vaudeville circuit. at one time serving as musical director for Sherman Dudley's The Smart Set company. In 1923 he toured Europe with Plantation Days. He also cut piano rolls for the QRS Music company during the 20s. During the 1930s and 1940s he performed as a soloist, led his own groups, and played with groups such as Fess Williams and "Wild Bill" Davis.
Johnson began writing songs and piano rags as early as 1914, the best known of which are "Harlem Strut" and "Carolina Shout." During the 1920s he wrote scores for musicals, including Plantation Days (1923), Runnin' Wild (1923), and Keep Shuffling (with Fats Waller, 1928). He wrote the song "Charleston," which was introduced in runnin' Wild along with the dance that became a fad. Other works include the musical Sugar Hill (1949), The Organizer (an opera with libretto by Langston Hughes), Symphonic Harlem (1932), and Yamekraw (1927), orchestrated by William Grant Still and adapted for film in 1930. Johnson wrote for radio and film as well, and performed in St. Louis Blues (1929) and wrote music for Emperor Jones (1933).
He was a major influence for Fats Waller, Duke Ellington, and Art Tatum.

Works

HARLEM SYMPHONY - Orchestra. Publisher: New York, Robbins Music, 1932.

JASMINE CONCERTO - Piano and orchestra. Publisher: New York, Mills, 1935.

THE ORGANIZER - Opera. Libretto by Langston Hughes.

YAMACRAW - Opera. Publisher: New York, Julius Rutin; Alfred & Co, 1928.

YAMEKRAW: A NEGRO RHAPSODY (1927) - Arranged for orchestra by William Grant Still. Publisher: Alfred & Co., 1928. Recording: The Symphonic Jazz of James P. Johnson, Musical Heritage Society, 4888W, 1984.

Sources

Anderson, E. Ruth. Contemporary American Composers: A Biographical Dictionary. Boston: G.K. Hall, 1982.

De Lerma, Dominique-René. Black Music in Our Society. Kent, OH: Kent State University Press, 1970. p. 175.

Southern, Eileen. Biographical Dictionary of Afro-American and African Musicians. Westport, CT: Greenwood Press, 1982.

JOHNSON, JOHN ROSAMOND (1873-1954)

Works

NOBODY KNOWS THE TROUBLE I SEE - Violin and piano. Arrangement by J. R. Johnson; transcribed with piano accompaniment by Maud Powell. Publisher: Oliver Ditson Co., 1921. Manuscript: Library Association of Portland, Oregon.

Sources

Anderson, E. Ruth. Contemporary American Composers: A Biographical Dictonary. Boston: G.K. Hall & Co., 1982, p. 264.

Carter, Madison H. An Annotated Catalogue of Composers of African Ancestry. New York: Vantage Press, 1986.

Southern, Eileen. Biogrpahical Dictionary of Afro-American and African Musicians. Westport, CT: Greenwood Press, 1982, pp. 210-11.

JONES, CHARLES (n.d.)

Works

SYMPHONY NO. 6 - Orchestra.

Source

De Lerma, Dominique-René. A Discography of Concert Music by Black Composers, 1st ed. Minneapolis, MN: AAMOA Press, 1973.

JONES, QUINCY DELIGHT, JR. (1933 -)

Quincy Delight Jones, Jr., was born March 14, 1933, in Chicago, Illinois.

He began to study trumpet in high school, and later attended Seattle University and the Berklee School of Music in Boston. He was influenced by artists Ray Charles, Joseph Pole, Clark Terry, and Billy Eckstine, and studied with Nadia Boulanger and Olivier Messiaen in France.

His honors include numerous awards from the music industry in the United States and abroad, and an honorary doctorate from the Berklee School of Music.

Jones has been active as a performer, arranger, musical director, and composer. Between 1961 and 1968 he was first music director, then vice president of Mercury Records. He has worked with such artists as Lionel Hampton, Dizzy Gillespie, Peggy Lee, Frank Sinatra, Ray Charles, and Roberta Flack. He has composed many film scores. including The Pawnbroker, In Cold Blood, For the Love of Ivy, Cactus Flower, The Getaway, and many others. He also composed music for such television shows as "Ironside," "Sanford and Son," and "Roots," and in 1973 he produced and directed the television show "Duke Ellington--We Love You Madly." In 1979 he co-founded the Institute for Black American Music.

Works

BLACK REQUIEM (1971) - Vocal solo, choir, and orchestra.

SOUNDPIECE (1962) - String quartet and contralto.

SOUNDPIECE (1964) - Jazz orchestra.

Sources

Anderson, E. Ruth. Contemporary American Composers: A Biographical Dictionary. Boston: G.K. Hall & Co., 1982, p. 266.

Southern, Eileen. Biographical Dictionary of Afro-American and African Musicians. Westport, CT: Greenwood Press, 1982, p. 219.

JOPLIN, SCOTT (1868-1917)

Scott Joplin was born in Texarkana, Texas, November 24, 1868, and died April 1, 1917 in New York City.
He came from a musical family and early revealed talent, teaching himself to play piano. He studied with private teachers during his adolescence and around 1894 he studied theory and composition at the George R. Smith College for Negroes in Sedalia, Missouri. A year earlier he had attended the 1893 Chicago World's Fair. where he came in contact with ragtime pianists Plunk Johnson, Henry Seymour, and Otis Sanders.
He worked extensively as a singer and pianist in his early years. Later he became famous for his rag pieces. During his lifetime he also wrote a ballet, The Ragtime Dance, and two operas, A Guest of Honor and Treemonisha. The former received at least one performance, if not more. However, despite several press announcements to the contrary, he was unable to find a producer for Treemonisha; it finally received its premiere in 1972, after a resurgence in Joplin's popularity. Some numbers from the opera were published separately: "A real slow drag" and the prelude to the third act in 1913 and "Frolic of the bears" in 1915. In 1973 his piano rags were featured in the score of the film The Sting.
Besides establishing the piano rag tradition, Joplin was the first American to write genuinely American folk operas and ballets and the first to successfully fuse the Afro-American folk technique with European art-music forms and techniques.

Works

A GUEST OF HONOR (1903) - Opera.

TREMONISHA (1905) - Opera. Publisher: Weston, Ont., Ragtime Society.

Sources

Blesh. BPIM 3 (Spring/Fall 1975).

De Lerma, Dominique-René. Black Music in Our Culture. Kent, OH: The Kent State University Press, 1970, p. 176.

Gammond, Peter. Scott Joplin and the Ragtime Era. New York, 1975.

Haskin, James. Scott Joplin. New York, 1978.

Reed, Addison. "The Life and Work of Scott Joplin." Dissertation (Ph.D.), University of North Carolina, 1973.

KAY, ULYSSES SIMPSON (1917 -)

Ulysses Simpson Kay was born January 7, 1917, in Tucson, Arizona.
He began to study piano at 6, violin at 10, and saxophone at 12, and in high school he sang in glee clubs and played in the marching band and dance orchestra. He attended the University of Arizona-Tucson (B.S. in public school music, 1938), the Eastman School of Music in Rochester, New York (M. Mus., 1940), the Berkshire Festival (Massachusetts), Yale, and Columbia University. Among those he studied with are John Lowell, Bernard Rogers, Howard Hanson, Paul Hindemith, and Otto Luening. William Grant Still encouraged him to become a composer.
During and after World War II (1942-45) he played saxophone in a Navy band and a dance orchestra; from 1949 to 1952 he studied in Rome as an associate of the American Academy. From 1953-68 he was an editorial adviser and music consultant for Broadcast Music.
He served as a visiting professor at Boston University (summer 1965) and UCLA (1966-67), and as a distinguished professor at Lehman College of the City University of New York (1968 -).
Kay was widely honored, receiving the Alice M. Ditson Fellowship in 1946, the Rosenwald Fellowship in 1947, a Fulbright Fellowship in 1950, a Guggenheim in 1964, and a grant from the National Endowment for the Arts in 1978. He won the Prix de Rome (1949, 1951), an award from the American Academy of Arts and Letters (1947), and an Alumni Award from the University of Rochester (1972). His orchestral piece A Short Overture won the George Gershwin Memorial Award in 1947. He received honorary doctorates from Lincoln College (1963), Bucknell University (1966), University of Arizona (1969), and Illinois Wesleyan University (1969). In 1979, he was elected to the American Academy of Arts and Letters.
He is a prolific composer with dozens of works in a variety of forms to his credit. He wrote his first film score for The Quiet One in 1948, and went on to write for film, documentaries, and television. Among his orchestral works are Portrait Suite which won the 1948 award for the best composition by a native Arizonan, Markings in memory of Dag Hammerskjold; and among his chamber works are Brass Quartet, Six Dances for String Orchestra, Aulos (for solo flute, two horns, string orchestra, and percussion), Facets for piano and woodwind quintet, and Quintet Concerto for five brass soli and orchestra. He wrote four operas: The Boor (1955, libretto adapted from Chekov), The Juggler of Our Lady (1956, libretto by Alexander King), The Capitoline Venus (1970, libretto after Mark Twain), and Jubilee (1976, libretto based on a novel by Margaret Walker). Other works include

Song of Jeremiah for baritone, chorus, and orchestra; Stephen Crane Set (chorus and thirteen instruments); Parables (chorus and chamber orchestra); Forever Free, Concert Sketches, and Four Silhouettes for band; Jersey Hours for voice and harps (text by Donald Door); The Western Paradise for narrator and orchestra (text by Donald Door); and Fugitive Songs and Triptych on Texts of Blake for solo voice and acompaniment.

Works

AMERICAN DANCES (1959) - See SIX DANCES FOR STRING ORCHESTRA

ANCIENT SAGA (1947) - Piano and string orchestra. Duration: 8 minutes. Note: Revision of an earlier work, THE ROPE.

ARIOSO (1948) - See CONCERTO FOR ORCHESTRA

AULOS (1967) - Solo flute, 2 horns, string orchestra, and percussion. Duration: 14 minutes. Commissioned by and dedicated to John Solum. Premiere: 1971, Indiana University (Bloomington); Indiana University Chamber Orchestra Wolfgang Vacano, Conductor; John Solum, flute.

BLEEKER STREET SUITE (1968) - Piano sketch for elementary orchestra with recorders, etc. Four movements: 1. Entrata; 2. Lullaby; 3. Novellette; 4. Ostinato. Duration: 7 minutes.

THE BOOR (1955) - Opera in one act; libretto from Anton Chekov, translated by Vladimir Ussachevsky and adapted by the composer. Three characters: soprano, tenor, and bass. Commissioned by the Koussevitsky Foundation of the Library of Congress. Dedicated to the memory of Serge and Netalie Koussevitsky. Premiere: 1968, University of Kentucky (Lexington).

BRIEF ELEGY (1946) - Oboe and strings. Duration: 5 minutes. Premiere: 1948; Washington, D.C.; National Gallery Orchestra, Richard Bales, Conductor.

CAPITAL LINE VENUS (1969) - Opera in one act; libretto by Judith Dvorak after Mark Twain. Duration: 45 minutes. Commissioned by the Quincy Society of Fine Arts. Premiere: 1971; Krannert Center for the Performing Arts, University of Illinois (Champaign-Urbana); University of Illinois Opera Group, Richard Aslanian, Conductor; David Barron, director; Laura Zirner, designer.

CHARIOTS, AN ORCHESTRAL RHAPSODY (1979). Duration: 15 minutes. Commissioned by Saratoga Performing Arts Center, Saratoga Springs, New York. Premiere: 8 August 1979; Philadelphia Orchestra, Ulysses Kay, Conductor.

CHORAL TRIPTYCH (1962) - Chorus (SATB) and string orchestra. Three songs: 1. Give Ear to My Words; 2. How Long Wilt Thou Forget Me, O Lord?; 3. Alleluia. Biblical text. Duration: 13 minutes. Commissioned by Daniel Pinkham under a Ford Foundation Grant. Publisher: Associated Music, 1967. Premiere: 1963; Museum of Modern Art, New York City; King's Chapel Choir of Boston, Daniel Pinkham, Director. Recording: King's Chapel Choir of Boston and Cambridge Festival Strings, Daniel Pinkham, Conductor; Cambridge Records, CRM-416: Four Contemporary Choral Works.

CONCERTO FOR OBOE AND ORCHESTRA (1940)

CONCERTO FOR ORCHESTRA (1948) - Duration: 18 minutes.   Publisher:
Duchess Music, 1948. Premiere: 1953; Venice, Italy; Teatro la Fenice
Orchestra, Jonel Perlea, Conductor. Recording: VC-81047, 1978.

A COVENANT FOR OUR TIME (1969) - Chorus and orchestra.

DANCES CALINDA SUITE (a.k.a. SUITE FROM THE BALLET "DANCE CALINDA")
(1947) - Orchestra. Duration: 14 minutes. Premiere: 1947; National
Orchestra Association, Leon Barzin, Conductor.

FANTASY VARIATIONS (1963) - Orchestra.   Introduction, theme, and 13
variations.   Duration: 15 minutes.   Commissioned by the Portland
(Maine) Symphony. Publisher: Duchess Music/MCA, 1966; parts on rental. Premiere: 1963; Portland (Maine) Symphony, Arthur Bennett Lipkin, Conductor. Recording: Oslo Philharmonic Orchestra, Arthur Bennett Lipkin, Conductor; Composers Recordings Inc. CRI SD-209.

FIVE PORTRAITS - Violin and piano.   Duration: 17 minutes.   Commissioned by the McKim Fund of the Library of Congress. Premiere: 1974;
Library of Congress; Ruggerio Ricci, violin; Leon Pommers, piano.

FREDERICK DOUGLASS (1983) - Opera in three acts.   Libretto by Donald
Dorr. Duration: full evening.

GUITARRA (1973; revised 1984) - Guitar.   Three movements: 1. Prelude;
2. Arioso; 3. Finale.   Duration: 12 minutes.   Commissioned by and
dedicated to Wilbur P. Cotton. Publisher: Carl Fischer.

HARLEM CHILDREN'S SUITE (1973) - Elementary orchestra.   Three movements: 1. Prelude; 2. Aria; 3. Finale.   Duration: 9 minutes.   Commissioned by the Harlem School of the Arts.   Dedicated to Dorothy
Maynor.

INSCRIPTIONS FROM WHITMAN (1963) - Chorus (SATB) and orchestra.   Text
by Walt Whitman. Two movements. Duration: 25 minutes. Commissioned
by the Tercentenary Commission of the State of New Jersey and the New
Jersey Symphony for the New Jersey Tercenterary.   Premiere: 1964;
Women's Chorus of Douglass College, New Jersey Oratorio Society Male
Chorus of Atlantic City, and New Jersey Symphony Orchestra, Kenneth
Schermerhorn, Conductor.

JERSEY HOURS (1978) - Voice and harp. Text by Donald Door.

JUBILEE (1974-76) - Opera in three acts.   Thirteen principals, double
chorus, and orchestra. Libretto by Donald Door, based on the novel by
Margaret Walker. Commissioned by Opera South. Premiere: 20 November
1976; Jackson, Mississippi; Opera South.

JUGGLER . . . (1956) - Opera. Libretto by Alexander King.

MARKINGS (1966) - Orchestra. Duration: 21 minutes. Commissioned by
the Meadow Brook Festival, Oakland University, Rochester Minnesota.
Written in memory of Dag Hammerskjold and dedicated to Oliver Daniel.
Publisher: Duchess Music/MCA 1968; parts on rental. Premiere:

1966; Meadow Brooks Festival. Oakland University Rochester, Minnesota; Detroit Symphony, Sixten Ehrling, Conductor.

OF NEW HORIZON (1944) - Orchestra. Duration: 8 minutes. Commissioned by Thor Johnson   PUblisher: C.F. Peters, 1961; parts on rental. Premiere: 1944; New York City; New York Philharmonic Symphony Orchestra Thor Johnson, Conductor. Recording: University of Arizona Records. Note: This work won the American Broadcasting Company Award in 1946.

ONCE THERE WAS A MAN (a.k.a. A COVENANT FOR OUR TIME) (1969) – Narrator, chorus (SATB), and orchestra. Text by Randal Caudill. Duration: 17 minutes. Commissioned by the 1969 Worcester (Massachusetts) Music Festival. Premiere: 1969; Detroit Michigan; Detroit Symphony, Sixten Ehrling, Conductor; William Warfield, narrator.

PARABLES (1970) - Chorus (SATB) and chamber orchestra. Two songs: 1. The Old Arm Chair; 2. The Hell-bound Train. Anonymous texts. Duration: 12 minutes. Commissioned by the American Choral Directors Association. Publisher: Duchess Music/MCA, 1970; parts on rental. Premiere: 1971; Kansas City, Missouri; Directors Association of the Kansas State University Concert Chorale, Rod Walker, Conductor, and Kansas State University Chamber Orchestra, Paul Roby, Conductor.

PARTITA IN A (1950) - Violin and piano. Four movements: 1. Prelude; 2. Burlesca; 3. Interlude; 4. Echo. Duration: 15 minutes. Premiere: 1952; American Academy, Rome, Italy.

PHOEBUS, ARISE (1959) - Soprano, bass, chorus (SATB), and Orchestra. Seven parts: 1. Prelude (text by composer); 2. No! (text by Thomas Hood); 3. Tears, Flow No More (text by Lord Herbert of Cherbury); 4. Phoebus, Arise (text by William Drummond); 5. Song (text by Thomas Middleton and William Rowley); 6. The Epicure (text by Abraham Cowley); 7. Epilogue (text by the composer). Duration: 30 minutes. Commissioned by the International Music Council of New York City. Premiere: 1959; Town Hall, New York City; International Fellowship Chorus and Orchestra, Harold Aks, Conductor.

PIETA (1950) - English horn and string orchestra. Duration: 7 minutes. Premiere: 1958; Annual Festival of American Music, Town Hall, New York City; Knickerbocker Chamber Orchestra, Herman Newman, Conductor; Doris Goltzer English horn.

PORTRAIT SUITE (1948) - Orchestra. Five parts: 1. Prologue; 2. Asymetric; 3. Reclining Figure; 4. Blossoming; 5. Epilogue. Duration: 18 minutes. Premiere: 1964; Erie, Pennsylvania; Erie Philharmonic, James Sample, Conductor. Note: This work won the 1948 award for best composition by a native Arizonan.

PRESIDENTIAL SUITE (1965) - Orchestra. Duration: 12 minutes. Commissioned by the Greater Boston Youth Symphony. Premiere: 1965; Boston Symphony Hall; Greater Boston Youth Symphony, Ulysses Kay, Conductor.

THE QUIET ONE SUITE (a.k.a SUITE FROM THE QUIET ONE)(1948) - Orchestra. Four movements: 1. Joy and Fears; 2. Street Wanderings; 3.

Interlude; 4. Crisis.   Premiere: 1948; New York Little Symphony, Ulysses Kay, Conductor.

QUINTET CONCERTO (1974) - Solo brass quintet (2 trumpets, F horn, 2 trombones; alternate part for tuba) and orchestra.   Three movements. Commissioned by the Juilliard School of Music.   Premiere: 1974; Juilliard School of Music; Walter Hendl, Conductor.

REVERIE AND RONDO (a.k.a TWO PIECES FOR ORCHESTRA) (1964) - Duration: 7 minutes.   Premiere: 1968; Flint, Michigan; Flint Symphony Orchestra, William Byrd, Conductor.

SCHERZI MUSICALI (1968) - Chamber orchestra.   Duration: 17 minutes. Commissioned by the Chamber Music Society of Detroit for its 25th anniversary.   Publisher: Duchess/MCA, 1971.   Premiere: 1969; Detroit, Michigan; Princeton Chamber Orchestra and Interlochen Arts Woodwind Quintet, Nicholas Harsanyi, Conductor.

SERENADE FOR ORCHESTRA (1954) - Four movements.   Commissioned by the Louisville Philharmonic Society.   Publisher: Associated Music, 1955. Premiere: 1954; Louisville Orchestra, Robert Whitney, Conductor. Recording: Louisville Orchestra, Robert Whitney, Conductor; First Edition Records LOU-545-8.

A SHORT OVERTURE (1946) - Orchestra.   Duration: 7 minutes.   Publisher: Duchess Music/MCA, 1973; parts on rental.   Premiere: 1947; New York City; New York City Symphony, Leonard Bernstein, Conductor. Recording: Oakland Youth Orchestra, Robert Hughes, Conductor; Desto DC-7101:   The Black Composer in America.   Note: This work won the Third Annual George Gershwin Memorial Contest in 1947.

SINFONIA IN E (1950) - Orchestra.   Four movements.   Duration: 20 minutes.   Publisher: Pembroke/Carl Fischer.   Premiere: 1951; Eastman--Rochester Symphony Orchestra, Howard Hanson, Conductor.   Recording: Oslo Philharmonic Orchestra, George Bariti, Conductor; Composers Recordings, Inc. CRI-139.

SIX DANCES FOR STRING ORCHESTRA (a.k.a. AMERICAN DANCES)(1954) - 1. Schottische; 2. Waltz; 3. Round Dance; 4. Polka; 5. Promenade; 6. Galop.   Duration: 18-19 minutes.   Publisher: Duchess Music (Leeds Contemporary Classics for String series), 1965. Premiere: CBS Radio, "String Serenade," conducted by Alfred Antonini.   Recording: Westphalian Symphony Orchestra, Paul Freeman, Conductor (Turnabout 34546); Round Dance and Polka: New Symphony Orchestra of London, Salvador Camarata, Conductor (Composers Recordings Inc. CRI-119).

SONG OF JEREMIAH (1945) - Baritone, chorus (SATB), and orchestra. Biblical text.   Duration: 19 minutes.   Premiere: 1954; Fisk University Choir, Harry Von Bergen, Conductor.

SOUTHERN HARMONY (1975) - Orchestra.   Duration: 21 minutes.   Based on themes and motives from William Walker's "The Southern Harmony" of 1835.   Four movements: 1. Prelude: Land of Beginnings; 2. Fifes and Drums; 3. Variants; 4. Elysium. Commissioned by the Southeastern Regional Metropolitan Orchestra Managers Association.   Publisher: Pembroke/Carl Fischer, 1976.   Premiere: 1976; North Carolina Symphony Orchestra, John Gosling, Conductor.

STRING QUARTET NO. 1 (1949) - withdrawn by the composer.

STRING QUARTET NO. 2 (1956) - Duration: 18 minutes. Four movements. Premiere: 1959; University of Illinois (Champaign-Urbana); Walden String Quartet.

STRING QUARTET NO. 3 (1961) - Duration: 15 minutes. Three movements. Commissioned by the University of Michigan. Dedicated to the Stanley Quartet. Premiere: 1962; Stanley Quartet.

STRING TRIPTYCH (1987) - String orchestra. Duration: 7 minutes. Publisher: Carl Fischer, Inc. Premiere: 23 January 1988; Missouri Allstate High School Orchestra; Paul Vermel conductor.

SUITE FOR ORCHESTRA (1945) - Duration: 17 minutes   Four movements: 1. Fanfare: Thirtyfour; 2. Scherzo; 3. Olden Tune; 4. Finale. Publisher: Associated, 1948. Premiere: 1950; Town Hall, New York City; American Youth Orchestra, Dean Dixon, Conductor.

SUITE FOR STRINGS (1947) - String orchestra. Duration: 14 minutes. Three movements. Publisher: C.F. Peters, 1961. Premiere: 1949; Baltimore Maryland; Baltimore Chamber Orchestra, Ulysses Kay, Conductor.

SYMPHONY (1967) - Orchestra. Duration: 25 minutes. Four movements. Commissioned by the Illinois Sesquicentennial Commission. Premiere: 1968; Chicago Symphony Orchestra. Jean Martinon, Conductor.

THEATER SET (1968) - Orchestra. Duration: 15 minutes. Three movements: 1. Overture; 2. Ballad--Chase Music; 3. Finale. Commissioned by the Junior League of Atlanta for Robert Shaw and the Atlanta Symphony Orchestra. Dedicated to Robert Shaw. Publisher: Duchess Music/MCA, 1971. Premiere: 1968; Atlanta Symphony Orchestra, Robert Shaw, Conductor.

THREE PIECES AFTER BLAKE (1952) - High voice and orchestra. Duration: 14 minutes. Text by Blake: 1. To the Evening Star; 2. Mad Song; 3. Contemplation. Premiere: 1955; David Broekman, Conductor; Shirley Emmons, soprano.

TRIPTYCH ON TEXTS OF BLAKE (1962) - High voice, violin, violoncello, and piano. Reduction of Three Pieces After Blake (To the Evening Star; Mad Song; Contemplation). Duration: 14 minutes. Commissioned by Kermit Moore. Publisher: Pembroke/Carl Fischer. Premiere: 1963; Winston-Salem Teachers College, Winston-Salem, North Carolina; Clarmoor Quartet.

UBRIAN SCENE (1963) - Orchestra. Duration: 12 minutes. Commissioned by Edward B. Benjamin. Publisher: Duchess Music/MCA, 1965; parts on rental. Premiere: 1964; New Orleans Philharmonic, Werner Torkanowsky, Conductor. Recording: Louisville Orchestra, Robert Whitney, Conductor; First Edition Records LOV-651.

THE WESTERN PARADISE (1976) - Narrator and orchestra. Text by Donald Door. Duration: 16 minutes. Five movements. Commissioned by the National Symphony for the Bicentennial. Premiere: 12 October 1976; Washington, D.C.; National Symphony, Antal Dorati, Conductor.

Sources

Baker, Theodore. Baker's Biographical Dictionary of Musicians, 1971 supplement to the 5th edition by Nicholas Slonimsky, s.v. "Kay, Ulysses Simpson."

Claghorn, Charles E. Biographical of American Music. West Nyack, NY: Parker Publishing Company, 1973.

De Lerma, Dominique-René. Black Music in Our Culture. Kent, OH: Kent State University Press, 1973, p. 176.

Groves Dictionary of Music and Musicians s.v. "Kay, Ulysses Simpson" by Eileen Southern vol. 9. Washington, D.C.: McMillan Pub. Ltd. 1980.

Hayes, Laurence Melton. "The Music of Ulysses Kay, 1939-63." Ph.D. dissertation, University of Wisconsin, 1971.

Southern, Eileen. Biographical Dictionary of Afro-American and African Musicians. Westport, CT: Greenwood Press, 1982.

KENNEDY, JOSEPH J., JR. (1923 -)

Joseph Kennedy, Jr. was born in Pittsburgh, Pennsylvania, in 1923.

He attended Carnegie Mellon University, Virginia State College, and Duquesne University (MA). Influences include Jimmie Lunceford and Ahmad Jamal.

He teaches at John Marshall High and Virginia Commonwealth University.

Among his works are A Lazy Atmosphere, Tempo for Two, Surrealism, You Can Be Sure, The Fantastic Vehicle, Illusions Opticas, Nothing to Fret About, Disenchantment, Hypnotic, Serious Moods, Charming Attitudes, Somewhat Eccentric, Suite for Trio and Orchestra, and Dialogue for Flute, Cello and Piano.

Works

DIALOGUE FOR FLUTE, CELLO, AND PIANO - Publisher: Mr. Vernon, New York, Hema Music Composition.

SUITE FOR TRIO AND ORCHESTRA - Premiere: 1965; Cleveland Summer Symphony, Joseph Kennedy, Conductor.

Sources

Information submitted by the composer.

Roach, Hildred. Black American Music: Past and Present, Vol. I. Miami: Krieger Publishing Co., 1985, pp. 93-94.

KING, BETTY JACKSON (1928 -)

Betty Jackson King was born in Chicago in 1928.

She attended Roosevelt University (B.M. and M.M.), Oakland University, Glassboro College, Peabody Institute, Westminister Choir College, and others. Her piano teachers include her mother, Gertrude Jackson Taylor, Saul Dorfman, and Maurice Dumesnil; organ: Joseph Lockett and Abba Leifer; composition: Karel B. Jarick; and voice: Thelma Waide Brown.

She has taught at the University of Chicago Laboratory School, Roosevelt University, Dillard University, and Wildwood High School.

Honors include a scholarship from the Chicago Umbrian Glee Club, awards from the National Association of Negro Musicians. Outstanding Leaders in Elementary and Secondary Education, and the International Black Writers Conference. She is past president of NANM.

Her compositions are the Biblical operas Saul of Tarus and My Servant Job; an Easter cantata, Simon of Cyrene; Requiem; the ballet The Kids in School With Me; Life Cycle (violin and piano); Vocalise (soprano, cello, and piano); and numerous others.

Works

THE KIDS IN SCHOOL WITH ME - Ballet.

LIFE CYCLE - Violin and piano.

MY SERVANT JOB - Sacred opera.

SAUL OF TARUS - Sacred opera.

VOCALISE - Soprano, violoncello, and piano.

Sources

Holly, Ellistine Perkins, ed. Biographies of Black Composers and Songwriters. Dubuque, IA: Wm. C. Brown Publishers, 1990, pp. 28-29.

Roach, Hildred. Black American Music: Past and Present, Vol. II. Miami: Krieger Publishing Co., 1985, pp. 60-62.

LAKE, OLIVER (1942 -)

Oliver Lake was born September 14, 1942, in Marianna, Arkansas.

As a child he played in a drum and bugle corps, and later studied saxophone and flute. He received his musical education at Lincoln University (BA, 1968), and Washington University-St. Louis. He also studied privately with Ron Carter and Oliver Nelson, and studied electronic music in Paris.

He helped found BAG--Black Artists Group--of St. Louis, and toured Europe in 1972-74 with a BAG band.

Among his best-known compositions are Violin Trio, Heavy Spirits, and Life Dance of Is, a multi-media theatre piece.

Lake taught in the public schools of St. Louis, at Webster College in 1969, and at the Creative Music Foundation at Woodstock, New York.

Works

SHADOW THREAD - Octet and cello.

SPACES (1972) - Violin trio.

SUITE FOR IMPROVISOR AND VIOLIN TRIO.

Sources

Anderson, E. Ruth. Contemporary American Composers: A Biographical Dictionary. Boston: G.K.Hall & Co., 1982, p. 301

Southern, Eileen. Biographical Dictionary of Afro-American and African Musicians. Westport, CT: Greenwood Press, 1982, p. 236.

LAMBERT, LUCIEN LEON GUILLAUME (1858-1945)

Works

ANDANTE ET FANTAISE - Piano and orchestra. Publisher: Paris, Heugel, 1892. Score: Biblioteque Nationale, Paris, France.

LES CLOCHES DE PORTO: TABLEAU MUSICAL - Orchestral reduction. Manuscript, 1912. Score: Biblioteque Nationale, Paris, France.

HYMNIS: DRAME ANTIQUE IN ACT V - Piano with flute or violin accompaniment. Publisher: Paris, Bruneau, 1889.

Sources

Southern, Eileen. Biographical Dictionary of Afro-American and African Musicians. Westport, CT: Greenwood Press, 1982.

Trotter, James M. Music and Some Highly Musical People. Chicago: Afro-Am Press, 1969. (reprint of 1878 ed.)

Wyatt, Lucius. "Composers Corner." BMR Newsletter 9.1.

Wyatt, Lucius. "Updated Music List--Six Composers of Nineteenth-Century New Orleans." BMR Newsletter 9.1.

LAMPLEY, CALVIN DOUGLAS (n.d.)

Works

FOUR LITTLE "INGS": PORTRAITS (ZENING, PRACTING, JAZZING, FUNING) (1982) - Flute and guitar. Commissioned by Frank Bahas. Premiere: 21 October 1982; Walter Art Gallery, Baltimore, Maryland; Frank Bahas, guitar; Janet Memsli, flute.

Source

Horne, Aaron. Woodwind Music of Black Composers. Westport, CT: Greenwood Press, 1990, p. 38.

LATEEF, YUSEF ABDUL (1920 -)

Yusef Abdul Lateef (a.k.a. William Evans) was born October 9, 1920, in Chattanooga, Tennessee.

He played alto and tenor saxophone in high school. He attended Wayne
University in Detroit. the Manhattan School of Music in New York (BA, M.
Mus. Ed.), and the University of Massachusetts at Amherst (D. Mus Ed.,
1975). He also studied at the Teal School of Music in Detroit for two
years, and privately in New York with various teachers, including Harold
Jones and John Wummer. He began playing flute in 1954 and later learned to
play oboe, bassoon, and such exotic instruments as the rabat, shanai, and
argole.
     He began to play jazz professionally after high school, and toured
with such notables as Lucius Millinder, Oran Page, and Dizzy Gillespie,
Charles Mingus, Babatundi Olatunji, and Julian Adderly, as well as playing
with groups of his own.
     Some of his best known compositions are Trio for Piano, Violin, and
Flute, Flute Book of the Blues, and Symphonic Blues Suite. He also composed music for film soundtracks. He identifies his music as "autophysio-
pschic."

Works

     SYMPHONIC BLUES SUITE - Quartet and orchestra.

     TRIO FOR PIANO, VIOLIN, AND FLUTE (1965)

     TRIO, VIOLONCELLO, AND PIANO

Sources

     Jeske, Lee. "Lateef, Yusef." The New Grove Dictionary of Jazz, Vol.
     2, pp. 12-13.

     Southern, Eileen. Biographical Dictionary of Afro-American and Afri-
     can Musicians. Westport, CT: Greenwood Press, 1982, pp. 237-238.

LAVERGNE, PATRIC (1955 -)

Works

     ELEGY - Violin.

     THREE MOVEMENTS - String bass.

Source

     Carter, Madison H.   An Annotated Catalogue of Composers of African
     Ancestry. New York: Vantage Press, 1986.

LAWRENCE, WILLIAM (1897-1966)

Works

     THREE NEGRO SPIRITUALS - String quartet.

Source

Carter, Madison H.   An Annotated Catalogue of Composers of African Ancestry. New York: Vantage Press, 1986.

LEE, BENJAMIN (n.d.)

Works

CONCERT FOR BRASS CHOIR AND ORCHESTRA - Premiere: 3 December 1989; Carnegie Hall; American Symphony Orchestra, James de Priest, conductor.

LEE, WILLIAM JAMES (1928 -)

William James Lee was born in Snow Hill, Alabama, July 23, 1928.
He came from a musical family: his father played trumpet/cornet, his mother was a concert singer, and his brother and sisters became professional musicians. Lee played drums in a family band at the age of 8, and began to study flute at 11. He attended the Snow Hill Institute and Morehouse College (B.A., 1951), and studied with Willis Lawrence James and Kemper Harreld.
He played string bass with various groups in the 1950s, including George Coleman, Johnny Griffin, Andrew Hill, and Clifford Jordan. During the 1960s he played with Ray Bryant, "Philly Joe" Jones, Phineas Newborn, Judy Collins, Theodore Bikel, Odetta, and Josh White, among others. In 1968 he founded the New York Bass Violin Choir, composed of Ron Carter, Richard Davis, Lisle Atkinson, Milt Hinton, Samuel Jones, Michael Fleming, and himself In 1972 he co-founded The Brass Company with Billy Higgins and Bill Hardman. He also toured and recorded with a family group called Descendants of Mike and Phoebe, which included his two sisters and his brother.
His works include the folk or jazz operas The Depot, One Mile East, Baby Sweets, and The Quarters and music for a stage play, A Hand Is On the Gate.

Works

BABY SWEETS - Folk or jazz opera.

THE DEPOT - Folk or jazz opera.

ONE MILE EAST - Folk or jazz opera.

THE QUARTERS - Folk or jazz opera.

Source

Southern, Eileen. Biographical Dictionary of Afro-American and African Musicians. Westport, CT: Greenwood Press, 1982, p. 224.

LEÓN, TANIA JUSTINA (1944 -)

Tania León was born May 14, 1944, in Havana, Cuba.

She began to study piano at the age of four, and attended the Carlos Alfredo Peyrellade Conservatory in Havana (B.A.), the National Conservatory in Havana (M.A.), and New York University (B.S., B.A., M.S.).

She became music director of Arthur Mitchell's Dance Theater of Harlem in 1970. During her tenure with the Dance Theater. she composed the ballets Tones and Haiku.

In 1978 she served as conductor and musical director for the Broadway musical The Wiz; and as musical director for a public television series, "Dance in America" (1977-78).

As guest conductor, León appeared with orchestras in Europe and the United States, including orchestra at the Festival of Two Worlds at Spoleto, Italy, and at the Nervi Festival in Genoa, Italy. In 1978 she was appointed musical director and conductor for the Brooklyn Philharmonia Community Concerts series; she also served as pianist for the Brooklyn Philharmonia Orchestra and assistant conductor to Lukas Foss.

Besides the ballets, she is also known for her composition Spiritual Suite and the score for a play by Mario Pena, La Ramera de la Cueva.

Works

BATÁ (1985) - Orchestra. Duration: 7 minutes. Commissioned by the Bay Area Women's Philharmonic. Dedication: "To My Father." Publisher: New York, Peer-Southern Concert Music.

THE BELOVED (1972) - Flute, oboe, clarinet, bassoon, piano, violoncello, and double bass. Duration: 10 minutes. Note: Ballet for the Dance Company of Harlem.

CONCERTO CRIOLLO (1980) - Solo timpani, solo piano, and orchestra. Duration: 20 minutes. Commissioned by the National Endowment of the Arts. Publisher: New York, Peer-Southern Concert Music.

FOUR PIECES FOR CELLO SOLO (1983) - Duration: 12 minutes. Publisher: New York, Peer-Southern Concert Music.

THE GOLDEN WINDOWS (1982) - Flute/piccolo/alto flute, oboe/English horn, trumpet, percussion. Duration: 30 minutes. Commissioned by the Byrd Hoffman Foundation. Ballet.

HAIKU (1974) - Ballet.

HEART OF OURS (1988) - Chorus and instruments.

KABIOSILE (1988) - Solo piano and orchestra. Duration: 8 minutes. Commissioned by the American Composers Orchestra. Publisher: New York, Peer-Southern Concert Music. Premiere: 4 December 1988, Carnegie Hall; The American Composers Orchestra; Ursula Oppens, piano.

MAGGIE MAGALITA (1980) - Flute, clarinet, violoncello, 2 percussion, pianoforte, and guitar. Theatre work.

NEW YORK - Piano and orchestra. Premiere: 4 December 1988, Carnegie Hall; American Composers Orchestra.

PAISANOS SEMOS! (WE'S HILLBILLIES) (1984) - Guitar. Duration: 4 minutes 30 seconds. Publisher: New York, Peer-Southern Concert Music.

PARAJOTA DELATE ("FROM T. TO J.") (1988) - Flute, clarinet, violin, violoncello, and piano. Duration: 4 minutes 30 seconds. Commissioned by the Da Capo Chamber Players.

PUEBLO MULATO: 3 SONGS ON POEMS BY NICOLAS GUILLEN (1987) - Soprano, oboe, guitar, double bass, percussion, piano. Duration: 12 minutes.

RABIOSILE (1988) - Piano and orchestra. Duration: 8 minutes. Publisher: Peer Southern, 1988. Premiere: 4 December 1988; Carnegie Hall, New York City; American Composers Orchestra.

SPIRITUAL SUITE - Ballet. Premiere: 1976; Marian Anderson, narrator.

TONES - Ballet. Commissioned by the Dance Theater of Harlem. Note: A collaboration with Arthur Mitchell.

Sources

Information submitted by the composer.

Southern, Eileen. Biographical Dictionary of Afro-American and African Musicians. Westport, CT: Greenwood Press, 1982, pp. 242-43.

LEWIS, JOHN AARON (1920 -)

John Aaron Lewis was born in La Grange, Illinois, May 3, 1920.
He received his B.M. (1942) from the University of New Mexico and M.M. (1953) from the Manhattan School of Music.
After serving in the Army, he played with various groups, including Dizzy Gillespie, Illinois Jacquet, Miles Davis, Lester Young, Charlie Parker, and Ella Fitzgerald.
In 1952 he co-founded the Modern Jazz Quartet (with Milton Jackson, Ray Brown, and Kenny Clarke), serving as pianist until 1977.
Lewis was president of MJQ Music, Inc., executive director of Lenox School of Jazz, and music director of Orchestra USA. He served as musical director for the annual Monterey Jazz Festivals. He taught at City College-CUNY.
His works include a ballet, Original Sin (1961); the film scores No Sun in Venice, Odds Against Tomorrow, and The Milanese Story; "Three Windows" from the film Sain-on Jamais and the jazz fugues "Concorde" and "Vendome."

Works

THE COMEDY - Soli: vibes, piano, bass, drums, with orchestra. Duration: 12 minutes. Publisher: New York, MJQ Music, Inc.

CONCERT PIECE (IN MEMORIAM) - Soli: vibes, piano, bass, and drums (solo piano) Orchestra. Duration: 20 minutes. Publisher: New York, MJQ Music, Inc.

DJANGO - Soli: vibes, piano, bass, drums, with string orchestra. Duration: 7 minutes 54 seconds. Publisher: New York, MJQ Music, Inc.

ENCOUNTER IN CAGNES - Soli: vibes, piano, bass, drums, with string orchestra. Duration: 12 minutes 28 seconds. Publisher: New York, MJQ Music, Inc.

ENGLAND'S CAROL - Soli: vibes, piano, bass, and drums, with orchestra. Duration: 7 minutes. Publisher: New York, MJQ Music, Inc.

FANFARE (SALUTE TO BASIE) - Orchestra. Duration: 5 minutes. Publisher: New York, MJQ Music Inc.

IN MEMORIAM (1971) - Jazz quartet and orchestra. Premiere: 13 November 1971; the Modern Jazz Quartet Albuquerque Symphony Orchestra, Y. Takeda, conductor.

JAZZ OSTINATO - Soli: vibes, piano, bass, and drums, with orchestra. Duration: 6 minutes. Publisher: New York, MJQ Music, Inc.

KANSAS CITY BREAKS - Soli: vibes, piano, bass, drums, with string orchestra. Duration: 6 minutes 29 seconds. Publisher: New York, MJQ Music, Inc.

MILANO - Soli: piano, bass, drums, with string orchestra. Duration: 6 minutes. Publisher: New York, MJQ Music, Inc.

NA DUBROYACKI NACIM - Soli: vibes, piano, drums, with strings. Duration: 20 minutes. Publisher: New York, MJQ Music, Inc.

ORIGINAL SIN - Ballet Duration: 24 minutes. Publisher: New York, MJQ Music, Inc.

THE QUEEN'S FANCY - Soli: vibes, piano, bass, with orchestra. Duration: 5 minutes. Publisher: New York, MJQ Music, Inc.

SKETCH FOR DOUBLE QUARTET - Jazz quartet and string quartet. Publisher: New York, MJQ Music, Inc.

THE SPIRITUAL - Soli: vibes, piano, bass, drums, with orchestra. Duration: 7 minutes. Publisher: New York, MJQ Music, Inc.

TALES OF THE WILLOW TREE - Orchestra. Duration: 10 minutes. Commissioned by the Atlanta Symphony Orchestra. Publisher: New York, MJQ Music, Inc. Premiere: 17 September 1987; Atlanta Symphony Orchestra.

THREE WINDOWS - Soli: vibes, piano, bass, drums, with string orchestra. Duration: 8 minutes 13 seconds. Publisher: New York, MJQ Music, Inc.

Sources

Information submitted by the composer.

Anderson, E. Ruth, ed. Contemporary American Composers: A Biographical Dictionary. Boston: G.K. Hall, 1982.

De Lerma Dominique-René. Black Music in Our Culture. Kent, OH: Kent State University Press, 1970, p. 176.

Southern, Eileen. Biographical Dictionary of Afro-American and African Musicians. Westport, CT: Greenwood Press, 1982.

LOGAN, WENDELL MORRIS (1940 -)

Wendell Logan was born November 24, 1940, in Thomson, Georgia.

He studied music with his father, a music teacher in the public school system, and was exposed to a wide variety of music performed at the community center, including shows by James Brown, Fats Domino, Little Richard, and Silas Green. He received his B.S. from Florida A&M University at Tallahassee, where he studied with Johnnie V. Lee, William Foster, and Olly Wilson. He also attended Southern Illinois University-Carbondale (M.Mus.), and University of Iowa-Iowa City (Ph.D.).

He received grants from the National Endowment for the Arts, the Martha Baird Rockefeller Fund, and the H.H. Powers Fund.

He contributed to professional journals, and published a book, Primer for Keyboard Improvisation in the Jazz/Rock Idiom.

Logan taught in the public schools of Rudyard, Michigan, and at Florida A&M, Ball State University, Western Illinois University, and the Oberlin School of Music.

His works often included electronic techniques, as in From Hell to Breakfast, a mixed media collaboration for dancers, speakers, lights, and magnetic tape, and In Memoriam: Malcolm X, for choir and magnetic tape. Others of his works include Proportions for Nine Players, Songs for our Times, Music for Brasses, Variations on a Motive by John Coltrane, Duo Exchanges, Five Pieces for Piano, and Three Pieces for Violin and Piano.

Works

CONCERT MUSIC FOR ORCHESTRA (1963) - Duration: 10 minutes. Premiere: 1965, Dallas Texas; Dallas Symphony.

THE EYE OF THE SPARROW (1978) - Flute, tenor saxophone, trumpet, double bass, piano, and drums. Duration: contains improvisational passages. Premiere: 1978, Oberlin Conservatory, Orberlin, Ohio.

MEMORIES OF . . . (1972; revised 1979) - Chamber orchestra. Duration: 12 minutes. Premiere: 24 February 1979, Oberlin Conservatory, Oberlin, Ohio.

OUTSIDE ORNETT'S HEAD (1979) - Trumpet, guitar, vibraphone, double bass, and drums. Duration: improvisational. Dedicated to Ornette Coleman.

PIECE FOR VIOLIN AND PIANO, THREE (1977) - Violin and electronic piano. Duration: 8 minutes. Dedicated to Richard Young. Premiere: 1977, Oberlin Conservatory, Oberlin, Ohio; Richard Young, violin; Sanford Margolis, piano. Recording: Orion, 1979.

POLYPHONY I (1968) - Orchestra. Duration: 20 minutes. Manuscript score (University of Iowa Music Library). Note: Ph.D. Dissertation, Dissertation Abstracts XXIX, 6, 1917-A.

PROPORTIONS FOR NINE PLAYERS AND CONDUCTOR (1968) - Flute, B-flat clarinet, B-flat trumpet, trombone, violin, cello, piano, and percussion (2 players). Duration: 16 minutes. Premiere: 1968, Ball State

University, Muncie, Indiana; New Music Ensemble. Recording: Orion, 1979. Reviewed: San Francisco Chronicle 7 February 1973; w/analysis, Perspectives of New Music, Vol. 9, p. 135.

REQUIEM FOR CHARLIE PARKER (1978) - Large orchestra, soloists, and jazz group. NOTE: Instrumentation includes soprano and tenor soloists and a choir of 3 male and 3 female singers.

SONG OF THE WITCHDOKTOR (1976) - Flute, violin, piano, and percussion. Duration: 12 minutes. Premiere: 1976, Oberlin Conservatory, Oberlin, Ohio.

STANZAS FOR THREE PLAYERS (1966) - Flute, cello, and piano. Duration: 16 minutes. Premiere: 1967, Center for New Music, Iowa City, Iowa. Reviewed: Daily Iowan, 1967.

TO MINGUS (1979) - Vibraphone (or other instrument capable of playing chords) and guitar. Duration: 6 minutes. Dedicated to Andre Whatley. Premiere: 24 February 1979 Oberlin Conservatory, Oberlin, Ohio. Note: Written in memory of Charles Mingus.

Sources

Information submitted by the composer.

Anderson, E. Ruth. Contemporary American Composers: A Biographical Dictoinary. Boston: G.K. Hall, 1976.

Clagburn, Charles Eugene. Biographical Dictionary of American Music. West Nyack, NY: Parker, 1973.

Jacobi, Hugh William. Contemporary American Composers Based at American Colleges and Universities. Paradise, CA: Paradise Arts, 1975.

Southern, Eileen. Biographical Dictionary of Afro-American and African Musicians. Westport, CT: Greenwood Press, 1982, p. 248.

Southern, Eileen. "Logan, Wendell." In The New Grove Dictionary of American Music, Vol. 3, p. 103.

Tischler, Alice. Fifteen Black American Composers: A Bibliography of Their Works. Detroit: Information Coordinators, Inc., 1981, pp. 179-87.

Wilson, Olly. "Wendell Logan: Proportions." Perspectives in New Music (1970): 135 42.

LOVINGOOD, PENMAN, SR. (1895 -)

Penman Lovingood, Sr., was born in Marshall, Texas, in 1895.
He attended Samuel Huston College, Temple University, and Compton College. He studied with William Happich at the Symphony Club in Philadelphia and with J. Rosamond Johnson in New York.
He received a Wanamaker Award (1930); the Bronze and Silver Medals in voice and composition by the Griffith Foundation (Newark, NJ); and an award from ASCAP for the performance of his opera Menelik of Abyssinia.

He was the author of <u>Famous</u> <u>Negro</u> <u>Musicians</u> (New York: Press Forum, 1921).
     Among his works are <u>Saturday's</u> <u>Child,</u> <u>Mass</u> <u>in</u> <u>B</u> <u>Flat,</u> <u>Twelve</u> <u>Spirituals,</u> <u>San</u> <u>Juan</u> <u>Overture,</u> the cantatas <u>The</u> <u>Romance</u> <u>of</u> <u>Noah</u> and <u>Supreme</u> <u>Deliverer,</u> and <u>Vitania</u> <u>Suite</u> for orchestra.

Works

CHACONNE - Viola and piano.

EVANGELINE AND GABRIEL - Opera.

MENELIK - Opera.

PRELUDE IN E-FLAT - Piano and orchestra.

SAN JUAN OVERTURE - Orchestra.

VITANIA SUITE - Orchestra.

Sources

Anderson, E. Ruth. <u>Contemporary</u> <u>American</u> <u>Composers:</u>   <u>A</u> <u>Biographical</u> <u>Dictionary</u>. Boston: G.K. Hall & Co., 1982, pp. 328-29.

Carter, Madison H.   <u>An</u> <u>Annotated</u> <u>Catalogue</u> <u>of</u> <u>Composers</u> <u>of</u> <u>African</u> <u>Ancestry</u>. New York: Vantage Press, 1986.

De Lerma, Dominique-Rene.   <u>Black</u> <u>Music</u> <u>in</u> <u>Our</u> <u>Culture</u>.   Kent, OH: Kent State University Press, 1970, pp. 176-77.

Roach, Hildred.   black <u>American</u> <u>Music:</u>   <u>Past</u> <u>and</u> <u>Present</u>, Vol. II. Miami: Krieger Publishing Co., 1985 pp. 36-37.

MARGETSON, EDWARD HENRY (1891-1962)

     Edward Henry Margetson was born December 31, 1891, in St. Kitts, British Virgin Islands. He died January 22, 1962, in New York City.
     Born into a musical family, he began his professional career as a church organist at the age of 15. He studied at Columbia University with Daniel Gregory Mason and Seth Bingham, and studied piano with Sam Lamberson.
     He received grants from the American Academy of Arts and Sciences, the Victor Baier Foundation, and the Rosenwald Foundation, and awards from the Harmon Foundation and the National Council of Negro Women.
     Margetson served as organist at the Episcopal Church of the Crucifixion between 1916 and 1954, and was an associate of the American Guild of Organists. In 1927 he founded a choral group, the Schubert Music Society, and served as its director until he retired in 1954.
     Among his best-known compositions are <u>Rondo</u> <u>Caprice</u> for orchestra, <u>Ballade-Valse-Serenade</u> for cello, and the song cycle <u>Echoes</u> <u>from</u> <u>the</u> <u>Caribbean</u>.

Works

BALLADE-VALSE-SERENADE - Cello.

Sources

Carter, Madison H.   An Annotated Catalogue of Composers of African Ancestry. New York: Vantage Press, 1986.

Hare, Maud Cuney. Negro Musicians and Their Music. Washington: Associated Press, 1936.

Southern, Eileen. Biographical Dictionary of Afro-American and African Musicians. Westport, CT: Greenwood Press, 1982. pp. 263-64.

McCREARY, RICHARD DEMING, JR. (1946 -)

Richard Deming McCreary, Jr., was born in Evergreen, Alabama, in 1946.
He studied at Florida A&M University (BS 1966), Southern Illinois University (M.M.Ed. 1970), and the University of Iowa (Ph.D. 1974).
He is currently Professor of Music at Governors State University.

Works

MYTH VS. REALITY - String ensemble and percussion.

PIECE FOR FLUTE, CLARINET, VIBRAPHONE, AND STRINGS. Publisher: SELF.

QUARTET - Bamboo flute, flute, 2 violins, cello, percussion. Publisher: SELF.

"Z" - Orchestra and tape. NOTE: Ph.D. thesis.

Source

Information submitted by the composer.

McCALL, MAURICE HENDERSON (1943 -)

Maurice Henderson McCall was born in Norfolk, Virginia, in 1943.
He receved his B.A. and M.F.A. from Carnegie-Mellon University and the Doctor of Musical Arts from the College Conservatory at the University of Cincinnati.   He studied with Nikolai Lopatnikoff, Carlos Surinach, Paul Cooper, and Scott Huston.
He has taught at the Hampton Institute, University of Cincinnati, and Virginia State University.
He served as director of the Hanarobi Contemporary Gospel Ensemble at the University of Cincinnati.
Among his works are the string pieces Petite Suite, Sinfonia Brevis, and Little Trio (two violins and double bass); the song cycle In Parting; Wedding Music (string quartet); Study No. 1 (piano); Olde Musick for recorder, cello, and harpsichord; and two songs for voice and piano, One Woman and Whom.

Works

DARK SYMPHONY - Soli, SATB, and orchestra without flutes or violins. Publisher: SELF.

LITTLE TRIO - 2 violins and double bass. Publisher: SELF.

OLDE MUSICK - recorder, cello, and harpsichord. Publisher: SELF.

PETITE SUITE - Young string orchestra. Publisher: SELF.

SINFONIA BREVIS - Young string orchestra. Publisher: SELF.

TWO SPIRITUALS (I WILL ARISE and SWING LOW) - Solo voice, oboe, and strings. Publisher: SELF.

WEDDING MUSIC (SUITE OF FOUR PIECES) - String quartet. Publisher: SELF.

Sources

Information submitted by the composer.

Holly, Ellistine Perkins. Biographies of Black Composers and Song Writers. Dubuque, IA: Wm. C. Brown Publishers, 1990, p. 31.

Roach, Hildred. Black American Music: Past and Present, Vol. II. Miami: Krieger Publishing Co., 1985, pp. 100-02.

McDANIEL, WILLIAM FOSTER (1940 -)

William Foster McDaniel, a graduate of Capital University in Columbus, Ohio, earned his M.M. at Boston University, where he studied with Bel Bo-sormenyi-Nagy, Lawrence Leighton-Smith, and Gardner Read. He also studied with Jacques Fevrier in Paris as a Fullbright Scholar. In 1965 he won the first prize in a national piano competition sponsored by the National Association of Negro Musicians.

Among his works are Concerto for Piano and Orchestra Nos. 1 and 2, Seven Songs for Soprano and Nonet, Flute Sonata, Brass Quintet, Five Songs With Debra, and Toccata for piano.

Works

CELLO SONATA - Duration: 22 minutes.

CONCERTO FOR ALTO SAXOPHONE AND ORCHESTRA - Duration: 19 minutes. Premiere: 17 February 1984, Carnegie Recital Hall, New York City; New York Housing Authority Orchestra, William Foster McDaniel, Conductor; Ken Adams, soloist.

CONCERTO FOR FLUTE AND ORCHESTRA - Duration: 22 minutes. Premiere: 22 April 1983, Freeport, New York; Brooklyn Philharmonic Orchestra, Tania Leon. Conductor; Ken Adams, soloist.

CONCERTO FOR PIANO AND ORCHESTRA NO. 1 - Duration: 35 minutes. Premiere: 13 December 1975, John Burroughs Jr. High School, Younkers, New York; Younkers Civic Philharmonic Orchestra Jerome Sala, Conductor; William Foster McDaniels, soloist.

CONCERTO FOR PIANO AND ORCHESTRA NO. 2 - Duration: 25 minutes.

CONCERTO FOR PIANO AND STRING ORCHESTRA - Duration: 14 minutes.
Premiere: 27 June 1975, Theodore Roosevelt Birthplace, New York City;
William Foster McDaniel, Conductor and soloist.

CONCERTO FOR TWO FLUTES AND STRING ORCHESTRA - Duration: 10 minutes.
Premiere: 28 January 1985, Carnegie Recital Hall, New York City; New
York Housing Authority Orchestra William Foster McDaniel, Conductor;
Hal Archer and Paula Bing, soloists.

STRING QUARTET - Duration: 12 minutes.

Sources

Information submitted by the composer.

Abdul, Raoul. Blacks in Classical Music. New York: Dodd, Mead &
Co., 1977, p. 66.

McLIN, EDWARD M. (1928 -)

Edward McLin was born in 1928 in Chicago.
He played trumpet and French horn in high school, and was awarded a
musical scholarship to Kentucky State College. He earned his B.M. (1950)
and M.M. (1951) from Chicago Musical College.
Between 1966 and 1968 he worked as staff arranger for Hansen Publications where he arranged or composed well over 100 pieces, including Drummin' Drummin' Drummin', Grand Hotel Jazz March, I Wanna Be Like You,
Spanish Flea/Lonely Bull, Circus March Medley, Calypso Carnival, Beatnick
Bounce Bongos, Theme for a Rock and Roller, and From These Halls. McLin
also composed, Chorales for strings, For Four B-flat Trumpets, and Matine
and March and Sourwood Mountain for band.

Works

CHORALES FOR STRINGS (1959) - Publisher: Pro Arts, 1959.

Source

Roach, Hildred. Black American Music: Past and Present, Vol. II.
Miami: Krieger Publishing Co., 1985, p. 60.

McLIN, LENA JOHNSON (1928 -)

Lena Johnson McLin was born September 5, 1928, in Atlanta, Georgia.
She attended Spelman College in Atlanta (B.A., 1951), Roosevelt Uni-
versity in Chicago, and Chicago State College.
She received awards from civic and community groups, from the National
Association of Negro Musicians, and from the NAACP. In 1975, Virginia
Union University presented her with an honorary doctorate.
She teaches in the public schools of Chicago, serving as head of the
music department at Kenwood High School for many years. She is active as a
choral conductor with school groups, church groups, and community groups,
worked with educational films, founded a small opera company (the McLin
Ensemble), and is a prolific composer of gospel music.

Works

BANCROFT

THE COLORS OF THE RAINBOW (1971) - 2 flutes, violin, violoncello, and oboe. Dedicated to Manford Byrd.

IMPRESSIONS NO. 1 - Orchestra.

IN THIS WORLD - Chorus, electric guitar, flute, violoncello, and electric piano. Publisher: Chicago, Neil Kjos, 1970.

THE MARRIAGE CANTATA (1974) - Flute, violin, violoncello, and piano or organ.

MEMORY (1976) - Flute, violin, violoncello, and piano or organ. Duration: 4 minutes. Publisher: Park Ridge, IL, KJOS Music Co.

Sources

Information submitted by the composer.

Ammer, Christine. Unsung: A History of Women in American Music. Westport, CT: Greenwood Press, 1980, pp. 158-59.

De Lerma, Dominique-Rene. Black Music in Our Culture. Kent, OH: Kent State University Press, 1970, p. 177.

Green, Mildred Denby. Black Women Composers: A Genesis. Boston: Twayne Publishers, 1983.

"McLin, Lena." In Keyboard Music by Women Composers: A Catalog and Bibliography. Compiled by Joan M. Meggett. Westport, CT: Greenwood Press, 1981, p. 117.

Southern, Eileen. Biographical Dictionary of Afro-American and African Musicians. Westport, CT: Greenwood Press, 1982.

MELLS, HERBERT FRANKLIN (1909-1953)

Works

MOTHERLESS CHILD. NEGRO SPIRITUAL. A SYMPHONIC POEM - Orchestra. Manuscript (1944) in U.S. Library of Congress.

QUINTET IN A MINOR (1944) - B-flat clarinet, 2 violins, viola. cello. University of Iowa Music Library. Score: University of Iowa Music Library; Center for Black Music Research, Columbia College-Chicago.

Source

Carter, Madison H. An Annotated Catalogue of Composers of African Ancestry. New York: Vantage Press, 1986.

MERRIFIELD, NORMAN LAVELLE (1906 -)

Norman Lavelle Merrifield was born in Louisville, Kentucky, in 1906.
He studied piano with Ellen T. Meriwether as a child. He received his
B.M. in 1927 and his M.M. in 1932 from Northwestern. He received a study
grant to attend Trinity College in London in 1946, and was awarded a Spe-
cial Study Fellowship to Northwestern University in 1964. He also studied
at Indiana, Jordon College of Music, Michigan State University, and Ball
State University.
He taught at Fisk University, Austin High School (Knoxville, Tennes-
see), Alabama State Teachers College, Florida A&M College, Crispus Attucks
High School (Indianapolis), and the Hampton Institute. He served as band
leader for seven Army bands, and organized and directed the 92nd Division
Artillery Band, the Fort Riley Cavalry Band, and the 1349 Engineer Band.
In 1968 he became coordinator of the Douglass South of Flanner House. He
contributed to Music Educators Journal, The School Musician, Choral Jour-
nal, and Sports Afield.
Some of his compositions are Ah Done Done, Motherless Child, Now Look
Away, Remember O Lord, Show Me Thy Way O Lord, Tryin' to Get Ready, And He
Never Said a Mumblin' Word, and Symphony.

Works

SYMPHONY - Orchestra.

Source

Roach, Hildred. Black American Music: Past and Present, Vol. II.
Miami: Krieger Publishing Co., 1985, pp. 43-44.

MITCHELL, ROSCOE (EDWARD, JR.) (1940 -)

Roscoe Mitchell was born August 3, 1940, in Chicago.
From 1961 he lead a hard-bop sextet, which included Joseph Jarman and
Henry Threadgill, and played in a free-jazz quartet with Jack DeJohnette
and in Muhal Richard Abram's Experimental Band. He led a sextet, then a
series of quartets and trios; in 1967, Malachi Favors, Lester Bowie, and
Phillip Wilson performed and recorded with him in the Roscoe Mitchell Art
Ensemble.   The group moved to Paris and was renamed the Art Ensemble of
Chicago. He returned to the US in 1971.
Mitchell was a founding member of the Association for the Advancement
of Creative Musicians (1965). In 1974 he established the Creative Arts
Collective in East Lansing, Michigan.

Works

VARIATIONS AND SKETCHES FROM THE BAMBOO TERRACE - Chamber orchestra,
piano, soprano voice. Commissioned by the Conimicut Foundation, the
Wisconsin Arts Board, and the Dane County Cultural Affairs Commission.
Premiere: 3 September 1988, Union Theatre, University of Wisconsin-
Madison; part of the Madison Festival of the Lakes.

Sources

Anderson, E. Ruth. Contemporary American Composers: A Biographical
Dictionary. Boston: G.K. Hall & Co., 1982, p. 486.

Holly, Ellistine Perkins. "Composers Notes." CBMR Digest, 1.2 (Winter 1988).

Roach, Hildred. Black American Music: Past and Present, Vol. I. Miami: Krieger Publishing Inc., 1985, pp. 113-14.

MOFFATT, RICHARD CULLEN (1927 - 1982)

Richard Cullen Moffatt was born April 14, 1927, in Colorado, Texas. He died in 1982.

He attended Lewis & Clark College and studied with Robert Stoltze, Leonard De Paur, and Margaret Notz Steinmetz.

Works

CINDERELLA - Opera

RUMPELSTILTSKIN - Opera.

SONATA - Violin.

A SONG FOR RUBY-JO - Opera in one act.

Sources

Carter, Madison H. An Annotated Catalogue of Composers of African Ancestry. New York: Vantage Press, 1986.

Claghorn, Charles Eugene. Biographical Dictionary of American Music. New York: Parker Publishing Co., 1973, p. 352.

MOORE, CARMAN LEROY (1936 -)

Carman Leroy Moore was born October 8, 1936, in Lorain, Ohio.

He studied piano as a child. He attended Ohio State University-Columbus (B. Mus., 1958) and Juilliard (M. Mus., 1966). Among his teachers were Lucio Berio, Hall Overton, Vincent Persichetti, and Stefan Wolpe.

As a music critic, he published regularly in the Village Voice, The New York Times, and The Saturday Review. He published Somebody's Angel Child: The Story of Bessie Smith in 1970 and The Growth of Black Sound in America in 1977.

He has been a teacher at Manhattanville College in Purchase, New York; Yale University; and Queens College and Brooklyn College of the City University of New York.

Among his best-known works are "Youth in a Merciful House" (1965) for piccolo, bassoons, percussions, vibraphone and viola; the two symphonies Gospel Fuse and Wild Fires and Field Songs; Solar Music for brass, percussion, and synthesizer; Follow Light for chorus, sopranos, bass viol, and percussion; and Quartet for saxophones and echoplex.

Works

BERENICE: VARIATIONS ON A THEME OF G.F. HANDEL (1984) - Violin, clarinet, cello, piano.

CATWALK (1967) - Ballet for orchestra. Duration: 15 minutes. Commissioned by the New York City Ballet. Unpublished score (IU).

CONCERTO FOR BLUES PIANO AND ORCHESTRA (1982)

CONCERTO FOR JAZZ VIOLIN AND ORCHESTRA (1987) - Commissioned by the Penfield High School Music Commission Project. Premiere: May 1987; Penfield High School Symphony.

FOUR MOVEMENTS FOR A FASHIONABLE FIVE-TOED DRAGON (1976) - Orchestra, Chinese instruments, and jazz quintet. Contents: 1. Overture; 2. Pastorale; 3. Urban Walk; 4. Colors; 5. Folk Energy. Duration: 55 minutes. Commissioned by the Hong Kong Trade Development Council. Premiere: 29 February 1976; Hong Kong. Recording: Vanguard (limited in-house pressing).

GOSPEL FUSE (1974) - Gospel quartet (SSSA), soprano solo, orchestra, saxophone, piano, electric organ. Text by Carman Moore. Duration: 22 minutes. Commissioned by the San Francisco Symphony. Dedicated to the memory of Hall Overton. Premiere: 22-25 January 1975; San Francisco, California; San Francisco Symphony. Note: Interview by Donal Henahan in New York Times, 19 January 1975, Section 2, p. 1.

THE GREAT AMERICAN NEBULA (1976) - Oratorio for string orchestra, narrator, concert band, gospel singer. chorus, and jazz trio. Text by Carman Moore. Contents: 1. The American Experiment; 2. Soft Shoe; 3. 17th Century; 4. Ghost Dance; 5. Terrestrial Revolutions; 6 March; 7. Home Is . . .; 8. Outer Space and Inner Grace. Duration: 30 minutes. Commissioned by the Elyria, Ohio, Bicentennial Committee. Premiere: 22 May 1976; Elyria, Ohio.

HIT: CONCERTO FOR PERCUSSION AND ORCHESTRA (1978) - Three movements. Duration: 20 minutes. Commissioned by the Rochester Philharmonic Orchestra through a NEA grant Premiere: 4 May 1978; Eastman Theater, Rochester. New York; Rochester Philharmonic Orchestra, Isaiah Jackson, Conductor.

THE MASQUE OF SAXOPHONE'S VOICE (1981) - Opera. Book and lyrics by composer.

A MOVEMENT FOR STRING QUARTET (1961) - Duration: 8 minutes. Unpublished score (IU). Premiere: 1963; New School for Social Research, New York City.

MUSEUM PIECE (1975) - Flute, cello, and tape. Duration: 12 minutes. Commissioned by Samuel Baron and Robert Sylvester. Publisher: New York, Peer-Southern. Premiere: April 1975; Guggenheim Museum, New York City; Samuel Baron, flute; Robert Sylvester, cello. Reviewed in New York Times, 24 April 1975, p. 42.

MUSIC FOR FLUTE ALONE (1981) - Flute, piano, double bass, and tape.

A MUSICAL OFFERING (1962) - Ballet.

SARATOGA FESTIVAL OVERTURE (1966) - Orchestra. Duration: 10 minutes. Commissioned by Lincoln Kirstein, director of the New York City Ballet.

SEAN-SEAN (1965) - French horn, 3 cellos, and tape. Duration: 10 minutes. Commissioned by Martha Clarke. choreographer. Dedicated to Sean O'Casey. Unpublished score (IU). Premiere: 1965; Juilliard School of Music, New York City. Note: Tape contains readings from Sean O'Casey.

SONATA FOR VIOLONCELLO AND PIANO (1965) - Two movements. Duration: 7 minutes. Premiere: 1965; Juilliard School of Music, New York City.

SONATA: VARIATIONS FOR MANDOLIN AND PIANO (1965) - Duration: 9 minutes. Unpublished score (IU). Premiere: 1965; New York Mandolin Society, New York City.

SYMFONIA [sic] (1964) - Chamber orchestra. Duration: 12 minutes.

TRYST (1964) - Clarinet, cello. and percussion. Duration: 8 minutes. Premiere: 1965; Juilliard School of Music, New York City.

VARIATIONS FOR MANDOLIN AND PIANO - Publisher: Plucked Strings, 1985. Premiere: 1981.

WILDFIRES AND FIELD SONGS (1974) - Orchestra. Commissioned by the New York Philharmonic through a grant from the New York State Council of the Arts. Premiere: 23-25, 28 January, 1975; Avery Fischer Hall, Lincoln Center, New York City; New York Philharmonic, Pierre Boulez, Conductor. Reviewed in New York Times, 24 January 1975, p. 18. Note: Interviewed by Donal Henahan in the New York Times, 19 January 1975, Section 2, p. 1.

YOUTH IN MERCIFUL HOUSE (1962) - Ballet for piccolo, 2 bassoons, viola, vibraphone, and percussion: cymbals, bongo drums, snare drum, and bass drum. Commissioned by Mary Barnett, choreographer. Unpublished score (IU). Premiere: 1965; Juilliard School of Music, New York City. Recordings: Desto (1975); Folkways 33902 (1976). Reviewed in Stereo Review vol. 37 no. 3 (September 1976), pp. 126-27.

Sources

Holly, Ellistine. "Composers Notes." CBMR Digest, 2.1 (Spring 1989).

Quist, Ned. "Moore, Carman (Leroy)." In The New Grove Dictionary of American Music, Vol. 3, p. 265.

Southern, Eileen. Biographical Dictionary of Afro-American and African Musicians. Westport, CT: Greenwood Press, 1982.

Tischler, Alice. Fifteen Black American Composers: A Bibliography of Their Works. Detroit Studies in Music Bibliography. Detroit: Information Coordinators, 1981.

Wyatt, Lucius R. "Composers Corner: Carman L. Moore." Black Music Research Bulletin, 10.2 (Fall 1988).

MOORE, DOROTHY RUDD (1940 -)

Dorothy Rudd Moore was born June 4, 1940, in New Castle, Delaware.

She received her B.A. from Howard University (1963), where she studied with Mark Fax. In the summer of 1963 she studied with Nadia Boulanger in Paris, and in 1965 with Chou Wen-chung in New York City.
She received a Lucy Moten Fellowship in 1963. In 1968 she became one of the founders of the Society of Black Composers.
Moore has taught at the Harlem School of the Arts (1965-66), at New York University (1969), and at the Bronx Community College (1971).
Among her best known works are Three Pieces for violin and piano (1967), Modes for string quartet (1968), Dirge and Deliverance for cello and piano (1971), Dream and Variations for piano (1974), and the song cycles Twelve Quatrains from the Rubaiyat (1962) and Songs from the Dark Tower (1970).

Works

Dorothy Rudd Moore works are unpublished and are available through American Composers Alliance.

BAROQUE SUITE FOR UNACCOMPANIED VIOLONCELLO (1964-65) - Duration: 15 minutes. Dedicated to Kermit Moore. Premiere: 21 November 1965, Harlem School of the Arts, New York City; Kermit Moore, cello.

DIRGE AND DELIVERANCE (1971) - Cello and piano. Duration: 16 minutes. Two movements; second movement has written-out cadenza. Commissioned by Kermit Moore. Premiere: 14 May 1972, Alice Tully Hall, Lincoln Center, New York City; Kermit Moore, cello; Zita Carno, piano. Reviewed: New York Times, 25 February 1975. NOTE: Must be played as a unit.

FREDERICK DOUGLAS - Opera in three acts   Libretto: Dorothy R. Moore. Premiere: 27 June 1985; Aaron Davis Hall, City College; Opera Ebony, Benjamin Matthews, director; James Butler, William Brown, William Drake, Alpha Floyd, Gurcell Henry, Kevin Maynor. Ronald Naldi, Carolyn Sebron, and Arthur Woodley, soloists.

FROM THE DARK TOWER (1970) - Voice (mezzo soprano), cello and piano. Texts by black American poets: Arno Bontemps, Countee Cullen, Waring Cuney, Langston Hughes, Goergia Douglas Johnson, Herbert Clark Johnson, and James Weldon Johnson. Contents: 1. O Black and Unknown Barbs (J.W. Johnson); 2. Southern Mansion (Bontemps); 3 Willow Bend and Weep (H.C. Johnson); 4. Old Black Men (G.D. Johnson); 5. No Images (Cuney); 6. Dream Variation (Hughes); 7. For a Poet (Cullen); 8. From the Dark Tower (Cullen). Duration: 34 minutes. Commissioned by Kermit Moore. Premiere: 8 October 1970, Norfolk State College, Norfolk, Virginia; Hilda Harris, mezzo-soprano; Kermit Moore, cello; Alan Booth, piano. Reviewed: Music Journal, January 1972; New York Times, 25 February 1975.

FROM THE DARK TOWER (1972) - Voice (mezzo soprano) and chamber orchestra: flute, oboe, clarinet, trumpet percussion, 2 violins, viola, cello, and double bass. Duration: 22 minutes. Contents: 1. O Black and Unknown Barbs (J.W. Johnson); 2. Willow Bend and Weep (H.C. Johnson); 3. Dream Variation (Hughes); 4. From the Dark Tower (Cullen). Commissioned by Hilda Harris. Premiere: 29 October 1972, Philharmonic Hall, Lincoln Center, New York City; Symphony of the New World, George Byrd, Conductor; Hilda Harris, mezzo soprano.

LAMENT FOR NINE INSTRUMENTS (1969) - Flute, oboe, clarinet, trumpet, trombone, percussion, violin, viola, and cello. Duration: 8 minutes. Premiere: 16 August 1969, Studio 58, New York City; Kermit Moore, Conductor. Note: Written for reading session of Society of Black Composers Performing New Works.

MODES FOR STRING QUARTET (1968) - Duration: 12 minutes. Three movements. Premiere: 28 May 1968, Harlem School of the Arts, New York City; Sanford Allen, violin; Selwart Clarke, violin; Alfred Brown, viola; Kermit Moore, cello. Reviewed: New York Times, 29 May 1968 and 25 February 1975.

MOODS (1969) - Viola and cello. Contents: 1. Agitated and Erratic; 2. Melancholic; 3. Frenetic. Duration: 15 minutes. Premiere: 20 May 1969, Intermediate School No. 201, New York City; Society of Black Composers concert; Selwart Clarke viola; Kermit Moore, cello. Note: Written on a Society of Black Composers grant; second movement written and performed in 1965.

PIECES FOR VIOLIN AND PIANO, THREE (1967) - Contents: 1. Vignette; 2. Episode; 3. Caprice. Duration: 10 minutes. Premiere: 2 March 1967, Carnegie Recital Hall, New York City; Richard Elias, violin; David Garvey, piano. Reviewed: New York Times 7 March 1967 and 24 February 1975.

SONNETS ON LOVE, ROSEBUDS, AND DEATH (1976) - Soprano, violin, and piano. Cycle of eight songs: 1 Sonnet: I had no thought of violets of late (Alice Dunbar Nelson); 2. Joy (Clarissa Scott Delany); 3. Sonnet: Some things are very dear to me (Gwendolyn B. Bennett; 4. Sonnett: He came in silvern armour (Gwendolyn B. Bennett); 5. Songs for a Dark Girl (Langston Hughes); 6. Idolatry (Countee Cullen); 7. Youth Sings a Song of Rosebuds (Arna Bontemps); 8. Invocation (Helen Johnson). Duration: 21 minutes. Commissioned by Miriam Burton and Sanford Allen. Premiere: 23 May 1976, Alice Tully Hall, Lincoln Center, New York City; Miriam Burton soprano; Sanford Allen, violin; Kelly Wyatt, piano.

SYMPHONY NO. 1 (1963) - In one movement. Duration: 15 minutes. Premiere: May 1963, Washington D.C.; National Symphony Orchestra.

TRIO FOR VIOLIN, CELLO, AND PIANO (1970) - Three movements. Duration: 15 minutes. Commissioned by the Reston Trio. Premiere: 26 March 1970, Carnegie Recital Hall, New York City; The Reston Trio. Reviewed: New York Times, 27 March 1970.

THE WEARY BLUES (1972) - Voice (baritone), cello, and piano. Text: "The Weary Blues, by Langston Hughes. Duration: 5 minutes. Commissioned by Rawn Spearman. Published in Patterson, Willis C., Anthology of Art Songs by Black Composers, New York: Marks, 1971. Premiere: 20 November 1972, Horace Mann Auditorium, New York City; Rawn Spearman, baritone; Kermit Moore, cello; Kelly Wyatt, piano.

THE WEARY BLUES (1979) - Voice (baritone) and orchestra: 2 flutes, 2 oboes/English horns, 2 clarinets/bass clarinets, 2 bassoons, 2 horns, timpani, piano, strings. Duration: 10 minutes. Premiere: 2 February 1979, Kleinhaus Hall, Buffalo, New York; Buffalo Philharmonic

Orchestra, Michael Tilson Thomas, Conductor; Benjamin Matthews baritone. Note: Orchestration of 1972 work.

Sources

Information submitted by the composer.

Davis Peter. "Retrospective Concert of Music by Dorothy Rudd Moore,
Performed by Group and Sung by Mrs. Moore." New York Times 25 February 1975: 28. Concert review.

McGinty, Doris Evans. "Moore, Dorothy Rudd." In The New Grove Dictionary of American Music, Vol. 3, pp. 265-66.

Southern, Eileen. Biographical Dictionary of Afro-American and African Musicians. Westport, CT: Greenwood Press, 1982, p. 279.

Tischler, Alice. Fifteen Black American Composers: A Bibliography of
Their Works. Detroit Studies in Music Bibliography. Detroit: Information Coordinators, 1981, pp. 201 210.

Williams, Ora. American Black Women in The Arts and Social Sciences:
A Bibliographic Survey. Metuchen, NJ: Scarecrow Press, 1978.

MOORE, KERMIT (1929 -)

Kermit Moore was born March 11, 1929, in Akron, Ohio.
He attended the Cleveland Institute of Music in Ohio (1951) New York
University (M.A.), the Paris Conservatory (artist diploma, 1956), and Juil-
liard. His teachers included Felix Salmond, Paul Bazelair, George Enesco,
Nadia Boulanger, and Pierre Pasquier.
His honors include the Lili Boulanger Award (1953), the Edgar Stillman
Kelly Award, and a Queen Elizabeth II Medal (1958). He was a founding
member of the Symphony of the New World in 1964, and of the Society of
Black Composers in 1968.
He has taught at the Hartt School of Music in Hartford, Connecticut.

Works

CELLO CONCERTO

CONCERTO - Timpani and orchestra.

FESTIVAL ESCAPADE (1987) - Symphony orchestra. Publisher: Rud/Mor
Publishing Company (1987). Premiere: 1987; Lincoln Center; Brooklyn
Philharmonic.

FOUR ARIAS - Adapted for soprano and orchestra.

MANY THOUSAND GONE - Flutes strings, percussion, and voices. Publisher: New York, Rudnor Publishing. Premiere: 28 October 1979, St.
Martin Episcopal Church of the City of New York; Kermit Moore, Conductor. Note: Based on Negro spiritual and African folk airs.

MOMBASA OSTINATA (1988) - Symphony orchestra. Duration: 15 minutes. Publisher: Rud/Mor Publishing Company (1988). Premiere: October 1988; United Nations Concert; APPOLO Theatre, New York.

MUSIC FOR CELLO AND PIANO - Recording: Cespicio Records.

MUSIC FOR TWO VIOLINS AND PIANO (1986) - Duration: 20 minutes. Publisher: Rud/Mor Publishing Company. Premiere: June 1986; New York City.

MUSIC FOR VIOLA, PIANO, AND PERCUSSION.

QUINCENTRA - String quartet and piano.

SONATA - Cello.

STRING QUARTET

Sources

Abdul, Raoul. "Kermit Moore at Alice Tully Hall." In Blacks in Classical Music. New York: Dodd, Mead & Co., 1977. pp. 181-83.

Horne Aaron. Woodwind Music of Black Composers. Westport, CT: Greenwood Press, 1990, pp. 48-49.

Roach, Hildred. Black American Music: Past and Present, Vol. II. Miami: Krieger Publishing Co., 1985 pp. 64-65.

Rosenberg, Deena, and Bernard Rosenburg. "Kermit Moore, Freelance Cellist." Music Makers. New York: Columbia University Press, 1979, pp. 277-88.

Southern, Eileen. Biographical Dictionary of Afro-American and African Musicians. Westport, CT: Greenwood Press, 1982, p. 279.

MOORE, PHIL (1918-1987)

Phil Moore was born February 20, 1918, in Portland, Oregon. He died May 13, 1987, in Los Angeles.
He studied at the Cornish Conservatory and the University of Washington.
He began his career as a classical pianist and composer, but in 1941 turned to Hollywood studio music, becoming a rehearsal pianist for MGM. He contributed music to fifty or more films and worked as a composer, arranger, conductor, and vocal coach in film and TV.

Works

CONCERTO FOR TROMBONE AND ORCHESTRA

Source

"Obituaries." The Black Perspective in Music 15.2 (Fall 1987).

MOORE, UNDINE SMITH (1904 - 1989)

Undine Smith Moore was born July 5, 1904, in Jarrat, Virginia, and died in 1989.

She studied piano with Lillian Allen Darden, piano and organ with Alice M. Grass, and with Howard Murphy. She received her B.A. and B. Mus. from Fisk University, and her M.A. and professional diploma from Columbia University Teachers College. She also studied at Juilliard and at the Manhattan School of Music, and at the Eastman School of Music in Rochester.

Moore received honorary doctorates from Virginia State University in 1972 and from Indiana University in 1976. Other honors include a Certificate of Appreciation from John Lindsay, Mayor of New York; the Seventh Annual Humanitarian Award from Fisk University in 1973; and the National Association of Negro Musicians Award in 1975. Also in 1975 April 13 was declared Undine Moore Day by Remmis Arnold, Mayor of Petersburg, Virginia.

She taught in the public schools of Goldsboro, North Carolina, and at Virginia State College in Petersburg (1924-1972). She also served as visiting professor at Carleton College, St. Benedict College, St. Johns University, and Virginia Union University.

With Altona Trent Jones, she co-founded and co-directed the Black Music Center at Virginia State (1969-72).

She was best known for her choral compositions, including "The Lamb," "Lord, we give thanks to Thee," and "Daniel, Daniel, servant of the Lord." Her Afro-American Suite for flute, cello, and piano is widely performed.

Works

AFRO-AMERICAN SUITE (1969) - Flute/alto flute, violoncello, and piano. Four movements: 1. Andante (Nobody Knows the Trouble I See, Lord); 2. Allegro Molto e marcato (I Heard the Preaching of the Elder); 3. Adagio ma appassionato (Who Is That Yonder?); Allegro molto e marcato (Shout All Over God's Heaven). Duration: 11 minutes 30 seconds. Commissioned by the Trio Pro Viva. Premiere: 1969, District of Columbia Teachers College, Washington, D.C.; Trio Pro Viva. Recording: Trio Pro Viva (D. Antoinette Handy, flute; Ronald Lipscomb, violoncello; Gladys Perry Norris, piano) on Eastern ERS-513 (Contemporary Black Images in Music for the Flute).

FUGUE IN F (1952) - String trio. Duration; 2 minutes 30 seconds. Premiere: 1952, Virginia State College, Petersburg, Virginia. Note: Three-voice 18th-century style fugue.

Sources

Information submitted by the composer.

Baker, David N., Lida M. Belt, and Herman C. Hudson. The Black Composer Speaks. Metuchen, NJ: Scarecrow Press, 1978.

Beckner, Steve. "Composer and Teacher--Mrs. Undine Smith Moore." The Progress-Index (Petersburg, Virginia), 5 January 1975.

De Lerma, Dominique-René, ed. Reflections on Afro-American Music. Kent, OH: Kent State University Press, 1973.

Harris, Carl G. "The Unique World of Undine Smith Moore." The Choral Journal 16 (January 1976): 6-7.

McGinty, Doris Evans. "Moore, Undine Smith." In The New Grove Dictionary of American Music, Vol. 3, p. 269.

MORGAN, WILLIAM ASTOR (1890 - ?) - Pseudonym: JEAN STOR

Works

ADAGIO - Opus 74. In Memory of our Friend, Franklin Delano Roosevelt. Orchestra. Manuscript (1945) in U.S Library of Congress.

Source

Carter, Madison H.   An Annotated Catalogue of Composers of African Ancestry. New York: Vantage Press, 1986.

MORRISON, GEORGE SUMNER, SR. (1891-1974)

Works

FIVE SOLOS - Violin and piano. Publisher: Handy brothers Music Co., Inc., 1947.

Source

Carter, Madison H.   An Annotated Catalogue of Composers of African Ancestry. New York: Vantage Press, 1986.

MOSELEY, JAMES ORVILLE (JOB) (1909 -)

James Orville Moseley was born September 21, 1909, in Alcorn College, Mississippi.
He received his AB from Morehouse College, a teachers certificate from Chicago Musical College, and his MM from the University of Michigan. He also attended New York University and the University of Southern California, and studied with Quincy Porter, Noble Cain, Ross Lee Finney, Eric Delamater, Wesley LaViolette, and Halsey Stevens.
Mosely has been a teacher at Natches College, Southern University, California State University-Long Beach, and Morgan State University.

Works

CONCERTO - Piano and orchestra. Three movements.

FORT HENRY - Orchestra. Tone poem.

HOW LONG THE ROAD - Opera.

SUITE - String orchestra. Five movements.

SYMPHONY IN A - Orchestra.

Sources

Carter, Madison H.   An Annotated Catalogue of Composers of African Ancestry. New York: Vantage Press, 1986.

Claghorn, Charles Eugene. Biographical Dictionary of American Music. New York: Parker Publishing Co., 1973.

NELSON, OLIVER EDWARD (1932-1975)

Oliver Edward Nelson was born June 4, 1932, in St. Louis, Missouri. He died in Los Angeles on October 27, 1975.

Born into a musical family, he began to study piano at the age of six and saxophone at eleven. He studied composition and theory at Washington University and at Lincoln University in Jefferson City, Missouri, and privately with Elliot Carter.   He was active as a performer beginning about 1950, when he played with the Jeter/Pillars band, George Hudson, Nat Towles, and Louis Jordan. In New York he played with various groups, including Erskine Hawkins, William Davis, and Louis Bellson.

He composed all kinds of music.   Some of his best known works are Soundpiece for jazz orchestra, Jazzhattan Suite, Dialogues for orchestra, and Suite for Narrator, String Quartet, and Jazz Orchestra. He also wrote music for films--including Death of a Gunfighter, Skullduggery, Istanbul Express, and Last Tango in Paris--and for television--including the series Six Million Dollar Man, It Takes a Thief, Ironside, and The Name of the Game.

Works

A BLACK SUITE FOR NARRATOR, STRING QUARTET, AND JAZZ ORCHESTRA (1970) - Text by Langston Hughes. Commissioned by Flying Dutchman Records for Mayor Carl B. Stokes of Cleveland.

COMPLEX CITY FOR ORCHESTRA (1966) - Commissioned by CBS

CONCERT PIECE FOR ALTO SAXOPHONE AND STUDIO ORCHESTRA (1972) - Commissioned by the Eastman School of Music.

DIALOGUES (1970) - Orchestra.

DIRGE FOR CHAMBER ORCHESTRA (1961) - Publisher: Nelson Music.

PIECE FOR ORCHESTRA (1969) - Orchestra and jazz soloist. Premiere: 1969, Washington University, St. Louis; the Little Symphony, Amerigo Marino, Conductor; Phil Woods, alto saxophone; Ron Carter, bass.

SOUNDPIECE FOR CONTRALTO, STRING QUARTET, AND PIANO (1963)

Sources

Baker, David N., Lida M. Belt, and Herman C. Hudson, eds. The Black Composer Speaks. Metuchen, NJ: Scarecrow Press, 1978.

Feather, Leonard. The New Edition of the Encyclopedia of Jazz. New York: Horizon Press, 1960.

Southern, Eileen. Biographical Dictionary of Afro-American and African Musicians (Westport, CT: Greenwood Press, 1982), p. 287.

PARKS, GORDON A. (1912 -)

Gordon Parks was born November 30, 1912, in Fort Scott, Kansas.
He is best known as a film director and producer, but he is also a composer, including a Piano Concerto in 1935, and The Learning Tree Symphony in 1967. He also wrote the music for the 1968 film, The Learning Tree.

Works

THE LEARNING TREE SYMPHONY (1967) - Orchestra.

MARTIN LUTHER KING - Ballet.

SYMPHONIC SETS - Piano and orchestra.

Sources

Carter, Madison H. An Annotated Catalogue of Composers of African Ancestry. New York: Vantage Press, 1986.

Cowans, Adger. "Evolution of a Composer: Gordon Parks." City Arts Quarterly 3.2. The Detroit Council of the Arts, Summer 1988.

Southern, Eileen. Biographical Dictionary of Afro-American and African Musicians. Westport, CT: Greenwood Press, 1982.

PERKINSON, COLERIDGE-TAYLOR (1932 -)

Coleridge-Taylor Perkinson was born June 14, 1932, in New York City.
He attended the High School of Music and Art in New York, New York University, and the Manhattan School of Music (B. Mus., 1953; M. Mus., 1954). He also studied at the Berkshire Music Center, the Mozarteum in Salzburg, Austria, and the Netherlands Radio Union in Hilversum. Among those who influenced his work were Hugh Ross, Dimitri Mitropoulos, Clarence Williams, and Dean Dixon.
His career is a varied one. He taught at the Professional Children's School in New York, at the Manhattan School of Music, and at Brooklyn College of the City University of New York.
He served as assistant conductor with the Dessoff Choir, as associate conductor of the Symphony of the New World (of which he was a founding member), and as conductor of the New York Mandolin Orchestra the Brooklyn Community Orchestra. He was the first composer-in-residence of the Negro Ensemble Company in New York.
Perkinson worked with the Alvin Ailey Dance Company and with Arthur Mitchell's Harlem Dance Company, for which he composed the ballet Ode to Otis.
He worked as musical director for such artists as Lou Rawls, Barbara McNair, Donald Byrd, and Max Roach, and for Martin Luther King Productions. He also wrote music for television, radio, and films, including A Warm December, Crossroads Africa, Amazing Grace, and The Education of Sonny Carson. In 1962-63, he composed Attitudes for George Shirley by commission from the Ford Foundation. He also wrote God Is A (Guess What)?, Song

of the Lusitanian Bogey, Ceremonies in Dark Old Men, Man Better Man, Nine
Elizabethan Love Lyrics, Thirteen Love Songs in Jazz Settings, Sinfonietta
for Strings, and Concerto for viola and orchestra.

Works

ATTITUDES (1962-63) - Solo cantata for tenor, violin, violoncello, and
piano. Five movements: 1. Sinfonia (Introduction) (text by the composer); 2. Ricercare I (On Aloneness) (texts by Tu Fu, Lawrence Fer-
linghetti, and e. e. cummings); 3. Ricercare II (On Death) (texts by
Dylan Thomas, John Donne, Mei Tao Chen, and Langston Hughes); 4.
Ground (On Love) (texts by John Dryden and Charles Cotton); 5. Finale
(On Freedom) (texts by Langston Hughes, Thomas Paine, Margaret Walker,
e.e. cummings, and Boris Pasternak). Commissioned by the Ford Foundation. Dedicated to George Shirley. Publisher: Tosci Music. Premiere: 1964, Metropolitan Museum of Art, New York City; George Shirley.

BLUE FORMS (1972) - Solo violin. Three movements: 1. Plain Blue/s;
2. Just Blue/s; 3. Jettin' Blue/s. Dedicated to Sanford Allen. Publisher: Tosci Music. Premiere: 1972, Carnegie Hall, New York City;
Sanford Allen, violin.

BLUES FORMS II - Solo trumpet and orchestra.

COMMENTARY (1964) - Violoncello and orchestra. Concert piece in two
parts. Commissioned by the National Association of Negro Musicians.
Dedicated to Kermit Moore. Publisher: Tosci Music. Premiere: 1967;
the Symphony of the New World, Benjamin Steinberg, Conductor; Kermit
Moore, violoncello.

CONCERTO FOR VIOLA AND ORCHESTRA (1953) - Three movements performed
without pauses. Dedicated to Selwart Clark. Publisher: Tosci Music.
Premiere: 1964; the Orchestra of America, Coleridge-Taylor Perkinson,
Conductor; Selwart Clark, viola. Note: This work was the composer's
Master's thesis.

DUNBAR - Solo voice, chorus, and orchestra. Texts by Countee Cullen
and Paul Lawrence Dunbar. Dedicated to Paul Lawrence Dunbar.

GRASS: A POEM FOR PIANO, STRINGS, AND PERCUSSION (1956) - Three movements performed without pauses. Publisher: Tosci Music. Note:
Inspired by and based on Carl Sandburg's poem "Grass."

HUNDREDTH PSALM (ca. 1949) - Chorus (SSA), brass, and strings. Biblical text. Publisher: Tosci Music. Premiere: 1951, Town Hall, New
York City; St. Cecelia Club, Hugh Ross, Conductor.

LAMENTATIONS: A BLACK/FOLK SONG SUITE FOR UNACCOMPANIED CELLO (1973)
- Four movements: 1. Fuging Tune; 2. Song Form; 3. Calvary Ostinato;
4. Perpetual Motion. Publisher: Tosci Music. Premier: 1973, Alice
Tully Hall, New York City; Ronald Lipscomb, violoncello.

ODE TO OTIS - Ballet.

SINFONIETTA NO. 1 FOR STRINGS (1956) - String orchestra. Three movements. Publisher: Tosci Music. Premiere: 1966, Hilversum, Netherlands; the Radio Kammer Orchest.

STRING QUARTET NO. 1: CALVARY (early 1950s) - Three movements. Publisher: Tosci Music. Premiere: early 1950s, Carnegie Hall; Cumbo
Quartet.

VARIATIONS AND FUGUE ON "THE ASH GROVE" (early 1950s) - Violin and
piano. Publisher: Tosci Music.

Sources

Baker, David N., Lida M. Belt, and Herman C. Hudson. The Black Composer Speaks. Metuchen NJ: Scarecrow Press, 1978.

Claghorn, Charles E. Biographical Dictionary of American Music. West
Nyack, NY: Parker Publishing Co., 1973.

Moore, Carman. "Perkinson, Coleridge-Taylor." In The New Grove Dictionary of American Music, Vol. 3, p. 536.

Roach, Hildred. Black American Music: Past and Preset, Vol. I.
Miami: Krieger Publishing Co., Inc., 1985.

Southern, Eileen. Biographical Dictionary of Afro-American and African Musicians. Westport, CT: Greenwood Press, 1982, p. 303.

PERRY, JULIA AMANDA (1924-1979)

Julia Amanda Perry was born March 25, 1924, in Lexington, Kentucky.
She died April 24, 1979, in Akron, Ohio.
Perry attended Akron University and Westminster Choir College in
Princeton, New Jersey (B. Mus., 1947 in voice; M. Mus. in composition,
1948), and studied at Juilliard and the Berkshire Music Center. She spent
the 1950s in Europe, where she studied with Nadia Boulanger, Luigi Dalla-
piccola, Henry Switten, Emanuel Balaban, and Alceo Galliera. During the
summers of 1956 and 57 she studied conducting at the Accademia Chigiana in
Siena, Italy.
She received Guggenheim Fellowships in 1954 and 1956, a Boulanger
Grand Prix, and an award from the National Institute of Arts and Letters in
1965.
While in Europe, she toured as a lecturer on American music for the
United States Information Service. She has taught at Florida A&M College
(1967-68) and Atlanta University (1968-69).
Among her best known works were the operas The Bottle, The Cask of
Amontillado, and The Selfish Giant; Stabat Mater (contralto and string
orchestra), Pastoral (flute and strings), Homage to Vivaldi for symphony
orchestra, Frammenti dalle lettere de Santa Caterina (soprano, chorus, and
orchestra), and Homunculus C.F. (soprano and percussions).

Works

THE BOTTLE (1953) - Opera in one act.

THE CASK OF AMONTILLADO - One act.   Adapted from the story by Edgar Allan Poe. Premiere: 1954.

CONTRETEMPS (1963) - Orchestra.

EPISODE - Orchestra.

FRAMMENTI DALLE LETTERE DE "SANTA CATERINA" - Mixed chorus, soprano solo, and small orchestra. Text: (Italian) Fragments from the Letter of St. Catherine. Publisher: New York, Southern Music Co.

HOMMAGE TO VIVALDI - Orchestra.

HOMUNCULUS C.F. (1966) - Ten percussion, harp, and piano.

PASTORAL (1962) - Flute and string quartet. Publisher: New York, Southern Music Co.

PIANO CONCERTO (1965) - Piano and orchestra.

REQUIEM FOR ORCHESTRA (1959)

SECOND PIANO CONCERTO (1965) - Piano and orchestra. Publisher: New York, Peer-Southern Organization.

THE SELFISH GIANT - Opera.

SHORT PIECE (1952) - Orchestra. Publisher: New York, Peer-Southern Organization.

STABAT MATER - Contralto and string orchestra or string quartet. Publisher: New York, Southern Music.

STUDY FOR ORCHESTRA (1952) - Premiere: Italy; Turin Symphony Orchestra, Dean Dixon, Conductor; 1956, New York Philharmonic Orchestra.

SYMPHONY NO. 1 (1959) - Orchestra.

SYMPHONY NO. 3 (1962) - Orchestra.

SYMPHONY NO. 4 (1964) - Orchestra.

SYMPHONY NO. 8 (1968) - Orchestra.

SYMPHONY NO. 9 (1965) - Orchestra.

SYMPHONY NO. 12 (1959) ("SIMPLE SYMPHONY") - Orchestra.

SYMPHONY USA (1967) - Chorus and small orchestra.

THREE WARNINGS - Opera.

VIOLIN CONCERTO (1966) - Violin and orchestra. Publisher: New York, Carl Fischer.

Sources

Abdul, Raoul. "Black Women in Music." In Blacks in Classical Music.
New York: Dodd, Mead & Co., 1977, pp. 55-56.

Ammer, Christine. Unsung: A History of Women in American Music.
Westport, CT: Greenwood Press, 1980, pp. 156-58.

Briscoe, James R., ed. Historical Anthology of Music by Women.
Bloomington, IN: Indiana University Press, 1987, pp. 333-34.

Green, Mildred Denby. Black Women Composers: A Genesis. Boston:
Twayne Publishers, 1983, pp. 71-98.

"Perry, Julia." In Keyboard Music by Women Composers: A Catalogue
and Bibliography. Compiled by Joan M. Meggett. Westport, CT: Greenwood Press, 1981, pp. 132-33.

Southern, Eileen. Biographical Dictionary of Afro-American and African Musicians. Westport, CT: Greenwood Press, 1982, pp. 303-04.

Southern, Eileen. "Perry, Julia." In The New Grove Dictionary of
American Music Vol. 3, p. 539.

Southern, Eileen. "Perry, Julia." In The New Grove Dictionary of
Music and Musicians Vol. 14, pp. 548-49.

PERRY, ZENOBIA POWELL (1914 -)

Zenobia Powell Perry was born in 1914 in Boley, Oklahoma.
She received her B.S. from Tuskegee Institute, Alabama, in 1938, and
her M.A. from Northern Colorado University in 1945; she also studied at
Wyoming University. Her teachers included Alan Willman, Darius Milhaud, R.
Nathaniel Dett, Gunnar Johnsen, Charles Jones, and Cortez Reece.
Perry taught at Arkansas A&M College (1946-1955) and Central State
University (1955 - ?).
Her compositions include Ships That Pass In the Night for orchestra,
Prelude and Danse for band, Sonatina for piano, and works for chamber en-
semble and for solo voice.

Works

FOUR HYMNS FOR THREE PLAYERS - Two sets of percussion, flute, piano,
narrator, and orchestra. Commissioned by the San Francisco Orchestra.

SHIPS THAT PASS IN THE NIGHT (1953) - Orchestra.

STRING QUARTET NO. 2 (1964)

Sources

Anderson, E. Ruth. Contemporary American Composers: A Biographical
Dictionary. Boston: G.K. Hall & Co., 1982, p. 403.

Holly, Ellistine Perkins. Biographies of Black Composers and Song
Writers. Dubuque, IA: Wm. C. Brown Publisher, 1990, p. 37.

Roach, Hildred. Black American Music: Past and Present, Vol. II.
Miami: Krieger Publishing Co.; 1985, p. 112.

PITTMAN, EVELYN LA RUE (1910 -)

Evelyn La Rue Pittman was born January 6, 1910, in McAlester, Oklahoma.
She received her BA from Spelman College in Atlanta, Georgia, in 1933;
a teaching certificate from Langston University; and her M. Mus. from University of Oklahoma at Norman in 1954.   She also studied at Juilliard with
Robert Ward, and in Paris with Nadia Boulanger.
She taught in the public schools of Oklahoma City, where she conducted
weekly broadcasts over the city-schools radio station with a 75-voice
choir, and in the Greenburg District of New York. She also directed a 350-
voice interdenominational choir sponsored by the YWCA.
Among her best known works are the opera Cousin Esther, written while
she was in France, the song collection Rich Heritage, and an opera about
the life of Martin Luther King, Freedom's Child.

Works

COUSIN ESTER (1954) - Opera. Premiere: May 1957, Paris.

FREEDOM'S CHILD (1971) - Opera. NOTE: about the life of Martin
Luther King, Jr.

Sources

Ammer, Christine. Unsung: A History of Women in American Music.
Westport, CT: Greenwood Press, 1980, p. 158.

Green, Mildred Denby. "Evelyn Pittman." In Black Women Composers: A
Genesis. Boston: Twayne Publishers, 1983, pp. 99-112.

Green, Mildred Denby. "A Study of the Lives and Works of Five Black
Women Composers in America." Ph.D. Dissertation, University of Oklahoma, 1975.

Southern, Eileen. Biographical Dictionary of Afro-American and African Musicians. Westport, CT: Greenwood Press, 1982, pp. 308-09.

PRICE, FLORENCE BEATRICE SMITH (1888-1953)

Florence Beatrice Smith Price was born April 9, 1888, in Little Rock,
Arkansas, and died June 3, 1953, in Chicago, Illinois.
Florence began to study piano at a very early age, and played in her
first recital at the age of four. She received her B.Mus. in 1906 from New
England Conservatory of Music in Boston, where she studied with George
Chadwick and H. M. Dunham, among others. She also attended the Chicago
Musical College, the American Conservatory in Chicago, Chicago Teachers
College, and the University of Chicago. After a brief teaching career
(Shorter College, 1906-1910 and Clark University, 1910-12), she got mar-
ried.

In 1927 she settled in Chicago, where she taught privately. To make money, she found publishers for her "teaching pieces" and wrote commerical music for radio.

In 1925 her piece "In the Land o' Cotton" won a prize in Opportunity Magazine's Holstein Prize competition. In 1932 she won first prize in the Wanamaker Music Contest for her Symphony in E Minor. The next year the Chicago Symphony performed the work at the Chicago World's Fair--the first time in history that a major orchestra had performed the symphony of an African American woman.

She composed four symphonies, a symphonic tone poem, two violin concertos, a piano concerto, two concert overtures based on Negro spirituals, the Chicago Suite for orchestra, Negro Folksongs in Counterpoint for string quartet, Moods (for flute, clarinet, and piano), Passacaglia and Fugue for organ, Lincoln Walks at Midnight and The Wind and the Sea for chorus and orchestra, the suites, Three Little Negro Dances and From the Canebrakes, and many piano pieces and songs which were performed by such artists as Marian Anderson, Roland Hayes, Leontyne Price, and Blanche Thebom.

Works

BY CANDLELIGHT - Violin and piano. Publisher: Chicago, McKinley Publishers.

CHICAGO SUITE - Orchestra.

COLONIAL DANCE SYMPHONY - Orchestra.

CONCERTO IN D - Violin and orchestra.

CONCERTO IN D MINOR - Piano and orchestra.

CONCERTO IN F MINOR - Piano and orchestra.

CONCERT OVERTURE NO. 1 - Orchestra. Based on Negro spirituals.

CONCERT OVERTURE NO. 2 - Orchestra. Based on three Negro spirituals.

THE DESERTED GARDEN - Violin and piano. Publisher: Bryn Mawr, Pennsylvania, Theodore Presser Co.

ETHIOPIA'S SHADOW IN AMERICA - Orchestra. Note: Received Honorable Mention in Redman Wanamaker Music Composition Contest.

LINCOLN WALKS AT MIDNIGHT - Chorus and orchestra.

MELLOW TWILIGHT - Violin and piano. Publisher: Chicago, McKinely Publishers.

MISSISSIPPI RIVER SYMPHONY - Orchestra.

MY SOUL'S BEEN ANCHORED IN DE LORD (1937) - Voice and piano; voice and orchestra. Publisher: New York, Carl Fischer.

NEGRO FOLKSONGS IN COUNTERPOINT - String quartet.

THE OAK - Orchestra. Tone poem.

QUINTET - Piano and strings.

RHAPSODY - Piano and orchestra.

SEA GULLS - Chorus (SSA) and string orchestra.

SONG OF HOPE - Voice and orchestra. Text by composer.

SONGS OF THE OAK - Orchestra. Tome poem.

SPRING JOURNEY - Chorus (SSA) and orchestra.

SUITE OF DANCE - Orchestra.

SYMPHONY IN D MINOR - Orchestra.

SYMPHONY IN G MINOR - Orchestra.

SYMPHONY NO. 1 IN E MINOR (1925) - Orchestra. Note: This piece won the 1932 Wanamaker Music Contest Award and was later performed by the Chicago Symphony (Fredrick Stock, Conductor) at the Chicago Worlds Fair.

THE WIND AND THE SEA - Mixed chorus and string orchestra.

Sources

Abdul, Raoul. "Black Women in Music." In Blacks in Classical Music. New York: Dodd, Mead & Co., 1977, pp. 52-53.

Ammer, Christine. Unsung: A History of Women in American Music. Westport, CT: Greenwood Press, 1980, pp. 152-53.

Carter, Madison H. An Annotated Catalogue of Composers of African Ancestry. New York: Vantage Press, 1986.

Green, Mildred Denby. Black Women Composers: A Genesis. Boston: Twayne Publishers, 1983.

Hare, Maud Cuney. Negro Musicians and Their Music. Washington: Associated Press, 1936.

Jackson, Barbara Green. "Florence Price, Composer." BPIM 5 (Spring 1977).

Nachman, Myrna S. [worklist prepared with Barbara Garvey Jackson] "Price [nee Smith], Florence Bea(trice)." In The New Grove Dictionary of American Music, Vol. 3, pp. 628-29.

Sizer, Sam. A Checklist of Source Materials by and about Florence B. Price. Fayetteville, AK: University of Arkansas Library, 1977. Lists 81 published and unpublished scores; 31 items of correspondence. [Meggett, p. 137]

Southern, Eileen. Biographical Dictionary of Afro-American and African Musicans. Westport, CT: Greenwood Press, 1982.

PRICE, JOHN ELWOOD (1935 -)

John Price was born June 21, 1935, in Tulsa, Oklahoma.   He began to study piano at 5, and learned to play orchestral instruments in high school. He attended Lincoln University (B.A., 1957), University of Tulsa (M. Mus., 1963), and Washington University. Among his teachers were Oscar Anderson Fuller, Augusta McSwain, William Penn, Bela Rozsa, Robert Wykes, and Harold Blumenfeld.

He taught at Karamu House in Cleveland, Ohio (1957-59), at Florida Memorial College in Miami (1964-74), at Eastern Illinois University (1974-) and presently at Tuskegee University, Alabama.

Works

ABENG (1983) - Horn and strings. Duration: 13 minutes 33 seconds.

ADAMS-CAMPBELL: "WHOSOEVER WILL" (1988-89) - Orchestra.

. . . AND SO FAUSTUS GAINED THE WORLD AND LOST HIS SOUL or WHATEVER HAPPENED TO HUMANITY? (1976) - Small orchestra. Duration: 14 minutes. Published: Floyd, Sam. An Anthology of Music by Black Contemporary Composers. Carbondale, IL: Southern Illinois University.

. . . AND SO FAUSTUS GAINED THE WORLD AND LOST HIS SOUL or WHATEVER HAPPENED TO HUMANITY? Version 2 (1989) - Orchestra. Duration: 14 minutes.

.   . AND MOSES . . . AND MIRIAM DANCED (1980) - Solo violin. Duration: 17 minutes 21 seconds.

THE BALLAD OF CANDY MAN BEECHUM (1962; revised 1964) - Incidental music for voice and guitar; revised version for chamber orchestra. Text by Ray McIver. Contents: 1. Ain't Nothin' Like Saturday Night (and dance); 2. Cat Fish; 3. Song with the Yella Gal; 4. Ballad of Candy Man Beechum; 5. I Work and Slave; 6. Candy Man's Funeral Dance and Lament. Duration: 1 hour. Revised version commissioned by AMS Players of Atlanta, Georgia.

CICADA (1980) - Solo violin. Duration: 14 minutes 30 seconds.

COLLEGE SONATA (1957) - Opera in two acts for chorus (SATB), soprano, mezzo soprano, 2 tenors, baritone, and bass-baritone, with orchestra and band. Text by John E. Price. Duration: ca. 2 hours. Note: A science fiction story about the last football game.

CONCERTO (1988-89) - Tuba and orchestra. Duration: 17 minutes 35 seconds. Dedicated to Tubist James Jenkins and the Alabama Symphony.

CONCERTO FOR PIANO AND ORCHESTRA (1969) - Duration: 25 minutes. Three movements. Dedicated to Ruth Norman Bostic.

CONCERTO FOR VIOLONCELLO AND ORCHESTRA (1959-74) - Duration: 27 minutes 30 seconds. Three movements: 1. Recitative; 2. Spiritual; 3. Variations. NOTE: Written for Donald White.

CONFESSION: Chorus, soloists, speakers, and orchestra.   Text: Nat Turner's confession.   Duration: 20 minutes.   NOTE: Incorporated into the revised version of BARELY TIME TO STUDY JESUS.

THE DAMNATION OF DOCTOR FAUSTUS (1962-63) - Chorus (SATB), tenor solo, and chamber orchestra.   Text by Christopher Marlowe (last scene). Duration: 33 minutes.   Dedicated to "My mother, Aunts Robbie, Jay, and Dr. Bela Rozsa."

DANCE FOR ENGLISH HORN AND ORCHESTRA (1952) - Duration: 14 minutes.

EDITORIAL I (1969) - Orchestra.   Duration: 16 minutes 25 seconds. NOTE: "A mirror is sounds after reading an editorial."

EPISODES (1956-57) - Piano and small orchestra.   Duration: 15 minutes 50 seconds.

THE FEAST OF UNITY (1969) - A stage review for chorus (SATB), soprano, alto, tenor, and baritone soloists, flute, oboe, alto saxophone, 2 trumpets, 2 trombones, tuba, piano/harp, percussion, and string octet, actors and dancers.   Text by Sam White, Sharon Lockhart, and others. Duration: 1 hours 27 minutes.   NOTE: "Comments on society and possible solutions for our problems."

FOR L'OVERTURE (1951) - Piano and orchestra.   Duration: 15 minutes. NOTE: "A kind of tone poem dedicated to Toussaint L'Overture."

FROM REMEMBERING THE VAINGLORIOUS LUMINESCENCE REVEALED ON THAT DAY AT THE OLDUVAI . . . (1979-80) - Orchestra.   Duration: 18 minutes 45 seconds.

HARAMBEE (1968-75) - Orchestra.   Duration: 11 minutes 47 seconds. NOTE: Title in Swahili means "Let's All Pull Together."

"HARRIET TUBMAN: BOOKER T. WASHINGTON SPEECH, AUBURN, NEW YORK . . . 1913" (1985-86) - Choir (SATB) and orchestra.   Duration: 52 minutes.

IMPULSE AND DEVIATION, NOS. 1-24 (1958; 1971-74; 1976) - Violoncello. No. 1 (1958) dedicated to Donald White and published in: Floyd, Sam. An Anthology of Music by Black Contemporary Composers.   Carbondale, IL: Southern Illinois University.   Premiere: 1971, Eastern Illinois University, Charleston, Illinois; Donald Tracy, cello.   Recording: Tape in IU Library (IU performance).   NOTE: Each piece is two movements.

A LIGHT FROM ST. AGNES (1968-70) - Opera for women's chorus (backstage), soprano, tenor, baritone solos, small orchestra, and Dixieland ensemble.   Duration: 1 hour.   Dedicated to Ann Flagg.   NOTE: Tragedy set in the backwoods of Louisiana.

A LITURGY FOR SEVEN MEMORIES (1973) - Chorus (SATB), mezzo-soprano and baritone solos, speakers, 2 flutes, 2 oboes, 2 clarinets, organ/piano, percussion, and string septet.   Text by John Tagliabue.   Duration: 1 hour 10 minutes.   Premiere: 1973, Florida Memorial College, Miami. Notes: Written for the James and Rosamond Johnson Ensemble of Florida Memorial College.   "A liturgy expounding the world's problems and thoughs about the Christ Child within the 20th century."

MANDOLIN (POEMS BY RITA DOVE) (1983-84) - Baritone/mezzo-soprano solo and small orchestra. Duration: 28 minutes 40 seconds.

MOURNING DOVE (1980) - Solo violin. Duration: 14 minutes 52 seconds.

NO IDEOLOGY IN THE WORLD (OR OUT OF IT) IS WORTH THE DEATH OF A WORM (1987) - Small orchestra. Duration: 16 minutes.

NOCTURNE FOR A WINTER NIGHT (1956) - French horn, harp, and strings. Duration: 7 minutes 48 seconds. Dedicated to Burton Hardin. NOTE: Inspired by a poem by John E Price.

O SUN OF REAL PEACE (1980-81) - Small orchestra. Duration: 21 minutes.

ON THE THIRD DAY . . . OSIRIS AROSE (1988) - Contrabass and piano. Duration: 13 minutes. Premiere: May 1988; New York City; Ortiz M. Walton, soloist.

THE OTHER FOOT (1972-74) - Opera in one act for large chorus (SATB), soprano and baritone soloists, 2 or 3 children's voices, orchestra, band, and marimba. Text by Ray Bradbury. Duration: 1 hour 16 minutes. Commissioned by Napoleon Reed of the Community of Artists.

OVERTURE (1972-73) - Orchestra. Duration: 7 minutes 42 seconds.

PIECE AND DEVIATION (1962) - Viola and piano. Duration: 9 minutes. Dedicated to Shirley M. Wall. Premiere: 1962, Vernon AME Church, Tulsa, Oklahoma.

PIECES, THREE (1970) - String orchestra. Duration: 25 minutes. Contents: 1. Blues; 2. Juba; 3. Dance. Dedicated to Eastern Illinois University String Orchestra; Donald Tracy, conductor.

PIECES, TWO (1955-75) - Strings and brass quartet. Duration: 12 minutes 32 seconds. Contents: 1. The Solent; 2. Inertia.

PIECES, TWO (1974-75) - Trumpet and strings. Duration: 13 minutes 32 seconds. Contents: 1. Spiritual; 2. Jumpin' Dance.

PIECES FOR MARCARBAR, NINE (1976-1978) - Violin and piano. Commissioned by Barbara Schlauch. Dedicated to the Schlauch family. NOTE: Six additional pieces (1977-78).

PRAYERS: IMHOTEP (1989) - Cello. Duration: 18 minutes.

A PTAH HYMN (1978) - Unaccompanied cello. Duration: 12 minutes. Commissioned by and dedicated to Gretchen Tracy. Premiere: 23 April 1979, Eastern Illinois University, Charleston, Illinois; Gretchen Tracy, cello.

QUARTET (1962) - Bassoon, french horn, violin, and viola. Duration: 13 minutes 30 seconds. Dedicated to Bela Rozsa. Premiere: 14 November 1967, Rutgers University, New Brunswick, New Jersey; Rutgers University Contemporary Chamber Ensemble. Recording: Tape available from composer.

RHAPSODY SYMPHONIQUE (1950) - Piano and orchestra.   Duration: 15 minutes 30 seconds. NOTE: Revised as SCHERZO II.

RIGHT ON, BABY! (1971-72) - Opera for soprano, tenor, baritone, and small orchestra. Text by Lewis Allan. Duration: 40 minutes 42 seconds. NOTE: Comedy about a very busy expectant mother.

SCARAB I (1980) - Solo violin. Duration: 16 minutes.

SCHERZO FOR CELLO AND ORCHESTRA (1973) - Duration: 11 minutes 32 seconds. Dedicated to Donald Tracy.

SCHERZO I FOR CLARINET AND ORCHESTRA (PIANO) (1952; revised 1953-54) - Duration: 15 minutes. Dedicated to James Tilman. Premiere (piano reduction): 1954, Lincoln University, Jefferson City, Missouri; 5 November 1971, Radio Station WTMI, Miami, Florida; Oakland Youth Symphony, Robert Hughes, Conductor; Alex Foster, clarinet. Recordings: Tape available from composer (with orchestra); tape of IU performance (with piano) in IU library. NOTE: Orchestrated in 1956.

SCHERZO II FOR CLARINET AND ORCHESTRA (1957) - Duration: 15 minutes 25 seconds. NOTE: Revision of RHAPSODY SYMPHONIQUE.

SCHERZO III FOR CLARINET AND ORCHESTRA (1969) - Duration: 17 minutes. NOTE: Uses smaller orchestra than that required for SCHERZO I and II.

SCHERZO IV FOR CLARINET AND ORCHESTRA (1968) - Duration: 14 minutes 27 seconds.

SERENADE FOR TULSA (1950) - Piano and orchestra. Duration: 13 minutes 21 seconds. Dedicated to the Tulsa (Oklahoma) Philharmonic.

SONG OF THE LIBERTY BELL (1976-78) - Chorus (SATB), baritone, 3 speakers, and orchestra. Text by Lewis Allan. Duration: 1 hour 10 minutes. Commissioned by Lewis Allan.

SPIRITUAL (1972-74) - Clarinet and string orchestra.   Duration: 6 minutes.

"STEADY WAH NO MO'" (1973) - String orchestra. Duration: 8 minutes 31 seconds. NOTE: Paraphrase on the spiritual.

SUGGESTION FOR THE CENTURY (1954; revised 1958) - Men's vocal quartet with orchestra. Duration: 5 minutes 42 seconds. Dedicated to Mr. and Mrs. Russell Jelliffe of Karamu House and President and Mrs. John F. Kennedy.

TARANTELLA (1952; revised 1955) - Violin and piano. Duration: 12 minutes 32 seconds. Dedicated to Kathryn Walker.

TEMPEST - (1965) - Incidental music for chorus (SATB), flute, guitar, and trumpet. Text by William Shakespeare. Premiere: 1965, Atlanta, Georga; AMS Players.

THREE ORCHESTRA PIECES (1980-81) - Orchestra. Duration: 32 minutes. Contents: 1. Arawak; 2. Citadel; 3. Makandal.

TO THE SHRINE OF THE BLACK MADONNA (1974) - String orchestra. Duration: 13 mintues 55 seconds. Dedicated to Donald Tracy and the Eastern Illinois University String Ensemble. NOTE: "Before Notre Dame in Paris was built, there were a Shrine to the Black Madonna."

TOBIAS AND THE ANGEL (1958) - Incidental music for a play for voice, harp, and percussion. Commissioned by Reuben Silver. Premiere: 1959, Karamu House, Cleveland, Ohio.

TRIO (1960; revised 1974) - Violin, cello, and piano. Two movements. Duration: 16 minutes 12 seconds. Dedicated to Shirley Wall, Floyd Jackson, and Betty Kimble.

TRIO (1982-83) - Violin, cello, and piano. Duration: 17 minutes 20 seconds.

VERSES FROM GENESIS AND PSALMS (1961) - Clarinet, percussion, cello, narrator, and dancers   Duration: 20 minutes 55 seconds. Commissioned by the youth department of Boston Avenue Methodist Church, Tulsa, Oklahoma. Dedicated to Mable Lynch. Premiere: October 1961, Boston Avenue Methodist Church, Tulsa, Oklahoma.

WATY: ANCIENT SINGER . . . WHO TRIED (1989) - Cello. Duration: 16 minutes 43 seconds.

Sources

Information submitted by the composer.

Anderson, E. Ruth. Contemporary American Composers: A Biographical Dictionary. Boston: G.K. Hall, 1976.

Composers of the Americas, Vol. 19. Washington, D.C.: Pan American Union Music Section, 1977.

Southern, Eileen. Biographical Dictionary of Afro-American and African Musicians. Westport, CT: Greenwood Press, 1982, p. 313.

Tischler, Alice. Fifteen Black American Composers: A Bibliography of Their Works. Detroit Studies in Music Bibliography. Detroit: Information Coordinators, 1981, pp. 213-57.

QAMAR, NADI ABU (1917 -)

Works

THE LIKEMBICAN PANORAMA - Chamber orchestra.

THE PHILOSOPHY OF THE SPIRITUALS - Orchestra and chorus.

Source

Matney, William C. Who's Who Among Black Americans. 5th ed. Lake Forest, IL: Ann Wolk Krouse, 1988, p. 1040.

RIVERS, CLARENCE JOSEPH (1931 -)

Clarence Joseph Rivers was born September 9, 1931, in Selma, Alabama.
He received his bachelors degree and his masters degree from St.
Mary's Seminary in Cincinnati, Ohio, and later studied at Xavier University
(Cincinnati), Catholic University (Washington, D.C.), Yale, and the Insti-
tute Catholique in Paris.
He founded the Department of Culture and Worship in the National Of-
fice for Black Catholics and became its first director in 1972.
In 1966 he received the Gold Medal of the Catholic Art Association.
Among his best known works are An American Mass Program, and Resurrection (for gospel/jazz soloist and chorus, piano or chamber orchestra). His
mass, Brotherhood of Man, was performed at the Newport Jazz Festival in
1967 with the Billy Taylor Trio.

Works

BROTHERHOOD OF MAN - Orchestra and jazz trio (piano, bass, and drums).

RESURRECTION - Gospel/jazz soloist, chorus, and piano or chamber orchestra.

Sources

Garcia, William. "Church Music by Black Composers." BPIM (Fall
1974).

Southern, Eileen. Biographical Dictionary of Afro-American and African Musicians. Westport, CT: Greenwood Press, 1982, p. 321.

ROBINSON, WALTER (1951 -)

Works

LOOK WHAT A WONDER JESUS HAS DONE (1989) - Gospel opera.

Source

Holly, Ellistine Perkins. Biographies of Black Composers. Dubuque,
IA: Wm. C. Brown Publishers, 1990.

ROXBURY, RONALD (1946 -)

Ronald Roxbury was born near Salisbury, Maryland, in 1946.
He received his Master's degree from the Peabody Institute, where he
studied with Earle Brown and Stefan Grove.
He taught at Tanglewood.
Besides composing, he has been a singer and served as intern for music
critic study for the Washington Star.
Among his works are Ave Maria and As Dew in Aprille for chorus; Combination Cyclops, Three Transcendental Etudes, Sonata, Hommage for Rick
Myers, Pictures of an Exhibitionist, and Preludes for piano; Chordorgel-
buchlien for organ; Haiku and Joe for guitar; Pygmies, Chants des Oiseaux,
and Insect Fear for voice; and for chamber Malcum Soul/Designs, Journey to

y-Ha'nth-lei, Ecstacies for Mi-Go/Several Bags of the Abominable Snowman, Briyga-ha, Requiem for Bill Null, Le Sofa des Folfeges; and others.

Works

ARIA FOR FRED - Cello and piano.

ECSTACIES FOR MI-GO/SEVERAL BAGS OF THE ABOMINABLE SNOWMAN - 14 guitars and 9 cellos with piccolo solo.

HAIKU AND JOE - Guitar.

PYGMIES - Violin.

QUASIMODO AT WITS' END - Flute, guitar, and double bass.

Sources

Anderson, E. Ruth. Contemporary American Composers: A Biographical Dictionary. Boston: G.K. Hall & Co., 1982.

Roach, Hildred. Black American Music: Past and Present, Vol. II. Miami: Krieger Publishing Co., 1985 p. 102.

RUSSELL, GEORGE ALLAN (1923 -)

George Allan Russell was born June 23, 1923, in Cincinnati, Ohio.
As a child, he played drums in a Boy Scout drum and bugle corps.   He received his musical education at the Wilberforce University High School in Xenia, Ohio, and studied privately in 1949 with Stephan Wolpe.
He began to play professionally while in high school, and later arranged for Benny Carter and Earl Hines.   In 1960 he formed a sextet that toured widely, and appeared on radio and television.
He taught at Lenox School of Jazz; Lund University in Oslo, Norway; Vaskilde Summer School in Denmark; and at the New England Conservatory of Music in Boston.
Russell developed the Lydian Chromatic concept of tonal organization, which explains Afro-American music in terms of its own history rather than by the laws of European music.   He published a book on the subject in 1953, taught the concept in New York (1953-68), and at the Festival of the Arts in Finland (1966, 1967).
He received Guggenheim fellowships in 1969 and 1972, grants from the National Endowment for the Arts in 1969 and 1976, and an American Music Conference Award in 1976.
Among his best known works are Othello Ballet Suite, Listen to the Silence, and Living Time.

Works

THE AFRICAN GAME - Jazz orchestra. Duration: 45 minutes. Commissioned by Massachusetts Council of the Arts and the Swedish Radio Company. Publisher: Russ-Hix. Premiere: 18 June 1983; Emmanuel Church, Boston, Massachusetts; Living Time Orchestra, George Russell, conductor. Recording: Blue Note, 1985.

CONCERTO FOR SELF-ACCOMPANIED GUITAR (1962) - Publisher: Russ-Hix
Music. Recorded by Rune Gustafsson (Sonet SLP-1441/1412: The Essence
of George Russell).

Sources

Baker, David N., Lida M. Belt, and Herman C. Hudson. The Black Composer Speaks. Metuchen, NJ: Scarecrow Press, 1978.

Feather, Leonard. The Encyclopedia of Jazz in the Sixties. New York:
Horizon Press, 1966.

Who's Who In America 39th ed. (1976-77), s.v. "Russell, George Allen"
[sic].

RYDER, NOAH FRANCIS (1914-1964)

Noah Francis Ryder was born April 10, 1914, in Nashville, Tennessee,
and died April 17, 1964, in Norfolk, Virginia. His father sang with the
Fisk Jubilee Singers, served as accompanist with Roland Hayes, and was a
college music teacher.
Ryder studied piano and violin as a child. He attended the University
of Cincinnati, Hampton Institute in Virginia (B.A., 1935), and the University of Michigan-Ann Arbor (M. Mus., 1947). While in college he led his
own jazz group, sang in the college choir, and organized a male quartet
(which turned professional as The Deep River Boys).
In 1946 he won the grand prize in the Navy War Writers' Board Contest
for his composition "Sea Suite for Male Voices."
Ryder taught at Palmer Memorial Institute in Sedalia, Missouri, Winston-Salem Teachers College in North Carolina, Hampton Institute, and Norfolk State College in Virginia (1947-62). At Norfolk he established a
music-degree program in 1960; led choral groups, including the Norfolk
Staters, a community male chorus composed of men from his college groups;
and chaired the music department.
He was best known for his spiritual arrangements and the piano works
Five Sketches for Piano and "Nocturne."

Works

SYMPHONY - Orchestra. Manuscript.

Sources

Johnson, Marjorie S. "Noah Francis Ryder (1914-1964): A Study of His
Life, Works, and Contributions to Music Education." Thesis (M.A.),
Catholic University, 1968.

---. "Noah Francis Ryder: Composer and Educator." The Black Perspective in Music (Spring 1978): 18-31.

McGinty, Doris Evans. "Ryder, Noah Francis." In The Grove Dictionary
of American Music, Vol. 4, p. 115.

Southern, Eileen. Biographical Dictionary of Afro-American and African Musicians. Westport, CT: Greenwood Press, 1982, pp. 328-329.

Tischler, Alice. "Noah Francis Ryder." In Fifteen Black American
Composers: A Bibliography of Their Works. Detroit, MI: Information
Coordinators, 1981, pp. 259-76.

SANTOS, HENRY JOSE (1927 -)

Henry Jose Santos was born August 29, 1927, in Lewiston, Maine.
He attended Boston University School of Fine and Applied Arts (B. Mus.
1952), Harvard University Summery School (1968), Boston College (1979), and
Boston University (M. Mus. 1980). He studied piano with Alfredo Fondacaro
(1952-60), conducting with Allan Lannom (1972-73), and composition with Dr.
Hugo Norden (1974-86).
He appeared with members of the Boston Symphony at Harvard for the
Albert Schweitzer Music Festival in 1950, and has performed in Paris and in
Lugano, Switzerland.
His honors include the Citizen's Achievement Award, Cape Verdean Bene-
ficient Society, 1968. In 1970 he was semi-finalist in the First Louis
Moreau Gottschalk International Competition for Pianists and Composers
sponsored by the Pan-American Union. He appeared in Who's Who Among Black
Americans First Edition, 1975-76.
He has been an instructor at the Perkins School for the Blind (1956-
70) and is current a professor in the Music Department of Bridgewater State
College.
Santos was appointed a member of the Ethnic Heritage Task Force of
Massachusetts in 1974. He served as Chairperson of the Community Re-
sources/Southeast Panel Merit Aid Program for the Massachusetts Council on
the Arts and Humanities in 1986, and in 1987 as a member of the General
Operating Support Panel for the Rhode Island Council for the Arts.

Works

LEOLA (1989) - Trumpet, alto saxophone, violin, cello, piano, and
drums. Duration: 3 minutes. Dedicated to T.J. Anderson for his 60th
Birthday Celebration Concert. Unpublished. Premiere: March 1989;
Sanders Theater, Harvard University, Cambridge, MA.

MASS IN G MAJOR (1987) - Soprano, contralto, and tenor soloists; chorus, orchestra, and electric piano. Duration: 20 minutes. Dedication: "In memory of my father." Unpublished. Premiere: 1987; Congregational Church, Middleboro, MA; the Mayflower Chorale, J. Fred
Thorton, Conductor.

Source

Information submitted by the composer.

SCHUYLER, PHILLIPPA DUKE (1932-1967)

Phillippa Duke Schuyler was born in New York City in 1932 and died in
Vietnam in 1967.
She began to study piano as a child, and made her debut at the age of
six at the 1939 New York World's Fair, playing her own works.
She won the Philharmonic Society's Notebook Contest prize eight times
before being barred because of her brilliance; and the National Guild prize
eight consecutive times. One piece Manhatten Noctourne, written when she

was 12, won first prize in the 1943 Grinnell Foundation Contest, and
another piece, Rumpelstiltskin, written at the age of 13, was awarded the
Wayne University and Grinnell Foundation prizes.

Besides her prodigious composing and career as a concert pianist,
Schuyler wrote several books: Who Killed the Congo?, Christ in Africa,
Good Men and Die, and Adventures in Black and White. At the time of her
death she was working as a correspondent for the Manchester (New Hampshire)
Union Leader.

Among her works are The Nile Fantasy, African Rhapsody, Three Little
Piano Pieces, and The Rhapsody of Youth.

Works

MANHATTAN NOCTOURNE - Orchestra. Symphonic Poem. Manuscript score in
Yale University James Weldon Johnson Memorial Collection. NOTE:
Received the Detroit Symphony Orchestra prize.

THE NILE FANTASY - Piano and orchestra. Three parts: 1. Inshallah or
Fate...Contemplation and Submission; 2. Violence and Terror; 3. The
Long Road to Peace. Arranged by Margaret A. Bonds.

RUMPELSTILTSKIN - Orchestra. NOTE: Received Wayne State University
Award.

SCHERZO - Orchestra.

SLEEPY HOLLOW SKETCHES - Orchestra.

WHITE NILE SUITE - Orchestra.

Sources

Anderson, E. Ruth. Contemporary American Composers: A Biographical
Dictionary. Boston: G.K. Hall & Co., 1982, p. 459.

Carter, Madison H. An Annotated Catalogue of Composers of African
Ancestry. New York: Vantage Press, 1986.

Cohen, Aaron I. International Encyclopedia of Women Composers. New
York: R. R. Bowker Co., 1981.

De Lerma, Dominique-René. "Schuyler, Philippa Duke." In The New
Grove Dictionary of American Music, Vol. 4, pp. 170-71.

Holly, Ellistine Perkins. Biographies of Black Composers and Song
Writers. Dubuque, IA: Wm. C. Brown Publishers, 1990, p. 41.

Roach, Hildred. Black American Music: Past and Present, Vol. II.
Miami: Krieger Publishing Co., 1985, pp. 67-68.

SHIRLEY, DONALD (1927 -)

Donald Shirley was born in Kingston, Jamaica, in 1927.

He studied at the Leningrad Conservatory at age nine, and graduated
from Harvard University, where he earned his Ph.D.

He has been a soloist with various symphony orchestras.

Works

LEGACY (1972) - String orchestra. Premiere: 3 December 1972; New York City; Symphony of the New World, D. de Coteau, Conductor.

SINGLETON, ALVIN (1940 -)

Alvin Singleton was born December 28, 1940, in Brooklyn, New York.
He attended New York University (B.Mus., 1967), Columbia University (1967-68), Juilliard (1967-68), the Berkshire Music Center (1969), and Yale (M. Mus., 1971). He also attended the Accademia Nazionale di Santa Cecilia in Rome on a Fulbright Scholarship (1971-72). In 1972 and 1974 he studied at Ferienkurse fuer neue Musik Darmstadt in West Germany and at the Instituto Musicaile in Vicenza, Italy.
His awards include an ASCAP Fellowship (1969), a Fulbright Scholarship (1971), a fellowship to the MacDowell Colony (summers 1987 and 1989). He won the Rena Greenwald Memoria Prize (1969-70), the Horation Parker Memorial Scholarship (1970-71), and the Woods Chandler Memorial Prize (1970-71) at Yale; and in Europe won the Kranichsteiner Musikpreis (1974), and two Musikprotokoll Composition Prizes (1979, 1981) by the Austrian Radio (GRAZ).
Among his works are the opera Dream Sequence '76 (1976) and Necessity is a Mother (1981), as well as a wide range of instrumental ensembles and solo works for piano, cello flute, viola, harpsichord, bass clarinet, and marimba.

Works

AFTER FALLEN CRUMBS (1988) - Orchestra. Duration: 7 minutes. Commissioned by the Atlanta Symphony Orchestra. Publisher: Valley Forge, PA, European American Music Corp. Recording: Nonesuch 79231-2 (CD), 79231-4 (cassette).

AGAIN (1979) - Chamber orchestra. Duration: 12 minutes. Publisher: Valley Forge, PA, European American Music Corp. Premiere: October 1979, London Sinfonietta.

AKWAABA (1985) - Flute, clarinet, bassoon, piano, percussion, violin, violoncello. Duration: 29 minutes; shorter version: 19 minutes. Publisher: Valley Forge, PA, European American Music Corp. Premiere: March 1985, Episteme ensemble.

ARGORU II (1970) - Cello. Duration: 13 minutes. Publisher: Valley Forge, PA, European American Music Corp.

ARGORU IV (1978) - Viola. Duration: 10 minutes. Publisher: Valley Forge, PA, European American Music Corp.

BE NATURAL (1974) - For any combination of three bowed strings. Duration: 10 minutes. Publisher: Valley Forge, PA, European American Music Corp.

DREAM SEQUENCE '76 (1976) - Opera in two parts for 8 singers, 2 actors, pantomime, 6 extras, chamber orchestra, and tape. Text by the composer. Duration: 68 minutes. Publisher: Valley Forge, PA, European American Music Corp. Premiere: August 1976, American Institute of Musical Studies.

EINE IDEE IST EIN STUECK STOFF ("AN IDEA IS A PIECE OF CLOTH") (1988) - String orchestra. Publisher: Valley Forge, PA, European American Music Corp. Premiere: 7 November 1988, Konzerthaus, Mozartsaal, Vienna; American Music Ensemble, Vienna, Hobart Earl, Conductor.

ET NUNC (1974) - Alto flute, bass clarinet, contrabass. Duration: 13 minutes. Publisher: Valley Forge, PA European American Music Corp.

KUIITANA (1974) - Concerto for piano, contrabass, percussion, and chamber orchestra. Duration: 17 minutes. Publisher: Valley Forge, PA, European American Music Corp. Premiere: October 1974, Vienna; Ensemble des 20 Jahrhunderts.

LA FLORA (1982) - Flute/alto flute, clarinet, percussion (2), violin, violoncello. Duration: 14 minutes. Publisher: Valley Forge, PA, European American Music Corp. Premiere: October 1983; Orchestra of Our Time.

MESSA (Italian language) (1975) - Flute, two guitars, electric organ, soprano solo, mixed choirs (four soprani, four alti, four tenori, four bassi), violoncello, and contrabass. Duration: 26 minutes. Publisher: Valley Forge, PA, European American Music Corp. Premiere: May 1985, the Vatican; Chiesa di S. Onofrio al Gianicolo.

MESTIZO II (1970) - Large orchestra. Publisher: Valley Forge, PA, European American Music Corp.

MOMENT (1968) - Large orchestra. Publisher: Valley Forge, PA, European American Music Corp.

NECESSITY IS A MOTHER (1981) - Three actresses (voices) and double bass with amplification. Text by the composer. Duration: 30 minutes. Publisher: Valley Forge, PA, European American Music Corp. Premiere: August 1981, Lenox Arts Center, Inc.

A SEASONING (1971) - Female or male voice, flute, E-flat alto saxophone, trombone, double bass (all doubling on percussion), and one percussion player. Text by the composer. Duration: 12 minutes. Publisher: Valley Forge, PA, European American Music Corp.

SECRET DESIRE TO BE BLACK (1988) - String quartet #2. Duration: 20 minutes. Publisher: Valley Forge, PA, European American Music Corp.

SHADOWS (1987) - Orchestra. Duration: 20 minutes. Publisher: Valley Forge, PA, European American Music Corp. Premiere: May 1987; Atlanta Symphony Orchestra. Recording: Nonesuch 79231-2 (CD); 79231-4 (cassette).

STRING QUARTET NO. 1 (1967) - Duration: 13 minutes. Publisher: Valley Forge, PA, European American Music Corp.

STRING QUARTET NO. 2

SUCH A NICE LADY (1979) - Clarinet violin, viola cello, and piano.
Duration: 15 minutes. Publisher: Valley Forge, PA, European American Music Corp.

A YELLOW ROSE PETAL (1982) - Orchestra. Duration: 20 minutes. Publisher: Valley Forge, PA, European American Music Corp. Premiere: May 1982, Houston Symphony Orchestra. Recording: Nonesuch 79231-2 (CD); 79231-4 (cassette).

Sources

Information submitted by the composer.

Montague, Stephen. "Singleton, Alvin (Elliot)." In The New Grove Dictionary of American Music, Vol. 4, p. 234.

SMITH, HALE (1925 -)

Hale Smith was born in Cleveland, Ohio, on June 29, 1925.
He began to study piano at the age of 7, and went on to obtain degrees from the Cleveland Institute of Music (B.Mus., 1950; M. Mus., 1952). He played in his first jazz groups as a teenager and was influenced by Earl Hines, Art Tatum, and Teddy Wilson.
He began to compose as a child, and in 1952 he received a BMI Student Composer's Award.
Besides composing, Smith worked as music editor/advisor for E.B. Marks, the Frank Music Corporation, Sam Fox Music Publishers, and C.F. Peters Corporation. During the 50s he was active as an arranger and worked with such artists as Chico Hamilton, Quincy Jones, Abbey Lincoln, and Ahmad Jamal. He toured as a lecturer and consultant and sometimes published articles in professional journals and anthologies, and taught at C.W. Post College (New York), and at the University of Connecticut at Storrs.
Smith wrote in a variety of forms and for a variety of mediums--work for radio, film, and television; chamber works; works for concert band, symphony orchestra, and chorus; songs set to texts from poets as widely differing as Langston Hughes, John Donne, and Lu Yun. Among his works are Contours, Orchestral Set, Ritual and Incantations and Innerflexions (for orchestra); Sonata for Piano and Cello; Music for Harp and Chamber Orchestra; By Yearning and by Beautiful (string orchestra); Comes Tomorrow (jazz cantata); and In Memoriam--Beryl Rubinstein (chorus and chamber orchestra).

Works

BLOOD WEDDING (1953) - Chamber orchestra. Play by Garcia Lorca (main characters are non-singing parts). Duration: 90 minutes. Commissioned by the Karamu Theatre, Cleveland, Ohio. Premiere: Karamu Theatre; Benno Frank, director.

BY YEARNING AND BY BEAUTIFUL (1961) - String orchestra. Duration: 6 minutes. Dedicated to Russell Atkins (suggested by his poem "By Yearning and by Beautiful"). Publisher: E.B. Marks, rental. Premiere: 1972; Richmond Symphony Orchestra, Joseph Kennedy Jr., Conductor.

CONCERT MUSIC FOR PIANO AND ORCHESTRA (1972) - Duration: 14 minutes. Dedicated to Jewel and Leon Thompson. Commissioned by Undine Smith

Moore and Altona T. Johns. Publisher: C.F. Peters, rental. Premiere: 1972; the Richmond Symphony Orchestra, Leon Thompson, conductor; Jewel Thompson, piano.

CONTOURS (1962) - Orchestra. Duration: 9 minutes. Commissioned by Broadcast Music Inc. in celebration of its 20th anniversary and dedicated to Carl Haverlin. Dedicated to the memory of Clarence Cameron White and Wallingford Rieger. Publisher: C.F. Peters, 1962. Premiere: 1962; Louisville Symphony Orchestra, Robert Whitney, Conductor. Recording: Louisville Symphony Orchestra Robert Whitney, Conductor (Louisville LOU 632).

DUO FOR VIOLIN AND PIANO (1953) - Three movements. Duration: 15 minutes. Publisher: C.F. Peter, rental. Premiere: 1955, Karamu Theatre, Cleveland, Ohio; Jeno Antal, violin; Betty Oberacker, piano.

EPICEDIAL VARIATIONS (1956) - Violin and piano. Duration: 12 minutes. Publisher: E.B. Marks, rental. Premiere: Cleveland, Ohio; Elliott Golub, violin, and John Ferritto, piano; and James Barrett, violin, and Jane Corner Young, piano.

IN MEMORIAM--BERYL RUBINSTEIN (1953; orchestrated in 1958) - Chorus (SATB) and chamber orchestra or piano. Three movements: 1. Moderato (text is a vocalise); 2. Poem D'Automne (text by Langston Hughes); 3. Elegy (text by Russell Atkins). Duration: 10 minutes 30 seconds. Publisher: Highgate Press (Galaxy Music), 1959; part of the Cleveland Composers Guild Publication Series. Recording: Kulas Choir and Chamber Orchestra, Robert Shaw, Conductor (Composers Recordings Inc., CRI SD-182: The Cleveland Composers Guild, Vol. I.).

INTRODUCTION, CADENZAS, AND INTERLUDES FOR EIGHT PLAYERS (1974) - Flute/ alto flute, oboe, clarinet, harp, piano, violin, viola, and violoncello. Duration: 12 minutes. Commissioned by the Nassau County Office of Cultural Development, John Maerhofer, Director. Publisher: E.B. Marks, 1976. Premiere: 1974; Sea Cliff Chamber Players.

MUSIC FOR HARP AND ORCHESTRA (1967) - Harp and chamber orchestra. Two movements. Duration: 13 minutes. Commissioned by the Symphony of the New World. Publisher: E.B. Marks, rental. Premiere: 1967, Carnegie Hall; Symphony of the New World, Benjamin Steinberg, Conductor; Gloria Agostini, harp.

NUANCES OF HALE SMITH (ca. 1967-68) - Small orchestra. TV and radio background music. Seven short pieces. Duration: 15 minutes. Commission: Sam Fox Music Publishers. Publisher: Sam Fox Publisher Recording: Sam Fox SF 1022 (side A), Synchrofox Music Library.

ORCHESTRA SET (1952) - Orchestra. Four piece. Duration: 15 minutes. Publisher: C.F. Peters, rental. Premiere: 1974; Symphony of the New World, Everett, Conductor. NOTE: This work was part of the composer's Master's thesis.

RITUAL AND INCANTATIONS (1974) - Orchestra. Duration: 15-18 minutes. Commissioned by the Thorne Music Fund. Dedicated to Francis Thorne. Publisher: C.F. Peters, rental. Premiere: 1974; Houston Symphony Orchestra, Paul Freeman, Conductor. Recording: The Detroit Symphony Orchestra Paul Freeman, Conductor; Columbia Black Composers Series.

SONATA FOR VIOLONCELLO AND PIANO (1955) - Three movements. Duration: 22 minutes. Commissioned by Kermit Moore. Dedicated to Kermit Moore. Publisher: C.F. Peters, rental. Premiere: In Europe by Kermit Moore. American Premiere: 1958, Donnell Auditorium, New York City; Benar Heifitz, violoncello, Ward Davenny, piano.

TWO LOVE SONGS OF JOHN DONNE (1958) - Soprano, string quartet, and woodwind quintet. Text by John Donne: Confined Love; The Computation. Duration: 8 minutes. Dedicated to Adele Addison. Publisher: E.B. Marks, rental. Premiere: 1958, Donnell Library Composer's Forum, New York City; Bethany Beardslee, soprano; Arthur Winograd, Conductor.

Sources

Information submitted by the composer.

Baker, David N., Lida M. Belt, and Herman C. Hudson. The Black Composer Speaks. Metuchen, NJ: Scarecrow Press, 1978.

"Black Composers." Newsweek 15 April 1974.

Breda, Malcolm Joseph. "Hale Smith: A Biographical and Analytical Study of the Man and His Music." Ph.D. Dissertation, University of Southern Mississippi, 1975.

Claghorn, Charles E. Biographical Dictionary of American Music. West Nyack, NY: Parker Publishing Co., 1973.

De Lerma Dominique-Rene. Black Music in Our Culture: Curricular Ideas on the Subjects, Materials, and Problems. Kent, OH: Kent State University Press, 1970.

Southern, Eileen. Biographical Dictionary of Afro-American and African Musicians. Westport, CT: Greenwood Press, 1982.

Southern, Eileen. "Smith, Hale." In The New Grove Dictionary of American Music, Vol. 4, p. 246.

Southern, Eileen. "Smith, Hale." In The New Grove Dictionary of Music and Musicians, Vol. 17, p. 414.

SMITH, NATHANIEL CLARK (1877-1933)

Nathaniel Clark Smith was born July 31, 1877, in Fort Levenworth, Kansas, and died October 8 1933, in St. Louis, Missouri.
Smith studied widely and long: Western University in Quindaro, Kansas; Guild Hall in London, England (1899); Chicago Musical College (where he received his B. Mus, in 1905); University of Kansas-Lawrence; Horner Institute of Fine Arts (Kansas City, Missouri, 1915-16); and the Sherwood School of Music (Chicago, 1928).
In between studies he was incredibly active. Beginning in the mid-1890s, he conducted a music studio, led a boy's band and organized a mail-carrier's band; served as bandmaster of the 8th Illinois Regiment Band during the Spanish-American War in 1898; and toured the world for 18 months with the M.B. Curtis All-Star Afro-American Minstrels. Upon his return to

the States in 1901, he plunged back into community activity, serving as bandmaster for the 8th Illinois State Militia attending Chicago Musical College, organizing Chicago's first black symphony orchestra (possibly the first in the nation), and founding a music publishing house with J. Berni Barbour (possibly the first to be completely African-American-owned), and organizing in 1904 Smith's Mandolin and String Instruments Club and the N. Clark Smith Ladies Orchestra. He was commissioned a captain in the Army in 1907 and joined the military faculty at Tuskegee Institite (Alabama, 1907-13), where he organized a band, an orchestra, glee clubs, and chamber ensembles, all of which toured widely in the South and Midwest. In 1919 he became a charter member of the National Association of Negro Musicians. In 1922 the Pullman Railroad Company hired him to organize musical groups among its black employees; beginning in Chicago and continuing in other large cities, he organized Pullman Porter Bands, Orchestras, and Glee Clubs.

Smith also taught, including tenures at Lincoln High School in Kansas City, Missouri (1916-22), Wendell Phillips High School (Chicago, 1925-26), and Sumner High School in St. Louis (1930-33). As an educator he exerted wide influence on the development of African-American music through his students and those whom he trained or coached--William Levi Dawson, Alonzo Lewis, Walter Dyette, Stanley Lee Henderson, Jasper Allen, Eddie Coles, Lionel Hampton, Alvis Hayes, Milton Hinton, Harlan Leonard, Walter Page, Quinn Wilson, Nelmatilda Ritchie Woodard, among many others.

As a composer he was best known for his band pieces and spiritual pieces, including "The Tuskegee Institute March," Negro Folk Suite, and Negro Choral Symphony.

Works

THE CHRISTIAN RECORDER MARCH - Piano or orchestra or brass band. Publisher: Kansas City, Missouri, Carl Hoffman. Score: In the Library of Congress and in photocopy format at the Center for Black Music Research, Columbia College, Chicago.

FREDERICK DOUGLASS FUNERAL MARCH - Publisher: Chicago, S. Brajnard's Sons Co. Score: In the Library of Congress and in photocopy format at the Center for Black Music Research, Columbia College, Chicago.

THE LINCOLN HIGH SCHOOL MARCH - Piano or orchestra or brass band or mandolin or guitar. Score: In the Library of Congress and in photocopy format at the Center for Black Music Research, Columbia College, Chicago.

NEGRO CHORAL SYMPHONY - Chorus and orchestra. Score: In the Library of Congress and in photocopy format at the Center for Black Music Research, Columbia College, Chicago.

NEGRO FOLK SUITE - Piano with arrangements by the composer for violin and piano; violin, cello, and piano, and full orchestra. Contents: 1. The Orange Dance (British Guinea); 2. The Pineapple Lament (Martinique); 3. The Banana Walk (St. Helena Island). Dedicated to Mr. Percy Granger. Publisher: Chicago Lyon and Healy, Inc. Score: In the Library of Congress and in photocopy format at the Center for Black Music Research, Columbia College, Chicago.

THE PICKANINNY BAND MARCH (1895) - Piano. Publisher: Kansas City, Missouri, Carl Hoffman. Score: In the Library of Congress and in photocopy format at the Center for Black Music Research, Columbia College, Chicago.

THE PRIMA DONNA SONG FROM NEGRO CHORAL SYMPHONY - Soprano, three parts female voices, four parts male voices, and orchestra. Publisher: Chicago, Lyon and Healy, Inc. Score: In the Library of Congress and in photocopy format at the Center for Black Music Research, Columbia College, Chicago.

SPIRITUAL JUBILEE FROM NEGRO CHORAL SYMPHONY - Solo, chorus, and orchestra. Publisher: Chicago, Lyon and Healy, Inc. Score: In the Library of Congress and in photocopy format at the Center for Black Music Research, Columbia College, Chicago.

TWO SONGS - Voice with piano and cello oblig. Dedicated to Mr. Rowland W. Hayes Boston. Score: In the Library of Congress and in photocopy format at the Center for Black Music Research, Columbia College, Chicago.

Sources

Carter, Madison H. An Annotated Catalogue of Composers of African Ancestry. New York: Vantage Press, 1986.

Scores at the Center for Black Music Research, Columbia College, Chicago.

SMITH, WILLIAM D. (n.d.)

Works

HAPPY LIFE MARCH (1901) - Piano or band or orchestra. Dedicated to Miss Lena Hill. Publisher: New York, Henry J. Wehman. Score: In the Library of Contress and in photocopy format at the Center for Black Music Research, Columbia College Chicago.

THE NEW CENTURY "NEGRO" MARCH - Piano or band or orchestra. Dedicated to the First Northern Colored Co-operative Banking Association of Philadelphia, PA. Publisher: Philadelphia Wm. D. Smith. Score: In the Library of Congress and in photocopy format at the Center for Black Music Research, Columbia College, Chicago.

Source

Scores at the Center for Black Music Research, Columbia College, Chicago.

SNAËR, SAMUEL (1832-1880?)

Samuel Snaër was born ca. 1832 in New Orleans and died sometime after 1880, also in New Orleans.
Little is known of his early life. He was highly regarded by his contemporaries as a pianist, violinist, and violoncellist. He conducted a music studio and was organist at St. Mary's Catholic Church in New Orleans. During the 1860s he directed the orchestra at the Theater D'Orleans.

His best known piece was the "Sous de fenetre."

Works

GRAZIELLA OVERTURE - Orchestra.

Sources

Southern, Eileen. Biographical Dictionary of Afro-American and African Musicians. Westport, CT: Greenwood Press, 1982.

Trotter, James M. Music and Some Highly Musical People. Chicago: Afro-Am Press, 1969. (reprint of 1878 ed.)

Wyatt, Lucius. "Composers Corner." CBMR Newsletter 9.1.

Wyatt, Lucius. "Updated Music List--Six Composers of Nineteenth-Century New Orleans." BMR Newsletter 9.1.

SOUTHALL, MITCHELL B. (1922-1989)

Mitchell B. Southall was born in Rochester, New York, in 1922.
He attended Langston University, the University of Iowa, and the Oklahoma College of Liberal Arts.
He conducted and performed jazz at night clubs and institutions and appeared as a classical pianist and guest conductor at concerts and choral festivals, and on radio and television broadcasts.
He served as theorist-conductor at Mississippi Valley State College.
His works include: Romance for Piano; Elf Dance; Impromptu; In Silet Night for mixed chorus; Piano Concerto; Intermezzo; De Lawd God A'mighty's On His Throne; Lady Be Good for male voices; and numerous spiritual arrangements for choral ensemble.

Works

ELF DANCE (1948) - Transcribed from the piano for symphony orchestra by the composer.

INTERMEZZO (1948) - Transcribed for string orchestra by the composer.

LOTUS LAND (1948) - Cyril Scott transcribed from the piano for symphony orchestra by Mitchell B. Southall.

Source

Information submitted by the composer.

STEWART, EARL LEWIS (1950 -)

Earl Stewart was born in Baton Rouge, Louisiana.
He received his formal music education at Southern University in Baton Rouge (B.S. 1973) and the University of Texas at Austin (M.M. in Composition 1976; D.M.A. in Composition 1981).

He has received numerous awards, including a study grant from the National Endowment of the Arts in 1975 and the Medal of Merit Award from the Junior Black Academy of the Arts in Dallas, Texas.

He has taught at the University of Texas at Austin and is presently Assistant Professor at the Berklee College of Music in Boston, Massachusetts. He is conductor of the Boston Orchestra and Chorale.

Works

AFRO FUGUES (1988-89) - Harp trio. Five fugues in African-derived styles: 1. Swing; 2. Afro-Latin; 3. Neo-New Orleans; 4 Calypso; 5. Ngoma.

AL-INKISHAFI - Choral/symphonic setting of an East African (Utenzi) poem. Oratoria for chorus, orchestra, English and Kiswahili narrators, mezzo-soprano soloist and ballet Premiere: 21 April 1984; University of Texas Performing Arts Center Grande Concert Hall; featuring Barbara Conrad of the Metropolitan Opera, actor Moses Gunn, Chuch Davis of the New York-based Chuch Davis Dance Company, the Southern University Chorus of Baton Rouge, and Maestro Sung Kwak and the Austin Symphony Orchestra.

AN APPROPRIATE TITLE (1974) - Concerto for soprano saxophone, three multiple percussionists, and multiple bassist. Premiere: February 1985; Second Annual Louisiana Composers Symposium, University of New Orleans; Jullian "Cannonball" Adderly; conducted by the composer

BLUES AND FUGUE (1989) - Orchestra.

EBONY SKETCHES (1989 90) - Orchestra.

GLIMPSES (1976; revised 1986) - Orchestra. NOTE: Master's thesis, a Neo-Classic Essay.

HOMAGE: TO DUKE, COUNT, JIMMY, TADD, AND THAD - Orchestra.

IDENTITY (1971; revised 1989) - Jazz orchestra, chorus, strings. Premiere: December 1971; Southern University Presidential Ball (without chorus).

IMPRINT OF JAMAICA (1986) (reggae essay) - Orchestra.

MCHANGANYIKO (SYMPHONY) (in progress) - Orchestra, chorus, and mezzo-soprano soloist.

OVERTURE OF PEACE (1978) - Symphonic poem. Orchestra.

SPIRITUALS (1987) - 1. "Deep River" for chorus and orchestra; premiered by the Community Music Center, Houston, Texas, 1987; 2. "Steal Away" for soprano soloist, chorus, and orchestra; premiered by the Boston Orchestra and Chorale.

UNDULATIONS (1986) (jazz ballad) - Flute or clarinet, harp, and strings.

VARIATIONS ON AN ORIGINAL LULLABY - Orchestra.

Source

Information submitted by the composer.

STILL, WILLIAM GRANT (1895-1978)

William Grant Still was born in Woodville, Mississippi, on May 11, 1895. He died in Los Angeles on December 3, 1978.

He began to play violin during high school in Little Rock Arkansas, where he was taught by Charlotte Andrews Stephens, and played in the University String Quartet when he attended Wilberforce College in Ohio (1911-14). He studied with Friedrich Lehmann and George Andrews at the Oberlin Conservatory of Music in Ohio (1917, 1919), and privately with Edgar Varese (1923-25) and George Whitefield Chadwick (1922), then director of the New England Conservatory of Music in Boston. Still was also strongly influenced by the example set by Samuel Coleridge-Taylor.

He received many honors during his long career including a Harmon Foundation Award (1928); fellowships from the Guggenheim Foundation (1934-35) and the Rosenwald Foundation; the Jubliee Prize of the Cincinnati Symphony (1944); a Freedom Foundation Award (1953); a prize from the U.S. Committee for the United Nations; and honorary doctorates from Howard University (1941), Oberlin (1947), Bates College (1954), University of Arkansas (1971), Pepperdine University (1973), the New England Conservatory of Music (1973), Peabody Conservatory (1974), and the University of Southern California at Los Angeles (1975).

Still was a prolific composer and arranger, beginning as early as 1916, when he began arranging for W. C. Handy in Oberlin (and made the first band arrangements of "Beale Street Blues" and "St. Louis Blues"). After a year of service with the Navy (1918), he moved to New York to work again for Handy, as performer, arranger, and road manager. In 1921, he became arranger and recording manager for Harry Pace's Phonograph Company (Black Swan recordings). During this time he wrote popular music, sometimes under the pseudonym Willy M. Grant.

During the 20s and 30s, he played in orchestras, including the pit orchestras for the Noble Sissle/Eubie Blake musical Shuffle Along (1921-23) and the musical Dixie to Broadway (1924, summer 1926). He also wrote arrangements for radio shows such as the "Old Gold Show" (1929) and the "Deep River Hour," and for individuals such as Earl Carroll, Artie Shaw, Donald Vorhees, and Sophie Tucker.

At the same time he was writing in the concert vein, and in 1926 the International Composers Guild sponsored a performance of his Levee Land, a three-movement work for orchestra and soloist Florence Mills. He produced three ballets--La Guiablesse (1927), Sahdji (1930), and Lenox Avenue (1937)- during this time, and his first symphony, the Afro-American, was performed on October 29, 1931, by the Rochester Philharmonic Orchestra. the first time in history that a major orchestra had played the full symphony of an African American composer. The 1949 performance of his first opera, Troubled Island (1941; libretto by Hughes), marked the first time a major company had performed the opera of an African American composer.

Still settled in Los Angeles in 1934, and began writing music for films, including Lost Horizon (1935), Pennies From Heaven (1936), and Stormy Weather (1943). Later he wrote for such television shows as "Gunsmoke" and the original "Perry Mason Show."

He was a prolific and versatile composer, among whose works are numbered 25 major works for symphony orchestra, 6 operas, 4 ballets, 8 works for voice and orchestra, 12 compositions for chamber groups, more than a dozen pieces for piano or accordion, and many songs. Among some of his best-known works, in addition to those noted above, are the suite A Deserted Plantation (1933); his second symphony Symphony in G Minor (1937); Old California (1941); In Memoriam: The Colored Soldiers Who Died for Democracy (1943), Festive Overture (1944), Danzas de Panama (1948), The Peaceful Land (1960). Among his compositions for voice and orchestra are And They Lynched Him on a Tree (1940, for black chorus, white chorus, narrator, and contralto; text by Katherine Garrison Chapin); Plainchant for America (1941; text by Chapin); and The Little Song That Wanted to be a Symphony (1954, for narrator, three female voices, and orchestra). Other works: From a Lost Continent (1948); Ennanga (harp concerto, 1956); From the Delta (1945) and Folk Suite for Band (1963) (band pieces); chamber compositions Suite for Violin and Piano (1943), Incantation and Dance (1945, oboe and piano), Pastorela (1946, violin and piano), Minatures (1948, flute, oboe, and piano); piano pieces Seven Traceries (1939) and Bells (1944); the song suite Songs of Separation (1949 using texts by Langston Hughes, Arna Bontemps Philippe-Thoby Marcelin, Paul Laurence Dunbar, and Countee Cullen); and the operas Highway I, USA (1962; libretto by Verna Arvey) and A Bayou Legend (1941; libretto by Arvey).

Works

AFRO-AMERICAN SYMPHONY (see SYMPHONY NO. 1)

THE AMERICAN SCENE (1957) - Orchestra. Suite cycle. Publisher: WGS Music.

AND THEY LYNCHED HIM ON A TREE (1940) - Narrator, contralto, two choruses, orchestra. Publisher: WGS Music.

ARCHAIC RITUAL SUITE (1946) - Orchestra. Publisher: WGS Music.

AUTOCHTHONOUS (see SYMPHONY NO. 4)

A BAYOU LEGEND (1941) - Opera. Manuscript.

BELLS (1944) - Orchestra. Suite. Publisher. MCA Music (miniature score available).

CHOREOGRAPHIC PRELUDE (1970) - Orchestra. Publisher: WGS Music.

COSTASO (1950) - Orchestra. Manuscript.

DANZAS DE PANAMA (1948) - String quartet or orchestra. Publisher: Southern Music Publishing Company. Recording: ORS7278.

DARKER AMERICA (1924) - Orchestra. Tone poem. Publisher: Carl Fischer, Inc. Recording: Turnabout 34546.

DISMAL SWAMP (1933) - Orchestra. Tone poem. Publisher: Theodore Presser Company.

ENNANGA (1956) - Harp, strings. piano. Publisher: WGS Music. Recording: Orion 7278.

FESTIVE OVERTURE (1944) - Orchestra. Publisher: WGS Music. Recording: CRI SD 259.

FOLK SUITE NO. 1 - Flute, piano, and string quartet. Publisher: Southern Music Publishing Co.

FOLK SUITE NO. 2 - Flute, clarinet, cello, piano. Publisher: Southern Music Publishing Co.

FOLK SUITE No. 4 - Flute, clarinet, cello, piano. Publisher: Southern Music Co.

FROM A LOST CONTINENT (1948) - Chorus and orchestra. Publisher: WGS Music.

FROM THE BLACK BELT (1926) - Orchestra. Suite. Publisher: Carl Fischer, Inc. Recording: Turnabout 35456.

HIGHWAY 1 USA (1962) - Vocal and Orchestra. Manuscript. Arias: "What does he know of dreams" and "You're wonderful, Mary." Recording: Columbia Records, Inc., Black Composers.

IN MEMORIAM: THE COLORED SOLDIERS WHO DIED FOR DEMOCRACY (1943) - Tone poem. Publisher: MCA Music (miniature score available).

KAINTUCK (1933) - Orchestra. Tone Poem.

LA GUIABLESSE (1927) - Ballet. Manuscript.

LENOX AVENUE (1937) - Ballet. Publisher: WGS Music.

LEVEE LAND (1925) - Soprano and orchestra. Manuscript.

THE LITTLE SONG THAT WANTED TO BE A SYMPHONY (1954) - Narrator, three female voices, orchestra. Publisher: Carl Fischer, Inc.

MINETTE FONTAINE (1958) - Opera. Manuscript.

MISS SALLY'S PARTY (1940) - Ballet   Manuscript.

MOTA (1951) - Opera. Manuscript.

OLD CALIFORNIA (1941) - Orchestra. Tone poem. Publisher: WGS Music.

PASTORELA (1946) - Violin and piano. Recording: ORS 7152.

PATTERNS (1960) - Orchestra. Suite. Publisher: WGS Music.

THE PEACEFUL LAND (1960) - Orchestra. Tone Poem. Publisher: American Music.

PLAIN-CHANT FOR AMERICA (1941) - Baritone, organ, orchestra; also arranged for chorus instead of baritone. Publisher: WGS Music.

POEM FOR ORCHESTRA (1944) - Publisher: MCA Music (miniature score available).

PRELUDES (1962) - Orchestra. Suite. Publisher: WGS Music. NOTE: This work has been transcribed for piano solo.

A PSALM FOR THE LIVING (1954) - Chorus and orchestra. Publisher: Bourne Company.

RHAPSODY (1955) - Soprano and orchestra. Manuscript.

SAHDJI (1930) - Choral ballet. Recording: Columbia Records, Inc., Black Composers Series, 1975.

SERENADE (1957) - Orchestra. Tone poem. Publisher: WGS Music.

A SONG A DUST (1936) - Orchestra. Tone poem.

SONG OF A CITY (1938) - Solo voice, chorus, orchestra. Manuscript. NOTE: Orchestral arrangement of the theme music for the 1939 New York World's Fair.

SUITE FOR VIOLIN AND PIANO (1943) - Publisher: MCA Music. Recording: Orion Records, ORS 7152.

THE SUNDAY SYMPHONY - See SYMPHONY NO. 3.

SYMPHONY NO. 1 (AFRO-AMERICAN SYMPHONY) (1930; revised 1969) - Orchestra. Duration: 24 minutes. Publisher: Novello and Company, 1970. Recordings: 1. New Records NRLP-105. ca. 1950; 2. American Musical Heritage MIA-118; 3. Black Composers Series, Vol. 2, Columbia M-32782 (1974).

SYMPHONY NO. 2 - Orchestra. Publisher: WGS Music.

SYMPHONY NO. 3 (THE SUNDAY SYMPHONY) (1958) - Orchestra. Duration: 25 minutes. Publisher: WGS Music. Recording: North Arkansas Symphony Orchestra Records (1984) (P. O. Box 1724, Fayetteville 72701).

SYMPHONY NO. 4 (AUTOCHTHONOUS)(1947) - Orchestra. Publisher: WGS Music.

SYMPHONY NO. 5 (WESTERN HEMISPHERE) (1945) - Orchestra. Publisher: WGS Music. NOTE: This symphony was originally THE THIRD SYMPHONY, but was later revised and renumbered.

THRENODY: IN MEMORY OF JAN SIBELIUS (1965) - Orchestra. Tone poem. Publisher: WGS Music.

TROUBLED ISLAND (1941) - Opera. Lyrics by Langston Hughes.

WESTERN HEMISPHERE - See SYMPHONY NO. 5.

WOODNOTES (1947) - Orchestra. Suite. Publisher: Southern Music Publishing Co.

Sources

Information submitted by Verney Arvey.

Cowell, Henry, ed. American Composers on American Music. New York: Frederick Unger Publishing Co., 1962, c. 1933.

De Lerma, Dominique-René. Black Music in Our Culture.   Kent, OH: Kent State University Press, 1970.

Haas, Robert Bartlett, ed. William Grant Still and the Fusion of Cultures in American Music. Los Angeles: Black Sparrow Press, 1972.

Southern, Eileen. Biographical Dictionary of Afro-American and African Musicians. Westport, CT: Greenwood Press, 1982.

Southern, Eileen. "Still, William Grant." In The New Grove Dictionary of American Music, Vol. 4, pp. 311-312.

Southern, Eileen. "Still, William Grant." In The New Grove Dictionary of Music and Musicians, Vol. 18, pp. 145-46.

STOKES, HARVEY (n.d.)

Harvey Stokes received his B.M. from East Carolina University, his M.M. from the University of Georgia, and his Ph.D. from Michigan State University.
He received the New England Conservatory of Music's New Works Competition, the Lancaster Summer Arts Festival Orchestral Composition, and the Jackie Robinson Foundation's Billy Taylor Music Merit Award.
He serves as a trustee of the Cincinnati Composer's Guild.
Stokes teaches at Miami University in Ohio.
Among his works are Values and Proposals Nos. 1, 2, and 3; Chamber Concerto No. 1, The Glory of Easter (song cycle), the oratorio The Second Act, and others.

Works

CHAMBER CONCERTO NO. 1 - Oboe and string quartet. Duration: 35 minutes. Publisher: Oxford, Ohio, Harkie-Coovey Music Co., 1988. Premiere: 25 April 1979, Greenville, North Carolina; David Hawkins, oboe; Paul Topper and Glen Davis, violins; Holly Hicks, viola; Daniel Mellado, cello.

THE GLORY OF EASTER - Soprano, tenor, piano, violin, violoncello, horn, and trumpet. Song cycle. Duration: 20 minutes

LYRIC SYMPHONY (1981), Opus 15 - Orchestra. Duration: 15 minutes. Premiere: 3 July 1983, Lancaster, Pennsylvania; Lancaster Symphony Orchestra, Steven Guzenhauser, Conductor.

A PSALM PRELUDE - Soprano, SATB, and orchestra. Publisher: Oxford, Ohio, Harkie-Coovey Music Co.

THE SECOND ACT - Oratorio. Soprano, tenor, baritone, bass, SATB, TTBB, orchestra, and brass septet. Duration: 30 minutes. Publisher: Oxford, Ohio, Harkie-Coovey Music Co.

SHORT SYMPHONY (1982), Opus 16 - Orchestra. Duration: 10 minutes.

Source

Information submitted by the composer.

SWANSON, HOWARD (1907-1978)

Howard Swanson was born August 18. 1907, in Atlanta. Georgia, and died November 12, 1978, in New York City.
As a child, Swanson won prizes in talent shows as a boy soprano. He began formal piano study at the age of 9. He studied with Ward Lewis and Herbert Elwell at the Cleveland Institute of Music (B. Mus., 1937), and with Nadia Boulanger at the American Academy in Fontainebleu, France (1938).
Honors he received include a Rosenwald Fellowship (1938), a Guggenheim Fellowship (1952), a National Academy of Arts and Letters Award (1952), and a William and Nona Copley Award (1958). His Short Symphony won the New York Critic's Circle Award as the best work performed during the 1950-51 concert season.
His songs first won distinction in the late 40s, particularly a 1949 Marian Anderson performance of "The Negro Speaks of Rivers" (Langston Hughes text) at Carnegie Hall. Other songs were recorded by such performers as Carl Stern, Eugene Haynes. and Elwood Peterson. Among his best known are "Montage" (text by Hughes), "Cahoots" (text by Carl Sandburg), "Death Song" (text by Paul Laurence Dunbar), "The Junk Man" (text by Sandburg), "In Time of Silver Rain" (text by Hughes), "Joy" (text by Hughes), and "Ghosts in Love" (text by Vachel Lindsay).
Other of his best known works are Night Music, Sound Piece for Brass Quintet (1952), Concerto for Orchestra (1954), and Concerto for Piano and Orchestra (1956); Piano Sonata No. 2 (1972); "The Cuckoo" for piano (1948); Fantasy Piece for saxophone and string orchestra (1969); Sonata for Violoncello and Piano (1973); Symphony No. 3 (1970); the song cycle Songs for Patricia (1951, texts by Norman Rosten); Trio for Flute, Oboe, and Piano (1976); and the anthem We Delighted, My Friend (1977, text by Leopold Senghor).

Works

CONCERTO FOR ORCHESTRA (1954) - Three movements. Duration: 19 minutes 30 seconds. Dedicated to Alma Morganthau. Commissioned by the Louisville Symphony. Publisher: Weintraub Music, 1970. Premiere: 1957; Louisville Symphony Orchestra. Robert Whitney, Conductor. Recording: Budapest Philharmonic Orchestra, Benjamin Steinberg, Conductor (Silhouettes in Courage SIL-K5001/5002: The Long Quest); tape of the premiere performance in the Amistad Research Center. NOTE: Tape recordings are deposited in the Howard Swanson Papers at the Amistad Research Center, Tulane University, New Orleans, Louisiana.

CONCERTO FOR PIANO AND ORCHESTRA (1956) - Commissioned by Humphry Noyes for Eugene Haynes. Manuscript.

DARLING, THOSE ARE BIRDS (1952) - Voice and strings. See SONGS FOR PATRICIA.

FANTASY PIECE FOR SOPRANO SAXOPHONE AND STRINGS (1969) - One movement. Duration: ca. 18-20 minutes. Commissioned by the Thorne Music Fund. Dedicated to Francis Thorne. Publisher: Weintraub Music, rental. NOTE: This work is listed in the Weintraub catalogue as FANTASY PIECE FOR CLARINET AND STRINGS.

GOODNIGHT (1952) - Voice and string orchestra. See SONGS FOR PATRICIA.

MUSIC FOR STRINGS (1952) - String orchestra. Duration: 12 minutes.
Publisher: Weintraub Music, rental. Premiere: 1952, Town Hall; the
Orchestra Society, Thomas Scherman, Conductor.

NIGHT MUSIC (1950) - Chamber orchestra Duration: 9 minutes. Publisher: Weintraub Music, rental Premiere: 1950; Locust Valley
Music Festival, Clara Roesch, Conductor. Recording: New York Ensemble of the Philharmonic Scholarship Winners, Dimitri Mitropoulos,
Conductor (Decca DL-8511; Decca DCM-Festival, Clara Roesch, Conductor).

NO LEAF MAY FALL (1952) - Voice and string orchestra. See SONGS FOR
PATRICIA.

NOCTURNE (1948) - Violin and piano. Duration: 3 minutes 20 seconds.
Publisher: Weintraub Music, 1951.

ONE DAY (1952) - Voice and string orchestra. See SONGS FOR PATRICIA.

SHORT SYMPHONY - Orchestra. Three movements. Duration: 11-12 minutes 30 seconds. Dedicated to Dimitri Mitropoulos. Publisher: Weintraub Music, rental. Premiere: 1950, Carnegie Hall; New York Philharmonic, Dimitri Mitropoulos, Conductor. Recordings: 1. Vienna
State Opera Orchestra, Franz Litschauer, Conductor (Composers Recordings, Inc. CRI SD-245);   2. American Recording Society Orchestra,
Dean Dixon, Conductor (American Recording Society ARS-116). NOTE:
This composition won the 1951 New York Critics Circle Award for the
best orchestral work of the 1950-51 season.

SONATA FOR VIOLONCELLO AND PIANO (1973) - Three movements. Duration:
20-25 minutes. Premiere: 1973, Alice Tully Hall, New York City;
Ronald Lipscomb, violoncello; Zita Carno, piano. Recording: Tape of
the premiere performance in the Amistad Research Center. NOTE: Tape
recordings are deposited in the Howard Swanson Papers at the Amistad
Research Center Tulane University, New Orleans, Louisiana.

SONGS FOR PATRICIA (1952) - Voice and string orchestra. Text by Nor-
man Rosten. Four songs: 1. Darling, Those are Birds; 2. No Leaf May
Fall; 3. One Day; 4. Goodnight. Duration: 6 minutes 25 seconds.
Publisher: Weintraub Music, rental.

SUITE FOR VIOLONCELLO AND PIANO (1949) - Four movements: 1. Prelude;
2. Pantomine; 3. Dirge; 4. Recessional. Duration: 13 minutes 45
seconds. Commissioned by and dedicated to Bernard Greenhouse. Publisher: Weintraub Music, 1951. Recording: Carl Stern, violoncello;
Abba Bogin, piano (Society of Participating Artists SPA-54).

SYMPHONY NO. 1 (1945) - Orchestra. Four movements. Duration: 25
minutes. Publisher: Weintraub Music rental. Premiere: 1969, Lincoln Center, New York City; Symphony of the New World, Benjamin Steinberg, Conductor. Recording: Tape of the premiere performance in the
Amistad Research Center. NOTE: Tape recordings are deposited in the
Howard Swanson Papers at the Amistad Research Center, Tulane University, New Orleans, Louisiana.

SYMPHONY NO. 2 (1948) - Orchestra. See SHORT SYMPHONY.

SYMPHONY NO. 3 (1970) - Orchestra. Three movements. Commissioned by the Symphony of the New World, Benjamin Steinberg, Conductor.

THRENODY FOR MARTIN LUTHER KING, JR. (1969) - String orchestra. Manuscript.

VISTA NO. II (1969) - String octet. Duration: 15 minutes. Dedicated to William and Barbara Holst. Commissioned by Gray College, State University of New York at Stony Brook. Manuscript. Weintraub Music, rental.

Sources

Baker, David N., Lida M. Belt, and Herman C. Hudson. The Black Composer Speaks. Metuchen, NJ: Scarecrow Press, 1978.

Baker, Theodore. Baker's Biographical Dictionary of Musicians, 5th ed. Completely revised by Nicholas Slonimsky. S.v. "Swanson, Howard."

Claghorn, Charles E. Biographical Dictionary of American Music. West Nyack, NY: Parker Publishing Company, 1973.

Reisser, Marsha J. "Howard Swanson: Distinguished Composer." The Black Perspective in Music 17.1, 2: 5-26.

Southern, Eileen. Biographical Dictionary of Afro-American and African Musicians. Westport, CT: Greenwood Press, 1982.

Southern, Eileen. "Swanson, Howard." In The New Grove Dictionary of American Music, Vol. 4, pp. 337.

Southern, Eileen. "Swanson, Howard." In The Grove's Dictionary of Music and Musicians, Vol. 18, pp. 396-97.

TAYLOR, WILLIAM ("BILLY") (1921 -)

William "Billy" Taylor was born in 1921.
He received his formal education at Virginia State (B.Mus. 1942) and the University of Massachusetts (D.M.E. 1975). His dissertation was The History and Development of Jazz Piano: A New Perspective for Educators.
He is the author of Jazz Piano: A Jazz History (1982) and has produced an educational filmstrip,, Listening to Jazz. He has also lectured on jazz performance and the music business at the University of D.C., Howard University, D.C. public schools, and New York schools, among others.
He received the New York Mayor's Award of Honor for Art and Culture. He has served as council member of the National Endowment and the Harlem Cultural Committee.
Among his works are ballet music for a musical, Your Arm's Too Short to Box with God; Suite for Jazz Piano and Orchestra; Bits of Bedlam; Cool and Caressing; A Live One; Muffle-Gruffle; Good Groove; and Cuban Caper.

Works

PEACEFUL WARRIOR - Jazz trio (piano, bass, drums), choir, and orchestra. Dedicated to Martin Luther King. Commissioned by the Atlanta
Symphony.

SUITE FOR JAZZ PIANO AND ORCHESTRA

YOUR ARM'S TOO SHORT TO BOX WITH GOD (Ballet music for the musical) -
Piano and orchestra.

Sources

Bennett, Bill. "Taylor, Billy (William)." In The New Grove Dictionary of Jazz, Vol. 2, p. 521.

Owens, Jimmy. "Billy Taylor: American Jazz Master." Jazz Educators
Journal 23.2 (Winter 1991): 31-33, 89, 95.

Roach, Hildred. Black American Music: Past and Present, Vol. II.
Miami: Krieger Publishing Co., 1985, pp. 19-20.

THOMAS, BLANCHE KATURAH (1885-1977)

Works

PLANTATION SONGS - In easy arrangement. Publisher: G. Schirmer,
Inc., 1937. Score in the Tacoma Public Library.

Source

Carter, Madison H.   An Annotated Catalogue of Composers of African
Ancestry. New York: Vantage Press, 1986.

TILLIS, FREDERICK CHARLES (1930 -)

Frederick Tillis was born in Galveston, Texas, on January 5, 1930.
Tillis began to study trumpet at the age of 7, and played trumpet and
saxophone during high school. He studied at Wiley College in Marshall,
Texas (B.A., 1949), North Texas State University (Denton; summers 1969 and
70), and at the University of Iowa (Iowa City; M.A., 1952; Ph.D., 1963).
He was director of the 356th Air Force Band; afterwards he went into
teaching, including tenures at Wiley College, Grambling College, Kentucky
State College-Frankfort, and University of Massachusetts-Amherst.
During the 1950s Tillis wrote primarily twelve-tone compositions;
later his style became more eclectic, drawing upon African American music,
African and Eastern idioms, and European styles.   Among his best known
works are Ring Shout Concerto, Spiritual Cycle, Freedom, and Metamorphosis
on a Scheme by J.S. Bach.

Works

AUTUMN CONCERTO FOR TRUMPET (1979) - Jazz orchestra. Duration: 10
minutes.

THE BLUE EXPRESS (1973) - Jazz orchestra. Duration: 5 minutes.

BLUE STONE DIFFERENCIA (1972) - Jazz orchestra. Duration: 5 minutes

CAPRICCIO FOR VIOLA AND PIANO (1960) - Duration: ca. 3 minutes 30 seconds. Publisher: New York, Composer Facsimile Edition.

CONCERTO FOR PIANO (1977) - Jazz orchestra. Duration: 19 minutes.

CONCERTO FOR PIANO (1979) - Jazz trio and symphony orchestra. Duration: ca. 20 minutes. Commissioned by Springfield Symphony Orchestra. Publisher: New York, Composer Facsimile Edition.

CONCERTO FOR TRIO PRO VIVA AND ORCHESTRA (1980) - Flute, violoncello, piano, and orchestra. Duration: 21 minutes 7 seconds. Commissioned by the Richmond (Virginia) Symphony Orchestra.

THE COTTON CURTAIN (1966) - Orchestra. Duration: 4 minutes 45 seconds. Publisher: New York, Composer Facsimile Edition. NOTE: Written for student orchestra.

DESIGNS FOR ORCHESTRA, NOS. 1 AND 2 (1963) - Duration: No. 1 ca. 7 minutes; No. 2 ca. 5 minutes 30 seconds. Publisher: New York, Composer Facsimile Edition.

ELEGY (1983) - Jazz orchestra. Duration: 5 minutes 6 seconds. Commissioned by the Howard University Jazz Ensemble.

FANTASY ON A THEME BY JULIAN ADDERLY (A Little Taste) (1975) - Jazz orchestra. Duration: 10 minutes.

INAUGURATION OVERTURE (1988) - Orchestra. Duration: ca. 6 minutes. Commissioned by Spellman College for the inauguration of Johnetta Betsch Cole.

IN MEMORY OF (1984) - Double quartet and trumpet, tenor saxophone, drum set, and string bass.

IN THE SPIRIT AND THE FLESH (1985) - Orchestra and mixed chorus. Duration: 20 minutes. Commissioned by the Atlanta Symphony Orchestra.

KCOR VARIATIONS (1977) - Jazz orchestra. Duration: 9 minutes 30 seconds.

MUSIC FOR ALTO FLUTE, CELLO, AND PIANO (1966) - Duration: ca. 3 minutes. Commissioned by Music Pro Viva. Publisher: Southern Music Co.

MUSIC FOR VIOLIN, CELLO, AND PIANO - Duration: 11 minutes. Publisher: New York, Composer Facsimile Edition.

NAYARAC (1974) - Jazz orchestra. Duration: ca. 6 minutes.

NIGER SYMPHONY (1975) - Chamber orchestra. Duration: 13 minutes. Comissioned by the Hartford (Connecticut) Chamber Symphony Orchestra. Publisher: New York, Composer Facsimile Edition.

NOBODY KNOWS (1986) - Double quartet (string quartet, trumpet, tenor saxophone, drum set, string bass). Duration: 8 minutes 8 seconds.

PHANTASY FOR VIOLA AND PIANO (1962) - Duration: 11 minutes. Publisher: Bryn Mawr, Pennsylvania, Theodore Presser Co.

QUARTET FOR FLUTE, CLARINET, BASSOON, AND CELLO (1952) - Duration: 8 minutes.

RING SHOUT CONCERTO FOR PERCUSSIONIST AND ORCHESTRA (1973-74) - Duration: 20 minutes. Publisher: New York, Composer Facsimile Edition.

SALUTE TO NELSON MANDELA - Chamber orchestra. Premiere: 17 March 1991, Fine Arts Auditorium Rosary College, River Forest, Illinois, and 19 march 1991, Orchestra Hall, Chicago, Illinois; Chicago Sinfonietta, Paul Freeman, conductor.

SATURN (1978) - Jazz orchestra.

SECRETS OF THE AFRICAN BAOBAB (VARIATIONS FOR JAZZ ORCHESTRA) (1976) - Modern dance/ballet. Duration: 10 minutes.

SEQUENCES AND BURLESQUE - String orchestra. Duration: 5 minutes 30 seconds. Publisher: New York, Composer Facsimile Edition. NOTE: Written for student ensemble.

SETON CONCERTO FOR TRUMPET (1973) - Jazz orchestra. Duration: 9 minutes. Comissioned by Richard Williams, New York.

SPIRITUAL CYCLE (1978) - Soprano and orchestra. Text by Robert Hayden. Contents: 1. On Lookout Mountain; 2. Lord Riot; 3. And All the Atoms Cry Aloud. Duration: 15 minutes. Commissioned by the Fine Arts Center, University of Massachusetts.

SPIRITUAL FANTASY NO. 2 FOR STRING BASS AND PIANO (1980) - Duration: 9 minutes 6 seconds. Publisher: New York, Composer Facsimile Edition.

SPIRITUAL FANTASY NO. 6 FOR TRUMPET AND SYMPHONY ORCHESTRA (1982) - Duration: 9 minutes.

SPIRITUAL FANTASY NO. 7 FOR CELLO AND PIANO (1983) - Duration: 9 minutes. Publisher: American Composers Alliance, 1984. Premiere: 1984; Washington, D.C.

SPIRITUAL FANTASY NO. 8 FOR VIOLIN, CELLO, AND PIANO (1987)

SPIRITUAL FANTASY NO. 12 (SUITE FOR STRING QUARTET) (1988) - Duration: 19 minutes 5 seconds.

SPIRITUAL FANTASY NO. 13 (1989) - Harp or piano. Duration: 8 minutes 5 seconds.

STRING TRIO (1961) - Duration: 4 minutes 45 seconds. Publisher: New York, Composer Facsimile Edition.

SYMPHONY IN THREE MOVEMENTS (NACIRFA NROH) (1969-70) -   Duration:
about 15 minutes.

THREE PLUS ONE (1969) - Violin, guitar, clarinet, and tape recorder.
Duration: 7 minutes 30 seconds. Publisher: New York, Composer Facsimile Edition.

THREE SHOWPIECES FOR VIOLA, UNACCOMPANIED (1966) - Duration: 4 minutes 30 seconds. Publisher: New York, Composer Facsimile Edition.

THREE SYMPHONIC SPIRITUALS (1978) - Orchestra. Duration: 11 minutes
6 seconds. Contents: 1. We Shall Overcome; 2. Deep River; 3. Swing
Low, Sweet Chariot. Commissioned by Columbia Records.

VARIANTS ON A THEME BY JOHN COLTRANE (NAIMA) (1979) - Jazz orchestra.
Duration: 6 minutes 30 seconds.

Sources

Information submitted by the composer.

Anderson, E. Ruth. Contemporary American Composers: A Biographical
Dictionary. Boston: G.K. Hall, 1976.

Claghorn, Charles Eugene. Biographical Dictionary of American Music.
West Nyack, NY: Parker, 1973.

Jacobi, William Hugh. Contemporary American Composers Based at American Colleges and Universities. Paradise, CA: Arts, 1975.

Moore, Carman. "Tillis, Frederick Charles." In The New Grove Dictionary of American Music, Vol. 4, pp. 394-95.

Southern, Eileen. Biographical Dictionary of Afro-American and African Composers. Westport, CT: Greenwood Press, 1982.

Tischler, Alice. fifteen Black American Composers: A Bibliography of
Their Works. Detroit Studies in Music Bibliography. Detroit: Information Coordinators, 1981.

TYLERS, WILLIAM H. (n.d.)

Works

THE CALL OF THE WOODS, Valse - Piano (arranged for orchestra or band
by the composer). Score in the Library of Congress and in photocopy
format at the Center for Black Music Research, Columbia College, Chicago.

MOCKINGBIRD RUBE, Characteristic March and Two - Piano or orchestra or
band. Publisher: New York, M. Witmark & Sons. Score in the Library
of Congress and in photocopy format at the Center for Black Music
Research, Columbia College, Chicago.

PANAMA, A Characteristic Novelty - Piano or band or orchestra. Publisher: New York, Leo Feist. Score in the Library of Congress and in

photocopy format at the Center for Black Music Research, Columbia College, Chicago.

Source

Scores at the Center for Black Music Research, Columbia College, Chicago.

WADE, MARCUS (n.d.)

Works

A MOORISH SONATA - Violin and piano.

Source

Carter, Madison H. An Annotated Catalogue of Composers of African Ancestry. New York: Vantage Press, 1986.

WALKER, CHARLES (n.d.)

Works

REQUIEM FOR BROTHER MARTIN (1968) - Chorus and orchestra. Commissioned by the Colgate Rochester Divinity School. Premiere: 15 January 1985; Franklin Plaza Hotel; M. Regina Black, choirmaster; Kermit Downes, Jr., instrumental coordinator.

Source

Wright, Josephine. "New Music." The Black Perspective in Music, 2.1 (Spring 1983): 198.

WALKER, GEORGE THEOPHILUS (1922 -)

George Theophilus Walker was born in Washington, D.C., June 27, 1922.
He began to study piano at the age of 5. Later he studied at the junior division of the Howard University School of Music, Oberlin Conservatory (B. Mus., 1941), the Curtis Institute in Philadelphia (artist diploma), the American Academy at Fontainbleau, France (artist diploma), and the Eastman School of Music in Rochester, New York (D. Mus., 1957). He studied under Rudolf Serkin, Rosario Scalero, Clifford Curzon, Robert Casadesus, Nadia Boulanger, William Primrose, Gregor Piatigorsky, and Gian-Carlo Menotti.
He won the Philadelphia Youth Auditions in 1941, and over the years received a Fulbright (1957), John Hay Whitney (1958), Bok Foundation grant for concerts in Europe (1963), Guggenheim (1969), MacDowell Colony (summers, 1966-69), Rockefeller (1971, 1974), the National Endowment for the Arts (1972, 1974), and the Hans Kindler Foundation (1975). He was the recipient of an Eastman School of Music Alumnus Citation (1961) and the Rhea A. Soslund Chamber Music Award (1967), and received grants from the American Music League and the Bennington Composers Conference.
After making his debut as a concert pianist at Town Hall in New York in 1945, Walker toured Europe and the United States during the 1950s.

He taught at Dillard University (New Orleans), the Dalcroze School of Music, the New School for Social Research, Smith College at Northampton, Massachusetts, University of Colorado-Denver, and Rutgers. He also served as guest professor at various institutes, including the Peabody Conservatory in Baltimore, Maryland, and the University of Delaware-Newark.

His first publication was Lament for Strings (later titled Lyric for Strings) in 1946. Among his best known works were Sonata for Cello and Piano; a blues song, "My luv is a red, red rose" (text by Burns); Spirituals for Orchestra; Address for Orchestra; Variations for Orchestra; Music for Brass--Sacred and Profane; and Trombone Concerto.

Works

ADDRESS FOR ORCHESTRA - Duration: 18 minutes.

ANTIFONYS FOR CHAMBER ORCHESTRA (ANTIFONYS FOR STRING ORCHESTRA) - Duration: 6 minutes

CANTATA FOR BOYS CHOIR, SOPRANO, TENOR, AND ORCHESTRA - Duration: 13 minutes.

CONCERTO FOR CELLO AND ORCHESTRA - Duration: 23 minutes.

CONCERTO FOR PIANO AND ORCHESTRA - Duration: 23 minutes.

CONCERTO FOR TROMBONE AND ORCHESTRA - Duration: 17 minutes.

CONCERTO FOR VIOLIN AND ORCHESTRA - Duration: 17 minutes.

DIALOGUE FOR CELLO AND ORCHESTRA - Duration: 13 minutes.

AN EASTMAN OVERTURE - Orchestra. Duration: 8 minutes.

IN PRAISE OF FOLLY (OVERTURE) - Duration: 8 minutes.

LYRIC FOR STRINGS - Duration: 6 minutes.

MASS FOR CHORUS AND SOLOIST AND ORCHESTRA - Duration: 23 minutes.

MUSIC FOR THREE - Piano trio. Duration: 7 minutes.

POEM FOR SOPRANO AND CHAMBER GROUP - Duration: 14 minutes.

SERENATA FOR CHAMBER ORCHESTRA - Duration: 13 minutes.

SINFONIA FOR ORCHESTRA (1984) - Duration: 10 minutes. Premiere: August 1984; Tanglewood, Massachusetts; Berkshire Music Festival Orchestra.

SONATA FOR CELLO AND PIANO - Duration: 15 minutes.

SONATA FOR VIOLA AND PIANO - Duration: 13 minutes.

SONATA FOR VIOLIN AND PIANO - Duration: 10 minutes.

SONATA NO. 2 FOR VIOLIN AND PIANO - Duration: 13 minutes.

STRING QUARTET NO. 2 - Duration: 15 minutes.

VARIATIONS FOR ORCHESTRA - Duration: 13 minutes.

Sources

Information submitted by the composer.

Abdul, Raoul. "George Walker's New Piece." In <u>Blacks in Classical Music</u>. New York: Dodd, Mead & Co., 1977, pp. 40-42.

De Lerma, Dominique-René. <u>Black Music in Our Culture</u>. Kent, OH: Kent State University Press, 1977, p. 180.

"George Theophilus Walker." <u>The Black Composer Speaks</u>. Ed. David N. Baker, Lida N. Belt, and Herman C. Hudson. Metuchen, NJ: Scarecrow Press, 1978, pp. 357-78.

Southern, Eileen. <u>Biographical Dictionary of Afro-American and African Musicians</u>. Westport, CT: Greenwood Press, 1982, p. 387.

Southern, Eileen. "Walker, George (Theophilus)." In <u>The New Grove Dictionary of American Music</u>, Vol. 4, p. 469.

Southern, Eileen. "Walker, George." In <u>The New Grove Dictionary of Music and Musicians</u>, Vol. 20, p. 173.

WESTON, HORACE (ca. 1825-1890)

Works

THE ALICE WESTON WALTZ - Banjo with piano accompaniment. Publisher: Philadelphia, S.S. Stewart, 1887. Score in the Library of Congress and in photocopy format at the Center for Black Music Research, Columbia College, Chicago.

THE BIRTHDAY PARTY WALTZ (1883) - 2 banjos. Publisher: Philadelphia, S.S. Stewart. Score in the Library of Congress and in photocopy format at the Center for Black Music Research, Columbia College, Chicago.

THE EGYPTIAN FANDANGO - Banjo. Publisher: Philadelphia, S.S. Stewart, 1882. Score in the Library of Congress and in photocopy format at the Center for Black Music Research, Columbia College, Chicago.

HORACE WESTON'S CELEBRATED POLKA - Banjo; 2 banjos. Arranged by John A. Lee. Publisher: Philadelphia, S.S. Stewart, 1887. Score in the Library of Congress and in photocopy format at the Center for Black Music Research, Columbia College, Chicago.

HORACE WESTON'S JIG - Banjo. Publisher: Philadelphia, S.S. Stewart. Score in the Library of Congress and in photocopy format at the Center for Black Music Research, Columbia College, Chicago.

HORACE WESTON'S NEW SCHOTTISCH - Banjo. Publisher: Philadelphia, S.S. Stewart, 1882. Score in the Library of Congress and in photocopy format at the Center for Black Music Research, Columbia College, Chicago.

HORACE WESTON'S OLD TIME JIG - Banjo. Publisher: Philadelphia, S.S. Stewart, 1883. Score in the Library of Congress and in photocopy format at the Center for Black Music Research, Columbia College, Chicago.

THE ROYAL SCHOTTISCHE - 2 banjos. Publisher: Philadelphia, S.S. Stewart. Score in the Library of Congress and in photocopy format at the Center for Black Music Research, Columbia College, Chicago.

THE SEEK NO FURTHER MARCH - Banjo. Publisher: Philadelphia, S.S. Stewart, 1883. Score in the Library of Congress and in photocopy format at the Center for Black Music Research, Columbia College, Chicago.

"SONG AND DANCE" MELODY - Banjo. Publisher: Philadelphia, S.S. Stewart, 1889. Score in the Library of Congress and in photocopy format at the Center for Black Music Research, Columbia College, Chicago.

WESTON'S GREAT MINOR JIG - Banjo. Publisher: Philadelphia, S.S. Stewart. Score in the Library of Congress and in photocopy format at the Center for Black Music Research, Columbia College, Chicago; S.S. Stewart Banjo and Guitar Journal, 2.2 (June 1883).

Source

Scores at the Center for Black Music Research, Columbia College, Chicago.

WHITE, ANDREW (NATHANIEL, III) (1942 -)

Andrew Nathaniel White was born in Washington, D.C. on September 6, 1942.
He began to study saxophone at the age of 12, and obtained his musical education at Tennessee A&I University (Nashville, 1958-60) and Howard University (B. Mus., 1964). He also studied at Dartmouth College, the Conservatoire in Paris, and the State University of New York at Buffalo.
He began playing professionally in 1960 and worked with various groups, including Kenny Clarke (1964-65 in Paris), Stanley Turrentine, and Stevie Wonder. He directed the John F. Kennedy Quintet from 1961 to 1964 and played in the Howard Theater house orchestra (1966-67); from 1968 to 1970 he played oboe and English horn with the American Ballet Theatre orchestra in New York. In 1970 he became bassist for the Fifth Dimension.
His honors include John Hay Whitney, Rockefeller, and Tanglewood fellowships.
He is the author of Hey Kid! Wanna Buy a Record? A Treatise on Self Production in the Music Business (Washington, 1982) and Andrew's X-rated Band Stories (Washington, 1984), and is the founder of Andrew's Music, a recording and publishing company.

Works

A JAZZ CONCERTO FOR ALTO SAXOPHONE AND SYMPHONY ORCHESTRA (1988) - Duration: 25 minutes. Publisher: Washington, D.C., Andrew's Musical Enterprises Inc., 1988. Premiere: 21 January 1989; Howard University, Washington, D.C.; Andrew White, Saxophone.

SHEPHERD SONG (1963) - Orchestra. Publisher: Washington, D.C., Andrew's Musican Enterprises, Inc.

Source

Information submitted by the composer.

WHITE, CLARENCE CAMERON (1880-1960)

Clarence Cameron White was born August 10, 1880, in Clarksville, Tennessee. He died in New York City on June 30, 1960.
He began to study music as a child in Oberlin, Ohio, and later studied violin under Joseph Douglas and Will Marion Cook in Washington, D.C. He attended Howard University (1894-95), the Oberlin Conservatory of Music in Ohio (1896-1901). He received an E. Azalia Hackley scholarship, enabling him to study in London during the summers of 1906 and 1908-10, where he studied composition with Samuel Coleridge-Taylor and violin with M. Zacharewitsch. Later he studied in Paris with Raoul Laparra (1930-32) and at Juilliard (summer 1940).
White was strongly influenced by Coleridge-Taylor. They corresponded while White was at Oberlin, and when Coleridge-Taylor visited the United States in 1904, White performed African Dances with Coleridge-Taylor at the piano. Later, he studied under Coleridge-Taylor in London and played in Coleridge-Taylor's String Players' Club. Another musical influence was a 1928 visit to Haiti.
White received a Harmon Foundation Award (1927), the Davis Bispham Medal for his opera Ouanga (1932), Rosenwald Fellowships (1930-32), the Benjamin Award for his orchestral Elegy (1954), and honorary degrees from Atlanta University (M.A., 1928) and Wilberforce University (D. Mus., 1933).
He was regarded as one of the leading African American violinists of the first two decades of the twentieth century and toured widely. However, he also taught, first in the public schools of Washington, D.C. (1902-05). There he helped Harriet Gibbs Marshall develop the program of her Washington Conservatory of Music; when it opened in 1903, he headed the strings department until 1907. Later he served as director of music at West Virginia State College at Institute (1924-30) and at Hampton Institute in Virginia (1932-35). He also taught for several summers at Pauline James Lee's Chicago University of Music.
He was one of the founders of the National Association of Negro Musicians in 1919, serving as its president from 1922-24, and as a member of the board of directors. In 1937-42 he organized community music programs for the National Recreational Association.
White also wrote, contributing articles to professional journals such as The Negro Music Journal (1902-03), Music and Poetry (1919-21), The Musical Observer, and The Etude.
Besides Ouanga, White's best known works include the violin compositions Bandanna Sketches (1919), Cabin Memories (1921), and From the Cotton Fields (1921); the ballet A Night in Sans Souci; the spiritual arrangements

Forty Negro Spirituals (1927) and Traditional Negro Spirituals (1940); Prelude, Dawn, Jublilee, Halleluja (1931, string quartet); Quatuor en do mineur (1931), Spiritual Suite (1956, for four clarinets), Fantasie (1954, violoncello), Legende d'Afrique (1955, commissioned and premiered by cellist Kermit Moore); and the orchestral works Piece for Strings and Timpanie, Kutamba Rhapsody (1942), Symphony in D Minor, Violin Concerto in G minor (1945), Concertino in D minor (1952), Dance Rhapsody (1955) and Poem (1955).

Works

BANDANA SKETCHES (1920) - Violin and piano. Publisher: New York, C. Fischer.

CABIN MEMORIES (1921) - Violin and piano.

CAPRICE, Opus 17, No. 2 - Violin and piano. Dedicated to Pauline Watson. Publisher: New York, Carl Fischer. Score in the Library of Congress and in photocopy format at the Center for Black Music Research, Columbia College, Chicago.

CHANT (NO-BODY KNOWS THE TROUBLE I'VE SEEN), Opus 12, No. 1 - Violin and piano. Publisher: New York, Carl Fischer. Score in the Library of Congress and in photocopy format at the Center for Black Music Research, Columbia College, Chicago.

CONCERTINO IN D MINOR (1952) - Orchestra.

CRADLE SONG - Violin and piano. Dedication: "To My Children, William and Clarence." Publisher: Boston, C.W. Thompson & Co. Score in the Library of Congress and in photocopy format at the Center for Black Music Research, Columbia College, Chicago.

DANCE RHAPSODY (1955) - Orchestra.

DIVERTIMENTO - Orchestra. Publisher: New York, Sam Fox.

ELEGY FOR ORCHESTRA

FANTASIE (1954) - Violoncello.

FROM THE COTTON FIELDS (1921), Opus 18 - Violin and piano. Publisher: New York, Carl Fischer. Score in the Library of Congress and in photocopy format at the Center for Black Music Research, Columbia College, Chicago.

HALLELUJAH (1931) - String quartet.

JUBILEE SONG - Violin and piano. Publisher: Philadelphia, Theodore Presser Co., 1924. Score in the Library of Congress and in photocopy format at the Center for Black Music Research, Columbia College, Chicago.

KUTAMBA RHAPSODY (1942) - Orchestra.

LEGENDE D'AFRIQUE (1955) - Violoncello. Commissioned and premiered by cellist Kermit Moore.

LEVEE DANCE, Opus 26, No. 2 - Violin and piano. Publisher: New York, Carl Fischer. Score in the Library of Congress and in photocopy format at the Center for Black Music Research, Columbia College, Chicago.

ON THE BAYOU, Opus 18, No. 2 - Violin and piano. Publisher: New York, Carl Fischer. Score in the Library of Congress and in photocopy format at the Center for Black Music Research, Columbia College, Chicago.

OUANGA (1932) - Opera. Premiere: 10 June 1949, South Bend, Indiana.

POEM (1955) - Orchestra.

PIECES FOR STRINGS AND TIMPANI - String orchestra.

SPIRITUAL, Opus 18, No. 3 - Violin and piano. Publisher: New York, Carl Fischer. Score in the Library of Congress and in photocopy format at the Center for Black Music Research, Columbia College, Chicago.

SUITE ON NEGRO THEMES - Orchestra. Publisher: New York, Sam Fox.

SYMPHONY IN D MINOR (1928) - Orchestra.

TUXEDO - Violin and piano. Dedication: "To Grandpa and Grandma." Publisher: Washington, D.C., Henry White. Score in the Library of Congress and in photocopy format at the Center for Black Music Research Columbia College, Chicago.

TWILIGHT, Opus 17, No. 1 - Violin and piano. Dedicated to Mayo Wadler. Publisher: New York, Carl Fischer. Score in the Library of Congress and in photocopy format at the Center for Black Music Research, Columbia College, Chicago.

VIOLIN CONCERTO NO. 2 - Violin and orchestra.

Sources

Anderson, E. Ruth. Contemporary American Composers: A Biographical Dictionary. Boston: G.K. Hall & Co., 1982, p. 552.

De Lerma, Dominique-René. Black Music in Our Culture. Kent OH: Kent State University Press, 1970.

Cuney-Hare Maud. Negro Musicians and Their Music. Washington: Associated Press, 1936.

Lemieux, Ramond. "White, Clarence Cameron." Dictionary of American Negro Biography. Ed. Rayford W. Logan and Michael R. Winston. New York: W.W. Norton, 1982, pp. 644-45.

Roach, Hildred. Black American Music: Past and Present, Vol. I. Miami: Krieger Publishing Co., 1985, pp. 98-99.

Scores at the Center for Black Music Research, Columbia College, Chicago.

Southern, Eileen. Biographical Dictionary of Afro-American and Afri-can Musicians. Westport, CT: Greenwood Press, 1982, pp. 398-400.

Southern, Eileen. "White, Clarence Cameron." In The New Grove Dic-tionary of American Music, Vol. 4, p. 515.

Southern, Eileen. "White, Clarence Cameron." In The New Grove Dic-tionary of Music and Musicians, Vol. 20, p. 382.

WHITE, JOSEPH (c. 1838-1890)

Joseph White was born around 1838 in New Orleans, and died in 1890.
He studied at the Paris Conservatory, and made a successful concert tour of the United States upon his return.

Works

VIOLIN CONCERTO (1867)

Source

Claghorn, Charles Eugene. Biographical Dictionary of American Music.
West Nyack, New York: Parker Publishing Co., 1973, p. 471.

WILLIAMS, JULIUS P. (1954 -)

Julius P. Williams was born in 1954 in New York City.
He was educated at the Hartt School of Music, Lehman College of the City University of New York, and the Aspen Music School.
He made his Carnegie Hall conducting debut in 1989 in the inaugural concerts of Symphony Saint Paulia. He has served as Assistant Conductor of the Brooklyn Philharmonic and the American Symphony under Lukas Foss, Artistic Director of the Festival of the Costa Del Sol in Spain, Conductor/Composer of the Connecticut Arts Awards on public television, and Conductor/Composer in Residence of the Nutmeg Ballet Company in Connecticut (which premiered his ballet Cinderella). He is currently Artistic Director of the New York State Summer School of the Arts School of Choral Studies and Visiting Associate Professor and Artist in Residence at the University of Vermont. During the 1989-90 season he appeared with the Dubrovnik Symphony at the Dubrovnik Festival in Yugoslavia in the performance of his opera Guenevere.
His Norman Overture was premiered by the New York Philharmonic under the baton of Zubin Mehta.   His numerous grants and awards include the distinguished alumnus award from Herbert H. Lehman College, an Honorary Distinguished Alumnus Award from Langston University, two major grants from the Astral Foundation, ASCAP Popular and Standard Awards (1979-80), Connecticut Commission on the Arts Grants, and the Key to the City of Dallas. He was profiled on CBS "Sunday Morning with Charles Kuralt" and "Nightwatch."

Works

CINDERELLA - Ballet. Premiere: Nutmeg Ballet Company in Connecticut.

GUINEVERE - Opera.

IN ROADS (1987) - Flute, oboe, and cello. Manuscript.

A NORMAN OVERTURE - Orchestra. Premiere: New York Philharmonic; Zubin Mehta, conductor.

TOCCATINA FOR STRING ORCHESTRA - Commissioned by the Camerata Youth Orchestra.

Source

Information submitted by the composer.

WILLIAMS, MARY LOU (1910-1981)

Mary Lou Williams (nee Mary Elfreida Scruggs) was born May 8, 1910, in Atlanta, Georgia. She died May 28, 1981, in Durham, North Carolina.
Her mother was a pianist, and Williams played piano as a child, play-ing for local social entertainments by the time she was 12. She obtained her musical education in the public schools of Pittsburgh and through private study. As a jazz pianist, she was influenced by Earl Hines and Art Tatum.
Among her honors are a Guggenheim Fellowship (1972) and honorary doc-torates from Fordham University, Manhattan College, and Loyola University.
She began to play professionally with bands on the vaudeville circuit, then with John Williams (1926-27), whom she married, and with Andy Kirk (1931-42). During the 30s she also arranged for jazz band-leaders Louis Armstrong, Tommy Dorsey, Earl Hines, Benny Goodman, and Glen Gray, among others. In 1942 she was co-leader of a group with her second husband, Harold ("Shorty") Baker. Thereafter she lead her own group, toured six months in 1943 with Duke Ellington as an arranger, then began performing in nightclubs as a soloist or with a trio.
Williams taught in the public schools of Pittsburgh, at the University of Massachusetts in Amherst (1975-77), and at Duke University (1977-81).
Among her best known works are the Zodiac Suite (performed by the New York Philharmonic in 1946), "Hymn in honor of St. Martin Porres" (1962), and "Mary Lou's Mass," which was adapted for ballet by the Alvin Ailey American Dance Theatre in 1971.

Works

ZODIAC SUITE - Orchestra. Premiere: 1946; New York Philharmonic.

Sources

Anderson, E. Ruth. Contemporary American Composers: A Biographical Dictionary. Boston: G.K. Hall & Co., 1982.

Feather, Leonard. The New Edition of the Encyclopedia of Jazz. New York: Horizon Press, 1960.

Southern, Eileen. Biographical Dictionary of Afro-American and Afri-can Musicians. Westport, CT: Greenwood Press, 1982, p. 406.

Roach, Hildred. Black American Music: Past and Present, Vol. II. Miami: Krieger Publishing Co., 1985, p. 88.

WILSON, OLLY WOODROW (1937 -)

    Olly Woodrow Wilson was born in St. Louis, Missouri, on September 7, 1937.
    He began to study piano at 8 and clarinet at 10. He played in the Sumner High School band under bandmaster Clarence Hayden Wilson. He studied with Earl Bates, Henry Lowe, and Robert Wykes at Washington University in St. Louis (B. Mus. 1959); at the University of Illinois-Urbana (M. Mus., 1960); with Robert Kelley and Phillip Bezanson at University of Iowa-Iowa City (Ph.D. 1964); and at the Studio for Experimental Music at the University of Illinois (1967). He was influenced by spirituals, gospel music, and blues, by the recordings of Bartok, Schoenberg, Stravinsky, Varese, Miles Davis, and Charlie Parker, and by playing with Oliver Nelson's jazz group. In 1971-72 and 1978 he studied African music in Ghana.
    He led a jazz group in high school. In college he played clarinet in the band then switched to string bass and played in the college chamber orchestra, the St. Louis Philharmonic, and the St. Louis Summer Players among others. In later years he played with the University of Illinois symphony orchestra and with the Cedar Rapids [Iowa] Symphony Orchestra.
    He taught at Florida A&M University (1960-62), the Oberlin Conservatory of Music (1965-70), and the University of California-Berkeley (1970-).
    His honors include Guggenheim fellowships (1971-72, 1977-78); awards from the National Academy of Arts and Letters (1974) and civic and professional organizations; and a prize for Cetus (for electronic tape) in 1968 in an international competition for electronic compositions sponsored by Dartmouth College.
    Among his best known works are Wry Fragments (1961) for tenor and percussions, "Chanson innocente" (1965) for contralto and two bassoons and "Soliloqy" for solo contrabass; Piece for Four (1966); SpiritSong (1973) for mezzo-soprano, women's chorus, orchestra with amplified instruemnts, and gospel chorus; and Sometimes (1976) for tenor and electronic tape, based on the spiritual "Sometimes I feel like a motherless child." Others are Black Martyrs (1972) for chorus and tape, written in memory of Martin Luther King Jr., Malcolm X, and Medgar Evers; Akwan (1972) for piano, electronic piano, and orchestra; The Eighteen Hands of Jerome Harris (1971), an electronic ballet work; Voices (1970) and Reflections (1978) for symphony orchestra; "Piano Piece" (1969); and Expansions (1979) for organ.

Works

    AKWAN (1972) - Piano/electric piano and orchestra. Duration: 16 minutes 35 seconds. Commissioned by Richard Bunger with a grant from the Martha Baird Rockefeller Foundation. Premiere: 1973; University of Claifornia (Berkeley) Orchestra. Michael Senturia, Conductor; Richard Bunger, piano. Recording: Richard Bunger, piano; Baltimore Symphony Orchestra, Paul Freeman, Conductor (Colubmia M-33434: Vol. 8, Black Composers series).

    EXPANSIONS II (1987-88) - Orchestra. Commissioned by the Koussevitsky Foundation. Premiere: 4-5 March 1988; University of California Symphony, Michael Senturia, Conductor.

    HOUSTON FANFARE (1986) - Orchestra. Commissioned by the Houston Symphony. Premiere: 25 October 1986.

    LUMINA (1981) - Orchestra. Commissioned by the American Composers Orchestra.

REFLECTIONS (1979) - Orchestra. Commissioned by the Oakland Youth Orchestra.

SINFONIA (1983-84) - Orchestra. Duration: 25 minutes. Commissioned by the Boston Symphony Orchestra. Premiere: 12 October 1984; Boston, Massachusetts; Boston Symphony Orchestra Seiji Ozawa, conductor. Recording: Boston Symphony Orchestra (1984).

SOLILOQUY (1962) - Bass viol.

SPIRIT SONG (1973) - Soprano, double chorus, and orchestra. Two movements.   Text adapted by the composer from traditional spirituals. Duration: 22 minutes. Commissioned by the Oakland Symphony Orchestra. Premiere: 1974; Oakland Symphony Orchestra, Castlemont High School Choir, and the Women's Voices of the Oakland Symphony Chorus; Harold Farberman, Conductor; Gwendolyn Lytle, soprano.

STRING QUARTET (1960) - Three movements. Duration: 20 minutes. Premiere: 1960; Graduate String Quartet of the University of Illinois.

STRUCTURE FOR ORCHESTRA (1960) - One movement.

THREE MOVEMENTS FOR ORCHESTRA (1964) - Duration: 22 minutes. Premiere: 1964, University of Iowa, Iowa City; University of Iowa Orchestra, James Dixon, Conductor.

TRILOGY FOR ORCHESTRA (1980) - Commissioned by the Oakland Symphony Orchestra.

TRIO FOR FLUTE, CELLO, AND PIANO (1959)

TRIO (1977) - Violin, violoncello, and piano. Commissioned by the San Francisco Chamber Music Society.

VIOLIN SONATA (1961) - Violin and piano. One movement. Premiere: 1961, the Contemporary Music Festival, Central State University, Wilberforce, Ohio; Elwin Adams, violin.

VOICES (1970) - Orchestra. Commissioned by the Boston Symphony Orchestra and the Fromm Foundation. Premiere: 1970; Tanglewood Festival Orchestra, Gunther Schuller, Conductor.

Sources

Information submitted by the composer.

Baker, David N., Lida M. Belt and Herman C. Hudson. The Black Composer Speaks. Metuchen, NJ: Scarecrow Press, 1978.

Brooks, Tilford. "A Historical Study of Black Music and Selected Twentieth Century Black Composers and Their Role in American Society." Ed.D. Dissertation, Washington University, 1972.

Claghorn, Charles E. Biographical Dictionary of American Music. West Nyack, NY: Parker Publishing Co., 1973.

De Lerma, Dominique-Rene, ed. Black Music in Our Culture: Curricular Ideas on the Subjects, Materials, and Problems. Kent, OH: Kent State University Press, 1970.

Southern, Eileen. Biographical Dictionary of Afro-American and African Musicians. Westport, CT: Greenwood Press, 1982.

Southern, Eileen. "Wilson, Olly." In The New Grove Dictionary of American Music, Vol. 4, p. 539.

Southern, Eileen. "Wilson, Olly." In The New Grove Dictionary of Music and Musicians, Vol. 20, p. 444.

WOODS, MICHAEL E. (1952 -)

Michael E. Woods was born February 4, 1952, in Akron, Ohio.
He received his B.A. in 1976 from the University of Akron and his M.M. from Berklee College of Music; he is working on a D.M.A. in composition at Oklahoma University.
He has received the Mary Miley Minority Grant (1988), Oklahoma State Regents Minority Grant (1988), and a National Endowment of the Arts Award (1978).
He has played bass with such artists as Lionel Hampton, Patti Page, Ramsey Lewis, and Dave Brubeck.
Among his 150 works are String Trio #1, String Quartet #1, Jazz Etudes for Viola and Bass, Psalm 93 and Quintet for Winds.

Works

ABRAHAM - Viola, clarinet, and flute. Duration: 3 minutes. Premiere: 1983, Oral Roberts University.

BLESS THE LORD - SATB, string orchestra. Duration: 6 minutes.

DOWNTOWN HEAVEN - Clarinet, bassoon, trumpet, trombone, percussion, violin, viola, electric bass. Duration: 6 minutes.

ENOCH - Viola, clarinet, flute. Duration: 3 minutes 30 seconds.

THE GATE IN THE EAST - Violin, oboe, and trombone. Duration: 3 minutes 30 seconds. Premiere: 1976, Akron University.

THE GATE IN THE SOUTH - Alto flute, violin, and clarinet. Duration: 3 minutes 50 seconds. Premiere: 1976, Akron University.

THE GATE IN THE WEST - Violin, viola. cello, and string bass. Duration: 4 minutes 30 seconds.

GOD'S CHOSEN MAN - SATB, rhythm section, string orchestra. Duration: 4 minutes. Commissioned by National Endowment of the Arts.

HIGHWAY 77 - Flute, clarinet, trombone, percussion, violin, viola, string bass. Duration: 8 minutes.

HOOPOSTOSIS - Violin, soprano saxophone, piano, bass, drums. Duration: 6 minutes. Premiere: 1984 Oral Roberts University.

JAZZ ETUDE FOR VIOLA AND BASS - Duration: 3 minutes 40 seconds.

JESUS ENTERS JERUSALEM - Flute, clarinet, bassoon, alto saxophone, trumpet, trombone, percussion, violin, viola, cello, string bass, guitar. Duration: 6 minutes 30 seconds.

THE JUDGEMENT HALL - Clarinet, bassoon, trumpet, trombone, percussion, violin, viola electric bass. Duration: 7 minutes. Premiere: 1985, Oral Roberts University.

NICODEMUS - Viola, clarinet, and flute. Duration: 4 minutes. Premiere: 1983, Oral Roberts University.

PROTEST - Tenor voice, SATB, rhythm section, string orchestra. Duration: 4 minutes. Commissioned by and dedicated to the National Endowment of the Arts.

PSALM #3 - Solo viola. Duration: 3 minutes 30 seconds. Premiere: 1978, Indiana University.

PSALM #4 - Solo violin. Duration: 4 minutes. Commissioned by Paul Bliss.

PSALM #5 - Solo violin. Duration: 3 minutes 30 seconds. Premiere: 1978, Indiana University.

PSALM #6 - Solo cello. Duration: 4 minutes. Premiere: 1978, Indiana University.

PSALM #23 - Soprano voice, electric bass, classical guitar, flute, violin viola, cello. Duration: 5 minutes. Premiere: 1981, Oral Roberts University.

PSALM #39 - Solo string bass, piano. Duration: 4 minuets. Premiere: 1976, Akron University.

PSALM #91 - Violin and viola. Duration: 4 minutes. Premiere: 1988, Oral Roberts University.

PSALM #92 - Violin and viola. Duration: 4 minutes. Premiere: 1988, Oral Roberts University.

PSALM #93 - Violin and viola. Duration: 6 minutes. Premiere: 1988, Oklahoma University.

PSALM #116 - SATB, string orchestra. Duration: 6 minutes 30 seconds.

PSALM #125 - SATB, classical guitar, electric bass, flute, violin, viola, cello. Premiere: 1976, Akron University.

QUESTION 85 - 2 violins, viola, cello. Duration: 9 minutes. Dedicated to questions on current events. Premiere: 1986, Oral Roberts University.

THE SAINTS CLUB - Clarinet, bassoon, trumpet, trombone, piano, percussion, violin, viola, electric bass. Duration: 6 minutes 30 seconds.

THE SERMON ON THE MOUNT - SATB, flute, classical guitar, violin, viola, cello, electric bass. Duration: 4 minutes.

STRING QUARTET NO. 1 - 2 violins, viola, cello. Duration: 12 minutes.

STRING SERENADE - String orchestra. Duration: 7 minutes. Dedicated to flood victims. Premiere: 1987, Oral Roberts University.

STRING TRIO NO. 1 - violin, viola, cello. Duration: 11 minutes 30 seconds.

STAND STILL - SATB, rhythm section, string orchestra. Duration: 4 minutes.

UNTO THY NAME BE GLORY - SATB, string orchestra. Duration: 7 minutes. Premiere: 1984, Oral Roberts Universitiy

WHAT SHALL I TELL MY CHILDREN WHO ARE BLACK - Clarinet, violin, string bass, spoken voice. Duration: 5 minutes. Commissioned by and dedicated to: Margaret Burroughs. Premiere: 1974, Akron University.

Sources

Information submitted by the composer.

Holly, Ellistine Perkins. Biographies of Black Composers and Songwriters. Dubuque, IA: Wm. C. Brown Publishers, 1990, pp. 48-49.

WORK, FREDERICK JEROME (1879-1942)

Frederick Jerome Work was born 1879 in Nashville, Tennessee, and died January 24, 1942, in Bordentown, New Jersey.

From a musical family (see also John Wesley Work III, and Julian C. Work), he obtained his musical education at Fisk University in Nashville, where he sang with the Fisk Jubilee Singers; at Columbia University Teachers College; and at Temple University.

He taught at Prairie View State College in Texas; in the public schools of Kansas City, Missouri; and at the New Jersey Manual Training School in Bordentown, where he was music director (1922-42).

He wrote and arranged for his school choir and composed instrumental work, of which the best known is Negro Suite (1936), but he was most noted for his spiritual arrangements and folksong collecting. Beginning in 1901 he and his brother John Wesley II published several collections of folksong arrangements; the first titled New Jubilee Songs as Sung by the Fisk Jubilee Singers.

Works

NEGRO SUITE (1936)

STRING QUARTET IN F

Sources

Roach, Hildred. Black American Music: Past and Present, Vol. II.
Miami: Krieger Publishing Co., 1985, p. 106.

Southern, Eileen. Biographical Dictionary of Afro-American and African Musicians. Westport, CT: Greenwood Press, 1982, pp. 413-14.

WORK, JOHN WESLEY, III (1901-1967)

John Wesley Work III was born June 14, 1901, in Tullahoma, Tennessee,
and died May 17, 1967, in Nashville.

He came from a family of musicians (see also John Wesley Work II,
Fredrick Jerome Work, and Julian C. Work), and received his musical training at the Fisk University laboratory school, Fisk High School, and Fisk
University (B.A., 1923). He also attended the Institute of Musical Art
(now Juilliard) in New York (1923-34), where he studied with Gardner Lamson; Columbia University Teachers College (M.A., 1930), where he sudied
with Howard Talley and Samuel Gardner; and Yale University (B.Mus., 1933),
where he studied with David Stanley Smith. He also studied voice privately
with Lamson (1924-27).

He taught at Fisk from 1927 through 1966, serving as director of choral groups, teacher, lecturer, and department chairman. He published articles in professional journals, including "Plantation Meistersingers" in
The Musical Quarterly (January 1940) and "Changing Patterns in Negro Folksongs" in Journal of American Folklore (October 1940). He also published
American Negro Songs and Spirituals (1940).

Honors include Julius Rosenwald fellowships (1931, 1932), first prize
in the 1946 competition of the Federation of American Composers for his
cantata The Singers, an award from the National Association of Negro Musicians (1947), and an honorary doctorate from Fisk University (1963).

Among his best known compositions are Yenvalou (1946), which used
Haitian themes; piano works Sassafras (1946), Scuppernong (1951), and Appa-
lachia (1954); the organ suite From the Deep South (1936); and the song
cycle Isaac Watts Contemplates the Cross (1962).

Works

NOCTURNE - Violin and piano. Three pieces.

TALIAFERO - Orchestra. Concert overture.

YENVALOU (1946) - Orchestra. NOTE: Uses Haitian themes.

Sources

De Lerma, Dominique-René. Black Music in Our Culture. Kent, OH:
Kent State University Press, 1973.

Roach, Hildred. Black American Music: Past and Present, Vol. I.
Miami: Krieger Publishing Co., 1982, p. 107-110.

Southern, Eileen. Biographical Dictionary of Afro-American and African Composers. Westport, CT: Greenwood Press, 1982, pp. 414-15.

WORK, JULIAN C. (1910 -)

Julian C. Work was born September 25, 1910, in Nashville, Tennessee.
From a musical family (see also John Wesley Work III, Frederick Jerome Work), he studied music with local teacher Mary E. Chamberlain and at Fisk University.
Among his best-known works are "Myriorama at Midnight" (performed in 1948 by the Los Angeles Philharmonic); Portraits from the Bible (1956); "Processional Hymn" (1957); "Autumn Walk (1957); "Driftwood Patterns" (1961); and "Stand the Storm" (1963).

Works

MYRIORAMA AT MIDNIGHT - Orchestra.

REQUIEM FOR TWO - Orchestra. Duration: 20 minutes 30 seconds.

Sources

Information submitted by the composer.

Roach, Hildred. Black American Music: Past and Present, Vol. II. Miami: Krieger Publishing Co., 1985, pp. 111-12.

Southern, Eileen. Biographical Dictionary of Afro-American and African Musicians. Westport, CT: Greenwood Press, 1982, p. 415.

Afro-European Composers

ALDRIDGE, AMANDA (1866-1956)

Works

THREE AFRICAN DANCES - Orchestra. Contents: 1. The Call to the Feast; 2. Luleta's Dance; 3. Dance of the Warriors. Publisher: London, Chappell, 1913, 8 pp. #23490. Piano-Conductor score and 12 parts. Score: Center for Black Music Research, Schomburg and Spingarn.

Source

De Lerma, Dominique-René. "Black Composers in Europe." Black Music Research Journal 10.2 (Fall 1990): 275-334.

BRIDGETOWER (BRIDGTOWER), GEORGE AUGUSTUS POLGREEN (1779? - 1860)

George Augustus Polgreen Bridgetower was born in Biala, Poland, about 1779, and died in London, February 29, 1860.

He made his debut as a violinist at the Concert Spirituel in Paris at the age of nine. His solo interpolations between the parts of Messiah at Drury Lane Theatre attracted the notice of the Prince of Wales (later King George IV), who took him under his patronage and had him taught the violin (by Barthelemon and Jarnowick) and composition (by Attwood).

He met Beethoven in Vienna in the spring of 1803, and the two performed Beethoven's three-movement Sonata in A for violin and piano in the Augarten on May 24.

Bridgetower returned to England and received his MusB from Cambridge in 1811, and played with the Philharmonic Society during its first season.

Works

MINUETS - Violin, mandolin, German flute, harpsichord.

SONATA MULATTICA - Violin and piano. Manuscript lost.

SYMPHONY - NOTE: Possibly spurious.

VIOLIN CONCERTO - Score: British museum.

Sources

"Bridgetower, George Augustus Polgreen." In The Dictionary of National Biography, Vol. 2. London: Oxford University Press, 1917, pp. 1231-32.

De Lerma. Dominique-René. "Black Composers in Europe." Black Music Research Journal 10.2 (Fall 1990): 275-334.

Groves, George. "Bridgetower, George (Augustus) Polgreen." In The New Grove Dictionary of Music and Musicians, Vol. 3, pp. 281-82.

Hare, Maud Cuney. Negro Musicians and Their Music. Washington: Associated Publishers, Inc., 1936, pp. 297-303.

Roach, Hildred. Black American Music: Past and Present, Vol. II. Miami: Krieger Publishing Company, 1985, p. 142.

Robinson, Wilhelmena S. Historical Afro-American Biographies (International Library of Afro-American Life and History). Washington, D.C.: Associated Publishers, 1976, pp. 55-56.

Scobie, Edward. Black Brittania: A History of Blacks in Britain. Chicago: Johnson Publishing Company, 1972, pp. 110-14.

Southern, Eileen. Biographical Dictionary of Afro-American and African Musicians. Westport, CT: Greenwood Press, 1982, pp. 47-48.

Wright, J.R.B. "George Polgreen Bridgetower: An African Prodigy in England 1788-1799." Musical Quarterly (January 1980): 65-82.

COLERIDGE-TAYLOR, AVRIL GWENDOLEN (1903 -)

Works

WYNDON - Chorus and orchestra. Publisher: London, J.W. Chester, 1936.

Source

De Lerma, Dominique-Rene. Black Concert and Recital Music: Provisional List. Bloomington, IN: Afro-American Music Opportunities, 1975.

COLERIDGE-TAYLOR, SAMUEL (1875-1912)

Samuel Coleridge-Taylor was born August 15, 1875, near London, England, and died September 1, 1912, in Croydon, England.

He began to study violin at the age of 5 and was a boy soprano in church choirs. He received his musical training at the Royal College of Music in London. Later, his interest in Negro folk music was stimulated by Paul Laurence Dunbar, whom he met in 1897 and with whom he gave a series of joint recitals, and by Frederick J. Loudin's Fisk Jubilee Singers.

He received a commission in 1898 from the Committee of the Three Choirs Festival at Gloucester, resulting in "Ballade in A minor."

He published his first composition, "In Thee, O Lord," when he was 16. His best-known works include the cantata Hiawatha's Wedding Feast, The Death of Minnehaha and Hiawatha's Departure (text from Longfellow's The Song of Hiawatha). Other compositions include Twenty-Four Negro Melodies Transcribed for Piano and Symphonic Variations on a African Air (based on the spiritual "I'm troubled in mind"); African Suite, The Atonement, Kubla Khan, and The Bamboula.

Coleridge-Taylor taught at the Croydon Conservatory, and part-time at the Crystal Palace School of Art and Music in South London and at the Guildhall School. He served as director of the Croydon Conservatory Orchestral Society, and from 1903 until his death he was professor of Music at Trinity College of Music in London.

Works

THE ATONEMENT (1902-03) - Opus 53. Sacred cantata for soprano, mezzo soprano, contralto, baritone and tenor soli, chorus and orchestra. Text by Alice Parsons. Five sections: 1. Prelude; 2. Gethsemane; 3. Prayer of the Holy Women and Apostles; 4. Pontius Pilate; 5. Calvary. Publisher: Novello, 1903. Premiere: 9 December 1903; Hereford Musical Festival, England.

BALLAD IN A MINOR (1898) - Opus 33. Orchestra. Duration: 15 minutes. Commissioned by the Committee of the Three Choirs Festival (1898) upon recommendation of Sir Edward Elgar. Dedicated to August J. Jaeger, musical advisor to the firm of Novello and Musical Times critic. Publisher: Novello, 1898. Premiere: 13 September 1898; Three Choirs Festival. Gloucester, England; Samuel Coleridge-Taylor, Conductor.

BALLAD IN C MINOR (1907) - Opus 73. Violin and piano. Five movements: 1. Molto moderato; 2. Allegro; 3. Pio andante e tranquillo; 4. Allegro vivace; 5. L'istesso tempo. Publisher: Augner, 1909. Premiere: 29 October 1907; Leeds England; Zacharewitsch. violinist; Coleridge-Taylor, piano.

BALLAD IN D MINOR (1895) - Opus 4. Violin and orchestra. Dedication: "To my friend Ruth Howell." Publisher: Novello, 1895.

THE BAMBOULA (A RHAPSODIC DANCE) (1910) - Opus 75. Orchestra. Duration: 9 minutes. Dedicated to Mr. and Mrs. Carl Stoeckel. Premiere: 1911; Norfolk Musical Festival, England.

THE BLIND GIRL OF CASTEL-CUILLE (1900-01) - Opus 43. Cantata for soprano and baritone soli, chorus and orchestra. Dedicated to Nicholas Kilburn. Esq. Publisher: Novello, 1901; revised edition by composer, 1902. Premiere: 9 October 1910; Leeds Musical Festival; Coleridge-Taylor, Conductor; Mme. Albani and Andrew Black. solists.

BON-BON SUITE (1908) - Opus 68. Cantata for baritone solo, chorus and orchestra. Six movements: 1. The Magic Mirror; 2. The Fairy Boat; 3. To Rosa; 4. Love and Hymen; 5. The Watchman; 6. Say What Shall We Dance. Dedication: "To Miss Sunshine (Doris)." Publisher: Novello, 1908. Premiere: 13 January 1909; Brighton Musical Festival, England; Coleridge-Taylor, Conductor; Henry Julien, soloist.

CONCERTO IN G MINOR (1911) - Opus 80. Violin and orchestra. Dedicated to Maud Powell, the American violinist. Publisher: Metzler,
1912. Premiere: 1911; Norfolk [Connecticut] Musical Festival. Editor: William I. Rend.

THE DEATH OF MINEHAHA (1899) - Opus 30. Cantata for soprano and baritone soli, chorus and orchestra. Duration: 40 minutes. Publisher:
Novello, 1898. Premiere: 26 October 1899; North Staffordshire Musical Festival, Hanley, England.

DREAM LOVERS (1898) - Opus 25. Operatic romance. Two male and two
female characters, chorus, and orchestra. Libretto by Paul Lawrence
Dunbar. Publisher: Boosey, 1898. Premiere: 18 December, 1898; Public Hall, Croydon, England.

ENDYMION'S DREAM (1909) - Opus 65. Opera in one act for soprano and
tenor soli, chorus, and orchestra. Text by C.R.B Barrett, based on
the work by John Keats. Publisher: Novello, 1910. Premiere: 4
February 1910; Brighton Music Festival, England.

ETHIOPIA SALUTING THE COLOURS (1902) - Opus 51. Orchestra. Dedicated
to the Treble Clef Club Washington, D.C. Publisher: Augener, 1902.
Premiere: Croydon Orchestral Society, Coleridge-Taylor, conductor.

FANTASIESTUCKE (1895) - Opus 5. String quartet. Five movements:
1. Prelude in E Minor (Allegro ma no troppo); 2. Serenade in G Major
(Andante molto); 3. Humoresque in A Minor (Presto); 4. Minuet and Trio
in G Major (Allegro moderato); 5. Dance in G Major (Vivace). Publisher: Augener, 1921. Premiere: 13 March 1895; Royal College of Music,
London, England.

FOUR AFRICAN DANCES (1902) - Opus 58. Violin and piano. Four move-
ments: 1. G Minor; 2. F Major; 3. A Major; 4. D Minor. Publisher:
Augener, 1904. Premiere: 1902; Rochester Choral Society, England;
Goldie Baker, violinist; Samuel Coleridge-Taylor, pianist.

FOUR CHARACTERISTIC WALTZES (1898) - Opus 22. Orchestra. Four movements: 1. Valse Bohemienne (Allegre ma non troppo); 2. Valse Rustique
(Tempo di valse); 3. Valse de la Reine (Andante con sentimento); 4.
Valse Mauresque (Furioso). Duration: 13 minutes. Publisher: Novello, 1899. Premiere: 16 December 1898; Public Hall, Croyden, England.

FOUR NOVELLETTEN (1902) - Opus 52   String orchestra. Four movements:
1. A Major; 2. C Major; 3. A Minor; 4. D Major. Duration: 21 minutes. Publisher: Novello, 1903.

FIVE CHORAL BALLADS (1904) - Opus 54. Baritone solo, chorus (SATB),
and orchestra. Five movements. Publisher: Breitkopf, 1904-5. Premiere: 25 October, 1905; Norwich Musical Festival. NOTE: Written
for and first performed in the United States by the Samuel Coleridge-
Taylor Choral Society in Washington.

GIPSY SUITE (1898) - Opus 20   Violin and piano. Four movements:
1. Lament and Tambourine; 2. A Gipsy Song; 3. A Gipsy Dance; 4. Waltz.
Publisher: Augener, 1898.

HEMO DANCE (1900) - Opus 47, No. 2. Orchestra. Duration: 7 minutes.
Publisher: Novello, 1900.

HIAWATHAN SKETCHES (1896) - Opus 16. Violin and piano. Three move-
ments: 1. A Tale; 2. A Song; 3. A Dance. Publisher: Augener 1908.
Premiere: 1896; the Salle Erard; joint concert with Paul Laurence
Dunbar.

HIAWATHA'S DEPARTURE (1899-1900) - Opus 30, No. 4. Cantata for soprano, tenor, and baritone soli chorus. and orchestra. Duration: 40
minutes. Publisher: Novello, 1900. Premiere: 22 February 1900;
Royal Choral Society, Royal Albert Hall England.

HIAWATHA'S WEDDING FEAST - Opus 30, No. 1. Cantata for tenor solo,
chorus, and orchestra. Duration: 32 minutes. Publisher: Novello,
1898. Premiere: 11 November 1898; Royal College of Music, England.
Recording: Royal Choral Society and Philharmonic Orchestra, Sir Malcolm Sargent, Conductor, Richard Lewis, Tenor (EMI-ASD 467, British
release); "Onaway! Awake Beloved", London Symphony, Paul Freeman,
Conductor, William Brown, tenor (Columbia Records Black Composers
series, COL M32782).

IDYLL (1901) - Opus 44. Orchestra. Duration: 5 minutes. Publisher:
Novelle, 1901. Premiere: 11 September 1901; Gloucester Musical Festival, England.

I'M TROUBLE IN MIND - Duration: 5 minutes 30 seconds.

INCIDENTAL MUSIC TO FAUST (1908) - Opus 70. Written and published for
piano in 1908 and for orchestra in 1909. Includes: 1. Dance of
Witches (Brocken Scene); 2. Four Visions--Helen; 3. Cleopatra; 4.
Messalina; 5. Margaret; 6. Dance and chant (Devil's Kitchen Scene).
Duration: 15 minutes. Publisher: Boosey.

INCIDENTAL MUSIC TO HEROD (1900) - Opus 47, No. 1. Orchestra. Commissioned by Beerbohm Tree. Publisher: Augener, 1901. NOTE: First
of five commissions by Beerbohn Tree for his London productions.

INCIDENTAL MUSIC TO THE MUSIC TO THE FOREST OF THE WILD THEME (1910-
1911) - Opus 74. Female voice and orchestra. Commissioned by Beerbohm Tree for a poetical fairy tale by Alfred Noyes. Publisher:
Boosey, 1911. NOTE: Play never performed.

INCIDENTAL MUSIC TO NERO (1906) - Opus 62. Orchestra. Text by
Stephen Phillips. Duration: 24 minutes. Dedicated to Beerbohm Tree.
Publisher: Novello, 1907. Premiere: 1906; Beerbohm Tree Production,
His Majesty's Theatre, London, England.

INCIDENTAL MUSIC TO OTHELLO (1911) - Opus 79. Orchestra. Based on
play by Shakespeare. Duration: 11 minutes 30 seconds. Dudicated to
Phyllis Neilson-Terry. Publisher: Metzler, 1911. Premiere: Her
Majesty's Theatre.

INCIDENTAL MUSIC TO ULYSSES (1901) - Opus 49. Orchestra, three vocal
sections, women's chorus. Published: Novello, 1902.

LEGEND FROM THE CONCERSTUCK (1893) - Opus 14. Violin and orchestra.
Dedicated to Miss Marie Motto. Publisher: Augener, 1897 and 1908.
NOTE: Coleridge-Taylor and his wife-to-be, Jessie S. Fleetwood
Walmisley, met for the first time when she accompanied the violinist
at the piano during a private family gathering when this composition
was performed.

A LOVELY LITTLE DREAM   - Strings and harmonium. In Volume II of "De
Groot and the Picadilly Orchestra series. Publisher: Metzler.

MEG BLANE (1902) - Opus 48. Mezzo-soprano solo, chorus, and orchestra. Publisher: Novello, 1902. Premiere: 3 October 1902; Sheffield
Musical Festival; Henry Wood, Conductor.

NONET IN F MINOR (1894) - Opus 2. Piano, violin, viola, violoncello,
double bass, clarinet, horn, and bassoon. Manuscript. Premiere: 5
July 1895; Royal College of Music, England. NOTE: Student work.

OVERTURE TO THE SONG OF HIAWATHA (1899) - Opus 30, No. 3. Orchestra.
Publisher: Novello, 1899. Premiere: 6 December 1899; Norwich Musi-
cal Festival. NOTE: Taylor used the Afro-American spiritual "Nobody
Knows the Trouble I see."

PETITE SUITE DE CONCERT (1911) - Opus 77. Orchestra. Four movements:
1. Le Caprice de Nanette (Allegro con brio); 2. Demande et Reponse
(Andante); 3. Un Sonnet d'Amour (Allegretto); 4. La Tarantelle Fretil-
lante (Vivace). Duration: 14 minutes 30 seconds. Publisher: Hawkes
(1911).

QUARTET IN D MINOR (1896) - Opus 13. Two violins, viola, violoncello.
Manuscript (unpublished).

QUINTET IN A MAJOR FOR CLARINET AND STRINGS (1895) - Opus 10. Clarinet, two violins, viola, cello. Four movements: 1. Allegro energico;
2. Larghetto affetuoso; 3. Scherzo, Allegro leggiero; 4. Finale, Allegro agitato. Duration: 30 minutes. Publisher: Brietkopf (Germany); presently available from Musica Rara, London. Premiere: 11
July 1895; Royal College of Music.

QUINTET IN G MINOR - Opus 1. Piano, 2 violins, viola, violoncello.
Manuscript (unpublished).

ROMANCE (1905?) - Opus 59, No. 2. Violin and piano. Publisher:
Augener, 1905(?).

ROMANCE IN G (1899) - Opus 39. Violin and orchestra. Publisher:
Novello, 1900. Premiere: 24 May 1899; Salle Erard, London; Coleridge-Taylor, violin; Jessie, piano.

SCENES FROM AN EVERYDAY ROMANCE (1900) - Opus 41, No. 1. Orchestra.
Suite in four movements: 1. E minor (Allegro); 2. G major (Andante);
3. B minor (Tempo di valse); 4. E minor (Presto). Duration: 12 minutes. Publisher: Novello, 1900. Premiere: 24 May 1900; Queen's
Hall, London; Philharmonic Society.

SONATA IN D MINOR (1898-9) - Opus 28. Violin and piano. Publisher: Hawkes, 1917; edited by A. Sammoni.

THE SOUL'S EXPRESSION (FOUR SONNETS) (1900) - Opus 42. Contralto solo and orchestra or pianoforte. Four movements: 1. The Soul's Expression; 2. Tears; 3. Grief; 4. Comfort. Text: "Four Sonnets" by Elizabeth Barrett Browning. Dedicated to Marie Brema. Publisher: Novello, 1900.

SYMPHONY IN A MINOR (1896) - Opus 8. Orchestra. Unpublished; manuscript at Royal College of Music. Premiere: 6 March 1896; St. James' Hall, Royal College of Music, London.

A TALE OF OLD JAPAN (1911) - Opus 76. Cantata. Soprano, contralto, tenor, and baritone soli, chorus and orchestra. Duration: 48 minutes. Dedicated to Mr. and Mrs. Carl Stoeckel. Publisher: Novello, 1911. Premiere: 6 December 1911; Queen's Hall, London; London Choral Society, Arthur Fagge, Conductor.

THELMA (1906-08) - Opus 72. Grand Opera. Publisher: Ascherbert-Hawkes, 1908(?). Though the opera itself was never performed, the New London Symphony performed the Prelude March 1910.

THREE HUMORESQUES (1897) - Opus 31. Orchestra; also written for piano solo. Three movements: 1. D major; 2. G minor; 3. A major. Publisher: Augener, 1897.

TOUSSAINT L'OUVERTURE (CONCERT OVERTURE) (1909)- Opus 46. Orchestra. Duration: 15 minutes. Publisher: Novello, 1901(?). Premiere: 21 October 1901; Queen's Hall Symphony Concerts; Henry Wood, Conductor.

TWO ROMANTIC PIECES (1896) - Opus 9. Violin and piano. Two movements: 1. Lament; 2. Dance-Merrymaking. Publisher: Augener, 1896. Premiere: 6 March 1896; Royal College of Music.

VALSE CAPRICE (1898) - Opus 23. Violin and piano. Publisher: Augener, 1898(?).

VARIATIONS IN B MINOR FOR VIOLONCELLO AND PIANO. Publisher: Augener, 1919. Premiere: 30 November 1907; Croydon, England; String Players Concert; Mr. C. A. Crabbe, violoncello.

ZARA'S EAR-RINGS (RHAPSODY) (1894?) - Soprano and orchestra. Unpublished. Premiere: 7 February 1895; college concert at the Imperial Institute; Miss Clementine M. Pierpoint soprano.

Sources

Banfield, Stephen. "Coleridge-Taylor, Samuel." In The New Grove Dictionary of Music and Musicians, Vol. 4 pp. 528-30.

Child, Harold Hannyngton. "Coleridge-Taylor, Samuel." In The Dictionary of National Biography, Twentieth Century 1912-1921. Eds. H.W.C. Davis and J.R.H. Weaver. London: Oxford University Press, 1927, pp. 122-23.

Coleridge-Taylor, Avril Gwendolyn. The Heritage of Samuel Coleridge-Taylor. London: Dobson, 1979. 160 pp.

Ewen, David. "Samuel Coleridge-Taylor, 1875-1912." In Composers Since 1900. New York: H.W. Wilson Co., 1969, pp. 132-34.

Sayers, William C. Berwick. Samuel Coleridge-Taylor, Musician: His Life and Letters. Arlington Heights, IL: Metro Books, 1969. (Reprint of 1915 ed.)

Scobie, Edward. Black Brittania: A History of Blacks in Britain. Chicago: Johnson Publishing Co., 1972. pp. 134-35.

Southern, Eileen. Biographical Dictionary of Afro-American and African Musicians. Westport, CT: Greenwood Press, 1982, pp. 78-79.

Tortolano, William. Samuel Coleridge-Taylor: Anglo-Black Composer, 1875-1912. Metuchen, NJ: Scarecrow Press, 1977.

MEUDE-MONPAS, THE CHEVALIER J. J. O. de (17?? - 17??)

Little is known of the Chevalier de Meude-Monpas. He was born in Paris and may have died in Berlin. He served Louis XVI of France as a musketeer, and went into exile at the onset of the Revolution. He studied music with Pierre La Houssaye and Francois Giroust, and published six concertos for violin and orchestra (1786), a Dictionnaire de Musique (1787), and a book entitled De l'influence de l'amour et de la musique sur les moeurs...

Works

SIX CONCERTOS (1786) - Violin and chamber orchestra. Scores of concertos I and IV held at the Library of Congress and the Center for Black Music Research.

Sources

BPIM 2 (Fall 1974): 233.

Southern, EIleen. Biographical Dictionary of Afro-American and African Musicians. Westport, CT: Greenwood Press, 1982, p. 233.

SAINT-GEORGES [SAINT-GEORGE], JOSEPH BOULOGNE, THE CHEVALIER DE (1749-1799)

The Chevalier de Saint-Georges was born Joseph Boulogne on December 25, 1749, near Basse Terre, Guadaloupe, West Indies. He died June 10, 1799, in Paris.
He began to study music at the age of five. Later, in France, he studied with Jean-Marie Leclair and François Gossec who appointed Saint-Georges concertmaster of the Concert des Amateurs in 1769. He succeeded Gossec in 1773 as Director of Instrumental Music.
During the 1770s and 1780s he performed as a concert violinist and in orchestral groups, in addition to composing. The onset of the French Revolution, during which he served as colonel of an all-black regiment, brought his musical career nearly to a halt until 1797.

Saint-George produced many pieces in a variety of forms: opera (Er-nestine and La Chasse), ten concertos for violin and orchestra, twelve string quartets, two symphonies, six "symphonies concertantes," twelve arias and duos with orchestra four sonatas (for flute and harp, keyboard, violin and keyboard, and two violins), and more than 100 songs with keyboard accompaniment.

Works

L'AMANT ANONIME: COMEDIE EN DEUX ACTES MELEE DE BALLETS REPRESENTEE A PARIS LE 8 MARS 1780. 152 pp. Text: Mme. de Genlis. Contents: 1. Despuis longtems (tenor); 2. Tant de circonstance (tenor and bass); 3. Son amour, son constance (soprano); 4. Chantons et celebrons (chorus); 5. Ballet (string orchestra); 6. Chanson (soprano); 7. Danse (string orchestra); 8. Quinque (two sopranos and two basses); 9. Amour devient mon propice (soprano); 10. Cesses, cesses (soprano and bass); 11. Aimer sans pouvoir le dire (bass); 12. Du tendre amour (soprano); 13. Non, non (soprano and tenor); 14. Ah quel trouble (soprano, tenor and bass); 15. Ballet (string orchestra); 16. Chorus; 17. Ballet; 18. Quatour (two sopranos, tenor, and bass); 19. Contredanse generale. Library: Bibliotheque Nationale.

L'AMANT ANONIME OVERTURE (a.k.a. SYMPHONY NO. 2)

LES AMOURS ET LA MORT DU PAUVRE OISEAU - Violin. Spurious?

AUPRES DE VOUS, MON COEUR SOUPIRE - Soprano, tenor, and string orchestra. Library: Bibliotheque Nationale (Conservatoire 4112).

L'AUTRE JOUR A L'OMBRAGE - Medium voice and guitar. Library: British Library (B.362.b (193.)), Bibliotheque Nationale (manuscript, 2pp., L4588).

CONCERTO FOR BASSOON AND ORCHESTRA (by 1782) - Premiere: 28 March 1782; Paris; Etienne Ozi, bassoon; Concert Spirituel. NOTE: Lost.

CONCERTO FOR CLARINET AND ORCHESTRA - NOTE: Lost.

CONCERTO FOR VIOLIN IN A MAJOR - Opus 5, No. 2. Violin and orchestra. Facsimile of parts. Master of the Violin, Vol. 3. Editor: Gabriel Banat. Publisher: Johnson Reprint Corp., 1981. Recording: Jean-Jacques Kantorow, violinist; Orchestre de Chambre, Bernard Thomas, Conductor; Arion [France] ARN 38-253.

CONCERTO FOR VIOLIN IN A MAJOR - Opus 7, No. 1. Violin and orchestra. Facsimile of parts. Master of the Violin, Vol. 3. Editor: Gabriel Banat Publisher: Johnson Reprint Corp., 1981.

CONCERTO FOR VIOLIN IN B-FLAT MAJOR - Opus 7, No. 2. Violin and orchestra. Facsimile of parts. Master of the Violin, Vol. 3. Editor: Gabriel Banat. Publisher: Johnson Reprint Corp., 1981.

CONCERTO FOR VIOLIN IN C MAJOR - Opus 5, No. 1. Violin and orchestra. Facsimile of parts. Master of the Violin, Vol. 3. Editor: Gabriel Banat. Publisher: Johnson Reprint Corp., 1981.

CONCERTO FOR VIOLIN IN D MAJOR - Opus 2, No. 2. Violin and orchestra. Facsimile of parts. Master of the Violin, Vol. 3. Editor: Gabriel Banat. Publisher: Johnson Reprint Corp., 1981.

CONCERTO FOR VIOLIN IN G MAJOR - Opus 2 No. 1. Violin and orchestra. Facsimile of parts. Master of the Violin, Vol. 3. Editor: Gabriel Banat. Publisher: Johnson Reprint Corp., 1981; Peer International.

DIEUX! QUEL PRESTIGE - High voice and string orchestra.

LE DROIT DU SEIGNEUR (1784?) - Opera. Contents: 1. D'l'instant qu'on nous mis en ménage; 2. L'autre jour jétois; 3. Vous enflammez; 4. Ce soir en votre honneur; 5. Colin, s'ra ce le dernier?; 6 Duo: Ah si parfois; 7. Duo: Dans la prairie. Publisher: Paris, Imbault, by 1792. NOTE: Possibly lost.

ERNESTINE (1777) - Opera in three acts. Text by Captain Valmont de Chderlos, revised by N. Desfontaines, after L'Histoire d'Ernestine ou les malheurs d'une jeune orpheline by Mme. Riccoboni. Premiere: 19 July 1777; Comédie Italienne. NOTE: Not located.

"Airs détaches d'ERNESTINE, comédie en trois actes mise en musique par M. de Saint-Georges. Chez M. Houbaut, 1 livre 16 sols." Only the following items have been found:

DE CLEMENGIS LA DOULOUREUSE IMAGE - Two sopranos and orchestra. Arranged by Dominique-René de Lerma. Premiere: February 1983; Joy Simpson, Alpha Floyd, sopranos; American Symphony Orchestra; Everett Lee, conductor.

IL N'EST POINT - Soprano, unaccompanied. In 1777 issue of the Journal de Paris.

LA SEULE ERNESTINE M'ENFLAME - Tenor and orchestra. Arranged by Dominique-René de Lerma. Premiere: 18 February 1984; Peabody/ Morgan Black Music Symposium, Friedburg Concert Hall, Peabody Conservatory of Music, Baltimore; Garymichael Murphy, tenor; Peabody Chamber Orchestra; Edward Polochick, conductor.

O CLEMENGIS, LIS DANS MON AME - Soprano and orchestra. Arranged by Dominique-René de Lerma. Publisher: New York, Peer International, 1978. Library: Library of Congress (79-771282). Premiere: 1974; Ford Auditorium, Detroit; Bonita Sanders, soprano; Detroit Symphony Orchestra; Paul Freeman, conductor. Recording: 1974, Columbia M-372781; Faye Robinson, soprano; London Symphony Orchestra, Paul Freeman, conductor.

SATISFAIT DU PLAISIR - Tenor and string orchestra. Edited by Dominique-René de Lerma. Premiere: 18 February 1984; Peabody/ Morgan Black Music Symposium, Friedburg Concert Hall, Peabody Conservatory of Music, Baltimore; Garymichael Murphy, tenor; Peabody Chamber Orchestra; Edward Polochick, conductor.

LA FILLE-GARÇON (1787) - Opera in two acts. Text: Desmaillot or Eve. Premiere: 8 August 1787. NOTE: Cast included Rose Renaud and Mlle. Carline; lost.

GUILLAUME TOUT COEUR (1790) - Opera. NOTE: Lost.

IMAGE CHÉRIE, ÉCRITS SI TOUCHANTS - Soprano and string orchestra.

LOIN DU SOLEIL - Soprano and orchestra.

LE MARCHAND DE MARRONS (1788) - Opera in two acts. Première: 1788;
Theatre de Beaujola Paris, or Théâtre des Petits Comédiens. NOTE:
Lost.

N'ÊTES VOUS PLUS LA TENDRE AMIE - Tenor and orchestra.

QUARTET FOR HARP AND STRINGS (1777) - Arranged by M. Deleplanque for
harp, violin, viola, and bass. Publisher: Paris, Sieber, ca. 1777.
NOTE: Advertisement appears in Mercure de France, September 1778.

QUARTETS FOR STRINGS, Op. 1 (1773) - Publisher: Paris, Sieber, 1773.
Library: Bibliothèque Nationale (Receuil 12; Arsenal, Mu. No. 197
bis; manuscript D 11175; Sketches perhaps for violin and keyboard, MS
9866).

   NO. 1, C MAJOR - Edited by Dominique-René de Lerma. Publisher:
   New York, Peer International, 1978. 15 pp. Contents: 1. Alle-
   gro assai; 2. Rondeau gratioso. Premiere: 1971; Black Music
   Seminar Bloomington, Indiana; Jacques Isvaelevitch, Zoltan
   Szabo, violins; Robert Swan, viola; unknown cellist. Recordings:
   1. Columbia M-32781, the Juilliard Quartet, 1974; 2. Musical
   Heritage Society MHS-3727, Quatour Jean-Noël Molard, 1977.

   NO. 2, E-FLAT MAJOR - Contents: 1 Allegro, 2. Rondeau. Recording: Musical Heritage Society MHS-3626, Quatour Jean-Noël
   Molard, 1977.

   NO. 3, G MINOR - Contents: 1. Allegro, 2. Rondeau. Recording:
   Musical Heritage Society MHS-3727, Quatour Jean-Noël Molard,
   1977.

   NO. 4, C MINOR - Contents: 1. Allegro moderato, 2. Rondeau.
   Recording: Musical Heritage Society MHS-3727, Quatour Jean-Noël
   Molard, 1977.

   NO. 5, G MINOR - Contents: 1. Allegro, 2. Rondeau. Recording:
   Musical Heritage Society MHS-3727, Quatour Jean-Noël Molard,
   1977.

   NO. 6, D MAJOR - Contents: 1. Allegro assai, 2. Rondeau. Recording: Musical Heritage Society MHS-3727, Quatour Jean-Noël
   Molard, 1977.

QUE ME FAIT À MOI LA RICHESSE - Tenor and string orchestra.

QU'IL EST CONTENT - Soprano and string orchestra.

SCENE FROM "ERNESTINE" - Soprano and orchestra. Publisher: Peer
International. Recording: Faye Robinson, soprano; London Symphony
Orchestra Paul Freeman, Conductor; Columbia M-32781, Black Composers
series, Vol. I, 1974.

SIX SONATES POUR LE VIOLON PAR ST. GEORGE - Violin solo with violin accompaniment. Oeuvre posthume. Publisher: Paris, Pleyel, ca. 1800. 2 vols. #258 contains sonatas 1-3; #259 contains sonatas 4-6. Library: British Library (g.422.f(5), Library of Congress (M219 .A25142). NOTE: "Gravées par Richomme."

NO. 1, B-FLAT MAJOR - Contents: 1. Allegro, 2. Aria con variazione.

NO. 2, E-FLAT MAJOR - Contents: 1. Allegro, 2. Aria con variazione.

NO. 3, A MAJOR - Contents: 1. Allegro, 2. Aria con variazione.

NO. 4, G MAJOR - Contents: 1 Allegro, 2. Gratioso con variazione.

NO. 5, B-FLAT MAJOR - Contents: 1. Allegro, 2. Aria con variazione. Library: Schomburg.

NO 6, A MAJOR - Publisher: Mainz, B. Schott's Sohne, n.d. Edited by Delphin Alard as Sonate III par le Chevalier de St. Georges. #19979. Les Maîtres Classiques du Violon, 37. Library; Library of Congress (M218.M23).

SONATA IN A MAJOR - Violin and piano. Edited by Dominique-Rene' de Lerma. Duration: 14 minutes. Publisher: Peer International (1984?).

SONATAS FOR VIOLIN AND KEYBOARD - Publisher: Paris, Le Duc, n.d. Library: Bibliothèque Nationale (VM75601).

NO. 1, B-FLAT MAJOR - Contents: 1. Allegro, 2. Tempo di Minuetto. Edited by Dominique-René de Lerma. Premiere: 26 February 1971; Boulder Unitarian Church, Boulder, Colorado; Stephen Shipps, violin; Paul Parmalee, piano. Recording: 1978; Arion ARN-38484; Jean Jacques Kantorow, violin; Brigitte Haudebourg, harpsichord.

NO. 3, G MINOR - Contents: 1. Allegro, 2. Rondeau gracioso. Recording: 1978; Arion ARN-38484; Jean Jacques Kantorow violin; Brigitte Haudebourg, harpsichord.

SONATE DE CLAVECIN [sic] IN G MAJOR - Keyboard with violin accompaniment. NOTE: This is a setting of the CONCERTO FOR VIOLIN, Op. 1, No. 1. In Choix de Musique.

SONATE POUR HARP ET FLUTE

STRING QUARTET IN C MAJOR - Opus 1, No. 1. Reconstructed and edited by Dominique-Rene' de Lerma. Publisher: Peer-Southern Organization, 1978.

SYMPHONIE CONCERTANTE (1775) - Opus 6. Two violins and orchestra. Publisher: Paris, Bailleux, 1775. Library: Bibliothèque Nationale (Collection Andre' Meyer; Conservatoire H295, lacking solo violin parts); Basel (KV X1165, No. 4, parts for solo cello, viola and two oboes only); Library of Congress.

   NO. 1, C MAJOR - Contents: 1. Allegro moderato; 2. Andante; 3. Rondeau.

   NO. 2, B-FLAT MAJOR. - Contents: 1. Allegro poco moderato; 2. Andante amoroso; 3. Rondeau.

SYMPHONIE CONCERTANTE (1777) - Opus 9. Two violins and orchestra.

SYMPHONIE CONCERTANTE (1778) - Opus 10.   Two violins, viola, and orchestra. Publisher: Paris, De la Chevardiere, 1778; Paris, Le Duc, 1791 (cited as Opus 11 in 1801 catalog). Library: Brussels (Fons Piron, lacks solo violin 1 and solo viola).

   NO. 1, F MAJOR - Contents: 1. Allegro; 2 Allegro.

   NO. 2, A MAJOR - Contents: 1. Allegro; 2. Rondeau. Library: Darmstadt.

SYMPHONIE CONCERTANTE (1784) - Three violins and orchestra. NOTE: The Journal de Paris (28 May 1784, p. 649) reports, "Une nouvelle symphonie concertante à trois violon au Concert Spirituel du dimanche 30 dans la salle occupée ci-devant par le Theâtre Français au Chateau des Tuileries," performed by Rodolfe Kreutzer, Guériollot, and Gervais. Barry Brook suspects this might have been a revision of one of the Symphonies Concertantes of the Opus 10 set.

SYMPHONIE CONCERTANTE IN D MAJOR - Two violins and orchestra. Contents: 1. Allegro; 2. Rondo. Library: Basel (Kr lv 188, lacking the solo parts). NOTE: The first movement is based on the first movement of the Violin Concerto Opus 2, No. 2.

SYMPHONIE CONCERTANTE IN E-FLAT MAJOR - Opus 12.   Orchestra. Facsimile of parts. Master of the Violin, Vol. 3.   Editor: Gabriel Banat. Publisher: Johnson Reprint Corp., 1981.

SYMPHONIE CONCERTANTE IN G MAJOR - Two violins and orchestra. Contents: 1. Allegro moderato. NOTE: Based on the Opus 2 Violin Concerto; no evidence of additional movements. Library: Basel.

SYMPHONIE CONCERTANTE IN G MAJOR FOR TWO VIOLINS AND ORCHESTRA (1782) - Opus 13. Duration: 15 minutes 15 seconds. Publisher: Frank Music; also in Barry S. Brook, La symphonie française dans la second moitié du siècle, Universite de Paris, Institute de Musique, 1962. Recordings: London Symphony Orchestra, Paul Freeman, Conductor; Columbia M-32781, Black Composers series, Vol. I, 1974. Orchestre de Chambre Jean-François Paillard; Erato ERA-9511, 1965, and Musical Heritage Society NHS CC-1, 1966. Instrumental Ensemble Jean-Marie Le Clair, Erato LDE-3037.

SYMPHONY NO. 1 IN G MAJOR - Opus 11, No. 1. Orchestra. Duration: 13 minutes, 25 seconds. Publisher: Peer International. Recordings: London Symphony Orchestra Paul Freeman, Conductor; Columbia M-32781, Black Composers series Vol I, 1974.   Instrumental Ensemble Jean-Marie Le Clair, Erato LDE-3037.

SYMPHONY NO. 2 IN D MAJOR (1779) - Opus 11, No. 2.   Contents: 1. Allegro presto; 2. Andante; 3. Presto.   Publisher: Paris, De la Chevardiere, n.d.   Library: Bibliothèque Nationale (Conservatoir H202).   Edited by Dominique-René de Lerma.   Rental: Bryn Mawr, Merron Music.   Premiere: February 1976; Ford Auditorium, Detroit; Detroit Symphony Orchestra; Paul Freeman, conductor.   NOTE: This is identical with the overture to L'AMANT ANONIME.

SYMPHONY IN G MAJOR - NOTE: Gentry, in his Essais sur la musique (vol. 2, p. 75) quotes a "refrain" from a symphony by "l'habile artiste Saint-Georges," which excerpt cannot be more fully identified and may relate to a work now lost.

TRIO (DUOS) - Violin and piano.   Dedicated to Mme. la Comtesse de Vauban.   Contents: 1. Adagio for violin and piano in F minor (for piano only), pp. 119-20; 2. Adagio for violin and piano in G minor, pp. 43-44; 3. Adagio for violin and piano in A major, pp. 47-48; 4. Allegro for violin and piano in C major, pp. 29-32; 5. Allegro for violin and piano in C major, pp. 67-70; 6. Allegro for violin and piano in C major, pp. 73-78; 7. Allegro for violin and piano in C major, pp. 91-92 (violin part was added later to first (18 of 77) measures only; 8. Allegro for violin and piano in D major, pp. 1-4; 9. Allegro for violin and piano in D major, pp. 93-96 (violin part was added later and is incomplete); 10. Allegro for violin and piano in D major, pp. 101-104; 11. Allegro for violin and piano in D major, pp. 150-52 (for piano); 12. Allegro for violin and piano in D major, pp. 181-86; 13. Allegro for violin and piano in E-flat major, pp. 55-58 (for piano only); 14. Allegro for violin and piano in E-flat major, pp. 33-42 (opening 10 measures of the violin part were added later); 15. Allegro for violin and piano in E-flat major, pp. 121-25 (for piano only); 16. Allegro for violin and piano in E-flat major, pp. 141-46 (violin part added later); 17. Allegro for violin and piano in F major, pp. 11-14; 18. Allegro for violin and piano in F major, pp. 135-39 (for piano only); 19. Allegro for violin and piano in F major, pp. 197-200 (for piano only); 20. Allegro for violin and piano in G major, pp. 45-50; 21. Allegro for violin and piano in G major, pp. 59-62; 22. Allegro for violin and piano in G minor, pp. 203-206; 23. Allegro for violin and piano in A major, pp. 53-54; 24. Allegro for violin and piano in B-flat major, pp. 173-76 (a draft of the first movement of the Violin Sonata in B-flat Major); 25. Allegro moderato for violin and piano in A major, pp. 167-70 (draft for the first movement of the Violin Sonata in A major); 26. Andante for violin and piano in D major, p. 149 (for piano only); 27. Andante for violin and piano in D major, pp. 155-56 (for piano only; the violin part was not added); 28. Andante for violin and piano in D minor, pp. 185-86; 29. Andante for violin and piano in E-flat major, pp. 37-38 (violin part added later); 30. Andante for violin and piano in E-flat major, pp. 85-86 (violin part added later); 31. Andante for violin and piano in F major, pp. 139-40 (for piano only); 32. Andante for violin and piano in F major, pp. 201-02 (for piano only); 33. Andante gratioso for violin and piano in C minor, p. 132; 34. Andantino for violin and piano in A major, pp. 171-72 (draft for second movement of the Violin Sonata in A Major); 35. Aria for violin and piano in C major, pp. 71-72; 36. Aria con variazione for violin and piano in D major, pp. 105-07 (contains three variations); 37. Arai con variazione for violin and piano in E-flat major, pp. 147-48 (contains four variations); 38. Aria con variazione for violine and piano in E-flat major, pp. 193-96 (contains for variations); 39 Aria con variazione for violin and piano in G major, pp. 23-24 (for piano only; contains two variations); 40. Aria con variazione for violin and piano in G major, pp. 63-66 (contains four variations. Recording: 1978; Arion ARN-38484; Jean-Jacques Kantorow, violin; Brigitte Haudebourg, harpsicord); 41. Grazioso for violin and piano in C major, pp. 33-36; 42. Minuetto gratioso for violin and piano in E-flat major, pp. 125-26 (for piano only); 43. Presto for violin and piano in E-flat major, pp. 87-88 (violin part added later); 44. Rondeau for violin and piano in C major, pp. 133-34 (violin part added later); 45. Rondeau for violin and piano in D major, pp. 19-20; 46. Rondeau for violin and piano in D major, pp. 99-100; 47. Rondeau for violin and piano in D major, pp. 153-54 (for piano only; violin part not added); 48. Rondeau for violin and piano in D major, pp. 157-58 (for piano only); 49. Rondeau gratioso for violin and piano in C major, pp. 79-80; 50. Rondeau gratioso for violin and piano in G major, pp. 163-66; 51. Rondo for violin and piano in C major, pp. 211-12; 52. Tempo di minuetto for piano in D major, pp. 15-16; 53. Tempo di minuetto for piano in D major pp. 26-27; 54. Tempo di minuetto for violin and piano in C major, pp. 127-31; 55. Tempo di minuetto for violin and piano in D major, pp. 97 98; 56. Tempo di minuetto for violin and piano in D major, pp. 187-88 (for piano only); 57. Tempo de minuetto for violin and piano in E-flat major, pp. 81-84 (violin part added later); 58. Tempo di minuetto for violin and piano in B-flat major, pp. 177-80 (draft for the second movement of the Violin Sonata in B-flat Major). Library: Bibliothèque Nationale (17725). NOTE: This manuscripte notebook contains sketches for violin and piano. In some instances the violin part was added later, in some, never added, but with a staff reserved.

Sources

Brooks, Barry S.   La Symphonie Française dans la second Moitie du XVIIIe Siècle. Paris: Institute de Musicologie de l'Universite de Paris 1962. 3 vols. (Brooks' documented biography, Vol. I, pp.375-86; Catalogue of Works, Vol. II, pp. 641-49; a transcription of the Symphonie Concertante in G, Catalogue No. 10 (1782) for strings with two solo violins, Vol. III, pp. 147-69.)

---. "Saint-Georges, Joseph Boulogne, Chevalier de." In Die Music in Geschichte und Gegenwart Vol. XI (Kassell: Bärenreiter-Ver. 1963) col. 1253.

De Lerma Dominique-René. "Black Composers in Europe." Black Music Research Journal 10.2 (Fall 1990): 275-334.

---. "The Chevalier de Saint-Georges." The Black Perspective in Music 1.1 (Spring 1976): 18-19.

Derr, Ellwood. "Saint-Georges, Joseph Boulogne, Chevalier de." In The New Grove Dictionary of Music and Musicians, Vol. 16 pp. 391-92.

Southern, Eileen. Biographical Dictionary of Afro-American and African Musicians. Westport, CT: Greenwood Press, 1982 pp. 330-31.

SANCHO, IGNATIUS (1729-1780)

Ignatius Sancho was born in 1729 on a slave ship in route from Guinea, West Africa, to Cartagena, Columbia, where he arrived as an orphan. He died December 14, 1780, in London, England.

At the age of two, he was sold or given to three maiden sisters who lived in Greenwich, England. Later he came to the attention of John, Second Duke of Montagu and formerly governor of Jamaica, who gave him a traditional classical education. After the Duke's death, the Duchess of Montagu became Sancho's patron.

Sancho was among the first composers of African ancestry to publish music in the European tradition. His works included: A Collection of New Songs Composed by an African, Humbly Inscribed to the Honorable Mrs. James Brudenell by Her Most Humble and Obedient Servant; Minuets, Cotillions & Country Dances for the Violin, Mandolin, German-Flute, and Harpsichord (dedicated to Henry, Duke of Buccleugh); Twelve Country Dances for the Year 1779, Set for the Harpsichord; and Minuets &c., &c., for the Violin, Mandolin, German-Flute, and Harpsichord, with obligato French horn parts, dedicated to his patron, John, Lord Montagu. He also published a Theory of Music, no longer extant, which he dedicated to Charlotte Augusta Matilda (later Queen of Wurttemburg).

Works

MINUETS, COTILLIONS & COUNTRY DANCES FOR THE VIOLIN, MANDOLIN, GERMAN FLUTE, AND HARPSICHORD (c. 1767) - Dedicated to Henry, Duke of Buc-cleugh.

MINUETS, COTILLIONS & COUNTRY DANCES FOR THE VIOLIN, MANDOLIN, GERMAN FLUTE AND HARPSICHORD WITH OBLIGATO FRENCH HORN (c. 1770) - Dedicated to John, Lord Montagu of Boughton.

Sources

Robinson, Wilhelmina S. Historical Afro-American Biographies (International Library of Afro-American Life and History). Washington, D.C.: Associated Publisher, 1976.

"Sancho, Ignatius." In The Dictionary of National Biography, Vol. 17, pp. 732-33.

Scobie, Edward. Black Brittania: A History of Blacks in Britain. Chicago: Johnson Publishing Company, 1972, pp. 95-100.

Southern, Eileen. Biographical Dictionary of Afro-American and African Musicians. Westport, CT: Greenwood Press, 1982, p. 331.

Wright, Josephine. Ignatius Sancho (1729-1780): An Early African Composer in England. The Collected Editions of His Music in Facsimile. New York: Garland Publishing Co., 1981. 90 pp.

Wright, Josephine R. B. "Ignatius Sancho: An African Composer (1729-1780)." BPIM 7 (Fall 1979).

Afro-Latino Composers

CERÓN, JOSÉ DOLORES (1897 -)

Works

    ENRIQUILLO (1941) - Orchestra.

    TRES PRELUDIOUS (1942) - Orchestra.

Source

    De Lerma, Dominique-René. Black Concert and Recital Music: Provi-
    sional List. Bloomington, IN: Afro-American Music Opportunities,
    1975.

CORDERO, ROQUE (1917 -)

    Roque Cordero was born in Panama City, Panama, on August 16, 1917.
    In Panama, he studied privately; later he received his B A from Ham-
line University in St. Paul, Minnesota (1947). He also studied at the
National Orchestral Association in New York and the Berkshire Music Center.
    He received his first compositional award, the National Prize of Pana-
ma, in 1937, for "The Spirit of Panama." Other honors and awards include
fellowships from the Institute of International Education (1943-44), Berkshire Music Center (1946), Panamanian Government (1946-48), and the Guggenheim Memorial Foundation (1949); and honorary doctorates from Hamline University (1966) and the University of Chile (1963). He received the 1974
Koussevitzky International Recording Award. Cordero also served as a dele-
gate to the International Music Council of UNESCO (1961-66, 1968).
    He has contributed widely to professional journals such as La Estrella
de Panama Revista Musical Chilena, Journal of Interamerican Studies, and
Buenos Aires Musical. He is the author of a manual, Curso de Solfeo, and
of "El Publico y la Musica Viva," published in Music in the Americas,
(Bloomington, 1967).
    He is best known for his orchestral and chamber works, including three
symphonies (1945, 1956, 1965), a violin concerto (1962), and Doble Concier-
to sin Orquesta (1979); a number of sonatas and sonatinas for violin and
piano, and cello and piano; and three string quartets. Other works are

Miniatures, Duo 1954, Cinco Mensajes Breves para Orquesta, Concertino, Dos Pequenas Piezas Corales, and Cantata for Peace.
Cordero taught in Panama at the Escuela de Artes y Oficios (1941-43) and the Conservatoria Nacional de Musica de Panama (now the Instituto Nacional de Musica de Panama). In the United States he taught at Indiana University in Bloomington (1966-69) and Illinois State University in Normal (1972 -).

Works

ADAGIO TRAGICO (1953) - Orchestra. Duration: 9 minutes. Publisher: New York, Peer-Southern Concert Music.

BALLET FOLKLORICO - Ballet. Commissioned by the National Institute of Tourism, Panama.

CANTATA PARA LA PAZ: CANTATA FOR PEACE (1979) - Bass-baritone solo, SATB chorus, orchestra. Duration: 35 minutes. Publisher: New York, Peer-Southern Concert Music.

CAPRICHO INTERIORANO: PANAMANIAN FOLK BALLET SUITE (1939) - Orchestra. Duration: 5 minutes. Publisher: New York, Peer-Southern Concert Music.

CINCO MENSAJES BREVES PARA ORQUESTRA: FIVE BRIEF MESSAGES FOR ORCHESTRA (1973) - Duration: 5 minutes. Publisher: New York, Peer-Southern Concert Music.

CONCERTINO FOR VIOLA AND STRING ORCHESTRA (1968) - Commissioned by the Catholic University of Chile.

CONCERTO FOR VIOLIN (1962) - Violin and orchestra. Duration: 29 minutes. Publisher: New York, Peer-Southern Concert Music.

DOS PIEZAS CORTAS: TWO SHORT PIECES (1945) - Violin and pianoforte. Duration: 5 minutes.

DOUBLE CONCERTO WITHOUT ORCHESTRA FOR VIOLIN AND PIANO - Commissioned by the Kennedy Center, Washington. D.C. Publisher: New York, Peer-Southern Concert Music.

ELEGY (1973) - String orchestra. Duration: 7 minutes. Publisher: New York, Peer-Southern Concert Music.

FIVE MESSAGES FOR FOUR FRIENDS (1983) - Guitar. Duration: 10 minutes. Publisher: Editions Salabert, 1985. Premiere: 27 September 1984; San Juan, Puerto Rico.

FIVE SHORT MESSAGES FOR ORCHESTRA (1958) - Commissioned by the Minneapolis Civic Orchestra.

MENSAJE FUNEBRE: FUNERAL MESSAGE (1961) - Clarinet solo and string orchestra. Duration: 9 minutes. Publisher: New York, Peer-Southern Concert Music.

MOMENTUM JUBILO: FANFARE (1973) - Orchestra. Duration: 2 minutes. Publisher: New York, Peer-Southern Concert Music.

MOVIMENTO SINFONICO: SYMPHONIC MOVEMENT (1946) - String orchestra. Duration: 16 minutes.   Publisher: New York, Peer-Southern Concert Music.

MUSICA VEINTE: MUSIC TWENTY - SSAA, baritone solo, orchestra.   Duration: 11 minutes 30 seconds.   Publisher: New York, Peer-Southern Concert Music.

OCHO MINIATURAS: EIGHT MINIATURES (1944, rev. 1948) - Orchestra. Duration: 11 minutes.   Publisher: New York, Peer-Southern Concert Music.

PANAMANIAN OVERTURE NO. 2 (1946) - Orchestra.   Duration: 12 minutes. Publisher: New York, Peer-Southern Concert Music.

PAZ, PAIX, PEACE (1969) -   Harp solo; flute, English horn, bass clarinet; alto flute, clarinet, bassoon; violin, viola, violoncello; 2 viola, double bass.   Duration: 18 minutes.   Publisher: New York, Peer-Southern Concert Music.

PERMUTACIONES 7 (1967) - Clarinet, trumpet, timpani, pianoforte, violin, viola, double bass.   Duration: 8 minutes 30 seconds.   Publisher: New York, Peer-Southern Concert Music.

QUINTETO (1949) - Flute, clarinet, violin, violoncello, pianoforte. Duration: 25 minutes.   Publisher: New York, Peer-Southern Concert Music.

SIX MOBILES FOR ORCHESTRA (1975) - Duration: 20 minutes.   Publisher: New York, Peer-Southern Concert Music.

SOLILOQUIOS NO. 5 - String bass solo.   Publisher: New York, North/ South Consonance, Inc.

SONATA (1963) - Violoncello and pianoforte.   Duration: 15 minutes. Publisher: New York, Peer-Southern Concert Music.

SONATINA (1946) - Violin and pianoforte.   Duration: 11 minutes. Publisher: New York, Peer-Southern Concert Music.

STRING QUARTET NO. 1 (1960) - Duration: 18 minutes 30 seconds.   Publisher: New York, Peer-Southern Concert Music.

STRING QUARTET NO. 2 (1968) - Duration: 23 minutes.   Publisher: New York, Peer-Southern Concert Music.

STRING QUARTET NO. 4 (1983) - Commissioned by the Illinois Arts Council.

SYMPHONY NO. 1 (1945) - Duration: 30 minutes.   Publisher: New York, Peer-Southern Concert Music.

SYMPHONY NO. 2 (1956) - Duration: 24 minutes.   Publisher: New York, Peer-Southern Concert Music.

SYMPHONY NO. 3 WITH THEME AND FIVE VARIATIONS (1965) - Duration: 16 minutes.   Publisher: New York, Peer-Southern Concert Music.

SYMPHONY NO. 4 (PANAMANIAN) (1986) - Duration: 35 minutes. Publisher: New York, Peer-Southern Concert Music.

THREE PERMUTATIONS 3 - Violin, violoncello, and string bass. Publisher: New York, North/South Consonance, Inc.

TRES MENSAJES BREVES: THREE BRIEF MESSAGES (1966) - Duration: 5 minutes. Publisher: New York, Peer-Southern Concert Music.

VIOLIN CONCERTO (1961) - Commissioned by the Serge Koussevitzky Music Foundation.

Sources

Information submitted by the composer.

Behague, Gerald. Music in Latin America. Englewood Cliffs, NJ: 1979.

Composers of the Americas, Vol. VIII. Washington, D.C., 1963, p. 59.

Southern, Eileen. Biographical Dictionary of Afro-American and African Musicians. Westport, CT: Greenwood Press, 1982, pp. 84-85.

GARCIA, JUAN FRANCISCO (n.d.)

Works

ADVENIMIENTO - Orchestra.

SYMPHONY, NO. 1; QUISQUEYANA (1941) - Orchestra.

SYMPHONY, NO. 2; POPULAR (1943) - Orchestra.

SYMPHONY, NO. 3 (1944) - Orchestra.

Source

De Lerma, Dominique-René. Black Concert and Recital Music: Provisional List. Bloomington, IN: Afro-American Music Opportunities Association, 1975.

GOMES, (ANTÔNIO) CARLOS (1836-1896)

Antônio Carlos Gomes was born July 11, 1836, in Campinas, Brazil, and died September 16, 1896, in Belem, Brazil.

He began to study music with his father, a provincial bandmaster, and began composing at an early age. He studied at the Imperial Conservatory of Music under Joaquim Giannini, and received a government scholarship in 1863 to study at the Milan Conservatory in Italy, under Lauro Rossi.

His opera Il Guarany brought him international fame. It debuted at La Scala on March 19 1870; it was produced in Rio de Janeiro on the Emperor's birthday (December 2, 1870), as well as in almost all European capitals in the next few years. Verdi referred to it as the work of a "truly musical genius."

After working in Italy most of his life, he returned to Brazil by 1892, when his last major work, the oratorio Colombo, was presented in Rio de Janeiro on October 12 (Columbus Day). He accepted an appointment to direct the local conservatory in Belem in 1896, but died a few months later.

Works

COLOMBO (1892) - Oratorio in four acts. Libretto: M. Canti. Recording: Sociedade Brasileira de Discos Historicos J. Léon TOB-1; J. Athor, bass.

CONDOR (1891) - Opera.

FANTASIA SOBRE A ALTA NOITE (c. 1859)

FOSCA (1873) - Opera. Libretto: A. Ghislanzoni.
INTENDITI CO DIO (1873) - Tenor and orchestra. Duration: 4 minutes 41 seconds. Publisher: Sao Paulo, Ricordi, n.d. Recording: Philips 9500 771 (1980); José Carreras, tenor; London Symphony Orchestra, Jesús López Cobos, conductor.

O TU SEI FRA GLI ANGELI - Tenor and orchestra. Recording: Sociedade Brasileira de Discos Historicos J. Léon TOB-1 and Associação Brasileiro dos Colectionadores de Discos 2; A. Colosimo, tenor.

OVERTURE - Orchestra. Recording: 1. Orquestra do Sindicato Musical do Rio de Janeiro; Leo Peracchi, conductor; 2 Odeon A-3252; Rio de Janeiro Symphony; Mignone, conductor.

IL GUARNAY (1870) - Opera. Libretto: Schalvini, C. d'Ormeville, after J. de Alencar. Publisher: Milano, Ricordi. Recordings: 1. Voce 48 (1980); Aurea Gomes (Cecilia), Benito Maresca (Pery), Paulo Fortes (Gonzales), Wilson Carrara (Il Cacico), Amin Feres (Don Antonio), Marcos Lousada (Don Alvaro), Manuel Pascoa (Alonso), Victor Prochei (Ruy Bento; Orchestra and Chorus of the Teatro Municipal, Rio de Janeiro, Mario Tavares, conductor; recorded 4 July 1980; 2. The Golden Age of Opera EJS 240 (n.d.); Gianna d'Angelo, Giorgio Gibin, Piero Cappuccilli, Miccola Zaccaria, Maximiliano Malaspina, Dino Crimi; Orchestra and Chorus of the Teatro Municipal, Rio de Janeiro, Francesco Molinari-Pradelli, conductor (recorded 1964); 3. Ember GVC-20 (n.d.); Lina Pagliughi, soprano; Orchestra Sinfonica di Rotino della Radiotelevisione Italiana (contains "O come e bello il ciel" only); 4. RCA VL-42433 (1978); Pasquale Amato, baritone (contains "Senza tetto" only) (recorded 22 March 1912).

AVE MARIA - Bass and orchestra. Recorded: Sociedade Brasileira de Discos Historics J. Léon TOB-1; Je Perrota, bass.

BALLET MUSIC - Orchestra. Recording: Odeon A-3253/4; Rio de Janeiro Symphony Orchestra; Mignone, conductor.

HIMMLISCHE MACHT, DIE MICH GEHANNT - Soprano and orchestra. Recording: 1914; Victor 6355-B; Emmy Destinn, soprano, with orchestra.

OVERTURE - Orchestra. Edited by Ross Jungnickel. Publisher: New York, Schirmer, 1912. Library: Spingarn. Recordings: 1. Columbia D-14457 and Columbia 52054-X; Milan Symphony Orchestra; Molajoli, conductor; 2. His Masters Voice S-10083; Orchestra del Teatro alla Scala; Sabjano, conductor; 3. Homochord 4-8802; Berlin Symphony Orchestra; Bohnke conductor; 4. Odeon O-26804 and Odeon 193577 and Parlophone 28053; Berlin State Opera Orchestra; Weissman, conductor; 5. Odeon 13028 and Parlophone CB-20526; Radio Italiana; Mignone, conductor; 6. Polydor 27347; unidentified orchestra; Gurlitt, conductor; 7. Odeon 5044; Rio de Janeiro Municipal Orchestra; Gouveia conductor; 8. Avellaneda Municipal Orchestra; Fauré, conductor; 9. Victor 119112; Boston Pops Orchestra; Arthur Fiedler, conductor; 10. Camden CAE-182 and Camden CAL-176; Boston Promenade Orchestra (i.e. Boston Pops Orchestra); Arthur Fiedler, conductor.

OVERTURE - Mandolin ensemble. Recording: Odeon 5117; Odeon Mandolin Orchestra.

PERY MA APPELLA - Tenor and orchestra. Recorded: 1900; Berliner 52566; Giovanni Cesarini, tenor.

REGINA DELLA TRIBU - Bass and orchestra. Recording: Sociedade Brasileira de Discos Historicos J. Léon TOB-1; N. Rossi-Lemeni, bass.

VANTO IO PUR SUPERBA CUNA - Tenor and orchestra. Recordings: 1. Victor 85-0000 and Victor B-5042; Beniamino Giglj, tenor; 2. Sociedade Brasileira de Discos Historicos J. Léon TOB-1; A. Pacheo, tenor.

HINO ACADEMICO (1859)

HYMNO TRIUMPHAL: A CAMÕES (1880) - Band and orchestra. Premiere: 10 June 1880; Imperial Teatro D. Pedro 2 Rio de Janeiro; for the 300th anniversary of the death of the poet Luis Vas de Camões (a.k.a. Camoens).

JOANA DE FLANDRES (1863) - Opera. Libretto: S. de Mendonca.

MARCHA DA INDUSTRIA (1860) - Orchestra.

MARIA TUDOR (1879) - Opera. Libretto: E. Praga after Hugo.

OVERTURE (?) - Orchestra. Recording: Odeon C-7269; Rio de Janeiro Symphony; Mignone, conductor.

ARIA DI MARIA - Soprano and orchestra. Recording: Sociedade Brasileiro de Discos Historicos J. Léon TOB-1; C. Gomes, soprano.

MASS (1854)

A NOITE DO CASTELO (1861) - Opera in three acts. Text: A.J. Fernades do Reis. Premiere: 4 September 1861; Rio de Janeiro.

IL SALUTO DEL BRASILE (1876)

SALVATOR ROSA (1874) - Opera. Libretto: Ghislanzoni.
     ARIA OF THE DUKE D'ARCOS - Bass and orchestra.   Recording: La
     Voce del Padrone 2-52558; Leo Sibiryakov, bass.

     E IL FAGLIO IO SEGNERO - Bass and orchestra.   Recording: Odeon
     3518-B and Fonotipia 152586; Luigi Mantrini (Manini?), bass.

     E QUANTO - Bass and orchestra. Recording: Sociedade Brasileira
     de Discos Historicos J. Léon LPP-3 and Columbia 5063-M; J. Mar-
     dones, bass.

     OVERTURE - Orchestra. Recordings: 1. Orchestra do Sindicato
     Musical do Rio de Janeiro; Leo Peracchi, conductor; 2. Parlophone
     CB-20525; Radio Italiana; Mignone, conductor.

     RECITATIVO - Bass and orchestra. Recording: G&T 52907 52907;
     Leo Sibiryakov, bass.

SE SA MINGA (1867) - Opera. Libretto: A. Scalvini.

LO SCHIAVO (1889) - Opera.   Libretto: R. Paravicini.   Published:
Milano, n.d.   Recording: Voce-39 (ca. 1980); Amin Feres (Rodrigo),
Benito Maresca (Américo), Leila Martins (Ilara), Fernando Texeira
(Iberé), Thereza Godoy (Boissy), Luiz Orefice (Gianfere), Jelvis
Mereschi (Leon and Botocudo), Boris Farina (Goitaca), João da Braz
(Guarudo), Luis Malheiro (Tapacoa), Odnilo Romanini (Tupinamba), Dori-
val Panzani (Carijo), Joao Batista (Caiapo), Roberto Binacardi
(Arari); Orchestra and Chorus of the Teatro Municipal, Sao Paulo,
David Machado, conductor (recorded 23 September 1979).

     ALVORADA - Orchestra. Recordings: 1. Orquestra do Sindicato
     Musical do Rio de Janeiro; Leo Peracchi, conductor; 2. Odeon
     C-7265; Rio de Janeiro Symphony Orchestra; Mignone, conductor.

     O CIEL DI PARAHYBA - Soprano and orchestra.   Recordings:
     1. ca. 1909; Victor 74112 and Sociedade Brasileira de Discos
     Historicos J. Leon G-4; Roxy King-Shaw, soprano; 2. Sociedade
     Brasieleira de Discos Historicos J. Léon TOB-1; M.C.N. de Freita,
     soprano.

     PRELUDE - Orchestra. Recording: Orquestra do Sindicato Musical
     do Rio de Janeiro; Leo Peracchi, conductor.

     PRELUDE, ACT IV - Orchestra. Recording: Parlophone CB-20527;
     Radio Italiana; Magnone, conductor.

     SOGNI D'AMORE - Bass and orchestra. Recording: Victor 33466; S.
     Vieira, bass.

Sources

Armond Marchant, Annie d'. "Carlos Gomes, Great Brazilian Composer,
July 11, 1836 - July 11, 1936." Pan American Union Bulletin (Washington, D.C.): 70 (1936): 767-76.

Behague, Gerard. "Gomes, (Antônio) Carlos." In The New Dictionary of
Music and Musicians, Vol. 7 , pp. 517-18.

Brito, J. Carlos Gomes. Rio de Janeiro, 1956.

De Lerma, Dominique-René. "Black Composers in Europe." Black Music Research Journal 10.2 (Fall 1990): 275-334.

De Lerma, Dominique-René. "A Concordance of Sources and Recordings of Music by Black Composers." Black Music Research Journal. Black Music Research Music Center, Chicago, 1984.

"Gomes, Antônio Carlos " In The Encyclopedia of Latin America. Ed. Helen Delpar. New York: McGraw-Hill, 1974, p. 252.

Hare, Maud Cuney. Negro Musicians and Their Music. Washington, D.C.: Associated Publishers, 1936, pp. 305-07.

Revista Brasileira de Musica, Vol. III (1936). Gomes Centenary issue.

Rogers, J.A. "Carlos Gomes: First Great Operatic Composer of the New World." In World's Great Men of Color, Vol. 2. New York: Macmillan, 1972, pp. 200-02.

White, Clarence Cameron. "Antônio Carlos Gomes." Negro History Bulletin, 4.5 (February 1941): 104, 110.

GUTIÉRREZ Y ESPINOSA, FELIPE (1825-1899)

Felipe Gutiérrez y Espinosa was born May 26, 1825, in San Juan, Puerto Rico, and died November 27, 1899, in San Juan.

As a child, he studied with his father and with Jose Alvarez, both members of the Regimiento Granada, and by the age of 20 he was able to play all the band instruments. Later, in 1876, the government of Puerto Rico sent him to study music in Europe.

He began his professional career as Principal Musician in the Regimiento Iberia. He served as chapel master of the San Juan Cathedral from 1858 to 1898, and as head of the San Juan music academy between 1871 and 1874.

He was the first Puerto Rican to write an opera, and wrote a total of five, including La palma del Cacique, El Bearnes, Guarionex, and Macias. His Tota Pulchra for chorus and orchestra marked the first time a saxophone was used in Puerto Rican composition. Other of his works include seventeen Masses, La Manganilla and Aire de Fandango, El Pasto de los Montes, Sonadina de violin and Las Siete Palabras.

Works

AGNUS DEI - High voice and orchestra.

AIRE DE FANDANGO - Orchestra.

EL AMOR DE UN PESCADOR (1857) - Zarzuela-opera. Text: Carlos Navarro y Alamansa.

EL BEARNÉS - Opera. Libretto by D. Antonio Biaggi.

LA FAMILIA - Orchestra.

GRAN SALVÉ Á NUESTRA SEÑORA DE LA PROVIDENCIA - SATB and orchestra.

GUARIONEX - Opera.

LITANIAS JESUITAS - SATB and orchestra.

MACIAS - Opera. Libretto by Martin Travieso. Premiere: 19 August 1877; San Juan. Note: Based on the novel Macias (1834) by Mariano Jose de Larra.

LA MANGANILLA - Orchestra.

MISERERE - Three part chorus and orchestra.

LA PALMA DEL CACIQUE (1856) - Opera.

EL PARTO DE LOS MONTES - Orchestra.

LA PESETA - Orchestra.

SAN JUAN - Mass. SATB and orchestra.

SANTA CECILIA - Mass. SATB and orchestra.

LAS SIETE PALABRAS - Chorus and orchestra.

SONADINA DE VIOLIN - with piano or orchestra.

TONIDÓN - Orchestra.

TOTA PULCHRA - Chorus, orchestra, and saxophone.

Sources

De Lerma, Dominique-René. "Black Composers in Europe." Black Music Research Journal 10.2 (Fall 1990): 275-334.

Southern, Eileen. Biographical Dictionary of Afro-American and African Musicans. Westport, CT: Greenwood Press, 1982, p. 155.

Stevenson, Robert. "Music in the San Juan, Puerto Rico, Cathedral to 1900," Revista/Review Interamericana 8 (Winter 1978-79).

HERNÁNDEZ, JULIO ALBERTO (1900 -)

Works

DANZA ORIENTAL - Orchestra.

3 ROMANZAS - Voice (or chorus?) and orchestra.

ROMANZA SIN PALABRAS - Orchestra.

SUITE ROMANTICA - Orchestra.

VALS TRISTE - Orchestra.

Source

De Lerma, Dominique-René. Black Concert and Recital Music: Provisional List. Bloomington, IN: Afro-American Music Opportunities Association, 1975.

NUNES-GARCIA, JOSÉ MAURICIO (1767-1830)

Jose Mauricio Nunes-Garcia was born September 22, 1767, in Rio de Janeiro, Brazil, and died April 18, 1830, in Rio de Janeiro.
Nunes-Garcia attended the Escola de Santa Cruz, was ordained a Roman Catholic priest in May 1792, and was appointed chapel master of the cathedral at Rio de Janeiro in 1798. In 1808 John VI appointed him musical director of the Royal Chapel. Called "the Father of Brazilian Music," he was influenced by the music of Mozart and Haydn.

Works

BEIJO A MÃO QUE ME CONDENA, M. 231 - Soprano and cello. Score in personal collection of Dr. Dominique-René de Lerma. Fundacao Nacional de Arte (Rua Araujo Porte Alegre, 80 Loja, 20030 Rio de Janeiro).

DIES SANCTIFICATUS, M. 130 (1793) - Chorus and orchestra. Fundacao Nacional de Arte (Rua Araujo Porte Alegre, 80 Loja, 20030 Rio de Janeiro).

LAUD SION SALVATOREM, M. 165 (1809) - Chorus and orchestra. Score in personal collection of Dr. Dominique-René de Lerma. Fundacao Nacional de Arte (Rua Araujo Porte Alegre, 80 Loja, 20030 Rio de Janeiro).

LAUDATE DOMINUM OMNES GENTES, M. 76 (1813) - Soloist, flute, 2 horns, strings. Score in personal collection of Dr. Dominique-René de Lerma. Fundacao Nacional de Arte (Rua Araujo Porte Alegre, 80 Loja, 20030 Rio de Janeiro).

LAUDATE PUERI, M. 77 (1813) - Soloist, flute, 2 horns, strings. Score in personal collection of Dr Dominique-René de Lerma. Fundacao Nacional de Arte (Rua Araujo Porte Alegre, 80 Loja, 20030 Rio de Janeiro).

MATINAS DO NATAL, M. 170 (1799) - Large orchestra, organ, continuo. Score in personal collection of Dr. Dominique-René de Lerma. Fundacao Nacional de Arte (Rua Araujo Porte Alegre, 80 Loja, 20030 Rio de Janeiro).

MISSA DA NOSSA SENHORA DA CONCIEÇÃO, M. 106 (1810) - Chorus and orchestra. Score in personal collection of Dr. Dominique-René de Lerma. Fundacao Nacional de Arte (Rua Araujo Porte Alegre, 80 Loja, 20030 Rio de Janeiro). Recording: Coro da Associacao de Canto Coral; Orquestra Sinfonica Nacional, Alceu Bocchino, conductor (Angel 3-CBX 410/412, n.d.).

OFICIO DOS DEFUNTOS, M. 186 (1816) - Soloists and orchestra. Score in personal collection of Dr. Dominique-René de Lerma. Fundacao Nacional de Arte (Rua Araujo Porte Alegre, 80 Loja, 20030 Rio de Janeiro).

OVERTURE IN D MINOR/MAJOR, M. 323 - Orchestra.   Score in personal collection of Dr. Dominique-René de Lerma.   Fundacao Nacional de Arte (Rua Araujo Porte Alegre, 80 Loja, 20030 Rio de Janeiro).

REQUIEM, M. 185 (1816) - Soprano, contralto, tenor, bass, chorus orchestra.   Score in personal collection of Dr. Dominique-René de Lerma.   Fundacao Nacional de Arte (Rua Araujo Porte Alegre, 80 Loja, 20030 Rio de Janeiro).

REQUIEM IN D MINOR (1816) - Chorus and orchestra.   Duration: 35 minutes.   Publisher: Associated Music Publishers. Recording: Black Composers Series, Vol. 5, Columbia M-33431, 1975.

SINFONIA FUNEBRE, M. 237 (1790) - Orchestra.   Score in personal collection of Dr. Dominique-René de Lerma.   Fundacao Nacional de Arte (Rua Araujo Porte Alegre, 80 Loja, 20030 Rio de Janeiro).

SINFONIA TEMPESTATE - Orchestra.   Fundacao Nacional de Arte (Rua Araujo Porte Alegre, 80 Loja, 20030 Rio de Janeiro).

STRING QUARTET - Fundacao Nacional de Arte (Rua Araujo Porte Alegre, 80 Loja, 20030 Rio de Janeiro).

TE DEUM LAUDAMUS, M. 93 (1811) - Chorus, soprano, tenor, bass, orchestra.   Score in personal collection of Dr. Dominique-René de Lerma. Fundacao Nacional de Arte (Rua Araujo Porte Alegre, 80 Loja, 20030 Rio de Janeiro).   Recording: [Musica na corte brasileira.]   Dircea de Amorim, soprano; Jose Evergisto Gomes Netto, tenor; Juan Thibault, bass; Orquestra Sinfonica Nacional, Alceu Bacchino, conductor.

TOTA PULCHRA ES MARIA, M. 1 (1783) - Obligato flute. solo (boy) soprano, chorus, strings.   Score in personal collection of Dr. Dominique-René de Lerma.   Fundacao Nacional de Arte (Rua Araujo Porte Alegre, 80 Loja, 20030 Rio de Janeiro).

ZEMIRA OVERTURE, M. 231 (1803) - Orchestra.

Sources

De Azevado, Luis H. Correa.   A Brief History of Music in Brazil. Washington, D.C., 1948.

De Lerma, Dominique-René.   "The Life and Works of Nunes-Garcia: A Status Report."   The Black Perspective in Music 14.2 (Spring 1986): 93-102.

Luper, Albert   The Music of Brazil.   Washington, D.C., 1943.

De Mattos, Cloefe Person.   Catalogo tematico des obras de Padre Jose Mauricio Nunes Garcia.   Rio de Janeiro, 1970.

Southern, Eileen.   Biographical Dictionary of Afro-American and African Musicians.   Westport, CT: Greenwood Press, 1982.

REPUBLICANO, ASSIS (1897 -)

Assis Republicano was born in Brazil in 1897.
He studied with Francisco Braga.
Among his works were Symphony of Multitudes for orchestra, chorus, and band; Improviso for cello and orchestra; and four operas: O Bandeirante, Natividade de Jesus, Amazonas, and O Ermitao de Gloria.

Works

AMAZONAS - Opera.

IMPROVISO - Cello and orchestra.

O BANDERIRANTE (THE PIONEER) - Opera.

O ERMITAO DE GLORIA (THE HERMIT OF GLORY) - Opera.

NATIVIDADE DE JESUS (BIRTH OF JESUS) - Opera.

SYMPHONY OF MULTITUDES - Orchestra, chorus, and band. In the Fleisher Collection, Philadelphia, Pennsylvania.

Source

Roach, Hildred. Black American Music: Past and Present, Vol. II. Miami: Krieger Publisher Co, 1985, p. 135.

ROLDÁN Y GARDES, AMADEO (1900-1939)

Amadeo Roldán y Gardes was born July 12, 1900, in Paris, and died March 2, 1939, in Havana, Cuba.
He began to study violin at the age of 5 at the Conservatory of Music in Madrid, Spain. Later he studied harmony and composition with Conrado el Campo, and after settling in Havana in 1919, he studied with Pedro Sanjuan, musical director of the Havana Orquesta Filarmonica.
In 1924 he was appointed concertmaster of the Filarmonica, and served as conductor after Sanjuan.
His best known works include Oberture sobre temas cubanos and Tres Pequenos Poemas; the ballets El Milagro de Anaquillé and La rebambaramba; and the chamber works Ritmicas I-VI, Tres toques, Danza negra, Motivos do son, Poema negro, and Curujey.

Works

DANZA NEGRA - Voice, 2 clarinets, 2 violas, percussion.

LLAMADA, PARA DESPERTAR A PAPA MONTERO - Clarinet, 2 violins, 2 violas, violoncello, Cuban timpani.

EL MILAGRO DE ANAQUILLE (1929) - Ballet.

POEMA NEGRO (1939) - String quartet.

LA REBAMBARAMBA (1928) - Ballet.

Sources

Carpentier, Alejo. La Musica en Cuba. Mexico, D.F., 1972. c. 1946.

Slonimsky, Nicholas. Music of Latin America. New York, 1972, c. 1945.

Southern, Eileen. Biographical Dictionary of Afro-American and African Musicans. Westport, CT: Greenwood Press, 1982. pp. 325-26.

WHITE Y LAFITTE, JOSE [JOSEPH] SILVESTRE DE LOS DOLORES (1836-1918)

Jose Silvestre de los Dolores White y Lafitte was born January 17, 1836, in Matanzas, Cuba. He died in Paris on March 15, 1918.

He began to study music at the age of 10 with his father, and later with Jose Maria Roman and Pedro Lecerf. In 1852, Louis Gottschalk encouraged him to study at the Paris Conservatory of Music, which he did in 1855, studying with Joseph Alard, Henri Reber, and Ferdinand Taite. In 1856 he won the Prix de Rome in Violin.

He toured in Europe, the Caribbean, South America, and Mexico, and after several years in Paris, toured in the United States between 1875-76. He spent 10 years (1881-1891) as a music teacher at the Imperial Court in Rio de Janeiro, then returned to Paris.

Works

AMOR HERMOSO - Two voices and orchestra. Unpublished.

AMOR HERMOSO - Two violins and piano. Publisher: Paris, Ch. Hayet, 1914. Library: Bibliotheque Nationale, 4Vm Y4975.

LA BELLA CUBANA - Violin and piano. Manuscript: Biblioteca Nacional, Havana. NOTE: A kind of Cuban national air based on rhythms of the old Haitian guaracha and merengue. Recording: Columbia CL-773.

BOLERO - Violin and orchestra. Dedicated to D. Carlos White. Unpublished.

CONCERTO IN F SHARP - Violin and orchestra. Revised and edited by Paul Glass and Kermit Moore. Piano reduction by John Ruggero. Publisher: Belwin-Mills Pub. Corp., 1976. Score: New York Public Library, University of New Mexico.

CONCERTO IN F SHARP MINOR (1864) - Violin and orchestra. Contents and Duration: 1. Allegro; 2. Adagio (16 minutes 56 seconds; 3. Allegro moderato (4 minutes 45 seconds). Publisher: Melville: Belwin-Mills, 1976 (edited by Paul Glass and Kermit Moore). Manuscript: Biblioteca Nacional, Havana. Recording: Columbia M-33432 (1975); Aaron Rosand, violin; London Symphony Orchestra, Paul Freeman, conductor (ed. by Paul Glass and Kermit Moore).

DUO CONCERTANTE ON THEMES FROM "FAUST" (ca. 1874) - Two violins (and orchestra?). Unpublished.

GRAND FANTASY ON THEMES FROM "LA TRAVIATA" (ca. 1866) - Violin (and piano?). Unpublished.

INVITATORIO - Four voices and orchestra. Unpublished.

LA JOTA ARAGONESA (CAPRICE) - Opus 5. Violin and piano. Edited by Paul Glass. Publisher: Associated Music Pub., Inc., 1975. Manuscript: Biblioteca Nacional, Havana.

LAMENTACIONES - Two voices and orchestra. Unpublished.

LAS LLAGES DE NUESTRA SENOR JESUCRISTO - Two voices and orchestra. Unpublished.

MELODIA SOBRE AIRES CUBANOS - Violin and piano. Unpublished.

MISERERE - Two voices and orchestra. Unpublished.

NOVELLES ÉTUDES, Opus 33 - Violin solo with violin accompaniment. Published: Paris, Burdilly, 1902. Library: Bibliothèque National, Vm8 213.

QUINTET - Flute, two violins, viola, and bass. Dedicated to J. José Garcia Aguirre. Unpublished.

ROMANCE-BARCAROLLE, Opus 2 - Violin and piano. Publisher: Paris, Gamboge Frères, 1861. Library: Bibliothèque Nationale, Vm 1f 6134.

ROMANCE SANS PAROLES, Opus 8, No. 2 - Violin and piano. Publisher: Paris, Gamboge Freres, 1863. Library: Bibliothèque Nationale, Vm 1f 6135.

ROMANCE SANS PAROLES, Opus 18 - Violin and piano. Publisher: Paris, Heugel, n.d. 5 pp. #9656. Library: Spingarn.

SIX GRANDE ÉTUDES, Opus 13 - Violin, unaccompanied. Publisher: Paris, Schonenberger, 1869. Library: Spingarn.

SIX GRANDE ÉTUDES - Violin. Publisher: Paris, Lemoine et Fils, 1898. 21 pp. #S2936. Library: Spingarn.

STRING QUARTET - Manuscript: Biblioteca Nacional, Havana.

STYRIENNE: MORCEAU DE CONCERT, Opus 11 - Violin and piano. Dedication: "A mon ami, Aimé Gros. Publisher: Paris, Froment; London: Schott, n.d., 2nd edition. 13 pp. #E.G.4460. Library: Spingarn.

VALSE-CAPRICE Opus 23 - Violin and piano. Dedication: A Monsieur le Marquis de Palmomares de Duero. Publisher: Paris, Hartmann, 1875. Library: Bibliothèque Nationale, Vm 1f 6137; Spingarn.

VARIATIONS ON A THEME FROM "NORMA" - Violin with (strings?) quartet or piano. Unpublished.

VARIATIONS ON AN ORIGINAL THEME - Violin and piano. Unpublished.

VIOLONESQUE, Opus 32 - Violin and piano. Publisher: Paris, Ulysse T. du Wast, 1897. 15 pp. #VTW377. Library: Bibliothèque Nationale, Vm 1f 6138; Spingarn.

ZAMACUECA: DANSE CHILENNE, Opus 30 - Violin and piano. Publisher: Paris, Ulysse T. du Wast, 1897, 7 pp. #VTW354; Paris, Rene Gilles, 1897. Library: Spingarn; Bibliotheque Nationale, Vm 1f 6139.

Sources

Abdul, Raoul. "A Master Violinist." In Blacks in Classical Music. New York: Dodd, Mead & Co., 1977, pp. 179-80.

Carter, Madison H . An Annotated Catalogue of Composers of African Ancestry. New York: Vantage Press, 1986.

De Lerma, Dominique-Rene. "Black Composers in Europe." Black Music Research Journal 10.2 (Fall 1990): 275-334.

De Lerma, Dominique-Rene. "A Concordance of Scores and Recordings of Music by Black Composers." Black Music Research Journal (1984): 60- 140. Black Music Research Center, Columbia College, Chicago.

De Lerma, Dominique-Rene. "Violinist Jose White in Paris, 1855-1875." Black Music Research Journal 10.2 (Fall 1990): 113-232.

Du Pont, Paul. Biography of Jose White. Paris: n.p., 1874.

Hare. Maud Cuney. Negro Musicians and Their Music. Washington, D.C.: Associated Publishers, 1936, pp. 303-05.

Southern, Eileen. Biographical Dictionary of Afro-American and African Musicians. Westport, CT: Greenwood Press, 1982, p. 400.

Trotter, James M. Music and Some Highly Musical People. Chicago: Afro-Am Press, 1968, pp. 224-40. (orig. 1878)

String Music Index

UNACCOMPANIED STRING SOLOS

BANJO

Weston, Horace

The Egyptian Fandango
Horace Weston's Celebrated Polka - banjo; 2 banjos
Horace Weston's Jig
Horace Weston's New Scottisch
Horace Weston's Old Time Jig
The Seek No Further March
"Song and Dance" Melody
Weston's Great Minor Jig

GUITAR

Bebey, Francis

Black Woman
The Chant of Ibadan: Black Tears
Christ Was Born in Bomba
Concert Pour Un Vieux Masque
Guitare d'une Autre Rime

Brouwer, Leo

Apuntes (1959)
Concerto for Guitar
Danza Caracteristica (1957)
Elogia de la Danza (1964)
La Espiral Eterna (1971)
Parabola
Pieza sin Titulo (1956)

Cordero, Roque   Five Messages for Four Friends (1983)

Casseus, Frantz Gabriel Dance of the Hounsies

Cunningham, Arthur   Jill Ellen (1977)

Dabney, Wendell Phillips Moments of Pleasure Waltz
The Mystic Shrine

| | Only a Dream |
| | Plantation Classic |

Holland, Justin	An Andante
	Carnival of Venice Fantaisie (1866)
	Chant Bohemien
	Choice Melodies for the Guitar (1867)
	Condellied
	Dearest Spot on Earth
	Flower Song, from Carmen
	Flowers of Spring: Waltzes
	Gems for the Guitar (1856?)
	Hunting Rondo
	Last Waltzes of a Lunatic
	March from Faust
	Shells of Ocean
	Sicilian Mariner's Hymn; O Sanctissima
	Spanish Fandango
	Two Arias from Lorezia

| Kay, Ulysses Simpson | Guitarra (1973) |

| León, Tania Justina | Paisanos Semos! (We's Hillbillies) (1984) |

| Roxbury, Ronald | Haiku and Joe |

| Russell, George Allan | Concerto for Self-Accompanied Guitar (1962) |

HARP

| Tillis, Frederick Charles | Spiritual Fantasy No. 13 (1989) - Harp or piano |

VIOLIN

Baker, David Nathaniel	Improvisation #1 for Unaccompanied Violin (1975)
	Improvisation #2 for Unaccompanied Violin (1975)
	Suite for Unaccompanied Violin (1975)

| Bland, Edward Osmund (Ed) | For Violin (1980) |

| Beckon, Lettie M. | Pulsations (1975) - Violin |

| Carter, John | Emblemes |

| Cooper, William Benjamin | Solo Violin |

| Jenkins, Leroy | Background to Life |

| Johnson, Frank (a.k.a. Francis Johnson) | Willig's Pocket Companion - Flute or violin |

| Johnson, Hall | Sonata in A Minor |

Lavergne, Patric	Elegy
Moffatt, Richard Cullen	Sonata
Perkinson, Coleridge-Taylor	Blue Forms (1972)
Price, John Elwood	...And Moses...and Marian Danced (1980) Cicada (1980) Mourning Dove (1980) Scarab I (1980)
Roxbury, Ronald	Pygmies
White y Lafitte, José [Joseph] (Silvester de los Dolores)	Six Grande Études, Opus 13
Woods, Michael E.	Psalm #4 Psalm #5

VIOLA

Fischer, William S.	Predilections (1963)
Hailstork, Adolphus Cunningham	Trapezium (1974)
Singleton, Alvin	Argoru IV (1978)
Tillis, Frederick Charles	Three Showpieces for Viola, Unaccompanied (1966)
Woods, Michael E.	Psalm #3

VIOLONCELLO

Cooper, William Benjamin	Chronikos (1977)
Cunningham, Arthur	Eclatette (1969) Violoncello Thisby Dying (1968) - Flute and cello or violoncello alone
Da Costa, Noel G.	Two Pieces for Unaccompanied Cello (1973)
Herbison, Jeraldine Saunders (Butler)	Sonata No. 1 (1977-78)
Holdridge, Lee	Fantasy Sonata (1972)
Jekins, Edmund Thorton	Sonata in A Minor
León, Tania Justina	Four Pieces for Cello Solo (1983)
Margetson, Edward Henry	Ballad-Valse-Serenade

McDaniel, William Foster Cello Sonata

Moore, Dorothy Rudd   Baroque Suite for Unaccompanied Violoncello
                           (1964-65)

Moore, Kermit   Sonata

Perkinson, Coleridge- Lamentations: A Black/Folk Song Suite for
Taylor   Unaccompanied Cello (1973)

Price, John Elwood   Impulse and Deviation, Nos. 1-24 (1958; 1971-74;
                           1976)
                      Prayers: Imhotep (1989)
                      A Ptah Hymn (1978)
                      Waty: Ancient Singer...Who Tried (1989)

Singleton, Alvin   Argoru II (1970)

White, Clarence Cameron Fantasie (1954)
                         Legende d'Afrique (1955)

Woods, Michael E.   Psalm #5

CONTRABASS

Baker, David Nathaniel Three Short Pieces for Solo Bass

Cordero, Roque   Soliloquios No. 5

Da Costa, Noel G.   In Space (1972)

Lavergne, Patric   Three Movements

TWO INSTRUMENTS

STRINGS

Anderson, T[homas]   Vocalise (1980) - Violin and harp
J[efferson]

Brouwer, Leo   Micropiezas - 2 guitars

Coleman, Charles DeWitt Suite - 2 violins

Cunningham, Arthur   Inventions, Two (1952) - 2 double basses

Da Costa, Noel G.   "Still Music" No. 1 (1965) - 2 violins
                      Time...On and On (1971) - Violin, tenor saxophone,
                           and pre-recorded electronic sounds

Dickerson, Roger Donald Music for String Trio (1957)

Hailstork, Adolphus   American Landscape No. 2 (1978) - Violin and
Cunningham   cello

Harris, Robert A.   Sonatine for Two Violins (1959-60)

Moore, Dorothy Rudd   Moods (1969) - Viola and cello

Saint-Georges [Saint-   Six Sonatas pour le Violon par St. George - Violin
George], Joseph   solo, with violin accompaniment
Boulogne, The
Chevalier de

White y Lafitte, José   Novelles Études, Opus 33 - Violin solo, with violin
[Joseph] (Silvester   accompaniment
de los Dolores)

Woods, Michael E.   Jazz Etude for Viola and Bass
                           Psalm #91 - Violin and viola
                           Psalm #92 - Violin and viola
                           Psalm #93 - Violin and viola

                    STRING WITH ANOTHER INSTRUMENT

Adams, Leslie   Intermezzo (1953) - Violin and piano
                           Night Song a.k.a. Night Music (1983) - Flute and
                               harp
                           Pastoral for Violin and Piano (1952)
                           Sonata for Cello and Piano (1964; completed in 1975)

Anderson, T[homas]   Bridging and Branching - Flute and double bass
J[efferson]   Variations on a Theme by Alban Berg (1977) - Viola
                               and piano

Atkins, Russell   Object-Forms (1953) - Violin and piano
                           Object-Forms (1958) - Violoncello and piano

Baker, David Nathaniel   Deliver My Soul (1968) - Violin and piano
                           The Dude (1962) - Violoncello and piano
                           Duo (1988) - Clarinet and violoncello
                           Electric Stere-Opticon (1975) - Violoncello and
                               electronic instruments
                           Ethnic Variations on a Theme of Paganini (1976) -
                               Violin and piano
                           Jazz Suite for Violin and Piano (1979)
                           Piece for Violoncello and Piano (1966)
                           Singer of Songs, Weaver of Dreams (1980) -
                               Violoncello and solo percussion
                           Sonata for Viola and Piano (1966)
                           Sonata for Violin and Cello (1974)
                           Sonata for Violin and Piano (1967)
                           Sonata for Violoncello and Piano (1973)
                           A Walk with a Child (1968) - Voice and guitar

Batiste, Alvin   Etude One - Solo clarinet and/or piano or bass
                           Picou - Clarinet and violoncello

Belafonte, Harry   Recognition (1968) - Voice and guitar

Bonds, Margaret Allision   I Want Jesus to Walk with Me - Cello and piano
                            Trouble Water - Cello and piano

Bridgetower   Sonata Mulattica - Violin and piano
[Bridgtower], George
(Augustus) Polgreen

Brown, Lawrence   Five Negro Folk Songs - Violoncello and piano
                            Spirituals - Violoncello and piano

Burleigh, Henry   Six Plantation Melodies for Violin and Piano (1901)
Thacker ("Harry")   Southland Sketches (1916) - Violin and piano

Chandler, Len H., Jr.   The Lovin' People (1967) - Voice and guitar

Clark, Edgar Rogie   Etude (1974) - Violin and piano
                            Figurine (1965) - Cello and piano

Clay, Omar   Chun Dynasty - Marima and violin

Coleridge-Taylor, Samuel   Ballad in C Minor (1907) - Violin and piano
                            Four African Dances (1902) - Violin and piano
                            Gipsy Suite (1898) - Violin and piano
                            Hiawathan Sketches (1896) - Violin and piano
                            Romance (1905?) - Violin and piano
                            Sonata in D Minor (1898-9) - Violin and piano
                            Two Romantic Pieces (1896) - Violin and piano
                            Valse Caprice (1898) - Violin and piano
                            Variations in B Minor for Violoncello and Piano

Cooper, William   Fantasy - Organ and cello
Benjamin

Cordero, Roque   Dos Piezas Cortas: Two Short Pieces (1945) -
                                 Violin and pianoforte
                            Double Concerto Without Orchestra for Violin and
                                 Piano
                            Sonata (1963) - Violoncello and pianoforte
                            Sonatina (1946) - Violin and pianoforte

Da Costa, Noel G.   Five Verses with Vamps (1968) - Violoncello and
                                 piano
                            Jes' Grew #1 Chant Variations for Violin (1973) -
                                 Violin and piano
                            Magnolia Blue (1975) - Violin and piano
                            Spaces (1966) - Trumpet and contrabass
                            Violin (1973) - Violin and electric piano

Dawson, WIlliam Levi   Sonata in A - Violin and piano
                            Sonata in A Minor for Violin and Piano

Dennis, Mark Andrew, Jr.   A Set of Three (1972) - Clarinet and violin

Elie, Justin   (4) African Suites
                            Haitian Legend - Violin and piano
                            Legende Creole - Piano and violin

Euba, Akin   The Wanderer - Violoncello and piano

Fischer, William S.   Movement for '65 (1965) - Flute and harp
                                  Music for Flute and Harp (1965)
                                  Piece (1955) - Viola and piano
                                  Short Piece (1962) - Violin and harpsichord
                                  Sonata (1962) - Violin and piano

Gutiérrez y Espinosa,   Sonadina de Violin - with orchestra
Felipe

Hailstork, Adolphus   Canto Carcelera (1978) - Oboe and guitar
Cunningham   Sonata for Violin and Piano (1972)
                                  Suite - Violin and piano

Hebron, J. Harvey   Sonata - Violin and piano

Herbison, Jeraldine   Fantasy in Three Moods (1971) - Cello and piano
Saunders (Butler)   Intermezzo for Cello and Piano (1969; revised 1975)
                                  Six Duos (1976) - Cello and piano

Jenkins, Edmund Thorton   Dance for Cello and Piano
                                  Rêverie; Fantasie pour Violin et Piano (1919)
                                  Romance (1915) - Violin and piano

Johnson, Frank (a.k.a.   Bingham's Cotillion - Piano, flute, or violin
Francis Johnson)   Johnson's March - Piano with accompaniment for
                                      flute or violin
                                  A New Spanish Dance - Piano with flute or violin
                                  Parade March - Piano with accompaniment for flute
                                      or violin

Johnson, John Rosamond   Nobody Knows the Trouble I See - Violin and piano

Kay, Ulysses Simpson   Five Portraits - Violin and piano
                                  Jersey Hours (1978) - Voice and harp
                                  Partita in A (1950) - Violin and piano

King, Betty Jackson   Life Cycle - Violin and piano

Lambert, Lucien Leon   Hymnis: Drame Antique in Act V - Piano with flute
Guillaume   or violin accompaniment

Lampley, Calvin Douglas   Four Little "Ings": Portraits (Zening, Practing,
                                      Jazzing, Funing) (1982) - Flute and guitar

Logan, Wendell Morris   Piece for Violin and Piano, Three (1977) - Violin
                                      and electric piano
                                  To Mingus (1979) - Vibraphone (or other instrument
                                      capable of playing chords) and guitar

Lovingood, Penman, Sr.   Chaconne - Viola and piano

Moore, Carman Leroy   Museum Piece (1975) - Flute, cello, and tape
                                  Sonata for Violin and Piano (1965)
                                  Sonata: Variations for Mandolin and Piano (1965)
                                  Variation for Mandolin and Piano

Moore, Dorothy Rudd	Dirge and Deliverance (1971) - Cello and piano Pieces for Violin and Piano, Three (1967)
Moore, Kermit	Music for Cello and Piano
Morrison, George Sumner, Sr.	Five Solos - Violin and piano
Nketia, Joseph Hanson Kwabena	Chamber Music in the American Idiom - Violin and piano w/partos
Nunes-Garcia, Jose Mauricio	Beijo a Mão Que Me Condena - Soprano and cello
Perkinson, Coleridge-Taylor	Variation and Fugue on "The Ash Grove" (early 1950s) - Violin and piano
Price, Florence Beatrice Smith	By Candlelight - Viola and piano The Deserted Garden - Violin and piano Mellow Twilight - Violin and piano
Price, John Elwood	On the Third Day...Osiris Arose (1988) - Contrabass and piano Piece and Deviation (1962) - Viola and piano Piece for Marcarbar, Nine (1976-1978) - Violin and piano Tarantella (1952; revised 1955) - Violin and piano
Roxbury, Ronald	Aria for Fred - Cello and piano
Saint-Georges [Saint-George], Joseph Boulogne, The Chevalier de	L'Autre Jour à l'Ombrage - Medium voice and guitar Sonata in A Major - Violin and piano Sonatas for Violin and Keyboard 　　No. 1, B-flat Major 　　No. 3, G Minor Sonate de Clavecin [sic] in G Major - Keyboard with violin acompaniment Sonate pour Harp et Flute
Smith, Hale	Duo for Violin and Piano (1953) Epicedial Variations (1956) - Violin and piano Sonata for Violoncello and Piano (1955)
Still, William Grant	Pastorela (1946) - Violin and piano Suite for Violin and Piano (1943)
Swanson, Howard	Nocturne (1948) - Violin and piano sonata Sonata for Violoncello and Piano (1923) Suite for Violoncello and Piano (1949)
Tillis, Frederick Charles	Capriccio for Viola and Piano (1960) Phantasy for Viola and Piano (1962) Spiritual Fantasy No. 2 for String Bass and Piano (1980) Spiritual Fantasy No. 7 for Cello and Piano (1983)

Wade, Marcus   A Moorish Sonata - Violin and piano

Walker, George   Sonata for Cello and Piano
Theophilus   Sonata for Viola and Piano
                                 Sonata for Violin and Piano
                                 Sonata No. 2 for Violin and Piano

White, Clarence Cameron   Bandana Sketches (1920) - Violin and piano
                          Cabin Memories (1921) - Violin and piano
                          Caprice, Op. 17, No. 2 - Violin and piano
                          Chant (No-Body Knows the Trouble I've Seen), Op.
                               12, No. 1 - Violin and piano
                          Cradle Song - Violin and piano
                          Jubilee Song - Violin and piano
                          Levee Dance, Op. 26, No. 12 - Violin and piano
                          On the Bayou, Op. 18, No. 2 - Violin and piano
                          Spiritual, Op. 18, No. 3 - Violin and piano
                          Tuxedo - Violin and piano
                          Twilight - Op. 17, No. 1 - Violin and piano

White y Lafitte, José   La Bella Cubana - Violin and piano
[Joseph] Silvestre de   Grand Fantasy on Themes from "La Traviata" (ca.
los Dolores   1866) - Violin and piano
                           La Jota Aragonesa, Caprice, Op. 5 - Violin and
                                piano
                           Melodia Sobre Aires Cubanos - Violin and piano
                           Romance-Barcarolle, Opus 2 - Violin and piano
                           Romance sans Paroles, Opus 8, No. 2 - Violin and
                                piano
                           Romance sans Paroles, Opus 18 - Violin and piano
                           Styrienne: Morceau de Concert, Opus 11 - Violin
                                and piano
                           Valse-Caprice, Opus 23 - Violin and piano
                           Variations on an Original Theme - Violin and piano
                           Violonesque, Opus 32 - Violin and piano
                           Zamacueca: Danse Chilenne, Opus 30 - Violin and
                                piano

Wilson, Olly Woodrow   Violin Sonata (1961) - Violin and piano

Woods, Michael E.   Psalm #39 - Solo string bass and piano

Work, John Wesley, III   Nocturne - Violin and piano

THREE INSTRUMENTS

PIANO TRIO (PIANO, VIOLIN, VIOLONCELLO)

Anderson, T[homas]   Ivesianna
J[efferson]

Baker, David Nathaniel   Blues Waltz (1976)
                           Contrasts (1976)
                           Roots (1976)
                           A Song (1976)
                           Walpurgisnacht (1976)

Dawson, William Levi   Trio in A Major for Violin, Violoncello, and Piano
                        (1925)

Fountain, Primous, III   Ricia (1977)

Hailstork, Adolphus   Trio for Violin, Cello, and Piano (1925)
Cunningham

Moore, Dorothy Rudd   Trio for Violin, Cello, and Piano (1970)

Price, John Elwood   Trio (1960; revised 1974)
                        Trio (1982-83)

Tillis, Frederick   Fantasy No. 8 for Violin, Cello, and Piano (1987)
Charles   Music for Violin, Cello, and Piano
                        Spiritual

Walker, George   Music for Three
Theophilus

Wilson, Olly Woodrow   Trio (1977)

                        STRINGS

Baker, David Nathaniel   Sonata for Viola, Guitar, and Contrabass (1973)

Beckon, Lettie M.   Head a Woe (1975) - 2 violins and cello

Cunningham, Arthur   Trio for Violin, Viola, and Violoncello (1968)

Cordero, Roque   Three Permutations 3 - Violin, violoncello, and
                        string bass

Lake, Oliver   Spaces (1972) - Violin trio

McCall, Maurice   Little Trio - 2 violins and double bass
Henderson

Moore, Undine Smith   Fugue in F (1952) - String trio

Singleton, Alvin   Be Natural (1974) - for any combination of three
                        bowed instruments

Stewart, Earl Lewis   Afro Fugues (1988-80) - Harp trio

Tillis, Frederick   String Trio (1961)
Charles

Woods, Michael E.   String Trio #1 - Violin, viola, and cello

                   STRINGS WITH OTHER INSTRUMENTS

Baiocchi, Regina A.   Two Zora Neale Hurston Songs (1990) - Mezzo-
Harris   soprano, violoncello, and piano

Baker, David Nathaniel	Ballad (1967) - F horn, alto saxophone, and violoncello
Cunningham, Arthur	Trio for Flute, Viola, and Bassoon (1952)
Dédé, Edmond	Rêverie Champêtre: Fantaisie - Violin and violoncello, or flute and bassoon, with piano accompaniment
Duncan, John	Black Bard - Flute, cello, and piano
el-Dabh, Halim	Thulathiya - Viola, oboe, and piano
Fischer, William S.	Suite for Three - Piano, flute, and violin Trio - Piano, clarinet, timpani, violin [sic]
Fountain, Primous	Movement - Flute, contrabass, and piano
Hakim, Talib Rasul	Lailatu'l-Quadr ("The Night of Power") (1984) - Bass, clarinet, percussion, and contrabass Set-Three (1970) - Soprano, violoncello, and piano Three Play Short Five (1965) - Bass clarinet, percussion, contrabass
Heard, Henry A.	Three Pieces (1977) - Flute, viola, and piano
Herbison, Jeraldine Saunders (Butler)	Trio (1979) - Guitar, violin, and flute Miniature Trio (1961) - Oboe, violin, and piano Nocturne (1961) - Oboe, violin, and piano
Holmes, Robert L.	Fantasy on a Negro Spiritual: Wade in the Water (1978) - Piano, flute, and violoncello Yesterday's Mansions (1972) - Flute, violoncello, and piano
Kebede, Ashenafi	Koturasia: Pentamelodic Exposition - Japanese koto, clarinet, and violin
Kennedy, Joseph J., Jr.	Dialogue for Flute, Cello, and Piano
King, Betty Jackson	Vocalise - Soprano, violoncello, and piano
Lateef, Yusef Abdul	Trio for Piano, Violin, and Flute (1965)
Logan, Wendell Morris	Stanzas for Three Players (1966) - Flute, cello, and piano
McCall, Maurice Henderson	Olde Musick - Recorder, cello, and harpsichord
Moore, Carman Leroy	Music for Flute Alone (1981) - Flute, piano, double bass, and tape Tryst (1964) - Clarinet, cello, and percussion
Moore, Dorothy Rudd	From the Dark Tower (1970) - Voice (mezzo-soprano), cello, and piano

	Sonnets on Love, Rosebuds, and Death (1976) - Soprano, violin, and piano

Sonnets on Love, Rosebuds, and Death (1976) - Soprano, violin, and piano
The Weary Blues (1972) - Voice (baritone), cello, and piano

Moore, Kermit   Music for Viola, Piano, and Percussion
Music for Two Violins and Piano (1986)

Moore, Undine Smith Afro-American Suite (1969) - Flute/alto flute, violoncello, and paino

Price, John Elwood Tobias and the Angel (1958) - Incidental music for a play for voice, harp, and percussion
Verses from Genesis and Psalms (1961) - Clarinet, percussion, cello, narrator, and dancers

Roxbury, Ronald   Quasimodo at Wits' End - Flute, guitar, and double bass

Saint-Georges [Saint-George], Joseph Boulogne The Chevalier de Trio (Duos) - Violin and piano

Singleton, Alvin   Et Nunc (1974) - Alto flute, bass clarinet, and contrabass

Tillis, Frederick Charles Music for Alto Flute, Cello, and Piano (1966)
Three Plus One (1969) - Violin, guitar, clarinet and tape recorder

White y Lafitte, Jose' [Joseph] (Silvester de los Dolores) Amor Hermoso - Two violins and piano

Williams, Julius P. In Roads (1987) - Flute, oboe, and cello

Wilson, Olly Woodrow Trio for Flute, Cello, and Piano (1959)

Woods, Michael E. Abraham - Viola, clarinet, and flute
Enoch - Viola, clarinet, and flute
The Gate in the East - Violin, oboe, and trombone
The Gate in the South - Alto flute, violin, and clarinet
Nicodemus - Viola, clarinet, and flute
What Shall I Tell My Children Who Are Black - Clarinet, violin, string bass, and spoken voice

FOUR INSTRUMENTS

STRING QUARTETS

Anderson, Walter F. String Quartet

Baiocchi, Regina A.   String Quartet (1979)
Harris

Baker, David Nathaniel   Pastorale (1959)
                          Religion (1972) - Soprano and string quartet
                          Some Not So Plain Ol' Blues (1990)
                          Sonata for Tuba and String Quartet (1971)
                          Songs of the night (1972) - Soprano, string
                                quartet, and piano
                          String Quartet No. 1 (1962)

Brown, John Harold   A Minor-String Quartet

Burris, Leslie   Song for Winnie

Cheatham, Wallace   String Quartet No. 1 (1987-88)
McClain

Clark, Edgar Rogie   Divertimento (1969)

Coleridge-Taylor, Samuel Fantasiestucke (1895)
                          Quartet in D Minor (1896)

Cordero, Roque   String Quartet No. 1 (1960)
                          String Quartet No. 2 (1968)
                          String Quartet No. 4 (1983)

Dett, Robert Nathaniel   Quartet

Dickerson, Roger Donald   String Quartet (1956)

Drew, James M.   String Quartet No. 1 (Lux Incognitus)

Duncan, John   Atavistic

Edward, Leo   String Quartet (1968; revised 1970)

Euba, Akin   Amici

Fischer, William S.   Quartet, No. 1 (1954)
                          Quartet, No. 2 (1962)
                          String Quartet (1957)

Furmam, James B.   String Quartet (1986)

Hakim, Talib Rasul   Currents (1967)

Harris, Robert A.   String Quartet No. 1 (1960-68)

Herbison, Jeraldine   Little Suite, Op. 1, C Major
Saunders (Butler)

Holt, Nora Douglas   String Quartet (four)

Johnson, Hall   G Major

Kay, Ulysses Simpson	String Quartet No. 1 (1949) - withdrawn by the composer String Quartet No. 2 (1956) String Quartet No. 3 (1961)
Lawrence, William	Three Negro Spirituals
McCall, Maurice Henderson	Wedding Music (Suite of Four Pieces)
McDaniel, William Foster	String Quartet
Moore, Carman Leroy	A Movement for String Quartet (1961)
Moore, Dorothy Rudd	Modes for String Quartet (1968)
Moore, Kermit	String Quartet
Nunes-Garcia, Jose Mauricio	String Quartet
Perkinson, Coleridge-Taylor	String Quartet No. 1: Calvary (early 1950s)
Perry, Zenobia Powell	String Quartet No. 2 (1964)
Price, Florence Beatrice Smith	Negro Folksongs in Counterpoint
Roldán y Gardes, Amadeo	Poema Negro (1939)
Saint-George [Saint-George], Joseph Boulogne, The Chevalier de	String Quartet in C Major Op. 1, No. 1
Singleton, Alvin	Secret Desire to Be Black (1988) String Quartet No. 1 (1967) String Quartet No. 2
Still, William Grant	Danzas de Panama (1948) - String quartet or orchestra
Tillis, Frederick Charles	Spiritual Fantasy No. 12 (Suite for String Quartet) (1988)
Walker, George Theophilus	String Quartet No. 2
White, Clarence Cameron	Hallelujah (1931)
White y Lafitte, Jose [Joseph] Silvestre de los Dolores	String Quartet
Wilson, Olly Woodrow	String Quartet (1960)

Woods, Michael E.   The Gate in the West - Violin, viola, cello, and
            string bass
           Question 85
           String Quartet No. 1

Work, Frederick Jerome String Quartet in F

STRINGS WITH OTHER INSTRUMENTS

Bland, Edward Osmund Sketches Set II (1964) - Clarinet, trumpet,
(Ed)   trombone, and violoncello

Bridgetower   Minuets - Violin, mandolin, German flute, and
[Bridgtower], George   harpsichord
(Augustus) Polgreen

Cunningham, Arthur   Basis (1968) - 4 double basses
          Jill Ellen (1975) - Violin, viola, violoncello,
           and guitar
          Perimeter (1965) - Flute, clarinet, vibraphone,
           and double bass

Da Costa, Noel G.   Blue Mix: A Composition in the Form of a Chart
           (1970) - Solo contrabass/fender bass,
           violoncello, contrabass, and percussion
          November Song (1974) - Soprano, violin, saxophone,
           and piano (with improvisation)

Euba, Akin   Music - Violin, horn, piano, and percussion

Hakim, Talib Rasul   Tone-Poem (1969) - Soprano, percussion,
           contrabass, and piano

Harris, Howard C., Jr. Pro Viva - Flute, piano, cello, and congas

Herbison, Jeraldine   I Heard the Trailing Garments of the Night (1975) -
Saunders (Butler)   Flute, violin, cello, and piano
          Introspection (1973) - Oboe, violin, cello, and
           piano

Kay, Ulysses Simpson Triptych on Texts of Blake (1962) - High voice,
           violin, violoncello, and piano

Lake, Oliver   Suite - Improvisor and violin trio

Logan, Wendell Morris Song of the Witch Doktor (1976) - Flute, cello,
           piano, and percussion

McLin, Lena Johnson   The Marriage Cantata (1974) - Flute, violin,
           violoncello, piano or organ
          Memory (1976) - Flute, violin, violoncello, piano
           or organ

Moore, Carman Leroy   Bernice: Variations on a Theme
                             G.F. Handel (1984) - Violin, clarinet, cello, and
                                 piano
                             Sean-Sean (1965) - French horn, 3 cellos, and tape

Perkinson, Coleridge-   Attitudes (1962-63) - Tenor, violin, violoncello,
Taylor   and piano

Price, John Elwood   Quartet (1962) - Bassoon, french horn, violin, and
                                 viola

Sancho, Ignatius   Minuets, Cotillions and Country Dances for the
                                 Violin, Mandolin, German Flute, and
                                 Harpsichord (c. 1767)

Still, William Grant   Folk Suite No. 2 - Flute, clarinet, cello, and piano
                             Folk Suite No. 4 - Flute, clarinet, cello, and piano

Tillis, Frederick   Quartet for Flute, Clarinet, Bassoon, and Cello
Charles   (1952)

FIVE INSTRUMENTS (STRINGS WITH OTHER INSTRUMENTS)

Baker, David Nathaniel   Sonata for Jazz Violin and String Quartet
                             Sonata for French Horn and String Quartet
                             Two Cello String Quintet (1987)

Bonds, Curtis Horace   Moon Circles (Tone Poem) - Piano and quartet

Bonds, Margaret Allison   Quintet F Major (1933) - Piano quintet

Carter, Warrick L.   Eric - Soprano saxophone or clarinet, 2 violins,
                                 viola, and violoncello (may be played by
                                 string orchestra)

Cloud, Lee Vernell   7 for 5 in 4 - Flute, clarinet, vibes, viola, and
                                 double bass

Coleridge-Taylor, Samuel   Quintet in A Major for Clarinet and Strings (1895) -
                                 Clarinet, 2 violins, viola and cello
                             Quintet in G Minor - Piano, violins, viola, and
                                 violoncello, pianoforte

Da Costa, Noel G.   Five Epitaphs (1956) - Soprano and string quartet

Duncan, John   Divertimento - Trombone and string quartet
                             Three Proclamations for Trombone and String
                                 Quartet

Hakim, Talib Rasul   Mutations (1964) - Bass clarinet horn, trumpet,
                                 viola, and violoncello

Hammond, Douglas   Suite in Two Colors - Flute violin, viola,
                                 violoncello, and piano

Hayes, Joseph   Quintet - Clarinet, bassoon, violin, violoncello,
                                    and piano

Herbison, Jeraldine   Metamorphosis (1978) - 2 violins, cello, guitar
Saunders (Butler)   and piano

Jekins, Leroy   Shapes, Textures, Rhythms, Moods, and Sounds -
                                    Violin, flute, clarinet, French horn, bass,
                                    and clarinet

Jones, Quincy Delight,   Soundpiece (1962) - String quartet and contralto
Jr.

León, Tania Justina   Porajota Delate ("From T. to J.") (1988) - Flute,
                                    clarinet, violin, violoncello, and piano

Logan, Wendell Morris   Outside Ornette's Head (1979) - Trumpet, guitar,
                                    vibraphone, double bass, and drums

McLin, Lena Johnson   The Colors of the Rainbow (1971) - 2 flutes,
                                    violin, violoncello, piano or organ

Mells, Herbert Franklin   Quintet in A Minor - B-flat clarinet, 2 violins,
                                    viola, and cello

Moore, Kermit   Quincentra - String quartet and piano

Perry, Julia Amanda   Pastoral (1962) - Flute and string quartet
                               Stabat Mater - Contralto and string orchestra or
                                    string quartet

Price, Florence   Quintet - Piano and strings
Beatrice Smith

Sancho, Ignatius   Minuets, Cotillions, and Country Dances for the
                                    Violin, Mandolin, German Flute, and
                                    Harpsichord with Obliagatto French Horn (c.
                                    1770)

Singleton, Alvin   Such a Nice Lady (1979) - Clarinet, violin, viola,
                                    cello, and piano

Stokes, Harvey J.   Chamber Concerto No. 1 - Oboe and string quartet

White y Lafitte, Jose   Quintet - Flute, two violins, viola, and bass
[Joseph] (Silvester   Variations on a Theme from "Norma" - Violin with
de los Dolores)   (strings?) quartet or piano

Woods, Michael E.   Hoopostosis - Violin, soprano saxophone, piano,
                                    bass, and drums

SIX INSTRUMENTS (STRINGS WITH OTHER INSTRUMENTS)

Baiocchi, Regina A.   Chase (1978) - Flute, alto flute, oboe, B-flat
Harris   clarinet, bassoon, and piano

Belaka, O'sai Tutu   Brother Malcolm - Piano, double bass, electric
(a.k.a. Charles   bass, flute, percussion, and violoncello
Henderson Bell, Sr.)

Bond, Curtis Horace   Rainbow (A Concertina) - Piano, string quartet,
                             and flute

Cunningham, Arthur   Two World Suite (1971) - 6 double basses

Da Costa, Noel G.   In the Circle (1970) - 4 electric guitars, fender
                             bass, and percussion
                        Occurrence for Six (1965) - Flute, clarinet, bass
                             clarinet, tenor saxophone, trumpet, and
                             contrabass

Hailstork, Adolphus   Sextet for Strings (1971)
Cunningham

Hakim, Talib Rasul   Contours (1966) - Oboe, bassoon, horn, trumpet,
                             violoncello, and contrabass
                        Elements (1967) - Flute/alto flute, clarinet/bass
                             clarinet, violin/viola, violoncello, piano,
                             and glass and bamboo wind and hand chimes

Hampton, Ralph   2 Songs, No. 2 - Voice, flute, clarinet, horn,
                             trumpet, trombone, violin, contrabass, and
                             piano

Hayes, Joseph   Hornotations, No. 1 (1970) - Horn and string
                             quartet, double bass

Leon, Tania Justina   Pueblo Mulato: 3 Songs on Poems by Nicolas
                             Guillen (1987) - Soprano, oboe, guitar,
                             double bass, percussion, piano

Logan, Wendell Morris   The Eye of the Sparrow (1978) - Flute, tenor saxo-
                             phone, trumpet, double bass, piano, drums

McCreary, Richard   Quartet - Bamboo flute, flute, 2 violins,
Deming, Jr.   violoncello, percussion

Nelson, Oliver Edward   Soundpiece for Contralto, String Quartet, and
                             Piano (1963)

Santos, Henry Jose   Leola (1989) - Trumpet, alto saxophone, violin,
                             cello, piano, drums

Singleton, Alvin   La Flora (1982) - Flute/alto flute, clarinet,
                             percussion (2), violin, violoncello

Still, William Grant   Folk Suite No. 1 - Flute, piano, string quartet

SEVEN INSTRUMENTS (STRINGS WITH OTHER INSTRUMENTS)

Anderson T[homas]
J[efferson]
Variations on a Theme by M.B. Tolson (1969) -
    Mezzo-soprano. alto saxophone. trumpet,
    violin, violoncello, piano

Brown, Uzee
Ebony Perspective - Bass voice, clarinet, trumpet,
    trombone, tuba, banjo, percussion

Cordero, Roque
Permutaciones 7 (1967) - Clarinet, trumpet,
    timpani, pianoforte, violin, viola, double
    bass

el-Dabh, Halim
Thulathiya - Soprano, flute, oboe, clarinet,
    bassoon, horn, viola

Hakim, Talib Rasul
Six Players and a Voice (1964) - Soprano,
    clarinet, trumpet, violoncello, 2 percussion,
    piano

Leon, Tania Justina
The Beloved (1972) - Flute, oboe, clarinet,
    bassoon, piano, violoncello, double bass

Logan, Wendell Morris
Maggie Magalita (1980) - Flute, clarinet,
    violoncello, 2 percussion, pianoforte, guitar

Roldan y Gardes, Amadeo
Llamada, Para Despertar a Papa-Montero - Clarinet,
    2 violins, 2 violas, violoncello, cuban
    timpani

Singleton, Alvin
Akwaaba (1985) - Flute, clarinet, bassoon, piano,
    percussion, violin, violoncello

Stokes, Harvey J.
The Glory of Easter - Soprano, tenor, piano,
    violin, violoncello horn, trumpet

Woods, Michael E.
Highway 77 - Flute, clarinet, trombone,
    percussion, violin, viola, string bass
Pslam #23 - Soprano voice, electric bass,
    classical guitar, flute, violin, viola, and
    cello

EIGHT INSTRUMENTS (STRINGS WITH OTHER INSTRUMENTS)

Coleridge-Taylor,
Samuel
Nonet in F Minor (1894) - Piano, violin, viola,
    violoncello, double bass, clarinet, horn,
    bassoon

Da Costa, Noel G.
Riff Time (1972) - Violin, violoncello, piano,
    percussion (5 players)

Hakim, Talib Rasul
Timelessness (1970) - Flugelhorn, horn. trombone,
    tuba, 2 percussion, contrabass, piano

Heard, Henry A.
Street Levels (1981) - Alto flute, jazz trio,
    string quartet, harp

Lewis, John Aaron	Sketch for Double Quartet
Smith, Hale	Introduction, Cadenzas, and Interludes for Eight Players (1974) - Flute/alto flute, oboe, clarinet, harp, piano, violin, viola, violoncello
Swanson, Howard	Vista No. II (1969) - String octet
Tillis, Frederick Charles	Nobody Knows (1986) - Double quartet (string quartet, trumpet, tenor saxophone, drum set, string bass)
Woods, Michael E.	Downtown Heaven - Clarinet, bassoon, trumpet, trombone, percussion, violin, viola, electric bass
	The Judgment Hall - Clarinet, bassoon, trumpet, trombone, percussion, violin, viola, electric bass

NINE INSTRUMENTS (STRINGS WITH OTHER INSTRUMENTS)

Bland, Edward Osmund (Ed)	Primo Counterpoint (1981) - Flute, clarinet, trumpet, trombone, 2 percussion, electric piano, violoncello, electric bass
Da Costa, Noel G.	Statement and Response (1966) - Flute, oboe, bass clarinet, trumpet, trombone, tuba, viola, violoncello, contrabass
Heard, Henry A.	Street Levels (1981) - Alto flute jazz trio, string quartet, harp
Johnson, James Louis ("J.J.")	Diversions (1968) - 6 trombones, celesta, harp, percussion
Lake, Oliver	Shadow Thread - Octet and cello
Logan, Wendell Morris	Proportions for Nine Players and Conductor (1968) - Flute, B-flat clarinet, B-flat trumpet, trombone, violin, cello, piano, percussion (2 players
Moore, Dorothy Rudd	Lament for Nine Instruments (1969) - Flute, oboe, clarinet, trumpet, trombone, percussion, violin, viola, cello
Woods, Michael E.	The Saints Club - Clarinet, bassoon, trumpet, trombone, piano, percussion, violin, viola, electric bass

TEN INSTRUMENTS (STRINGS WITH OTHER INSTRUMENTS)

Bland, Edward Osmund   Magnetic Variations (1982) - Solo clarinet, flute,
(Ed)   clarinet, oboe/English horn, 2 percussion,
                                electric piano, violoncello, electric bass,
                                violin (amplified)

Fletcher, John   Suite (1973) - Organ, flute, clarinet, bassoon,
                                violin, cello, brass quartet

Smith, Hale   Two Love Songs of John Donne (1958) - Soprano,
                                string quartet. woodwind quintet

ELEVEN INSTRUMENTS (STRINGS WITH OTHER INSTRUMENTS)

Bland, Edward Osmund   Paean for An Endangered Planet (1989) - Flute,
(Ed)   oboe, clarinet, bassoon, 2 percussion,
                                guitar, harp, piano/electric piano. violin
                                (amplified), violoncello

Cordero, Roque   Paz, Paix, Peace (1969) - Harp solo, flute,
                                English horn, bass clarinet, alto flute,
                                clarinet, bassoon, violin, 2 viola, double
                                bass

Da Costa, Noel G.   The Blue Mountains (1962) - Mezzo-soprano, flute,
                                oboe, clarinet, bass clarinet, F-horn,
                                trumpet, viola violoncello, contrabass,
                                percussion
                            In the Landscape of Spring (1962) - Mezzo-soprano,
                                flute, oboe, clarinet, bass clarinet, F-horn,
                                trumpet, viola, violoncello, contrabass,
                                percussion

TWELVE INSTRUMENTS (STRINGS WITH OTHER INSTRUMENTS)

Bland, Edward Osmund   Passa in Blue (1987) - Flute, oboe, clarinet,
(Ed)   bassoon, 2 percussion, guitar, harp,
                                piano/electric piano. violin (amplified),
                                viola (amplified), violoncello

Perry, Julia Amanda   Homunculus C.F. (1966) - Ten percussion, harp,
                                piano

Tillis, Frederick   In Memory Of (1984) - Double quartet and trumpet,
Charles   tenor saxophone, drum set, string bass

Woods, Michael E.   Jesus Enters Jerusalem - Flute, clarinet, bassoon,
                                alto saxophone, trumpet, trombone,
                                percussion, violin, viola, cello, string
                                bass, guitar

STRINGS WITH WOODWINDS

Adams, Leslie   Night Song, a.k.a. Night Music (1983) - Flute and
                                       harp

Anderson, T[homas]   Bridging and Branching - Flute and double
J[efferson]   bass
                                  Six Pieces for Clarinet and Chamber Orchestra
                                       (1962)

Baker, David Nathaniel   Sonata for Violin, Violoncello, and Four Flutes
                                       (1980)

Batiste, Alvin   Etude One - Solo clarinet and/or piano or bass
                                  Picou - Clarinet and violoncello

Bland, Edward Osmund   Magnetic Variations (1982) - Solo clarinet, flute,
(Ed)   clarinet, oboe/English horn, 2 percussion,
                                       electric piano, violoncello, electric bass,
                                       violin (amplified)
                                  Paean for an Endangered Planet (1989) - Flute,
                                       oboe, clarinet, bassoon, 2 percussion,
                                       guitar, harp, piano/electric piano, violin
                                       (amplified), viola (amplified), violoncello
                                  Primo Counterpoint (1981) - Flute, clarinet,
                                       trumpet, trombone, 2 percussion, electric
                                       piano, violoncello, electric bass
                                  Sketches Set I (1965) - Clarinet, trumpet, 2
                                       celli, timpani
                                  Sketches Set II (1964) - Clarinet, trumpet,
                                       trombone, violoncello

Bond, Curtis Horace   Rainbow (A Concertina) - Piano, string quartet,
                                       flute

Bridgetower   Minuets - Violin, mandolin, German flute,
[Bridgtower], George   harpsichord
(Augustus) Polgreen

Brown, Uzee   Ebony Perspective - Bass voice, clarinet, trumpet,
                                       trombone, tuba, banjo, percussion

Carter, Warrick L.   Eric (1977) - Soprano saxophone or clarinet, 2
                                       violins, viola, cello (may be played by
                                       string orchestra)

Cloud, Lee Vernell   7 for 5 in 4 - Flute, clarinet, vibes, viola,
                                       double bass
                                  Survival - Flute, string quartet, double bass, 8
                                       voices, percussion

Coledrige-Taylor, Samuel   Quintet in A Major for Clarinet and Strings (1895)
                                  Nonet in F Minor (1894) - Piano, violin, viola,
                                       violoncello, double bass, clarinet, horn,
                                       bassoon

Cordero, Roque	Paz, Paix, Peace (1969) - Harp solo, flute, English horn, bass clarinet, bassoon, alto flute, clarinet, violin, violoncello, 2 viola, double bass
Cunningham, Arthur	Minakesh (1969) - a. oboe and piano; b. violoncello and strings; c. voice and piano (1970) Perimeters (1965) - Flute, clarinet, vibraphone,, double bass Thisby Dying (1968) - Flute and violoncello or violoncello alone Trio for Flute, Viola, and Bassoon (1952)
Da Costa, Noel G.	The Blue Mountains (1962) - Mezzo-soprano, flute, oboe, clarinet, bass clarinet, contrabass, percussion Epigrams (1965) - Solo violin and flute, clarinet, bassoon, vibraphone, piano In the Landscape of Spring (1962) - Mezzo-soprano, flute, oboe, clarinet, bass clarinet, F-horn, trumpet, viola, violoncello, contrabass, percussion November Song (1974) - Concert scene for soprano, violin, saxophone, piano (with improvisation) Sitting Quietly, Doing Nothing (1962) - Mezzo-soprano, flute, oboe, clarinet, bass clarinet, F-horn, viola, violoncello, contrabass, percussion Statement and Response (1966) - Flute, oboe, bass clarinet, trumpet, trombone, tuba, viola, violoncello, contrabass Time...On and On (1971) - Violin, tenor saxophone, pre-recorded electronic sounds
Dédé, Edmond	Rêverie Champêtre: Fantaisie - Duet for violin and violoncello or flute and bassoon, with piano accompaniment
Dennis, Mark Andrew, Jr.	A Set of Three (1972) - Clarinet and violin
Duncan, John	Black Bards - Flute, cello, and piano
el-Dabh, Halim	Tahmeela - Soprano, flute, oboe, clarinet, bassoon, horn, viola Thulathiya - Viola, oboe, piano
Fletcher, John	Suite (1973) - Organ, flute, clarinet, bassoon, violin, cello, bass
Fischer, William S.	Suite for Three - Piano, flute, violin
Hailstork, Adolphus Cunningham	Canto Carcelera (1978) - Oboe and guitar From the Dark Side of the Sun (1971) - Flutes, alto flute, soprano saxophone, marimbas, vibraphones, glockenspiel, celeste, triangles, bongo drums, strings

Hakim, Talib Rasul

Three Play Short Five - Bass clarinet, percussion,
    contrabass
Lailatu'l-Qadr ("The Night of Power") (1984) -
    Contrabass and percussion

Hammond, Douglas

Suite in Two Colors - Flute, violin, viola,
    violoncello, piano

Harris, Howard C., Jr.

Pro Viva - Flute, piano, cello, congas

Heard, Henry A.

Three-Piece (1977) - Flute, viola, piano

Herbison, Jeraldine
Saunders (Butler)

I Heard the Trailing Garments of the Night (1975) -
    Flute, violin, cello, piano
Introspection (1973) - Oboe, violin, cello, piano
Trio (1979) - Guitar, violin, flute

Kay, Ulysses Simpson

Aulos (1967) - Solo flute, 2 horns, string
    orchestra, percussion
Brief Elegy (1946) - Oboe and strings
Concerto for Oboe and Orchestra (1940)
Pieta (1950) - English horn and string orchestra

Kebede, Ashenafi

Koturasia: Pentamelodic Exposition - Japanese
    koto, clarinet, violin

León, Tania Justina

The Beloved (1972) - Flute, oboe, clarinet,
    bassoon, piano, violoncello, double bass
Maggie Magalita (1980) - Flute, clarinet,
    violoncello, 2 percussion, pianoforte, guitar
Parajota Delate (1988) - Flute, clarinet, violin,
    violoncello, piano

Logan, Wendell Morris

The Eye of the Sparrow (1978) - Flute, tenor
    saxophone, trumpet, double bass, piano, drums
Song of the Witchdoktor (1976) - Flute, violin,
    piano, percussion
Stanzas for Three Players (1966) - Flute, cello,
    piano

McCreary, Richard
Deming, Jr.

Piece for Flute, Clarinet, Vibraphone, and Strings
Quartet - Bamboo flute, flute, 2 violins,
    violoncello, and percussion

McLin, Lena Johnson

The Colors of the Rainbow (1971) - 2 flutes,
    violin, violoncello, oboe
The Marriage Cantata (1974) - Flute, violin,
    violoncello, piano or organ
Memory (1976) - Flute, violin, violoncello, piano
    or organ

Moore, Carman Leroy

Berenice: Variations on a Theme of G.F. Handel
    (1984) - Violin, clarinet, cello, piano
Museum Piece (1975) - Flute, cello, tape
Music for Flute Alone (1981) - Flute, piano,
    double bass, tape
Tryst (1964) - Clarinet, cello, percussion

Roldán y Gardes, Amadeo Danza Negra - Voice, 2 clarinets, 2 violas,
                              percussion
                         Llamada, Para Despertar a Papa-Montero - Clarinet,
                              2 violins, 2 violas, violoncello, Cuban
                              timpani

Sancho, Ignatius   Minuets, Cotillions, and Country Dances for the
                              Violin, Mandolin, German Flute, and
                              Harpsichord (c. 1767)
                         Minuets, Cotillions, and Country Dances for the
                              Violin, Mandolin, German Flute, and
                              Harpsichord with Obligatto French Horn (c.
                              1770)

Singleton, Alvin   Akwaaba (1985) - Flute, clarinet, bassoon, piano,
                              percussion, violin, violoncello
                         Et Nunc (1974) - Alto flute, bass clarinet,
                              contrabass
                         La Flora (1982) - Flute/alto flute, clarinet, 2
                              percussion, violin, violoncello
                         Such a Nice Lady (1979) - Clarinet, violin, viola,
                              violoncello, piano

Stewart, Earl Lewis   An Appropriate Trifle (1974) - Concerto for
                              soprano saxophone, three multiple
                              percussionists, multiple bassists
                         Undulation (Jazz Ballad) (1986) - Flute or
                              clarinet, harp, strings

Stokes, Harvey J.   Chamber Concerto No. 1 - Oboe and string quartet

Still, William Grant   Folk Suite No. 1 - Flute, piano, string quartet
                         Folk Suite No. 2 - Flute, clarinet, cello, piano
                         Folk Suite No. 4 - Flute, clarinet, cello, piano

White y Lafitte, José   Quintet - Flute, two violins, viola, bass
[Joseph] (Silvester
de los Dolores)

Woods, Michael E.   Abraham - Viola, clarinet, flute
                         Enoch - Viola, clarinet, flute
                         The Gate in the South - Alto flute, violin, clarinet
                         Nicodemus - Viola, clarinet, flute
                         What Shall I Tell My Children Who Are Black -
                              Clarinet, violin, string bass, spoken voice

                         STRINGS WITH BRASS

Baker, David Nathaniel   Ballad (1967) - F-horn, alto saxophone,
                              violoncello
                         Fantasy (1954) - Soprano, brass ensemble, harp
                         Sonata for Tuba and String Quartet (1971)
                         Suite for French Horn, String Quartet, and
                              Contrabass (1985)

Bland, Edward Osmund   Primo Counterpoint (1981) - Flute, clarinet,
(Ed)   trumpet, trombone, 2 percussion, electric
                                piano, violoncello, electric bass
                           Sketches Set I (1965) - Clarinet, trumpet, 2
                                cellos, timpani
                           Sketches Set II (1964) - Clarinet, trumpet,
                                trombone, violoncello

Brown, Uzee   Ebony Perspective - Bass voice, clarinet, trumpet,
                                trombone, tuba, banjo, percussion

Da Costa, Noel G.   The Blue Mountain (1962) - Mezzo-soprano, flute,
                                oboe, clarinet, bass clarinet, F-horn,
                                trumpet, viola, violoncello, contrabass,
                                percussion
                           In the Landscape of Spring (1962) - Mezzo-soprano,
                                flute, oboe, clarinet, bass clarinet, F-horn,
                                trumpet, viola, violoncello, contrabass,
                                percussion
                           Occurrence for Six (1965) - Flute, bass clarinet,
                                tenor saxophone, trumpet, contrabass
                           Sitting Quietly, Doing Nothing (1962) - Mezzo-
                                soprano, flute, oboe, clarinet, bass
                                clarinet, F-horn, trumpet, viola,
                                violoncello, contrabass, percussion
                           Spaces (1966) - Trumpet and contrabass
                           Statement and Response (1966) - Flute, oboe, bass
                                clarinet, trumpet, trombone, tuba, viola,
                                violoncello

Duncan, John   Divertimento - Trombone and string quartet
                           Three Proclamations for Trombone and String Quartet

Fletcher, John   Suite (1973) - Organ, flute, clarinet, bassoon,
                                violin, cello, brass quartet

Hakim, Talib Rasul   Sound Images (1969) - Brass (2 trumpets, 2
                                flugelhorns, 4 horns, 3 trombones, tuba), 3
                                percussion, strings, female chorus
                           Timelessness (1970) - Flugelhorn, horn, trombone,
                                tuba, 2 percussion, contrabass, piano

Hayes, Joseph   Hornotations, No. 1 (1970) - Horn, string quartet,
                                double bass

Johnson, James Louis   Diversion (1968) - 6 trombones, celeste, harp,
("J.J.")   percussion

Kay, Ulysses Simpson   Quintet Concerto (1974) - Solo brass quintet (2
                                trumpets, F-horn, 2 trombones; alternate part
                                for tuba) and orchestra

Logan, Wendell Morris   Outside Ornett's Head (1979) - Trumpet, guitar,
                                vibraphone, double bass, drums

Moore, Carman Leroy   Sean-Sean (1965) - French horn, 3 cellos, tape

Price, John Elwood   Abeng (1983) - Horn and strings
                            Nocturne for a Winter Night (1956) - French horn,
                                harp, strings
                            Pieces, Two (1955-75) - Strings and brass quartet
                            Pieces, Two (1974-75) - Trumpet and strings

                            STRINGS WITH PERCUSSION

Baker, David Nathaniel   Concerto for Fours (1980) - Solo quartet (flute,
                                cello, tuba, contrabass), tuba quartet,
                                contrabass quartet, percussion quartet
                            Singers of Songs, Weavers of Dreams (1980) -
                                Violoncello and solo percussion

Beckon, Lettie M.   Symphonic Essay (1977) - String orchestra and
                                percussion

Belaka, O'sai Tutu   Brother Malcolm - Piano, double bass, electric
(a.k.a. Charles   bass, flute, percussion, violoncello
Henderson Bell, Sr.)

Clay, Omar   Chun Dynasty - Marimba and violin

Da Costa, Noel G.   Riff Time (1972) - Violin, violoncello, piano,
                                percussion (5 players)

Fischer, William S.   Trio - Piano, clarinet, timpani, violin [sic]

Hailstork, Adolphus   From the Dark Side of the Sun (1971) - Flute,
Cunningham   alto flute, soprano saxophone, marimbas,
                                vibraphones, glockenspiel, celeste,
                                triangles, bongo drums, strings

Hakim, Talib Rasul   Three Play Short Five (1965) - Bass clarinet,
                                percussion, contrabass
                            Timelessness (1970) - Flugelhorn, horn, trombone,
                                tuba, 2 percussion, contrabass, piano
                            Lailatu'l-Qadr ("The Night of Power") (1984) -
                                Bass clarinet, string bass, percussion

Harris, Howard C., Jr.   Pro Viva - Flute, piano, cello, congas

McCreary, Richard   Myth vs. Reality - String ensemble and percussion
Deming, Jr.

Moore, Carman Leroy   Tryst (1964) - Clarinet, cello, percussion

Moore, Kermit   Music for Viola, Piano, and Percussion

Perry, Julia Amanda   Homunculus C.F. (1966) - 10 percussion, harp,
                                piano

Price, John Elwood   Tobias and the Angel (1958) - Incidental music for
                                a play for voice, harp, percussion
                            Verses from Genesis and Psalms (1961) - Clarinet,
                                percussion, cello, narrator, dancers

STRINGS WITH TAPE/ELECTRONIC INSTRUMENTS

Baker, David Nathaniel	Electric Ster-Opticon (1975) - Violoncello and electronic instruments
Da Costa, Noel G.	Time ... On and On (1971) - Violin, tenor saxophone, pre-recorded electronic sounds
Dennis, Mark Andrew, Jr.	Serene (1973) - Harp, electronic tape, voice
el-Dabh, Halim	Ush Ka Masriya - Harpsichord and tape
Fischer, William S.	Gift of Lesbos (1968) - Cello, piano, tape Time I (1966) - Saxophone, viola, violoncello, percussion, electronic sounds Time II (1967) - Saxophone, viola, violoncello, percussion, electronic sounds
McCreary, Richard Deming, Jr.	"Z" - Orchestra and tape
Moore, Carman Leroy	Museum Piece (1975) - Flute, cello, tape Music for Flute Alone (1981) - Flute, piano, double bass, tape Sean-Sean (1965) - French horn, 3 cellos, tape
Tillis, Frederick Charles	Three Plus One (1969) - Violin, guitar, clarinet, tpae recorder

STRING ORCHESTRA

Adams, Leslie	Sketch: "Sarabande" (1951)
Akpabot, Samuel	Three Nigerian Dances (1975)
Baker, David Nathaniel	Baker's Shuffle (1970) Black Eyed Peas and Cornbread '1970) Blue Strings (1970) Blues (1966) Calypso - Nova No. 1 (1970) Calypso - Nova No. 2 (1971) Evening Song (1970) An Evening Thought First Day of Spring (1969) The Jamaican Strut Little Price Waltz (1959) Mod Waltz (1970) Reflection on a Summer Day - Cello choir Slow Grove (1970) Somber Time (1970) The Sunshine Boogaloo (1970) Triplet Blues (1970)
Batiste, Alvin	The Kheri Herbs - Clarinet and string orchestra
Barnett, Willis L.	Perspectives (1981)

Beckon, Lettie M.   Symphonic Essay (1977) - String orchestra and
                              percussion

Clark, Edgar Rogie   Elegia (1968)
                           Larghetto (1970)

Coleridge-Taylor, Samuel   Four Novelletten (1902)
                           A Lively Little Dream - Strings and harmonium

Cordero, Roque   Elegy (1973)
                           Mensaje Funebre: Funeral Message (1961) -
                              Clarinet solo and string orchestra
                           Movimento Sifonico: Symphonic Movement (1946)
                           Movement (1946)

Dickerson, Roger Donald   Concert Pieces for Beginning String Players Ten
                              (1973)

Ekweume, Lazarus Edward   Negro Rhapsody
Nnanyelu

el-Dabh, Halim   Concerto - Derabucca or timpani and string
                              orchestra
                           Tahmeela for Derabucca and Strings (1959)

Euba, Akin   Ice Cubes

Fox, James Ingram   Andante Con Moto
                           Quartet

Freeman, Paul (Douglas)   Geisterlied (1960) - String orchestra with
                              percussion

Furman, James B.   Cantilena for Strings (1976)
                           Fantasia and Chorale for Strings (1971)

Hailstork, Adolphus   Capriccio for a Departed Brother: Scott Joplin
Cunningham   (1869-1917) (1969)
                           Essay for Strings (1986)
                           Sextet for Strings (1971)
                           Sport for Strings (1986)
                           Two Struts with Blues (1985)

Harris, Robert A.   Adagio for String Orchestra (1966)

Herbison, Jeraldine   Suite No. 1 in C (1960: revised 1977)
Saunders (Butler)   Suite No. 2 (1963)
                           Suite No. 3 (1969)
                           Theme and Variations

Johnson, Hall   Suite

Kay, Ulysses Simpson   Six Dances for String Orchestra
                           String Triptych (1987)
                           Suite for Strings (1947)

McCall, Maurice Henderson	Petite Suite - Young string orchestra Sinfonia Brevis - Young string orchestra
McCreary, Richard Deming, Jr.	Myth vs. Reality - String ensemble and percussion
McDaniel, William Foster	Concerto for Piano and String Orchestra Concerto for Two Flutes and String Orchestra
McLin, Edward M.	Chorales for Strings (1959)
Moseley, James Orville (JOB)	Suite
Perkinson, Coleridge-Taylor	Sinfonia No. 1 for Strings (1956)
Price, John Elwood	Pieces Three (1970) - String orchestra "Steady Wah No Mo" (1973) To the Shrine of the Black Madonna (1974)
Shirley, Donald	Legacy (1972)
Singleton, Alvin	Eine Idee Ist Ein Steuck Stoff ("An Idea Is A Piece of Cloth") (1988)
Smith, Hale	African Suite (African Themes)
Southall, Mitchell B.	Intermezzo (1948)
Still, William Grant	Ennanga (1956) - Harp, strings, piano
Swanson, Howard	Fantasy Piece for Soprano Saxophone and Strings (1969) Music for Strings (1952) Threnody for Martin Luther King, Jr. (1969) Vista No. II (1969) - String octet
Tillis, Frederick Charles	Sequences and Burlesque
Walker, George Theophilus	Antifonys for Chamber Orchestra Lyric for Strings
White, Clarence Cameron	Pieces for Strings and Timpani
Williams, Julius P.	Toccatina for String Orchestra
Woods, Michael E.	String Serenade

SOLO/SOLI CONCERTI WITH ORCHESTRA

Adams, Alton Augustus	The Governor's Own (March) - Small orchestra and piano or full orchestra and piano or band
Adams, Leslie	Concerto for Piano and Orchestra (1965)

Anderson, T[homas] J[efferson]	Concerto for Two Violins and Chamber Orchestra (1988) Six Pieces for Clarinet and Chamber Orchestra (1962)
Anderson, Walter F.	Concerto for Harmonica and Orchestra
Atkins, Russell	Object-Form (1977) - Concerto for piano and orchestra
Baker, David Nathaniel	Concerto (1986) - Clarinet and orchestra Concerto (1987) - Tenor saxophone and orchestra Concerto (1988) - Alto saxophone and orchestra Concerto for Brass Quintet and Orchestra (1987) Concerto for Cello and Chamber Orchestra (1975) Concerto for Saxophone and Chamber Orchestra (1987) Ellingtones: A Fantasy for Saxophone and Orchestra (1987)
Batiste, Alvin	Musique d'Afrique Nouvelle Orleans - Clarinet and orchestra North American Idiosyncrasies - Clarinet, piano, double bass, drums, orchestra Planetary Perspective for Grass-Root Players and Orchestra - Clarinet and various ethnic instruments and orchestra
Belaka, O'Sai Tutu (a.k.a. Charles Henderson Bell, Sr.)	Concerto - Piano, drums, orchestra
Bland, Edward Osmund (Ed)	Atalanta's Challenge (1988) - Solo soprano saxophone, chamber orchestra, percussion, electric piano Concerto for Electric Violin and Chamber Orchestra Romantic Synergy (1987) - Solo flute and chamber orchestra
Bledsoe, Jules	African Suite - Violin and orchestra
Beckon, Lettie M.	Integrated Concerto (1978) - Piano and orchestra
Bonds, Margaret Allison	The Niles Fantasy - Piano and orchestsra
Bridgetower [Bridgtower], George (Augustus) Polgreen	Violin Concerto
Carter, John	Piano Concerto
Coleridge-Taylor, Samuel	Ballad in D Minor (1895) - Violin and orchestra Concerto in G Minor (1911) - Violin and orchestra Legend from the Concerstuck (1893) - Violin and orchestra Romance in G (1899) - Violin and orchestra
Cordero, Roque	Concertino for Viola and String Orchestra (1968) Concerto for Violin (1962) - Violin and orchestra Violin Concerto

Cunningham, Arthur	Adagio (1954) - Oboe and strings
	Concerto for Double Bass (1971) - Double bass and
	    orchestra
	Dialogue for Piano and Orchestra (1966)
	Dim Du Mim (Twilight) (1968-69) - English horn or
	    oboe and chamber orchestra
	Pataditos (1970) - Piano and orchestra
	Rooster Rhapsody (1975) - Orchestra and narrator
	Sun Bird (1974-75) - Voice, chamber orchestra,
	    guitar

Davis, Anthony	Maps (198?) - Concerto for violin and symphony orchestra Violin and Concerto (1988) Wyang V (1985) - Piano and orchestra
Ekwueme, Lazarus Edward Nnanyelu	Piano Concerto in RE (1963) - Piano and chamber orchestra
Fax, Mark	Music (1947) - Piano and orchestra
Fountain, Primous, III	Concerto for Cello and Orchestra
Gutiérrez y Espinosa, Felipe	Sonadina de Violin - with piano and orchestra
Hagan, Helen Eugenia	Concerto in C Minor - Piano and orchestra
Hailstork, Adolphus Cunningham	Concerto for Violin, Horn, and Orchestra (1975) Songs of the Magi (1987) - Oboe and strings Three Romances for Viola and Chamber Orchestra (1988)
Handy, John Richard	Concerto for Jazz Soloist and Orchestra (1970)
Harris, Margaret Rosezarian	Concerto No. 2 - Piano and orchestra
Harris, Robert A.	Concert for Bassoon and Chamber Orchestra (1965) Concert Piece for Horn and Orchestra (1964) Contrasts for Four Winds and String Orchestra (1966)
Hayes, Joseph	On Contemplating a Flower - Solo oboe, chamber choir, strings
Holmes, Robert L.	Concerto for Pro Viva (1980) - Flute, violoncello, piano, chamber orchestra

Jenkins, Edmund Thorton	Concerto for Clarinet and Orchestra
	Prelude Religieuse (1917) - Piano and orchestra
	Romance (1915) - 2 violins and orchestra
	The Saxophone Strut (1926) - Saxophone and piano.
	    Scored for saxophone and orchestra with the
	    title Milano Strut

Johnson, James Louis   Scenario (1962) - Trombone and orchestra
("J.J.")   Sketch - Trombone and orchestra

Johnson, James Price   Jasmine Concerto - Piano and orchestra

Kay, Ulysses Simpson   Ancient Saga (1947) - Piano and string orchestra
                            Aulos (1967) - Solo flute, 2 horns, string
                                 orchestra, percussion
                            Brief Elegy (1946) - Oboe and strings
                            Concerto for Oboe and Orchestra (1940)
                            Pieta (1950) - English horn and string orchestra
                            Quintet Concerto (1974) - Solo brass quintet (2
                                 trumpets, F-horn, 2 trombones; alternate part
                                 for tuba) and orchestra

Kennedy, Joseph J., Jr.   Suite for Trio and Orchestra

Lambert, Lucien Leon   Andante et Fantaisie (illegible) - Piano and
Guillaume   orchestra

Lateef, Yusef Abdul   Symphonic Blues Suite - Quartet and orchestra

Lee, Benjamin   Concert for Brass Choir and Orchestra

León, Tania Justina   Concerto Criollo (1980) - Solo timpani, solo
                                 piano, orchestra
                            Kabiosile (1988) - Solo piano and orchestra
                            New York - Piano and orchestra
                            Rabiosile (1988) - Piano and orchestra

Lewis, John Aaron   The Comedy - Soli: vibes, piano, bass, drums;
                                 with orchestra
                            Concert Piece (In Memoriam) - Soli: vibes, piano,
                                 drums (solo piano); with orchestra
                            Django - Soli: vibes, piano, bass, drums; with
                                 orchestra
                            England's Carol - Soli: vibes, piano, bass,
                                 drums; with orchestra
                            Jazz Ostinato - Soli: vibes, piano, bass, drums;
                                 with orchestra
                            Milano - Soli: piano, bass, drums, strings
                            Na Dubroyacki Nacim - Soli: vibes, piano, drums,
                                 strings
                            The Queen's Fancy - Soli: vibes, piano, bass;
                                 with orchestra
                            The Spiritual - Soli: vibes, piano, bass, drums;
                                 with orchestra
                            Three Windows - Soli: vibes, piano, bass, drums;
                                 with string orchestra

Lovingood, Penman, Sr.   Prelude in E-Flat - Piano and orchestra

McDaniel, William   Concerto for Alto Saxophone and Orchestra
Foster   Concerto for Flute and Orchestra
                            Concerto for Piano and Orchestra No. 1
                            Concerto for Piano and Orchestra No. 2

| | Concerto for Piano and String Orchestra |
| | Concerto for Two Flutes and String Orchestra |

| Meude-Monpas, The Chevalier J.J.O. de | Six Concertos (1786) - Violin and chamber orchestra |

Moore, Carman Leroy	Concerto for Blues Piano and Orchestra (1982)
	Concerto for Jazz Violin and Orchestra (1987)
	Hit: Concerto for Percussion and Orchestra (1978)

| Moore, Kermit | Cello Concerto |
| | Concerto - Timpani and orchestra |

| Moore, Phil | Concerto for Trombone and Orchestra |

| Moseley, James Orville (JOB) | Concerto - Piano and orchestra |

| Nelson, Oliver Edward | Concerto Piece for Alto Saxophone and Studio Orchestra (1972) |

| Parks, Gordon A. | Symphonic Sets - Piano and orchestra |

Perkinson, Coleridge-Taylor	Blues Forms II - Solo trumpet and orchestra
	Commentary (1964) - Violoncello and orchestra
	Concerto for Viola and Orchestra (1953)

Perry, Julia Amanda	Piano Concerto (1965) - Piano and orchestra
	Second Piano Concerto (1965) - Piano and orchestra
	Violin Concerto (1966) - Violin and orchestra

| Perry, Zenobia Powell | Four Hymns for Three Players - 2 sets of percussion, flute, piano, narrator, orchestra |

Price, Florence Beatrice Smith	Concerto in D - Violin and orchestra
	Concerto in D Minor - Piano and orchestra
	Concerto in F Minor - Piano and orchestra
	Rhapsody - Piano and orchestra

Price, John Elwood	Concerto (1988-89) - Tuba and orchestra
	Concerto for Piano and Orchestra (1969)
	Concerto for Violoncello and Orchestra (1959-74)
	Dance for English Horn and Orchestra (1952)
	Episodes (1956-57) - Piano and small orchestra
	For L'Overture - Piano and orchestra
	Rhapsody Symphonique (1950) - Piano and orchestra
	Scherzo for Cello and Orchestra (1973)
	Scherzo I for Clarinet and Orchestra (Piano) (1952; revised 1953-54)
	Scherzo II for Clarinet and Orchestra (1957)
	Scherzo III for Clarinet and Orchestra (1968)
	Scherzo IV for Clarinet and Orchestra (1968)
	Serenade for Tulsa (1950) - Piano and orchestra
	Spiritual (1972-74) - Clarinet and string orchestra

| Republicano, Assis | Improviso - Cello and orchestra |

Saint-Georges [Saint-
George], Joseph
Boulogne, The Chevalier
de

Concerto for Bassoon and Orchestra
Concerto for Clarinet and Orchestra
Concerto for Violin in A Major, Opus 5, No. 2 -
    Violin and orchestra
Concerto for Violin in A Major, Opus 7, No. 1 -
    Violin and orchestra
Concerto for Violin in B-flat Major, Opus 7, No. 2 -
    Violin and orchestra
Concerto for Violin in C Major, Opus 5, No. 1 -
    Violin and orchestra
Concerto for Violin in D Major, Opus 2, No. 2 -
    Violin and orchestra
Concerto for Violin in G Major, Opus 2, No. 1 -
    Violin and orchestra
Symphonie Concertante, Opus 6 (1775) - Two violins
    and orchestra
Symphonie Concertante, Opus 9 (1777) - Two violins
    and orchestra
Symphonie Concertante, Opus 10 (1778) - Two violins
    and orchestra
Symphonie Concertante (1784) - Three violins and
    orchestra
Symphonie Concertante, D Major - Two violins and
    orchestra
Symphonie Concertante in G Major for Two Violins
    and Orchestra, Opus 13 (1782)
Symphonie Concertante, G Major - Two violins and
    orchestra

Schuyler, Phillippa Duke   The Nile Fantasy - Piano and orchestra

Singleton, Alvin   Kuiitana Concerto for Piano (1974) - Contrabass,
    percussion, chamber orchestra

Smith, Hale   Concert Music for Piano and Orchestra (1972)
Music for Harp and Orchestra (1967)

Swanson, Howard   Concerto for Piano and Orchestra (1956)
Fantasy Piece for Soprano Saxophone and Strings (1969)

Taylor, William
("Billy")

Suite for Jazz Piano and Orchestra
Your Arm's Too Short to Box With God (Ballet music
    for the musical) - Piano and orchestra

Tillis, Frederick
Charles

Concerto for Trio Pro Viva and Orchestra (1980) -
    Flute, violoncello, piano, orchestra
Ring Shout Concerto for Percussionist and
    Orchestra (1973-74)
Spiritual Fantasy No. 6 for Trumpet and Symphony
    Orchestra (1982)

Walker, George
Theophilus

Concerto for Cello and Orchestra
Concerto for Piano and Orchestra
Concerto for Trombone and Orchestra
Concerto for Violin and Orchestra
Dialogue for Cello and Orchestra

White, Andrew
(Nathaniel, III)

A Jazz Concerto for Alto Saxophone and Symphony
    Orchestra (1988)

White, Clarence Cameron

Violin Concerto No. 2 - Violin and orchestra

White y Lafitte, Jose
[Joseph] Silvestre de
los Dolores

Bolero - Violin and orchestra
Concerto, F Sharp Minor (1864) - Violin and
    orchestra
Due Concertante on Themes from "Faust" - Two
    violins (and orchestra?)
Las Llages de Nuestra Senor Jesucristo - Two voices
    and orchestra

White, Joseph

Violin Concerto (1867)

Wilson, Olly Woodrow

Akwan (1972) - Piano/electric piano and orchestra

CHAMBER ORCHESTRA

Adams, Alton Augustus

The Governors Own (March) - Small orchestra and
    piano or full orchestra and piano or band

Adams, Leslie

All the Way (1965)
A Kiss in Xanadu (1954; orchestration revised,
    1973)

Bland, Edward Osmund
(Ed)

Piece for Chamber Orchestra (1979)

Beckon, Lettie M.

Piece (1977)

Bonds, Curtis Horace

Flowers

Bonds, Margaret Allison

Scripture Reading

Ekwueme, Lazarus Edward
Nnanyelu

Flow Gently Sweet Niger (1962) - Tone poem for
    chamber orchestra

Fountain, Primous, III

Cadences - Chamber ensemble
Three Pieces - Chamber ensemble
Variations on Titles - Chamber ensemble

Furman, James B.

Concerto for Chamber Orchestra

Hakim, Talib Rasul

Arkan-5 (1980-81)
Reflections on the 5th Day (1972) - Narrator and
    chamber orchestra
Shapes (1965)

Hancock, Eugene Wilson

Suite - Organ, strings, oboe, timpani

Heard, Henry A.

Cadences (1986)

Heath, James E. (Jimmy)

The Afro-American Suite of Evolution

Herbison, Jeraldine Saunders (Butler)	Promenade (1982)
Johnson, James Louis ("J.J.")	Rondo - Vibraphone, piano, contrabass, drum, chamber orchestra
Kay, Ulysses Simpson	Scherzi Musicali (1968)
Logan, Wendell Morris	Memories of... (1972; revised 1979)
Mitchell, Roscoe (Edward, Jr.)	Variations and Sketches from the Bamboo Terrace - Chamber orchestra, piano, soprano voice
Moore, Carman Leroy	Symfonia [sic] (1964)
Nelson, Oliver Edward	Dirge for Chamber Orchestra (1961)
Perkinson, Coleridge-Taylor	Grass: A Poem for Piano, Strings, and Percussion (1956)
Price, John Elwood	...And So Faustus Gained the World and Lost His Soul, or Whatever Happened to Humanity? (1976) The Ballad of Candy Man Beechum (1962; revised 1964) - Incidental music for voice and guitar; revised version for chamber orchestra No Ideology in the World (or Out of It) Is Worth the Death of a Worm (1987) O Sun of Real Peace (1980-81)
Qamar, Nadi	The Likembican Panorama
Singleton, Alvin	Again (1979) Kuiitana (1974) - Concerto for piano, contrabass, percussion, and chamber orchestra
Swanson, Howard	Night Music (1950)
Tillis, Frederick Charles	Niger Symphony (1975) Salute to Nelson Mandela (1990)
Walker, George Theophilus	Serenata for Chamber Orchestra

ORCHESTRA

Adams, Alton Augustus	The Governor's Own (March) - Small orchestra and piano or full orchestra and piano or band
Adams, Leslie	Ode to Life (1979; revised 1982) Romance (from Contrasts for Piano) (1961) Symphony No. 1 (1979)
Akpabot, Samuel	Cynthia's Lament Nigeria in Conflict

	Overture for a Nigerian Ballet Scenes from a Nigerian Ballet
Aldridge, Amanda	Three African Dances
Anderson, T[homas] J[efferson]	Chamber Concerto (Remembrances) (1988) Chamber Symphony (1968) Classical Symphony (1961) Intervals (1970-71) Introduction and Allegro (1959) Messages, A Creole Fantasy (1979) New Dances (1960) Pyknon Overture (1958) Squares: An Essay for Orchestra (1965) Symphony in Three Movements (1963)
Anderson, Walter F.	Symphonic Variations (Lord, Lord, Lord)
Baker, David Nathaniel	Birdsong (1984) Jeanne Marie at the Picture Show (1982) Lima Beba Samba
Ballata-Taylor, Nicholas George Julius	The Music of Africa - Symphony Overture on African Themes
Barnett, Willis L.	Symphony No. 1 (1982)
Billups, Kenneth Brown	American in the 40's
Bland, Edward Osmund (Ed)	Let Peace Be Free (1984)
Bonds, Margaret Allison	Montgomery Variations (1965)
Bridgetower, [Bridgtower], George (Augustus) Polgreen	Symphony (possibly spurious)
Carter, John	In Memoriam, Medgar Evers
Carter, Warrick L.	Life Part I (1963)
Cerón, José Dolores	Enriguillo (1941) Tres Preludios (1942)
Cheatham, Wallace McClain	Portraits (1982) Symphony (1986)
Clark, Edgar Rogie	Fete Creole (1970)
Coleridge-Taylor, Samuel	Ballad in A Minor (1898) The Bamboula (A Rhapsodic Dance) (1910) Ethiopia Saluting the Colours (1902) Four Characteristic Waltzes (1898) Hemo Dance (1900) Idyll (1901) Incidental Music to Faust (1908)

	Incidental Music to Herod (1900)
	Incidental Music to Nero (1906)
	Incidental Music to Othello (1911)
	Overture to The Song of Hiawatha (1899)
	Petite Suite de Concert (1911)
	Scenes from an Everyday Romance (1900)
	Symphony in A Minor (1896)
	Three Humoresques (1897)
	Toussaint L'Ouverture (Concert Overture) (1909)

Cook, Will Marion   In Dahomey (1902)

Cooke, Charles L.   Pro Arte, An Overture

Cordero, Roque   Adagio Tragico (1953)
Capricho Interiorano: Panamanian Folk Ballet
    Suite (1939)
Cinco Mensajes Breves Para Orquestra: Five Brief
    Messages for Orchestra (1973)
Five Short Messages for Orchestra (1958)
Momentum Jubilo: Fanfare (1973)
Ocho Miniaturas: Eight Miniatures (1944; revised
    1948)
Panamanian Overture No. 2 (1946)
Six Mobiles for Orchestra (1975)
Symphony No. 1 (1945)
Symphony No. 2 (1956)
Symphony No. 3 (With Theme and Five Variations)
    (1965)
Symphony No. 4 (Panamanian) (1986)

Cunningham, Arthur   Concentrics (1968)
Lights Across the Hudson (1956)
Lullabye for a Jazz Baby (1969)
Night Lights (1955)
Rooster Rhapsody (1975) - Orchestra and narrator
Theatre Piece (1966)

Da Costa, Noel G.   Quiet . . . Vamp It and Tag It (1971)

Davis, Anthony   Notes from the Underground (1988)
Still Waters (1982)

Dawson, William Levi   Negro Folk Symphony (1931; revised in 1952)
A Negro Worksong for Orchestra (1941)
Scherzo (1920)

Dédé, Edmond   Arcadia Overture
Chant Dramatique
Chicago: Grande Valse à l'Américaine
En Chasse: Mazurka Elégante
Mephisto Masque: Polka Fantastique
Mon Sous Off'cier: Quadrille Brilliant
Le Palmier Ouverture
Symphony ("Quasimodo") (by 1865)

Dett, Robert Nathaniel   Enchantment Suite
                          In the Bottoms: Juba Dance

Dickerson, Roger Donald   Concert Overture for Orchestra (1957)
                          A Musical Service for Louis (A Requiem for Louis
                              Armstrong) (1972) - Orchestra with optional
                              mixed chorus (no text)
                          Orpheus and His Slide Trombone (1974-75) -
                              Orchestra and narrator

Diton, Carl Rossini   Symphony in C Minor

Drew, James M.   Symphony No. 2
                          West Indians Lights (1973)

Edward, Leo   Fantasy Overture (1972)

Elie, Justin   Aboriginal Suite
                          Grande Valse de Concert
                          Quisqueye-Symphonic Suite

el-Dabh, Halim   Agamemnon
                          Baccanalia
                          Citadelle
                          Clytemnestra
                          Fantasia-Tahmeel - Timpani and string orchestra
                          Iphigenia (Ballet Suite)
                          One More Gaudy Night
                          Symphony Epilogue
                          Symphony No. 1
                          Symphony No. 2
                          Symphony No. 3
                          Tonography (1980)
                          Unity at the Cross Roads (1978)

Euba, Akin   Abik
                          Four Pieces for African Orchestra (1966)
                          Legend of Olurounbi
                          Olurounbi (1967)

Fax, Mark Oakland   Short Piece (ca. 1946)

Fiberesima, Adam   Concerto Overtunes
                          Symphony No. 1
                          Symphony No. 2
                          Symphony No. 3
                          Symphony No. 4

Fischer, William S.   Introduction and Song (1959)
                          Variations (1961)
                          Variations No. 2 (1964)

Fountain, Primous, III   The Art of Frustration
                          Auxiliary 2
                          Evolutio Quaestionis
                          Incoherent
                          Irrelevance

Huh
Manifestation
Movement
Ritual Dance of the Amaks (1973)
Saturn
Symphony No. 1 ("Epitome of the Oppressed")
Transition and/or Reformation
Triptych

Fox, James Ingram

African Ceremonial Dance Suite
Bornu Farewell
Symphony No. 1
Symphony No. 2
Symphony No. 3
Symphony No. 4 ("Emancipation")

Freeman, Harry Lawrence

The Slave (1925 or 1932)
Zulu King (1934)
Zuluki

Furman, James B.

Declaration of Independence (1977) - Orchestra and
        narrator
Moments in Gospel (1985)

Garcia, Juan Francisco

Advenimiento
Symphony No. 1: Quisqueyana (1941)
Symphony No. 2: Popular (1943)
Symphony No. 3 (1944)

Gomes, (Antônio) Carlos

Marcha da Indústria (1860)
Maria Tudor Overture [?]
Lo Schiavo Alvorada

Grider, Joseph William

Suite

Gutiérrez y Espinosa,
Felipe

Aire de Fandango
Elpasto de los Montes
La Familia
La Manganilla
La Peseta
Tonidón

Hailstork, Adolphus
Cunningham

An American Fanfare (1985)
An American Port of Call (1984)
Bellevue (1974)
Celebration (1974)
Epitaph (1979)
Phaedra (Tone Poem) (1966)
Statement, Variation, and Fugue (1966)
Symphony No. 1 (1988)

Hakim, Talib Rasul

Az-Zaahir-Al Batin (The Outward-The Inward) (1985-
        86)
Concepts (1974)
Recurrences (1974)
Visions of Ishwara (1970)

Harris, Howard C., Jr.   An American Music Tree Folk Psalm (1973)

Handy, William   Blue Destiny Symphony
Christopher

Harris, Robert A.   Moods for Orchestra (1968-69)
                          Two Moods in Miniature

Heard, Henry A.   Conjectures (1982)

Herbison, Jeraldine   Genesis I (1980)
Saunders (Butler)   Genesis II (1980)

Hernández, Julio Alberto Danza Oriental
                          Romanza Sin Palabras
                          Suite Romantica
                          Valse Triste

Jenkins, Edmund Thorton   African War Dance
                          American Folk Rhapsody: Charlestonia (1925)
                          Folk Rhapsody (1923?) [Rhapsodie Spirituelle,
                              Negro Folk Rhapsody, No. 27]
                          Folk Rhapsody (1919) [Negro Folk Rhapsody, No. 1?]

Johnson, Hall   Festival March (To the Black Soldiers of America)
                          Norfolk

Johnson, James Price   Harlem Symphony
                          Yamekraw: A Negro Rhapsody (1927)

Jones, Charles   Symphony No. 6

Kay, Ulysses Simpson   Bleeker Street Suite (1968)
                          Chariots, An Orchestra Rhapsody (1979)
                          Concerto for Orchestra (1948)
                          Dance Calinda Suite (1947)
                          Fantasy Variations (1963)
                          Harlem Children's Suite (1973)
                          Markings (1966)
                          Of New Horizon (1944)
                          Portrait Suite (1948)
                          Presidential Suite (1965)
                          The Quiet One Suite (1948)
                          Reverie and Rondo (1964)
                          Serenade for Orchestra (1954)
                          A Short Overture (1946)
                          Sinfonia in E (1950)
                          Southern Harmony (1975)
                          Suite for Orchestra (1945)
                          Symphony (1967)
                          Theater Set (1968)
                          Ubrian Scene (1963)
                          The Western Paradise (1976) - Narrator and
                              orchestra

Lambert, Lucien Leon   Les Cloches de Porto: Tableau Musical -
Guillaume   Orchestra reduction

León, Tania Justina	Batá (1985)
Lewis, John Aaron	Fanfare (Salute to Basie) Tales of the Willow Tree
Logan, Wendell Morris	Concert Music for Orchestra (1968) Polyphony I (1968)
Lovingood, Penman, Sr.	San Juan Overture Vitania Suite
Margetson, Edward Henry	Rondo Caprice
McCreary, Richard Deming, Jr.	"Z" - Orchestra and tape
McLin, Lena Johnson	Impressions No. 1
Mells, Herbert Franklin	Motherless Child, Negro Spiritual. A Symphonic Poem
Merrifield, Norman Lavelle	Symphony
Moore, Carman Leroy	Saratoga Festival Overture (1966) Wildfires and Field Songs (1974)
Moore, Dorothy Rudd	Symphony No. 1 (1963)
Moore, Kermit	Festival Escapade (1987) Mombasa Ostinata (1988)
Morgan, William Astor	Adagio - Opus 74
Moseley, James Orville (Job)	Fort Henry Symphony in A
Nelson, Oliver Edward	Complex City for Orchestra (1966) Dialogues (1970) Piece for Orchestra (1969) - Orchestra and jazz soloist
Nunes-Garcia, José Mauricio	Matinas do Natal (1799) - Large orchestra, organ, and continuo Overture Sinfonia Funebre Sinfonia Tempestate Zemira Overture (1803)
Nzewi, Emeka Meki	Symphonic Poem (1966)
Parks, Gordon A.	The Learning Tree Symphony (1967)
Perry, Julia Amanda	Contretemps (1963) Episode Homage to Vivaldi Requiem for Orchestra (1959)

Short Piece (1952)
Study for Orchestra (1952)
Symphony No. 1 (1959)
Symphony No. 2 (1962)
Symphony No. 4 (1964)
Symphony No. 8 (1968)
Symphony No. 9 (1965)
Symphony No. 12 (1959) ("Simple Symphony")

Perry, Zenobia Powell   Ships That Pass in the Night (1953)

Price, Florence Beatrice   Chicago Suite
Smith   Colonial Dance Symphony
                           Concert Overture No. 1
                           Concert Overture No. 2
                           Ethiopia's Shadow in America
                           Mississippi River Symphony
                           The Oak
                           Songs of the Oak
                           Suite of Dance
                           Symphony in D Minor
                           Symphony in G Minor
                           Symphony No. 1 in E Minor (1925)

Price, John Elwood   Adams-Campbell: "Whosoever Will" (1988-89)
                      . . . And So Faustus Gained the World and Lost His
                             Soul, or Whatever Happened to Humanity?
                             (1976; Version 2 1989)
                      Editorial I (1969)
                      From Remembering the Vainglorious Luminescence
                             Revealed on That Day at the Olduvai . . .
                             (1979-80)
                      Harambee (1968-75)
                      Overture (1972-73)
                      Three Orchestral Pieces (1980-81)

Ryder, Noah Francies   Symphony

Saint-Georges [Saint-   L'Amant Anonime Overture (a.k.a. Symphony No. 2)
George], Joseph   Symphonie Concertante in E-Flat Major, Opus 12
Boulogne, The Chevalier Symphony in G Major
de   Symphony No. 1 in G Major, Opus 11, No. 1
                         Symphony No. 2 in D Major (1799), Opus 11, No. 2

Schuyler, Phillippa Duke Manhattan Nocturne
                          Rumpelstiltskin
                          Scherzo
                          Sleepy Hollow Sketches
                          White Nile Suite

Singleton, Alvin   After Fallen Crumbs (1988)
                    Mestizo II (1970) - Large orchestra
                    Moment (1968) - Large orchestra
                    Shadows (1987)
                    A Yellow Rose Petal (1982)

Smith, Hale   Contours (1962)
                             Orchestra Set (1952)
                             Ritual and Incantations (1974)

Smith, Nathaniel Clark   The Christian Recorder March - Piano or orchestra
                                  or brass band
                             Frederick Douglass Funeral March - Piano or
                                  orchestra or brass band
                             The Lincoln High School March - Piano or orchestra
                                  or brass band or mandolin or guitar
                             Negro Folk Suite - Piano with arragements by the
                                  composer for violin and piano; violin, cello,
                                  and piano, and full orchestra

Smith, William D.   Happy Life March (1901) - Piano or band or
                                  orchestra
                             The New Century "Negro" March - Piano or band or
                                  orchestra

Snaër, Samuel   Graziella Overture

Southall, Mitchell B.   Elf Dance - Trans. for orchestra
                             Lotus Land - Trans. for orchestra

Sowande, Olufela   Africana
("Fela")   Folk Symphony (Nigerian Themes)
                             Nigerian Miniatures (An Orchestral Suite)

Stewart, Earl Lewis   Blues and Fugue (1989)
                             Ebony Sketches (1989-90)
                             Glimpses (1976; revised 1986)
                             Homage: To Duke, Count, Jimmy, Tadd, and Thad
                             Imprint of Jamaica (1986)
                             Overture of Peace (1978)
                             Variations on an Original Lullaby

Still, William Grant   Afro-American Symphony
                             The American Scene (1957)
                             Archaic Ritual Suite (1946)
                             Autochthonous (see Symphony No. 4)
                             Bells (1944)
                             Choreographic Prelude (1970)
                             Costaso (1950)
                             Danzas de Panama (1948)
                             Darker America (1924)
                             Dismal Swamp (1933)
                             Festive Overture (1944)
                             Kaintuck (1933)
                             Old California (1941)
                             Patterns (1960)
                             The Peaceful Land (1960)
                             Poem for Orchestra (1944)
                             Preludes (1962)
                             Serenade (1957)
                             A Song A Dust (1936)
                             The Sunday Symphony (see Symphony No. 3)

	Symphony No. 1 (Afro-American Symphony) (1930; revised 1969) Symphony No. 2 Symphony No. 3 (The Sunday Symphony) (1958) Symphony No. 4 (Autochthonous) (1947) Symphony No. 5 (Western Hemisphere) (1945) Threnody: In Memory of Jan Sibelius (1965) Woodnotes (1947)
Stokes, Harvey J.	Lyric Symphony (1981) Short Symphony (1982)
Swanson, Howard	Concerto for Orchestra (1954) Short Symphony Symphony No. 1 (1945) Symphony No. 2 (1948) Symphony No. 3 (1970)
Tillis, Frederick Charles	The Cotton Curtain (1966) Designs for Orchestra, Nos. 1 and 2 (1963) Inauguration Overture (1988) Symphony in Three Movements (Nacirfa Nroh) (1969-70) Three Symphonic Spirituals (1978)
Tyers, William H.	The Call of the Woods - Piano (arranged for orchestra or band by the composer) Mockingbird Rube - Piano or orchestra or band Panama - Piano and band or orchestra
Walker, George Theophilus	Address for Orchestra In Praise of Folly (Overture) Sinfonia for Orchestra (1984) Variations for Orchestra
White, Clarence Cameron	Concertino in D Minor (1952) Dance Rhapsody (1955) Divertimento Elegy for Orchestra Kutamba Rhapsody (1942) Poem (1955) Suite on Negro Themes Symphony in D Minor (1928)
William, Julius P.	A Norman Overture
Williams, Mary Lou	Zodiac Suite
Wilson, Olly Woodrow	Expansions II (1987-88) Houston Fanfare (1986) Lumina (1981) Reflections (1979) Sinfonia (1983-84) Structure for Orchestra (1960) Three Movements for Orchestra (1964) Trilogy for Orchestra (1980) Voices (1970)

Work, John Wesley, III   Taliafero
                             Yenvalou (1946)

Work, Julian C.   Myriorama at Midnight
                             Requiem for Two

SOLO VOICE WITH STRINGS AND OTHER INSTRUMENTS

Anderson T[homas]   Variations on a Theme by M.B. Tolson (1969) -
J[efferson]   Mezzo-soprano, alto saxophone, trumpet,
                                 trombone, violin, violoncello, piano

Baiocchi, Regina A.   Two Zora Neale Hurston Songs (1990) - Mezzo-
Harris   soprano, violoncello, piano

Baker, David Nathaniel   Fantasy (1954) - Soprano, brass ensemble, harp
                             Give and Take (1975) - Soprano and chamber
                                 ensemble (flute/alto flute, oboe/English
                                 horn, viola, violoncello, percussion)
                             Songs of the Night (1972) - Soprano, string
                                 quartet, piano
                             Through This Vale of Tears - Tenor and string
                                 quartet

Belafonte, Harry   Recognition (1968) - Voice and guitar

Chandler, Len H.   The Lovin' People (1967) - Voice and guitar

Cunningham, Arthur   Violetta (1963) - Musical for soprano, tenor,
                                 baritone, and bass, with string quartet and
                                 string octet

Da Costa, Noel G.   The Blue Mountains (1962) - Mezzo-soprano, flute,
                                 oboe, clarinet, bass clarinet, F-horn,
                                 trumpet, viola, violoncello, contrabass,
                                 percussion
                             Five Epitaphs (1956) - Soprano and string quartet
                             In the Landscape of Spring (1962) - Mezzo-soprano,
                                 flute, oboe, clarinet, bass clarinet, F-horn,
                                 trumpet, viola, violoncello, contrabass,
                                 percussion
                             November Song (1974) - Concert scene for soprano,
                                 violin, saxophone, and piano (with
                                 improvisation)
                             Sitting Quietly, Doing Nothing (1962) - Mezzo-
                                 soprano, flute, oboe, clarinet, bass
                                 clarinet, F-horn, trumpet, viola,
                                 violoncello, contrabass, percussion

Dennis, Mark Andrew, Jr. Serene (1973) - Harp, electronic tape, voice

el-Dabh, Halim   Tahmeela - Soprano, flute, oboe, clarinet,
                                 bassoon, horn, viola

Hakim, Talib Rasul   Set-Three (1970) - Soprano, violoncello, piano

Six Players and A Voice (1964) - Soprano,
    clarinet, trumpet, violoncello, 2 percussion,
    piano
Tone-Poem (1969) - Soprano, percussion,
    contrabass, piano

Hampton, Ralph

2 Songs, No. 2 - Voice, flute, clarinet, horn,
    cello, percussion

Heard, Henry A.

Street Levels (1981) - Soprano voice, flute,
    clarinet, horn, trumpet, violin, viola, piano

Jones, Quincy Delight,
Jr.

Soundpiece (1962) - String quartet and contralto

Kay, Ulysses Simpson

Triptych on Texts of Blake (1962) - High voice,
    violin, violoncello, piano

King, Betty Jackson

Vocalise - Soprano, violoncello, piano

León, Tania Justina

Pueblo Mulato: 3 Songs on Poems by Nicholas
    Guillen (1987) - Soprano, oboe, guitar,
    double bass, percussion, piano

McCall, Maurice
Henderson

Two Spirituals (I Will Arise and Swing Low) - Solo
    voice, oboe, strings

Moore, Dorothy Rudd

From the Dark Tower (1970) - Voice (mezzo-
    soprano), cello, piano
Sonnets on Love, Rosebuds, and Death (1976) -
    Soprano, violin, piano
The Weary Blues (1972) - Voice (baritone), cello,
    piano

Nelson, Oliver Edward

Soundpiece for Contralto, String Quartet, and
    Piano (1963)

Nunes-Garcia, José
Mauricio

Beijo a Mão que Me Condena - Soprano and cello

Perkinson, Coleridge-
Taylor

Attitudes (1962-63) - Tenor, violin, violoncello,
    piano

Perry, Julia Amanda

Stabat Mater - Contralto and string orchestra or
    string quartet

Roldán y Gardes, Amadeo

Danza Negra - Voice, 2 clarinets, 2 violas,
    percussion

Singleton, Alvin

Necessity Is A Mother (1981) - 3 actresses
    (voices) and double bass with amplification
A Seasoning (1971) - Female or male voice, flute,
    E-flat alto saxophone, trombone, double bass
    (all doubling on percussion, and one
    percussion)

Smith, Hale   Two Love Songs of John Donne (1958) - Soprano,
                              string quartet, and woodwind quintet

Stokes, Harvey J.   The Glory of Easter - Soprano, tenor, piano,
                              violin, violoncello, horn, trumpet

Woods, Michael E.   Psalm #23 - Soprano voice, electric bass,
                              classical guitar, flute, violin, viola, cello

VOCAL SOLO/SOLI WITH ORCHESTRA

Adams, Leslie   Dunbar Songs (1981) - High soprano or tenor voice
                              and chamber orchestra
                            Five Songs (1960) - High soprano or tenor voice
                              and chamber orchestra
                            Hymn to Freedom (1989) - Soprano, tenor, baritone,
                              chamber orchestra
                            The Meadowlark (from Dunbar Songs) (1980) - Solo
                              high voice and orchestra
                            Six Songs (a.k.a Afro-American Songs) (1961) -
                              Medium--mezzo-soprano or baritone--solo voice
                              and strings

Anderson, T[homas]   Horizon '76 (1975) - Soprano and orchestra
J[efferson]   In Memorian Malcolm X (1974) - Soprano and orchestra

Bonds, Margaret Allison   Ezekiel Saw the Wheel (1959) - Voice and orchestra
                              (or voice and piano)
                            Five Spirituals (1946) - Voice and orchestra (or
                              voice and piano)
                            He's Got the Whole World in His Hands (1965) -
                              Voice and piano or voice and orchestra
                            I Got A Home in That Rock (1959) - Voice and
                              orchestra (or voice and piano)
                            Joshua Fit Da Battle of Jericho - Voice (medium)
                              and orchestra (or voice and piano)
                            Spirituals Five (1942) - Voice (high) and orchestra

Carter, John   Cantata (1964) - Voice and orchestra or piano
                            Requiem Seditiosam: In Memory of Medgar Evers
                              (ca. 1967) - Baritone/bass with orchestra

Clark, Edgar Rogie   Kaffir Drinking Song (1976) - Voice (baritone) and
                              orchestra
                            The Wicked Race (1976) - Voice (baritone) and
                              orchestra

Coleridge-Taylor, Samuel   Incidental Music to the Music to the Forest of the
                              WIld Theme (1910-1911) - Female voice and
                              orchestra
                            The Soul's Expression (Four Sonnets (1900) -
                              Contralto solo and orchestra and piano
                            Zara's Ear-Rings (Rhapsody) (1894?) - Soprano and
                              orchestra

Cooper, William Benjamin   Cantata (1975) - Soprano and orchestra

Dawson, William Levi   Out in the Fields - Voice and piano (orchestra)

Dickerson, Roger Donald   New Orleans Concerto (1976) - Piano, orchestra,
                                 with soprano solo

Edward, Leo   Psalm 150 - Soprano and orchestra

Ekwueme, Lazarus   Psalm 23 for Contralto (or Baritone) and Chamber
Edward Nnanyelu   Orchestra (1962)

el-Dabh, Halim   Pierre Jusqu' Au Ciel - Male voice and orchestra

Gomes, (Antônio) Carlos   Salvator Rosa Air of the Duke d'Arcos - Bass and
                                 orchestra

Gutiérrez y Espinosa,   Agnus Dei - High voice and orchestra
Felipe

Heath, James E.   Afro-American Suite of Evolution - Soli voice, 6
(Jimmy)   (STBB), orchestra

Hernández, Julio Alberto   3 Romanzas - Voice (or chorus?) and orchestra

Jenkins, Edmund Thorton   Prayer (1925) - Low voice and orchestra
                            That Place Called Italie (1925) - Voice and piano;
                                 manuscript score for orchestra

Kay, Ulysses Simpson   Three Pieces After Blake (1952) - High voice and
                                 orchestra

McCall, Maurice   Two Spirituals (I Will Arise and Swing Low) - Solo
Henderson   voice, oboe, strings

Mitchell, Roscoe   Variations and Sketches from the Bamboo Terrace -
(Edward, Jr.)   Chamber orchestra, piano, soprano voice

Moore, Dorothy Rudd   From the Dark Tower (1972) - Voice (mezzo-soprano)
                                 and chamber orchestra
                            The Weary Blues (1979) - Voice (baritone) and
                                 orchestra

Moore, Kermit   Four Arias - Adapted for soprano and orchestra

Nunes-Garcia, Jose   Laudate Dominum Omnes Gentes (1813) and Laudate
Mauricio   Pueri (1813) - Soloist, flute, 2 horns,
                                 strings
                            Oficio Dos Defuntos (1816) - Soloists and orchestra

Perry, Julia Amanda   Stabat Mater - Contralto and string orchestra or
                                 string quartet

Price, Florence   My Soul's Been Anchored in De Lord (1937) - Voice
Beatrice Smith   and piano; voice and orchestra
                            Song of Hope - Voice and orchestra

Price, John Elwood   Mandolin (Poems by Rita Dove) (1983-84) - Baritone/
                                 mezzo-soprano solo and small orchestra

Suggestions for the Century (1954; revised 1958) -
     Men's vocal quartet with orchestra

Saint-Georges [Saint-   Aupres de Vous, Mon Coeur Soupire - Soprano, tenor,
George], Joseph   string orchestra
Boulogne, The Chevalier Dieux! Quel Prestige - High voice and string
de   orchestra
                    Image Cherie, Ecrits si Touchants - Soprano and
                        string orchestra
                    Loin du Soleil - Soprano and orchestra
                    N'etes Vous Plus la Tendre Amie - Tenor and
                        orchestra
                    Que Me Fait a Moi la Richesse - Tenor and string
                        orchestra
                    Qu'il Est Content - Soprano and string orchestra
                    Scene from "Ernestine" - Soprano and orchestra

Still, William Grant   Highway 1 USA (1962) - Vocal and orchestra
                    Levee Land (1925) - Soprano and orchestra
                    The Little Song That Wanted to Be a Symphony
                        (1954) - Narrator, 3 female voices, orchestra
                    Plain-Chant for America (1941) - Baritone, organ,
                        orchestra; also arranged for chorus
                    Rhapsody (1955) - Soprano and orchestra

Swanson, Howard   Darling, Those Are Birds (1952) - Voice and
                      orchestra
                    Goodnight (1952) - Voice and string orchestra
                    No Leaf May Fall (1952) - Voice and string
                      orchestra
                    One Day (1952) - Voice and string orchestra
                    Songs for Patricia (1953) - Voice and string
                      orchestra

Tillis, Frederick   Spiritual Cycle (1978) - Soprano and orchestra
Charles

Walker, George   Poem for Soprano and Chamber Group
Theophilus

White y Lafitte, Jose   Amor Hermoso - Two voices and orchestra
[Joseph] Sylvester de   Initatorio - Four voices and orchestra
los Dolores   Lamentaciones - Two voices and orchestra
                    Las Llages de Nuestra Senor Jesucristo - Two voices
                      and orchestra
                    Miserere - Two voices and orchestra

CHOIR AND ORCHESTRA

Adams, Leslie   The Righteous Man (Cantata No. 1) (Cantata to the
                    Memory of Dr. Martin Luther King) (1985)

Akinwole, Obataiye   The Road to Freedom - Chorus, soli, narrator,
                    dancers, piano, orchestra

Akpabot, Samuel   Verba Christi (1975) - Cantata for soloist,
                              chorus, narrator, orchestra

Anderson, T[homas]   What Time Is It? - Boys choir and jazz orchestra
J[efferson]

Ballanta-Taylor,   Cantata - Chorus and orchestra
Nicholas George Julius

Beckon, Lettie M.   Help (1976) - Women's choir and string quartet

Billups, Kenneth Brown   Spiritual - String orchestra and chorus

Boatner, Edward Hammond Julius Sees Her in Rome, Georgia (1935; revised
                              1975) - Chorus, soloist, orchestra

Bonds, Margaret Allison Credo - Chorus (SATB), baritone solo, orchestra
                         Hold On - Chorus (SATB) and orchestra
                         I Wish I Knew How It Would Feel To Be Free -
                              Voice, chorus, orchestra
                         Mass in D Minor (Latin text) - Chorus and orchestra
                         Peter Go Ring Dem Bells - Chorus and string quartet
                         Sinner Please Don't Let This Harvest Pass - Voice,
                              chorus (SATB), orchestra
                         Standin in the Need of Prayer - Voice, chorus
                              (SATB), orchestra
                         This Little Light of Mine - Voice, chorus (SATB),
                              orchestra

Burleigh, Henry   Every Time I Feel the Spirit - Orchestra and
Thacker ("Harry")   chorus

Coleridge-Taylor, Avril Wyndon - Chorus and orchestra
Gwendolen

Coleridge-Taylor, Samuel The Atonement (1902-03) - Sacred cantata for
                              soprano, mezzo-soprano, contralto, baritone,
                              and tenor soli; chorus; orchstra
                         The Blind Girl of Castel-Cuille (1900-01) -
                              Cantata for soprano and baritone soli,
                              chorus, orchestra
                         The Death of Minehaha (1899) - Cantata for soprano
                              and baritone soli, chorus, orchestra
                         Dream Lovers - Two male and two female characters,
                              chorus, orchestra
                         Five Choral Ballads (1904) - Baritone solo, chorus
                              (SATB), orchestra
                         Hiawatha's Departure (1899-1900) - Cantata for
                              soprano, tenor, and baritone soli, chorus,
                              orchestra
                         Hiawatha's Wedding Feast - Cantata for tenor solo,
                              chorus, orchestra
                         Incidental Music to Ulysses (1901) - Orchestra and
                              women's chorus
                         Meg Blane (1902) - Mezzo-soprano solo, chorus,
                              orchestra

A Tale of Old Japan (1911) - Cantata, soprano,
   contralto, tenor, and baritone soli; chorus;
   orchestra

Cordero, Roque   Cantata para la Paz: Canata for Peace (1979) -
   Bass-baritone solo, chorus (SATB), orchestra
   Musica Veinte: Music Twenty - SSAA, baritone
   solo, orchestra

Cunningham, Arthur   Litany (1972) - Chorus (SATB) and orchestra
   Mundy Man (1970) - Chorus (SATB), orchestra,
   harmonica
   Night Song (1973) - Chorus (SATB), soloist,
   orchestra

Da Costa, Noel G.   Ceremony of Spirituals (1976) - Soprano,
   soprano/tenor saxophone, orchestra, chorus
   The Confession Stone (1969)- Soprano, trio (SSA),
   chamber ensemble

Dawson, William Levi   Break, Break, Break - Chorus and orchestra
   Out in the Fields - Chorus (SATB) and piano
   (orchestra); women's chorus (SSA) and piano
   (orchestra)

Dennis, Mark Andrew, Jr. Black Mirrors (1972-73) - Instrumental ensemble
   and choir

Dett, Robert Nathaniel   The Chariot Jubilee - Tenor, chorus, orchestra
   Music in the Mine (1916)
   The Ordering of Moses - Chorus and orchestra

Dickerson, Roger Donald A Musical Service for Louis (A Requiem for Louis
   Armstrong) (1972) - Orchestra with optional
   mixed chorus (no text)

Dorsey, James Elmo   An American Vignette - Chorus, contralto solo,
   orchestra

Ducander, Sten   Five Negro Spirituals for Male Choir, Flute, and
   Guitar

Euba, Akin   Chaka (1970) - Soloists, chorus, and orchestra

Fischer, William S.   Statement (1964) - Speaking chorus with orchestra
   Trilogy (1964) - Women's chorus (three part) and
   orchestra

Freeman, Harry Lawrence The Slave Ballet from Salome (1925) - Chorus and
   orchestra

Gutiérrez y Espinosa,   Gran Salve a Nuestra Señora de la Providencia -
Felipe   SATB and orchestra
   Litanias Jesuitas - SATB and orchestra
   Miserere - Three part chorus and orchestra
   San Juan - SATB and orchestra
   Santa Cecilia - SATB and orchestra

	Las Siete Palabras - Chorus and orchestra
	Tota Pulchra - Chorus, orchestra, saxophone
Hailstork, Adolphus Cunningham	Serenade (1971) - Women's chorus (SSA), soprano solo, violin, solo, piano
	Done Made My Vow: A Ceremony (1985) - Chorus, soloists, orchestra
Hakim, Talib Rasul	Sound Images (1969) - Brass (2 trumpets, 2 flugelhorns, 4 horns, 3 trombones, tuba), 3 percussion, strings, female chorus
Handy, William Christopher	They That Sow in Texas - SATB, TTBB, orchestra
Harris, Robert A.	Psalm 47 (1960-61) - Women's voices and 5 instruments: flute, clarinet, violin, viola, cello
Hayes, Joseph	On Contemplating a Flower - Solo oboe, chamber choir, and strings
Heath, James E. (Jimmy)	Afro-American Suite of Evolution - Soli voices, 6 (STBB), orchestra
Herbison, Jeraldine Saunders (Butler)	Little Brown Baby (1967) - SAT, 2 violins, piano
Hernández, Julio Alberto	3 Romanzas - Voice (or chorus?) and orchestra
Johnson, Bessie	Ode to Faith - Chorus, solos, orchestra
Jones, Quincy Delight, Jr.	Black Requiem (1971) - Vocal solo, choir, orchestra
Kay, Ulysses Simpson	Choral Triptych (1962) - Chorus (SATB) and string orchestra
	A Covenant of Our Time (1969) - Chorus and orchestra
	Inscriptions from Whitman (1963) - Chorus (SATB) and orchestra
	Once There Was A Man (1969) - Narrator, chorus (SATB), orchestra
	Parables (1970) - Chorus (SATB) and chamber orchestra
	Phoebus, Arise (1959) - Soprano, bass, chorus (SATB), orchestra
	Song of Jeremiah (1945) - Baritone, chorus (SATB), orchestra
León, Tania Justina	Heart of Ours (1988) - Chorus and instruments
McCall, Maurice Henderson	Dark Symphony - Soli (SATB) and orchestra without flutes or violin
McLin, Lena Johnson	In This World - Chorus, electric guitar, flute, violoncello, electric piano

Moore, Carman Leroy

Gospel Fuse (1974) - Gospel quartet (SSSA),
    soprano solo, orchestra, saxophone, piano,
    electric organ

Nunes-Garcia, Jose'
Mauricio

Dies Sanctificatus (1793) - Chorus and orchestra
Laud Sion Salvatorem (1809) - Chorus and orchestra
Missa da Nossa Senhora da Conciecao - Chorus and
    orchestra
Requiem (1816) - Soprano, contralto, tenor, bass,
    chorus, orchestra
Te Deum Laudamus (1811) - Chorus, soprano, tenor,
    bass, orchestra

Perkinson, Coleridge-
Taylor

Dunbar - Solo voice, chorus, orchestra
Hundredth Psalm (ca. 1949) - Chorus (SSA), brass,
    strings

Perry, Julia Amanda

Frammenti Dalle Lettere de "Santa Caterina" -
    Mixed chorus, soprano solo, small orchestra
Symphony USA (1967) - Chorus and small orchestra

Price, Florence
Beatrice Smith

Lincoln Walks at Midnight - Chorus and orchestra
Sea Gulls - Chorus (SSA) and string orchestra
Spring Journey - Chorus (SSA) and orchestra
The Wind and the Sea - Mixed chorus and string
    orchestra

Price, John Elwood

Confession - Chorus, soloist speakers, orchestra
The Damnation of Doctor Faustus (1962-63) - Chorus
    (SATB), tenor solo, chamber orchestra
"Harriet Tubman: Booker T. Washington Speech,
    Auburn, New York . . . 1913" (1985-86) -
    Choir (SATB) and orchestra
Song of the Liberty Bell (1976-78) - Chorus (SATB),
    baritone, 3 speakers, orchestra
Suggestion for the Century (1954; revised 1958) -
    Men's vocal quartet with orchestra
Tempest (1965) - Incidental music for chorus
    (SATB), flute, guitar, trumpet

Qamar, Nadi

The Philosophy of the Spirituals - Orchestra and
    chorus

Rivers, Clarence

Resurrection - Gospel/jazz soloist, chorus, and
    piano or chamber orchestra

Santos, Henry Jose'

Mass in G Major (1987) - Soprano, contralto, and
    tenor soloists; choir; orchestra; electric
    piano

Singleton, Alvin

Messa (Italian language) (1975) - Flute, 2
    guitars, electric organ, soprano solo mixed
    choirs (four soprani, four alti, four tenori,
    four bassi), violoncello, contrabass

Smith, Hale   In Memoriam--Beryl Rubinstein (1953; orchestrated
                                in 1958) - Chorus (SATB) and chamber
                                orchestra or piano

Stewart, Earl Lewis   Al-Inkishafi - Chorus, orchestra, English and
                                Kiswahili narrators, mezzo-soprano soloist,
                                ballet
                           Identity (1971; revised 1989) - Jazz orchestra,
                                chorus, strings
                           Mchanganyiko - Mezzo-soprano, chorus, orchestra
                           Spirituals (1987) - Soprano soloist, chorus,
                                orchestra

Stokes, Harvey J.   A Psalm Prelude - Soprano, SATB, orchestra
                           The Second Act (Oratorio) - Soprano, tenor,
                                baritone, bass, SATB, TTBB orchestra, brass
                                septet

Still, William Grant   And They Lynched Him On A Tree (1940) - Narrator,
                                contralto, 2 choruses, orchestra
                           From A Lost Continent (1948) - Chorus and orchestra
                           A Psalm for the Living (1954) - Chorus and
                                orchestra
                           Song of a City (1938) - Solo voice, chorus,
                                orchestra

Tillis, Frederick   In the Spirit and the Flesh (1985) - Orchestra and
Charles   mixed chorus

Walker, Charles   Requiem for Brother Martin (1968) - Chorus and
                                orchestra

Walker, George   Cantata for Boys Choir, Soprano, Tenor, and
Theophilus   Orchestra
                           Mass for Chorus and Soloist and Orchestra

Wilson, Olly Woodrow   Spirit Song (1973) - Soprano, double chorus, and
                                orchestra

Woods, Michael E.   Bless the Lord - SATB, string orchestra
                           God's Chosen Man - SATB, rhythm section, string
                                orchestra
                           Protest - Tenor voice, SATB, rhythm section,
                                string orchestra
                           Psalm #116 - SATB, string orchestra
                           Psalm #125 - SATB, classical guitar, electric
                                bass, flute, violin, viola, cello
                           The Sermon on the Mount - SATB, flute, classical
                                guitar, violin, viola, cello, electric bass
                           Stand Still - SATB, rhythm section, string
                                orchestra
                           Unto Thy Name Be Glory - SATB, string orchestra

ORCHESTRA WITH JAZZ GROUP

Baker, David Nathaniel
Concerto for Bass Viol and Jazz Band (1972) - Bass
     viol, jazz ensemble, string quartet solo
     violin
Concerto for Cello and Jazz Band (1987)
Concerto for Flute and Jazz Band (1971) - Flute/
     alto flute, jazz ensemble, string quartet
Concerto for Trumpet, String Orchestra, and Jazz
     Band
Concerto for Trombone, Jazz Band, and Chamber
     Orchestra (1972)
Concerto for Trumpet, Orchestra, and Jazz Band
Concerto for Two Pianos, Jazz Band, Chamber
     Orchestra, and Percussion (1976)
Concerto for Violin and Jazz Band (1969)
Le Chat Qui Peche (1974) - Orchestra, soprano,
     jazz quartet
Quintet for Jazz Violin and String Orchestra (1987)
Reflections (1969) - Jazz ensemble and orchestra
Sangre Negro (1974) - Orchestra and jazz trio
Suite of Little Ethnic Pieces (1983) - String
     orchestra and jazz quartet
Two Improvisations for Orchestra and Jazz Combo
     (1974) - Orchestra and jazz trio (piano,
     bass, drums)

Batiste, Alvin
North American Idiosyncrasies - Clarinet, piano,
     double bass, drums, orchestra

Carter, Warrick L.
The Hampton Thought (1977) - Jazz ensemble and
     strings
Keisha Z (1972) - Jazz ensemble with strings
Love All Living Thins (1976) - Jazz ensemble with
     strings
Magnolia Thunderpussy (1973) - Jazz ensemble with
     strings
Monique (1973) - Jazz ensemble with strings
Ponta de Areia (1976) - Jazz ensemble with strings
Thursday's Love (1974) - Jazz ensemble with strings

Coleman, Ornette
Skies of America (1972) - Jazz quartet and
     orchestra

Cunningham, Arthur
Night Bird (1978) - Jazz quintet, solo voice,
     chamber orchestra

Davis, Nathan
The United Spirited - Jazz orchestra string
     quartet, choir

Fischer, William S.
Concerto Grosso No. 1 (1968) - Jazz ensemble with
     orchestra
Concerto Grosso No. 2 ("Blues") - Jazz ensemble
     with orchestra
Experience in E - Jazz quintet and orchestra

Hailstork, Adolphus   Two Struts with Blues (1985) - String orchestra,
Cunningham   flute, horn, jazz quartet

Johnson, James Louis   Rondo - Vibraphone, piano, contrabass, drums,
("J.J.")   chamber orchestra

Jones, Quincy Delight,   Soundpiece (1964) - Jazz orchestra
Jr.

Lewis, John Aaron   The Comedy - Soli: Vibes, piano, bass, drums; with
                                 orchestra
                             Concert Piece (In Memoriam) - Soli: Vibes, piano,
                                 bass drums (solo piano); orchestra
                             Django - Soli: Vibes, piano, bass, drums; string
                                 orchestra
                             Encounter in Cagnes - Soli: Vibes, piano, bass,
                                 drums; orchestra
                             England's Carol - Soli: Vibes, piano, bass,
                                 drums; orchestra
                             In Memoriam (1971) - Jazz quartet and orchestra
                             Jazz Ostinato - Soli: Vibes, piano, bass, drums;
                                 orchestra
                             Kansas City Breaks - Soli: Vibes, piano, bass,
                                 drums; orchestra
                             Milano - Soli: Piano, bass, drums; orchestra
                             Na Dubroyacki Nacim - Soli: Vibes, piano, drums;
                                 strings
                             The Queen's Fancy - Soli: Vibes, piano, bass;
                                 orchestra
                             Sketch for Double Quartet - Jazz quartet and
                                 string quartet
                             The Spiritual - Soli: Vibes, piano, bass;
                                 orchestra
                             Three Windows - Soli: Vibes, piano, bass, drums;
                                 string orchestra

Logan, Wendell Morris   Requiem for Charlie Parker (1978) - Large
                                 orchestra, soloist, jazz group (includes
                                 soprano and tenor soloists and choir of 3
                                 male and 3 female singers)

Moore, Carman Leroy   Concerto for Blues Piano and Orchestra (1982)
                             Concerto for Jazz Violinist and Orchestra (1987)
                             Four Movements for a Fashionable Five-Toed Dragon
                                 (1976) - Orchestra, Chinese instruments, jazz
                                 quintet

Nelson, Oliver Edward   Black Suite for Narrator, String Quartet, and Jazz
                                 Orchestra (1970)
                             Piece for Orchestra (1969) - Orchestra and jazz
                                 soloist

Rivers, Clarence   Brotherhood of Man - Orchestra and jazz trio
                                 (piano, bass, and drums)

Stewart, Earl Lewis   Identity (1971; revised 1989) - Jazz orchestra,
                                 chorus, orchestra

Undulations (jazz ballad) (1986) - Flute or
     clarinet, harp, strings

Taylor, William   Peaceful Warrior - Jazz trio (piano, bass, drums),
("Billy")   choir, orchestra
                               Suite for Jazz Piano and Orchestra

Tillis, Frederick   Autumn Concerto for Trumpet (1979) - Jazz orchestra
Charles   The Blue Express (1973) - Jazz orchestra
                               Blue Stone Differencia (1972) - Jazz orchestra
                               Concerto for Piano (1977) - Jazz orchestra
                               Concerto for Piano (1979) - Jazz trio and symphony
                                    orchestra
                               Elegy (1983) - Jazz orchestra
                               Fantasy On a Theme by Julian Adderly (A Little
                                    Taste) (1975) - Jazz orchestra
                               In Memory Of (1984) - Double quartet and trumpet,
                                    tenor saxophone, drum set, and string bass
                               KCOR Variations (1977) - Jazz orchestra
                               Nayarac (1974) - Jazz orchestra
                               Nobody Knows (1986) - Double quartet string
                                    quartet, trumpet, tenor saxophone, drum set,
                                    string bass
                               Saturn (1978) - Jazz orchestra
                               Seton Concerto for Trumpet (1973) - Jazz orchestra
                               Variants On a Theme by John Coltrane (Naima)
                                    (1979) - Jazz orchestra

                          MULTI-ENSEMBLES AND ORCHESTRA

Akinwole, Obataiye   The Road to Freedom - Chorus, soli, narrator,
                                    dancers, piano, orchestra

Anderson, T[homas]   Spirituals (1979) - Orchestra, jazz quartet,
J[efferson]   chorus, children's choir, tenor, narrator
                               Thomas Jefferson's Orbiting Minstrels and
                                    Contraband - String quartet, woodwind
                                    quintet, jazz sextet, dancers, soprano,
                                    computer, visuals, keyboard synthesizer

Baker, David Nathaniel   The Beatitudes (1968) - Chorus (SATB), soloists,
                                    narrator, jazz ensemble, string orchestra,
                                    dancers
                               Black America: To the Memory of Martin Luther
                                    King, Jr. (1968; has undergone several
                                    revisions) - Jazz ensemble, narrators, chorus
                                    (SATB), soloists, string orchestra
                               Concerto for Fours (1980) - Solo quartet (flute,
                                    cello, tuba, contrabass), tuba quartet,
                                    contrabass quartet, percussion quartet
                               Concerto for Trombone, Jazz Band, and Chamber
                                    Orchestra (1972)
                               Concerto for Trumpet, Orchestra, and Jazz Band
                               Concerto for Two Pianos, Jazz Band, Chamber
                                    Orchestra, and Percussion (1976)

Deliver My Soul (1966) - Chorus (SATB), narrators,
jazz ensemble, string orchestra, dancers
I Will Tell Thy Name (1966) - Chorus (SATB),
narrators, jazz ensemble, string orchestra,
dancers
Kaleidoscope (1968) - Jazz ensemble, narrators,
chorus (SATB), soloist, string orchestra
Levels: A Concerto for Solo Contrabass, Jazz
Band, Flute Quartet, Horn Quartet, and String
Quartet (1973)
Psalm 22 (1962) - Chorus (SATB), narrators, jazz
ensemble, string orchestra, dancers
A Song of Mankind (1970) - Chorus (SATB),
orchestra, jazz ensemble, rock band, vocal
soloist, lights, sound effects

Cloud, Lee Vernell   Survival - Flute, string quartet, double bass, 8
voices, percussion

el-Dabh, Halim   Black Epic (1968) - Voice, dancers, actors,
orchestra

Furman, James B.   I Have A Dream (1970; revised 1971) - Chorus
(SATB), gospel choir, baritone, folk and
gospel solos, orchestra, gospel piano, organ,
guitar, banjo, combo organ, electric bass,
electric guitar, drum set

Gomes, (Antônio) Carlos   Hymno Triumphal: A Camões (1880) - Band and
orchestra

Logan, Wendell Morris   Requiem for Charlie Parker (1978) - Large
orchestra, soloist, jazz group (includes
soprano and tenor soloists and choir of 3
male and 3 female singers)

Moore, Carman Leroy   The Great American Nebula (1976) - Oratorio for
string orchestra, narrator, concert band,
gospel singer, chorus, jazz trio

Moore, Kermit   Many Thousand Gone - Flutes, strings, percussion,
voices

Price, John Elwood   The Feast of Unity (1969) - Chorus (SATB);
soprano, alto, tenor, and baritone soloists;
flute, oboe, alto saxophone, 2 trumpets, 2
trombones, tuba, piano/harp, percussion,
string octet, actors, dancers
A Liturgy for Seven Memories (1973) - Chorus
(SATB), mezzo-soprano and baritone solos,
speakers, 2 flutes, 2 oboes, 2 clarinets,
organ/piano, percussion, string septet

Republicano, Assis   Symphony of Multitudes - Orchestra, chorus, band

Stokes, Harvey J.   The Second Act - Oratorio - Soprano, tenor,
                              baritone, bass, SATB, TTBB, orchestra, brass
                              septet

Taylor, William   Peaceful Warrior - Jazz trio (piano, bass, drums),
("Billy")   choir, orchestra

OPERA

Adams, Leslie   Blake (1984)

Akpabot, Samuel   Jaja of Opobo (1972) (operetta)

Allen, Gilbert   Steal Away

Anderson, T[homas]   Soldier Boy, Soldier (1979)
J[efferson]

Baker, David Nathaniel   Malcolm

Bledsoe, Jules   Bondage

Boatner, Edward Hammond   Trouble in Mind (1975-78)

Brooks, Harry   Connie's Hot Chocolates (1929)

Brown, Oscar, Jr.   Kirk and Co.

Capers, Valerie   Sojourner

Clark, Edgar Rogie   The Stranger (1967)
                           Ti Yette (1940)

Coleridge-Taylor, Samuel   Dream Lovers (1898) (operatic romance)
                           Endymion's Dream (1909)
                           Thelma (1906-08) (grand opera)

Cook, Will Marion   Clorindy, The Origin of the Cakewalk (1898)
                              (operetta)

Cunningham, Arthur   House by the Sea (1966)
                           St. Louis Woman (1929) (folk opera)

Dafora Horton, Asadata   Africa (1944) (tribal opera)
                           Kykuntor (The Witch Woman) (folk opera)
                           Zunguru (1940) (dance opera)

Dédé, Edmond   L'Antropohage (1880) (operetta)
                           Aprè le Miel (1880) (opera comique)
                           Une Aventure de Télèmaque
                           Chik-King-Fo (1878) (operetta)
                           Le Noye (opera comique)
                           Sultan d'Ispahan (opera)

Dubois, Shirley Graham   Little Black Sambo (1938)
(Graham, Shirley Lola)   Tom-Tom (1932)
(Mrs. McCanns, Mrs.
W.E.B. Dubois)

Duncan, John   Gideon and Eliza
                            The Hellish Bandit Banditi (1974)

Ekwueme, Lazarus   A Night in Bethlehem (1963) (Christmas chamber
Edward Nnanyelu   opera)

el-Dabh, Halim   Clytemnestra (dance opera)
                            Opera Flies (1971)
                            The Twelve Hours Trip (1973)

Fax, Mark Oakland   A Christmas Miracle (1958)
                            The Lost Zoo
                            Merry Go Round
                            Till Victory is Won (1967)

Fiberesima, Adam   Opu Jaja

Fischer, William S.   Jesse

Freeman, Harry Lawrence   African Kraal (1903; revised 1934)
                            African Romance (1927)
                            Athalia (1916)
                            The Flapper (1929)
                            Leah Kleschna (1931)
                            The Martyr (1893)
                            The Octoroon (1904)
                            The Plantation (1915)
                            The Prophecy (1911)
                            The Slave (1925 or 1932)
                            Slaying of the Lion
                            The Tryst (1909)
                            Uzziah (1934)
                            Valdo (1905)
                            Vendetta (1923)
                            Voodoo (1914)
                            Zuluki (1898)
                            Zululand (1947)

Gomes, (Antônio) Carlos   Condor (1891)
                            Fosca (1873)
                            Il Guarany (1870)
                            Joana de Flandres (1863)
                            Marcha da Industria (1860)
                            Maria Tudor (1879)
                            A Noite do Castelo (1861)
                            Salvator Rosa (1874)
                            Lo Schiavo (1889)
                            Se Sa Minga (1867)

Gutiérrez y Espinosa,   El Amor de un Pescador (1857)
Felipe   El Bearnés
                            Guarionex

	Macias La Palma del Cacique (1856)
Heywood, Donald	Africana (1934)
Johnson, Hall	Fi-yer (operetta)
Johnson, James Price	The Organizer Yamacraw
Joplin, Scott	A Guest of Honor (1903 Treemonisha (1905)
Kay, Ulysses Simpson	The Boor (1955) Capital Line Venus (1969) Frederick Douglas (1983) Jubilee (1974) Juggler. . . (1956)
King, Betty Jackson	Saul of Tarus: A Sacred Opera My Servant Job: A Sacred Opera
Lapido, Duro	Eda (folk opera) Moremi (folk opera) Oba Kosa (folk opera) Oba Moro (folk opera) Oba Waja (folk opera)
Lee, William James	Baby Sweets (folk or jazz opera) The Depot (folk or jazz opera) One Mile East (folk or jazz opera) The Quarters (folk or jazz opera)
Lovingood, Penman, Sr.	Evangeline and Gabriel Menelik
Moffatt, Richard Cullen	Cinderella Rumpelstiltskin A Song for Ruby-Jo
Moseley, James Orville (Job)	How Long the Road
Nzewi, Emeka Meki	The Lost Finger (1970) (opera-drama) Mystery is Illusion (1974) (operetta) Ogbunigwe (1968) (opera-drama) The Ordeal for Regeneration (1980) (opera-drama)
Perry, Julia Amanda	The Bottle (1953) The Cask of Amontillado The Selfish Giant Three Warnings
Pittman, Evelyn La Rue	Cousin Ester (1954) Freedom's Child (1971)

Price, John Elwood   College Sonata (1957)
                            A Light from St. Agnes (1968-70)
                            The Other Foot (1972-74)
                            Right On, Baby (1971-72)

Republicano, Assis   Amazonas
                            O Banderirante (The Pioneer)
                            O Ermitao de Gloria (The Hermit of Glory)
                            Natividade de Jesus (Birth of Jesus)

Robinson, Walter   Look What a Wonder Jesus Has Done (1989) (gospel
                                 opera)

Saint-George [Saint   Le Droit du Seigneur (1784?)
George], Joseph   Ernestine (1777) - Opera in three acts
Boulogne The   La Fille-Garçon (1787) - Opera in two acts
Chevalier de   Guillaume Tout Coeur (1790)
                            Le Marchand de Marrons (1788) - Opera in two acts

Singleton, Alvin   Dream Sequence '76 (1976)

Still, William Grant   A Bayou Legend (1941)
                            Minette Fontaine (1958)
                            Mota (1951)
                            Troubled Island (1941)

White, Clarence Cameron   Ouanga (1932)

Williams, Julius P.   Guinevere

                            BALLET

Carter, John   Epigrams

Cordero, Roque   Ballet Folklorico

Cunningham, Arthur   Ballet (string quartet with jazz quartet)
                            Harlem Suite (1969) - Chorus, solo voices, piano,
                                 electric bass, drums, orchestra, dancers

Dédé, Edmond   Les Canotiers de Lorment (1880)
                            Caryatis
                            Diana et Actéon
                            Ellis
                            Les Faux Mandarins
                            Néhana, Reine des Fées (1862)
                            Les Nymphes et Chasseurs (1880)
                            La Sensitive (1877)
                            Spahis et Grisettes (1880)
                            Le Triomphe de Bacchus (1880)

el-Dabh, Halim   Fluries in Hades
                            Lucifer

Elie, Justin   Voudou

Euba, Akin	Alatangana
Fountain, Primous, III	Manifestation (1969)
Freeman, Harry Lawrence	Slave Ballet from Salome (1932) Zulu King (1934)
Jenkins, Edmond Thorton	Ballet No. 1: Processional Ballet No. 3
King, Betty Jackson	The Kids in School with Me
León, Tania Justina	The Golden Windows Haiku (1974) Spiritual Suite Tones
Lewis, John Aaron	Original Sin
Moore, Carman Leroy	Catwalk (1967) A Musical Offering (1962) Youth in Merciful House (1962)
Parks, Gordon A.	Martin Luther King
Perkinson, Coleridge- Taylor	Ode to Otis
Roldán y Gardes, Amadeo	El Milagro de Anaquille (1929) La Rebambaramba (1928)
Saint-Georges [Saint- George], Joseph Boulogne, The Chevalier de	L'Amant Anonime
Stewart, Earl Lewis	Al-Inkishafi
Still, William Grant	La Guiablesse (1927) Lenox Avenue (1937) Miss Sally's Party (1940) Sahdji (1930) (choral ballet)
Tillis, Frederick Charles	Secrets of the African Baobab (Variations for Jazz Orchestra) (1976) (modern dance/ballet)
Williams, Julius P.	Cinderella

Discography

Anderson, Thomas Jefferson. CHAMBER SYMPHONY (1968). Recording: Composers Recordings, Inc., SD-258, ca. 1970; Royal Philharmonic Orchestra; James Dixon, conductor.

---. SQUARES: AN ESSAY FOR ORCHESTRA (1965). Recording: Black Composers Series, vol. 8, Columbia M-33434; Baltimore Symphony Orchestra; Paul Freeman, conductor.

---. VARIATIONS ON A THEME BY M. B. TOLSON (1969). Recording: Nonesuch H-71303, 1974; Jan de Gaetani, mezzo-soprano; Al Regni, alto saxophone; Allan Dean, trumpet; John Swallow, trombone; Jeanne Benjamin, violin; Fred Sherry, violoncello; Gilbert Kalish, piano; Arthur Weisberg, conductor.

Baker, David Nathaniel. ETHNIC VARIATIONS ON A THEME OF PAGANINI (1976). Recording: Ruggerio Ricci for Vox, 1976.

---. GIVE AND TAKE (1975). Recording: Laurel LP-115, 1982; Edith Anne Diggory, soprano; Michelle Milter, flute and alto flute; Emily Agnew, oboe and English horn; Glenn Mellow, viola; Patrick Binford, violoncello; Rich Dimond, percussion and wind machine.

---. SINGERS OF SONGS, WEAVERS OF DREAMS. Recording: (1) Laurel LP-117, 1981; Janos Starker, violoncello; George Gaber, percussion; (2) Golden Crest 4223, n.d.; Cooke, violoncello; Brown, percussion.

---. SONATA FOR PIANO AND STRING QUINTET (1971). Recording: AAMOA NS-7401; Helena Freire, pianist.

---. SONATA, TUBA AND STRING QUARTET (1971). Recording: Gold Crest CRS-4122, n.d. (ca. 1974); Harvey Phillips, tuba; the Composers String Quartet.

---. SONATA FOR VIOLONCELLO AND PIANO (1973). Recording: Black Composers Series, vol. 6, Columbia M-33432; Janos Starker, violoncello; Alain Plaes, piano.

Bebey, Francis. BLACK WOMAN. Guitar. Recording: Ocara in France; Compositions for Solo Guitar.

---. THE CHANT OF IBADAN: BLACK TEARS. Guitar. Recording: Ocara in France; Compositions for Solo Guitar.

---. CHRIST WAS BORN IN BOMBA. Guitar. Recording: Ocara in France; Compositions for Solo Guitar.

---. CONCERT POUR UN VIEUX MASQUE. Guitar. Recording: Philips, France.

Bland, Edward Osmund (Ed). FOR VIOLIN (1980). Recording: Cambria Records #1026, 1986.

---. PIECE FOR CHAMBER ORCHESTRA (1979). Recording: Cambria Records C-1026, 1986; Members of the Speculum Musicae and the Group for Contemporary Music.

---. SKETCHES SET I (1965). Clarinet, trumpet, two cellos, timpani. Recording: Cambria Records #1026, 1986.

Bland, James A. CARRY ME BACK TO OLD VIRGINNY. Recording: (1) Victor LM-1703; Marian Anderson, contralto; Gregory Piatigorsky, cello; (2) Renee Chemet, violin; (3) Bidu Sayao, soprano; Milne Charnley, piano; (4) Helen Traubel, soprano; male chorus; orchestra; Charles O'Connell, conductor.

Bonds, Margaret Allison. I WISH I KNEW HOW IT WOULD FEEL TO BE FREE. Recording: RCA Victor LSC-3183. NOTE: Arranged for Leontyne Price.

---. SINNER PLEASE DON'T LET THIS HARVEST PASS. Recording: RCA Victor LSC-3183. NOTE: Arranged for Leontyne Price.

---. STANDIN' IN THE NEED OF PRAYER. Recording: RCA Victor LSC-3183. NOTE: Arranged for Leontyne Price.

---. THIS LITTLE LIGHT OF MINE. Recording: RCA Victor LSC-3183. NOTE: Arranged for Leontyne Price.

Brouwer, Leo. APUNTES (1959). Recording: Inter-American Musical Editions, OAS-012, 1981; Everton Gloeden, guitar.

---. DANZA CARACTERISTICA (1957). Recording: Musical Heritage Society, MHS-3777, 1973; Oscar Cáceres, guitar.

---. DANZAS CONCERTANTES (1958). Guitar and orchestra. Recording: Musical Heritage Society MHS-3777, 1973; Oscar Cáceres, guitar; instrumental ensemble; Leo Brouwer, conductor.

---. ELOGIA DE LA DANZA (1964). Recording: (1) Musical Heritage Society, MHS-3839, 1972; Leo Brouwer, guitar; (2) Musical Heritage Society, MHS-3777, 1973; Oscar Cáceres, guitar.

---. MICROPIEZAS (ca. 1954). 2 guitars. Recording: Musical Heritage Society, MHS-3777, 1973; Oscar Cáceres and Leo Brouwer. guitars.

---. PIEZE SIN TITULO (1956). Recording: Musical Heritage Society,   MHS-
3777, 1973; Oscar Cáceres, guitar.

Burleigh, Harry Thacker. DEEP RIVER. Recording: (1) Decca A-385; Jascha
Heifetz, violin; Milton Kaye, piano; (2) Decca DL-5214; Jascha Heifetz, violin; Milton Kaye, piano.

---. EVERY TIME I FEEL THE SPIRIT. Recording: RCA LSC-2600, 1962; Leontyne Price, soprano; orchestra and chorus; Leonard De Paur, conductor
(and arranger).

---. I STOOD ON DE RIBBER OB JORDON. Recording: (1) RCA LM/LSC-2592,
1962; Marian Anderson, contralto; Franz Rupp, piano; (2) London
LPS-182, 1950; Ellabelle Davis, soprano; orchestra; Victor Olof, conductor.

---. WERE YOU THERE? Recording: (1) RCA ARL 1-1403, n.d.; Sherrill
Milnes, baritone; Jon Sprong, organ; (2) RCA AVM 1-1735, 1976 (recorded May 1947); Marian Anderson, contralto; Franz Rupp, piano; (3) London LPS-182, 1950; Ellabelle Davis, soprano; orchestra; Victor Olof,
conductor; (4) Starline SRS-5192, n.d.; Paul Robeson, bass; Rutland
Clapham, piano; (5) RCA LM-3292, 1972 (recorded 27 July 1925); Paul
Robeson, bass; Lawrence Brown, piano; (6) BRC Productions, 1980; Ver-
onica Tyler, soprano; Ernest Regongini, piano; (7) PRC CC-4, n.d.;
Illinois Wesleyan University Choir; Lewis E. Wikehart, conductor.

Burrs, Leslie. SONG FOR WINNIE.   String quartet. Recording: Phillip
Records, August 1989.

Coleridge-Taylor, Samuel. AFRICAN SUITE, Op. 35, No. 4, DANSE NEGRE
(1898). Recording: Columbia M-32782, 1974; London Symphony Orchestra; Paul Freeman, conductor.

---. CHARACTERISTIC WALTZES, Op. 22. Piano. Recording: HMV B-8378/9; New
Light Symphony Orchestra.

---. THE DEATH OF MINNEHAHA. Recording: HMV C-2210/3; Elsa Suddaby, soprano; George Baker, baritone; Howard Fry, bass; Royal Choral Society;
Royal Albert Hall Orchestra; Malcolm Sargent, conductor.

---. DEEP RIVER. Recording: Victor 74246; Maud Powell, violin.

---. DREAM DANCES Op. 74, No. 2. Piano. Recording: HMV B-8876/7. Recording: London Paladium Orchestra; Greenwood, conductor; arranged by
P. Fletcher.

--- FAUST, Op. 70, Nos. 1, 2. Recording: Boosey & Hawkes, 1922; Regent
Concert Orchestra.

---. THE FOREST OF WILD THYME: CHRISTMAS OVERTURE. Recording: BBC Symphony Orchestra; Pitt, conductor.

---. HIAWATHA'S BALLET. Recording: Columbia L-1450/1; New Queen's Hall
Orchestra; Alick MacLean, conductor.

---. HIAWATHA'S WEDDING FEAST, Op. 30, No. 1 (1898). Recording: (1) His
Master's Voice ASD 467, 1962; Philharmonic Orchestra; Royal Choral

Society; Richard Lewis, tenor; Sir Malcolm Sargent, conductor; (2) Columbia M-32782, 1974 (contains "Onaway, awake, awake, beloved" only); William Brown, tenor; London Symphony Orchestra; Paul Freeman, conductor.

---. HIAWATHA'S WEDDING FEAST, selections. Recording: (1) HMV PES-5264; Alexandria Choir; Sinfonia of London; Charles Proctor, conductor; (2) Angel S-35900; Richard Lewis, tenor; Royal Choral Society; Philharmonica Orchestra; Malcolm Sargent, conductor; (3) HMV ASD-467; Richard Lewis, tenor; Royal Choral Society; Philharmonica Orchestra; Malcolm Sargent, conductor; (4) HMV C-1931/4; Walter Glynne, tenor; Royal Albert Hall Orchestra; Royal Choral Society; Malcolm Sargent, conductor.

---. INTERMEZZO, Op. 74, No. 3. Orchestra. Recording: J.B. 8113.

---. OTHELLO SUITE, Op. 79. Recording: HMV B-4273/4; New Symphony, Malcolm Sargent, conductor.

---. PETITE SUITE DE CONCERT, Op. 77 (1900). Recording: (1) HMV C-2372/3; London Symphony Orchestra; Malcolm Sargent, conductor; (2) Victor 11283/4; London Symphony Orchestra; Malcolm Sargent, conductor; (3) Columbia 9340/1; Ansell, conductor; (4) Columbia DX-651/2; Bournemouth Municipal Orchestra; Godfrey, conductor; (5) Columbia DB-2478/80; Queen's Hall Light Orchestra; (6) HMV SKLP-30123; Philharmonia Orchestra; Weldon, conductor; (7) Columbia L-1808/O; New Queen's Hall Orchestra; Alick MacLean, conductor; (8) Columbia ML-2180; Queen's Hall Light Orchestra or City of Birmingham Orchestra; Sidney Troch, conductor; (9) New Queen's Hall Orchestra; Alick MacLean conductor; (10) RCA Victor 13792 (n.d.) (contains nos. 1 and 2 only); London Symphony Orchestra; Malcolm Sargent, conductor.

---. PETITE SUITE DE CONCERT: DEMANDE ET RESPONSE. Recording: (1) London LPB-196; Richard Crean, conductor; (2) Decca LF-1010; Richard Crean, conductor; (3) HMV E-310; arr. Cedric Sharp, violoncello; (4) Boosey and Hawks, S-2096; J. Wilbur String Ensemble.

---. QUINTET F SHARP MINOR, Op. 10 (1895). Clarinet and strings. Recording: (1) Chantry Recordings ABM-23, 1976; Georgina Dobree, clarinet; Amici String Quartet; (2) Spectrum SR-127, 1980; Ramon Kireilis, clarinet; Lamont String Quartet.

---. SONATA, D MINOR, Op. 28. Violin and piano. Recording: Columbia L-1396/7; Albert Sammons, violin; William Murdoch, piano.

---. SONGS OF HIAWATHA, Op. 82. Recording: (1) Boosey and Hawkes, 1916, Nos. 2 and 4; Regent Concert Orchestra; arranged by A. Lotter; (2) Boosey and Hawkes, 1922, No. 4; Regent Concert Orchestra; arranged by A. Lotter.

---. ST. AGNES EVE, nos. 1 and 2. Recording: Boosey and Hawkes, 1909; Regent Concert Orchestra.

---. VALSE SUITE, Op. 71, Nos. 2 and 6. Piano. Recording: Columbia DB-2212; Palm Court Orchestra; Sandler, conductor.

Cordero, Roque. CONCERTO (1962). Violin. Recording: Columbia M-32784, 1974; Sanford Allen, violin; Detroit Symphony Orchestra; Paul Freeman, conductor.

---. 8 MINIATURAS (1948). Recording: Columbia M-32784, 1974; Detroit Symphony Orchestra; Paul Freeman, conductor.

---. QUINTET (1949). Piano, flute, clarinet, violin, violoncello. Recording: Turnabout TV-S34505, 1973; John Wion, flute; Arthur Bloom, clarinet; Kees Kooper violin; Fred Sherry, violoncello; Mary Louise Boehm, piano.

---. SYMPHONY NO. 2 (1957). Recording: First Edition Records LS-765, 1979; Louisville Orchestra; Jorge Mester, conductor.

Cunningham, Arthur. HARLEM SUITE: LULLABYE FOR A JAZZ BABY (1969).   Recording: Desto DC-7107, ca. 1971; Oakland Youth Orchestra; Robert Hughes, conductor.

Da   Costa, Noel G. GENERATA (1958). Recording: Adama 1, 1981; Lorna McDaniel organ; Leo Ahramjian and Sylvia Ahramjian, violins; Phyllis McKinney, viola; Karen Ahramjian, violoncello; Dominic Fiore, double bass.

Davis, Anthony. MAPS (198?). Concerto for violin and symphony orchestra. Recording: Gramavision 18-8807; Kansas City Symphony Orchestra; Shem Guibbory, violin; William McGlaughlin, conductor.

---. WAYGANG NO. 5 (1988). Concerto for piano and orchestra. Recording: Gramavision 18-8807; Anthony Davis, piano; Pheeron akLaff, percussion; William McClaughlin, conductor.

Dawson, William Levi. NEGRO FOLK SYMPHONY (1983; revised 1952). Recording: Decca DL-710077, 1963; American Symphony Orchestra; Leopold Stokowski, conductor.

---. OUT IN THE FIELDS (ca. 1929). Recording: (1) Desto DC-7101, 1971; Cynthia Bedford mezzo-soprano; Oakland Youth Orchestra; Robert Hughes, conductor; (2) Silver Crest MOR-111977, 1977; Morgan State University Choir; Patricia Singer, piano; Nathan Carter, conductor.

Dett, Robert Nathaniel. IN THE BOTTOMS: JUBA DANCE. Recordings: (1) MGM E-3195; Hamburg Philharmonia; (2) Music Sound Books MSB-78028; Hamburg Philharmonia; (3) Victor 21750; Victor Orchestra.

---. THE ORDERING OF MOSES (1932). Recording: Silver Crest TAL-42868-5, 1968; Jeanette Walters, soprano; Carol Brice, contralto; John Miles, tenor; John Work IV, baritone; Talladega College Choir; Mobile Symphony Orchestra; William L. Dawson, conductor.

Duncan, John. BLACK BARDS. Recording: Eastern ERS-513.

Fischer, William S. A QUIET MOVEMENT (1966). Recording: Desto DC-7107, ca. 1971; Oakland Youth Orchestra; Robert Hughes, conductor.

Gomes, (Antônio) Carlos. FOSCA:, INTENDITI CON DIO (1873). Recording:
     Philips 9500 771, 1980; José Carreras, tenor; London Symphony Orches-
     tra; Jesús Lopez Cobos, conductor.

---. FOSCA: O TU SEI FRA GLI ANGLEI. Tenor and orchestra. Recording:
     Sociedade Brasileira de Discos Historicos J. Léon TOB-1 and Associacão
     Brasileiro dos Colectionadores de Discos 2; A. Colosimo, tenor.

---. FOSCA: OVERTURE. Orchestra. Recording: (1) Orquestra do Sindicato
     Musical do Rio de Janeiro; Leo Peracchi, conductor; (2) Odeon A-3252;
     Rio de Janeiro Symphony; Mignone, conductor.

---. IL GUARANY (1970). Recording: (1) Voce 48, 1980 (recorded 4 July
     1980); Aurea Gomes (Cecilia); Benito Maresca (Pery); Paulo Fortes
     (Gonzales); Wilson Carrara (Il Cacico); Amin Feres (Don Antonio);
     Marcos Louzada (Don Alvaro); Manuel Pascoa (Alonso); Victor Prochei
     (Ruy Bento); Orchestra and Chorus of the Teatro Municipal, Rio de
     Janeiro; Mario Tavares, conductor; (2) The Golden Age of Opera EJS240,
     n.d. (recorded 1964); Gianna d'Angelo; Giorgio Gibin; Pero Cappuccil-
     li; Niccola Zaccaria; Maximiliano Malaspina; Dino Crimi; Orchestra and
     Chorus of the Teatro Municipal, Rio de Janeiro; Francesco Molinari-
     Pradelli, conductor; (3) Ember GVC-20, n.d. (contains "O come è bello
     il ciel" only); Lina Pagliughi, soprano; Orchestra Sinfonica di Rotino
     della Radiotelevisione Italiana; (4) RCA VL-42433, 1978 (contains
     "senza tetto" only; recorded 22 March 1912); Pasquale Amato, baritone.

---. IL GUARANY [HIMMLISCHE MACHT, DIE MICH GEHANNT]. Soprano and orches-
     tra. Recordings: Victor 6355-B, 1914; Emmy Destinn, soprano, with
     orchestra.

---. IL GUARANY: OVERTURE. Orchestra. Recordings: (1)Columbia D-14457
     and Columbia 52054-X; Milan Symphony Orchestra; Molajoli, conductor;
     (2) His Master's Voice S-10083; Orchestra del Teatro alla Scala; Sab-
     jano, conductor; (3) Homochord 4-8803; Berlin Symphony Orchestra;
     Bohnke, conductor; (4) Odeon O-26804 and Odeon 193577 and Parlphone
     28053; Berlin State Opera Orchestra; Weissman, conductor; (5) Odeon
     13028 and Parlophone CB-20526; Radio Italiana; Mignone, conductor; (6)
     Polydor 27347; unidentified orchestra; Gurliti, conductor; (7) Odeon
     5044; Rio de Janeiro Municipal Orchestra; Gouveia, conductor; (8)
     Avellaneda Municipal Orchestra; Fauré, conductor; (9) Victor 119112;
     Boston Pops Orchestra; Arthur Fiedler, conductor; (10) Camden CAE-182
     and Camden CAL-186; Boston Promenade Orchestra [i.e. Boston Pops Or-
     chestra]; Arthur Fiedler, conductor.

---. IL GUARANY: OVERTURE. Mandolin ensemble. Recording: Odeon 5117;
     Odeon Mandolin Orchestra.

---. IL GUARANY: PERRY MA APPELLA. Tenor and orchestra. Recording:
     Berliner 52566, 1900; Giovanni Cesarini tenor.

---. IL GUARANY: REGINA DELLA TRIBÙ. Bass and orchestra, Recording:
     Sociedade Brasileira de Discos Historicos J. Léon TOB-1; N.
     Rossi-Lemeni, bass.

---. IL GUARANY: VANTO IO PUR SUPERBA CUNA. Tenor and orchestra. Record-
     ings: (1) Victor 85-0000 and Victor B-5042; Beniamino Gigli, tenor;

(2) Sociedade Brasileira de Discos Historicos J. Léon TOB 1; A. Pacheo, tenor.

---. MARIA TUDOR: OVERTURE [?]. Orchestra. Recording: Odeon C-7269; Rio de Janeiro Symphony; Mignone. conductor.

---. MARIA TUDOR: ARIA DI MARIA. Soprano and orchestra. Recording: Sociedad Brasileiro de Discos Historicos J. Léon TOB-1; C. Gomes, soprano.

---. SALVATOR ROSA: ARIA OF THE DUKE D'ARCOS. Bass and orchstra. Recording: La Voce del Padrone 2-52558; Leo Sibiryakov, bass.

---. SALVATOR ROSA: E IL SAGLIO IO SEGNERO. Bass and orchestra. Recording: Odeon 3518-B and Fonotipia 152586; Luigi Mantrini (Manini?), bass.

---. SALVATOR ROSA: E QUANTO. Bass and orchestra. Recording: Sociedade Brasileira de Discos Historicos J. Léon LPP-3 and Columbia 5063-M; J. Mardones, bass.

---. SALVATOR ROSA: OVERTURE. Orchestra. Recordings: (1) Orquestra do Sindicato Musical do Rio de Janeiro; Leo Peracchi, conductor; (2) Parlophone B-20525; Radio Italiana; Mignone, conductor.

---. SALVATOR ROSA: RECITATIVO. Bass and orchestra. Recording: G&T 52907 52907; Leo Sibiryakov, bass.

---. LO SCHIAVO: ALVORADA. Orchestra. Recordings: (1) Orquestra do Sindicato Musical do Rio de Janeiro; Leo Peracchi, conductor; (2) Odeon C-7265; Rio de Janeiro Symphony Orchestra; Mignone conductor

--- LO SCHIAVO: O CIEL DI PARAHYBA. Soprano and orchestra. Recordings: (1) Victor 74112 and Sociedade Brasileira de Discos Historicos J. Léon G-4, ca. 1909; Roxy King-Shaw, soprano; (2) Sociedade Brasileira de Discos Historicos J. Léon TOB-1; M.C.N. de Freita, soprano.

---. LO SCHIAVO: PRELUDE. Orchestra. Recording: Orquestra do Sindicato Musical do Rio de Janeiro; Leo Peracchi conductor.

---. LO SCHIAVO: PRELUDE. ACT IV. Orchestra. Recording: Parlophone CB-20527; Radio Italiana; Magnone, conductor.

---. LO SCHIAVO: SOGNI D'AMORE. Bass and orchestra. Recording: Victor 33466; S. Vieira, bass.

Hailstork, Adolphus Cunningham. CELEBRATION (1974). Orchestra. Recording: Columbia M34556 1978; Detroit Symphony Orchestra; Paul Freeman, conductor.

---. TWO STRUTS WITH BLUES (1985). Recording: Blue Note, 1985.

Hakim. Talib Rasul. SHAPES (1965). Recording: The Black Composer in America, Desto DC 7107; Oakland Youth Orchestra; Robert Hughes, conductor.

---. VISIONS OF ISHWARA (1970). Recording: Black Composer Series, vol. 8, Columbia M-33434; Baltimore Symphony Orchestra; Paul Freeman, conductor.

Holmes, Robert L. YESTERDAY'S MANIONS (1972). Flute, violoncello, piano. Recording: Eastern RS-513, ca. 1972; Trio Pro Viva.

Johnson, Hall. HONOR, HONOR. Recording: (1) Black Heritage Recordings 90671, ca. 1975; Virginia State College Choir; Eugene Thamon Simpson, conductor; (2) RCA AVM 1-1735, 1976 (recorded May 1947); Marian Anderson, contralto; Franz Rupp piano; (3) Tioch Digital TD-1009, 1982; Wilhelmenia Fernandez, soprano; George Darden, piano; (4) Marble Arch LS-1181, ca 1981; Paul Spencer Adkins tenor, with piano; (5) RCA LSC-2600, 1962; Leontyne Price, soprano; orchestra and chorus; Leonard De Paur, conductor.

---. RIDE ON KING JESUS. Recording: (1) Tioch Digital TD-1009, 1982; Wilhelmenia Fernandez, soprano; George Darden, piano; (2) RCA-LSC-2600, 1962; Leontyne Price, soprano; orchestra and chorus; Leonard De Paur conductor (and arranger).

Johnson, John Rosamond. LIFT EVERY VOICE AND SING. Recording: (1) Recall Records, n.d.; St. Augustine's College Choir; Jack L. Biggers, organ; Addison W. Reed, conductor; (2) RCA ARC 1-4421, 1982; Leontyne Price, soprano; National Philharmonic Orchestra; Charles Gerhardt, conductor (and arranger); (3) Sound 80, ca. 1975; Sounds of Blackness; Gary Hines conductor; (4) Columbia JC-36267, 1979; William A. Brown, tenor; Royal Philharmonic Orchestra; Paul Freeman, conductor (arranged by Hale Smith).

Jones, Charles. SYMPHONY NO. 6. Recording: Silhouettes in Courage K-5001/2, 1970.

Joplin, Scott. TREEMONISHA (1911). Recording: (1) Deutsche Grammophone 2707 083, 1976; Carmen Balthrop, soprano (Treemonisha); Betty Allen, mezzo-soprano (Monisha); Curtis Rayam, tenor (Remus); Willard White, bass (Ned); Ben Harney baritone (Zodzetrick); Cora Johnson, soprano (Lucy); Kenneth Hicks, tenor (Andy); Dorceal Duckens, baritone (Luddud); Dwight Ransom, tenor (Cephus); Raymond Bazemore, baritone (Simon); Edward Pierson, bass (Parson All-Talk); orchestra; Gunther Schuller, conductor (and arranger); (2) Smithsonian Collection P-12974, 1975; April Curtis, soprano; Margaret Lindsey, soprano; Morgan State University Chorus; Nathan Carter, conductor (arranged by T.J. Anderson, contains "A Real Slow Drag" only).

Kay Ulysses Simpson. CONCERTO FOR ORCHESTRA (1948). Recording: (1) Varèse Sarbande VC-81047; Orchestra Sinfonica del Teatro La Fenice; (2) Remington Musirama R-199-173; Teatro La Fenice orchestra; Jonel Perlea conductor.

---. DANCES: ROUND DANCE AND POLKA. String orchestra. Recording: CRI 119; New Symphony Orchestra; Tutti Camerata conductor.

---. FANTASY VARIATIONS (1957). Recording: (1) Composers Recording, Inc.. CRI-SD-209, 1965; Oslo Philharmonic Orchestra; Arthur Bennett Lipkin, conductor; (2) Remington Musirama R-199-173; Teatro La Fenice orchestra; Jonel Perlea, conductor.

---. MARKINGS (1966). Recording: Black Composers Series. vol. 3, Columbia M-32783, 1974; London Symphony Orchestra; Paul Freeman, conductor.

---. OF NEW HORIZONS. Recording: University of Arizona Records.

---. SERENADE (1954). Orchestra. Recording: LOU 548-9, ca. 1954; Louisville Orchestra; Robert Whitney, conductor.

---. SINFONIA, E (1950). Recording: CRI 139, n.d.; Oslo Philharmonic Orchestra; George Barati, conductor.

---. SIX DANCES (1954). String orchestra. Recording: (1) Turnabout TV-S 34546, 1974; Wesphalian Symphony Orchestra Recklinghausen; Paul Freeman, conductor; (2) CRI-119, ca. 1955; New Symphony Orchestra London; Tutti Camerata, conductor (contains nos. 3 and 4).

---. A SHORT OVERTURE (1946). Recordng: The Black Composer in America, Desto DC-7101, 1971; Oakland Youth Orchestra; Robert Hughes, conductor.

---. UMBRIAN SCENE (1963). Recording: LOU 651, ca. 1965; Louisville Orchestra; Robert Whitney, conductor.

Kennedy, Joseph J., Jr. DIALOGUE (1970). Recording: Eastern ERS-513; Trio Pro Viva.

Ladipo, Duro. EDNA (1965). Folk opera. Recording: Nigerial Cultural Records 5-6, 1971 (recorded 1965); Duro Ladipo National Theatre.

---. OBA KOSO Folk opera. Recording: Kaleidoscope KS-2201, 1975; Duro Ladipo (Shango); Abiodun Ladipo (Oya); Adebisi; Fasanu (Gbonka); Lasisi Gbebaolaja (Timi); Duro Ladipo National Theatre; Duro Ladipo, conductor.

Lateef, Yusef. TRIO NO. 1. Piano, flute, violin. Recording: Eastern ERS-513.

Moore, Carman Leroy. FOUR MOVEMENTS FOR A FASHIONABLE FIVE-TOED DRAGON (1976). Recording: Vanguard (limited in-house pressing).

---. YOUTH IN MERCIFUL HOUSE (1962). Recording: (1) Desto, 1975; (2) Folkways 33902, 1976.

Moore, Dorothy Rudd. DIRGE AND DELIVERANCE (1962). Recording: Performance Records CR-77001, 1981; Kermit Moore, violoncello; Raymond Jackson, piano.

---. FROM THE DARK TOWER (1970). Recording: Performance Records CR-77003, 1980; Hilda Harris, mezzo-soprano; Kermit Moore, violoncello; Wayne Sanders, piano.

Moore, Undine Smith. AFRO-AMERICAN SUITE (1969). Recording: Contemporary Black Images in Music for the Flute, Eastern ERS-513; Trio Pro Viva (D. Antoinette Handy, flute; Ronald Lipscomb, violoncello; Gladys Perry Norris, piano).

Nunes-Garcia, José Mauricio. MISSA DA NOSSA SENHORA DA CONCIECAO (1810).
    Recording: Angel 3-CBX 410/412, n.d.; Coro da Associacao de Canto
    Coral; Orquestra Sinfonica Nacional; Alceu Bocchino, conductor.

---. REQUIEM, D MINOR, M. 185 (1816).   Recording: (1) Columbia M-33431,
    1975; Doralene Davis, soprano; Betty Allen, mezzo-soprano; William
    Brown, tenor; Mattil Tuloisela, bass-baritone; Helsinki Philharmonic
    Orchestra; Morgan State University Chorus; Paul Freeman, conductor
    (arranged by Dominique-René de Lerma); (2) Audio House AHS-30F75,
    1975; Morgan State College Choir; WIlliam Partridge, organ; Nathan
    Carter, conductor (contains Nos. 1 and 2 only; arranged by Dominique-
    René de Lerma); (3) Desta LDR-5012, n.d.; Margarida Martins Maia,
    soprano; Carmen Pimental, contralto; Isuardo Camino, tenor; Jorge
    Bailly, bass; Coro de Assoçiascao de Canto Coral; Orquestra do Theatro
    Municipal, Rio de Janeiro; Edoardo de Guarnieri, conductor.

---. TE DEUM LAUDAMUS (1811).   Recording: Musica na Corte Brasileira;
    Dirce a de Amorim, soprano; Jose Evergisto Gomes Netto, tenor; Juan
    Thibault, bass; Orquestra Sinfonica Nacional; Alceu Bocchino, conduc-
    tor.

Perry, Julia.   SHORT PIECE.   Orchestra.   Recording: CRI 145, ca. 1965;
    Imperial Philharmonic of Tokyo; William Strickland, conductor.

---. STABAT MATER.   Recording: CIR 133, 1960; Makiko Askura, mezzo-
    soprano; Japan Philharmonic Symphony Orchestra; William Strickland,
    conductor.

Roldán, Amadeo. CONCIONES POPULARES CUBANAS. Recording: Adolfo Odnopo-
    soff, cello; Bertha Huberman, piano.

Russell, George Allan.   THE AFRICAN GAME.   Jazz orchestra.   Recording:
    Blue Note, 1985.

---. CONCERT FOR SELF-ACCOMPANIED GUITAR (1962).   Recording: The Essence
    of George Russell, Sonet SLP-1411/1412; Rune Gustafson.

Saint-Georges, Chevalier de.   ERNESTINE: O CLEMENGIS, LIS DANS MON ÂME.
    Soprano and orchestra.   Recording: Columbia M372781, 1974; Fay Robin-
    son, soprano; London Symphony Orchestra; Paul Freeman, conductor.

---. ERNESTINE: ERNESTINE, QUE VAS-TU FAIRE? (1777).   Recording: Columbia
    M-32781, 1974; Faye Robinson, soprano; London Symphony Orchestra; Paul
    Freeman, conductor; arranged by Dominique-Rene de Lerma.

---. SONATA FOR VIOLIN AND KEYBOARD NO. 1, B-FLAT MAJOR.   Recording: Arion
    ARN-38484, 1978; Jean Jacques Kantorow, violin; Brigitte Haudebourg,
    harpsichord.

---. SONATA FOR VIOLIN AND KEYBOARD NO. 3, G MINOR.   Recording: Arion ARN-
    38484, 1978; Jean Jacques Kantorow, violin; Brigitte Haudebourg, harp-
    sichord.

---. STRING QUARTET IN C MAJOR, Op. 1, No. 1 (1773).   Recording: (1) Co-
    lumbia M-32781, 1974; Juilliard Quartet; edited by Dominique-René de
    Lerma; (2) Musical Heritage Society NHS-3727, 1977; Jean-Noël Molard
    String Quartet.

---. STRING QUARTET NO. 3, G MINOR. Recording: Musical Heritage Society
MHS-3727, 1977; Quartour Jean-Noël Molard.

---. STRING QUARTET NO. 4, C MINOR. Recording: Musical Heritage Society
MHS-3727, 1977; Quartour Jean-Noël Molard.

---. STRING QUARTET NO. 5, G MINOR. Recording: Musical Heritage Society
MHS-3727, 1977; Quartour Jean-Noël Molard.

---. STRING QUARTET NO. 6, D MAJOR. Recording: Musical Heritage Society
MHS-3727, 1977; Quartour Jean-Noël Molard.

---. SYMPHONIE CONCERTANTE IN G MAJOR, Op. 13 (1782). Recording: (1)
Columbia M-32781, 1974; Miriam Fried and Jaime Laredo, violins; London
Symphony Orchestra; Paul Freeman, conductor; cadenza by Dominique-René
de Lerma; (2) Erato ERA-9511, 1965, and Musical Heritage Society
MHS CC-1, 1966; Huguette Fermandez and Ginette Carles, violins; Orchestre de Chambre; Jean-François Paillard, conductor; (3) Erato LDE-
3037, n.d.; Micheline Blanchard and Germaine Raymond, violins; Ensemble Instrumental Jean-Marie Leclair; Jean-François Paillard, conductor.

---. SYMPHONY NO. 1 IN G MAJOR, Op. 11, No. 1 (1779). Recording: (1) Columbia M-32781, 1974; London Symphony Orchestra; Paul Freeman, conductor; edited by Dominique-René de Lerma; (2) Erato LDE-3037, n.d.;
Ensemble Instrumental Jean-Marie Leclair; Jean-Francois Paillard,
conductor.

Singleton, Alvin. AFTER FALLEN CRUMBS (1988). Recording: Elektra/None-
such Records, 9 79231-2 (CD), 9 79231-4 (cassette); Atlanta Symphony
Orchestra; Robert Shaw, conductor.

---. SHADOWS (1987). Recording: Elektra/Nonesuch Records, 9 79231-2 (CD),
9 79231-4 (cassette); Atlanta Symphony Orchestra; Louis Lane, conductor.

---. A YELLOW ROSE PETAL. Recording: Elektra/Nonesuch Records, 9 79231-2
(CD), 9 79231-4 (cassette); Atlanta Symphony Orchestra; Louis Lane,
conductor.

Smith, Hale. CONTOURS (1962). Recording: Louisville LOU-632; Louisville
Symphony Orchestra; Robert Whitney, conductor.

---. IN MEMORIAM BERYL RUBINSTEIN (1953; orchestrated 1958). Recording:
The Cleveland Composers' Guild, vol. 1, Composers Recordings Inc.
CRI Sd-182; the Kulas Choir and Chamber Orchestra; Robert Shaw, con-
ductor.

---. NUANCES OF HALE SMITH (ca. 1967-68). Recording: Sam Fox SF 1022
(side A), Synchrofox Music Library.

---. RITUAL AND INCANTATION (1974). Recording: Columbia Black Composers
Series, Columbia M-34556; The Detroit Symphony Orchestra; Paul Freeman, conductor.

Sowande   Olufela   ("Fela").   AFRICAN SUITE.   Recording: (1) Columbia
    M-33433, 1975; London Symphony Orchestra; Paul Freeman, conductor; (2)
    London LS-425; Harvey, conductor.

Still, William Grant.   CARMELA.   Recording: Orion ORS-7152, 1971; Louis
    Kaufman, violin; Annette Kaufman, piano.

---. DANZAS DE PANAMA (1948).   String quartet.   Recording: Orion ORS 7278,
    1972; George Berres, Terry King, Louis Kaufman, Alex Neiman.

---. DARKER AMERICA.   Tone poem, orchestra.   Recording: Turnabout TV-S
    34546, 1974; Seigried Landau and the Westchester Symphony Orchestra.

---. ENNANGA (1956).   Harp, strings, piano.   Recording: Orion 7278; Lois
    Craft, harp; Annette Kaufman, piano; strings.

---. FESTIVAL OVERTURE (1944).   Orchestra.   Recording: Composer's Record-
    ings Inc. CRI SD 259, 1970; Arthur Lipkin and the Royal Philharmonic
    of London.

---. FROM THE BLACK BELT (1926).   Suite, orchestra.   Recording: Turnabout
    TV-S 34546, 1974; Siegried Landau and the Westchester Symphony Orches-
    tra.

---. HERE'S ONE.   Recording: (1) Vox 627, 1948; Louis Kaufman, violin;
    Annette Kaufman, piano; arrangements by Louis Kaufman; (2) Orion
    ORS-7152, 1971; Louis Kaufman, violin; Annette Kaufman, piano; ar-
    rangement by Louis Kaufman.

---. LENOX AVENUE: BLUES (1937).   Recording: (1) New Records NRLP-105,
    ca. 1950; Gordon Manley, piano; (2) Orion ORS-7152, 1971; Louis Kauf-
    man, violin; Annette Kaufman, piano; arrangement by Louis Kaufman; (3)
    Concert Hall Society CHC-58; Louis Kaufman, violin; Annette Kaufman,
    piano; arrangement by Louis Kaufman; (4) Concert Hall Society CHC
    1140, 1950; (5) Victor 27411; Artie Shaw and His Orchestra; (6) Vox
    627, 1948; Louis Kaufman, violin; Annette Kaufman, piano; arrangement
    by Louis Kaufman

---. LENOX AVENUE: FLIRTATION (1937).   Recording: Hancock Foundation,
    University of Southern California 395, 1942; Hancock Ensemble; Loren
    Powell, conductor.

---. PASTORELA (1946).   Violin and piano.   Recording: Orion ORS 7152,
    1971; Louis Kaufman, violin; Annette Kaufman, piano.

---. SAHDJI (1930).   Choral ballet   Recording: (1) Black Composers
    Series, Columbia Records, 1975; London Symphony Orchestra; Paul Free-
    man, conductor; (2) Eastman-Rochester Symphony Orchestra; Eastman
    School Chorus; Howard Hanson, conductor.

---. SONGS OF SEPARATION (1949).   Recording: (1) Desto DC-7107, ca. 1971;
    Cynthia Bedford, mezzo soprano; Oakland Youth Orchestra; Robert
    Hughes, conductor; (2) Orion ORS-7278, 1972; Claudine Carlson, mezzo-
    soprano; Georgia Akst, piano.

---. SUITE (1943).   Violin and piano.   Recording: Orion ORS-7152, 1971;
    Louis Kaufman, violin; Annette Kaufman, piano.

--- SYMPHONY NO. 1: "AFRO-AMERICAN SYMPHONY" (1930; revised 1969). Orchestra. Recording: (1) New Records NRLP-1-5, ca. 1950; Vienna Symphony; Karl Kreuger, conductor; (2) Instrumental Music in the Twentieth Century, Society for the Preservation of the American Music Heritage MLA-118; The Royal Philharmonic of London; Karl Kreuger, conductor; (3) Black Composers Series, vol. 2, Columbia M-32782, 1974; The London Symphony; Paul Freeman, conductor; (4) Columbia 119920D, 1944; All American Youth Orchestra; Leopold Stokowski, conductor ("Scherzo" only); (5) Eastman-Rochester Symphony Orchestra; Howard Hanson, conductor ("Scherzo" only).

---. SYMPHONY NO. 3: "THE SUNDAY SYMPHONY" (1958). Orchestra. Recording: North Arkansas Symphony Orchestra Records, 1984; North Arkansas Symphony Orchestra.

---. 3 VISIONS (1936). Recording: (1) Da Camera Magna SM-93144, 1975; Felipe Hall, piano; (2) Desto DC-7102/3, ca. 1971; Natalie Hinderas, piano; (3) New Records NRLP-105, ca. 1950; Gordon Manley, piano; (4) Opus One 39 (ca. 1978); Ruth Norman, piano (contains No. 2 only); (5) Orion ORS-7152, 1971; Louis Kaufman, piano; Annette Kaufman, piano (contains No. 2 only).

Swanson, Howard. CONCERTO FOR ORCHESTRA (ca. 1957). Recording: The Long Quest, Silhouettes in Courage SIL-K5001/5002; Budapest Philharmonic Orchestra; Benjamin Steinberg, conductor.

---. NIGHT MUSIC (1950). Recording: (1) Decca UAT-273045; New York Ensemble of the Philharmonic Scholarship Winners; Dimitri Mitropoulous, conductor; (2) Decca DL-3215; (3) Brunswick AXTL-1054; New York Ensemble of the Philharmonic Winners; Dimitri Mitropoulous, conductor.

---. SHORT SYMPHONY (1948). Recording: (1) Composers Recordings Inc. CRI SD-254, 1969; Vienna State Opera Orchestra; Franz Litschauer; (2) American Recording Society ARS-116; American Recording Society Orchestra; Dean Dixon, conductor; (3) American Recording Society ARS-7; American Recording Society Orchestra; Dean Dixon, conductor; (4) Vanguard VRS-434; Vienna State Opera Orchestra; Franz Litschauer, conductor.

---. SUITE. Violoncello and piano. Recording: American Recording Society ARS-1; Carl Stern, violoncello; Abba Bogin, piano.

--- SUITE FOR VIOLONCELLO AND PIANO (1949). Recording: Society of Participating Artists SPA-54. ca. 1953; Carl Stern, violoncello; Abba Bogin, piano.

Tillis, Frederick Charles. MUSIC FOR ALTO FLUTE, CELLO, AND PIANO (1966). Recording: Eastern ERS-513, ca. 1973; Trio Pro Viva.

Walker, George. ADDRESS FOR ORCHESTRA (1959). Recording: Desto DC-7107, ca. 1971; Oakland Youth Orchestra; Robert Hughes, conductor.

---. CONCERTO FOR TROMBONE AND ORCHESTRA (1957). Recording: Columbia M-32783, 1974; Denis Wick trombone; London Symphony Orchestra; Paul Freeman, conductor.

---. AN EASTMAN OVERTURE (1983). Recording: Mercury 289-411 31-1, 1983; Eastman Philharmonia; David Effron, conductor.

---. LYRIC FOR STRINGS (1946). Recording: Columbia M-33433, 1975; London Symphony Orchestra; Paul Freeman, conductor.

---. VARIATIONS FOR ORCHESTRA (1971). Recording: Serenus SRS-12077, 1977; New York Philharmonic Orchestra; Paul Freeman, conductor.

White. Clarence Cameron. CONCERTO, Op. 63. Violin. Recording: Stark Recordings; Zimmer violin.

---. LEVEE DANCE. Recording: (1) Decca DL 5214; Jascha Heifetz, violin; Milton Kay, piano; (2) Brunswick AXL-2017; Jascha Heifetz.

---. NOBODY KNOWS THE TROUBLE I'VE SEEN. Recording: HMV DA-278, ca. 1971; Fritz Kreisler, violin.

White y Lafitte, José Silvestre de los Delores. CONCERTO IN F-SHARP MINOR (1864). Recording: Columbia M-33432, 1975; Aaron Rosand, violin; London Symphony Orchestra; Paul Freeman, conductor; edited by Paul Glass and Kermit Moore.

Wilson, Olly Woodrow. AKWAN (1972). Recording: Columbia M-33434, 1975; Richard Bunger. piano and electric piano; Baltimore Symphony Orchestra; Paul Freeman, conductor.

---. PIECE FOR FOUR (1966). Recording: CRI SD-264, ca. 1975; Robert Willoughby, flute; Gene Young, trumpet; Joseph Schwartz, piano; Bertram Turetzky, double bass.

Bibliography

Articles

1. Ardoin J. "A Black Composers Concert." American Musical Digest 1.5 (1970): 5-6. (Reprinted from The Dallas Morning News 31 Jan. 1970.)

2. Armond Marchant, Annie d. "Carlos Gomes, Great Brazilian Composer, July 11, 1836-July 11, 1936." Pan American Union Bulletin (Washington, D.C) 70 (1936): 767-776.

3. Beckner, Steve. "Composer and Teacher--Mrs. Undine Smith Moore." The Progress-Index (Petersburg, VA), 5 January 1975.

4. Blair, Gwenda. "Evening the Score." Daily News Magazine (28 September 1986): 2024. Interviews with Anthony, Christopher, and Thulani Davis on their collaboration "X," about the late civil rights leader Malcolm X.

5. Blesh. BPIM 3 (Spring/Fall 1975).

6. Clemons, J.G. "Classical Composer Primous Fountain, ed." Black Enterprise (July 1980): 24.

7. Davis, Peter. "Retrospective Concert Music by Dorothy Rudd Moore, performed by group and sung by Mrs. Moore." New York Times 25 February 1975: 28. Concert review.

8. De Lerma, Dominique-René, ed. AAMOA Reports 7.2,3 (March/June 1975).

9. ---. "Black Composers in Europe." Black Music Research Journal 10.2 (Fall 1990): 275-334.

10. ---. "A Concordance of Scores and Recordings of Music by Black Composers." Black Music Research Journal 1984: 22-59.

11. ---. "The Chevalier de Saint-Georges." The Black Perspective in Music 1.1 (Spring 1976): 18-19.

12. ---. "Violinist Jose White in Paris, 1855-1875." Black Music Research Journal 10.2 (Fall 1990): 113-232.

13. "Dr. Paul Freeman Is to Symphony Music What Jackie Robinson Was to Baseball." Sepia April 1968.

14. Freeman, Paul. "Black Symphonic Music Will Now Be Heard." Symphony News 24.6 (1973-74): 7-10.

15. Harris, Carl G. "The Unique World of Undine Smith Moore." The Choral Journal 16 (January 1975): 6-7.

16. Henahan, Donal. "Conductor Brings to Light Blacks' Symphonic Works." New York Times 8 May 1974: 39.

17. Hillman, Betty. "In Retrospect: Edmund Thorton Jenkins, American Composer: At Home Abroad." The Black Perspective in Music 14.3 (Spring 1986): 143-180.

18. Hunt, J. "Conversation with Thomas J. Anderson: Blacks and the Classics." The Black Perspective in Music 1.2 (Fall 1973): 156-65.

19. Johnson, Marjorie S. "Noah Francis Ryder: Composer and Educator." The Black Perspective in Music (Spring 1978): 18-31.

20. Johnson, Tom. "Music: Talib Rasul Hakim Has Found His Music." Village Voice 20 February 1978: 80.

21. Kerner, Leighton. "The Overhaul of 'X.'" Village Voice 21 October 1986: 78.

22. Mandell, Howard. "Caught: X (The Life and Times of Malcolm X) New York City Opera/New York." Down Beat January 1987: 50.

23. Owens, Jimmy. "Billy Taylor: American Jazz Master." Jazz Educators Journal 23.2 (Winter 1991).

24. Peterson, B.L. "Shirley Graham DuBois: Composer and Playwright." The Crisis (May 1977): 177-79.

25. Piccarella, John. "Malcolm in Midtown: The Terrain of Recent Black, American History Shifts Beneath X's Operatic Conventions." Village Voice 21 October 1986: 77-78.

26. Revista Brasileira de Musica 3 (1936). Antônio Carlos Gomes Centenary issue.

27. Rockwell, John. "Malcolm X--Hero to Some, Racist to Others--Is Now the Stuff of Opera." New York Times 28 September 1986: 2.1, 21.

28. Rowes, B. "For Composer Anthony Davis, X Marks the Premiere of What May Be the First Major Black Opera." People 6 October 1986: 129-30.

29. Schneider, Steve. "Cable TV Notes: Series Explores Contemporary Composers and Choreographers." New York Times 21 September 1986: 2. Short notice on video profile of Anthony Davis' opera "X (The Life and Times of Malcolm X)."

30. Sears, Ann. "John William 'Blind' Boone, Pianist-Composer: Merit, Not Sympathy, Wins." Black Music Research Journal 9.2 (Fall 1989): 225-47.

31. Seligman, G. "The Road to X." Opera News September 1986: 28-30.

32. Sims, D. Maxine. "An Analysis and Comparisosn of Piano Sonatas by George Walker and Howard Swanson." The Black Perspective in Music 4 (Spring 1976): 70-81.

33. Southern, Eileen. "America's Black Composers of Classical Music." Music Educators Journal 62 (November 1975): 46-59.

34. Sullivan, Lester. "Composers of Color of Nineteenth-Century New Orleans: The History Behind the Music." Black Music Research Journal 8.1 (1988): 51-82.

35. Trythall, Gilbert. "T.J. Anderson." BMI: The Many Worlds of Music April 1969: 17.

36. White, Clarence Cameron. "Antônio Carlos Gomes." Negro History Bulletin 4.5 (February 1941): 104, 110.

37. Wilson, Olly. "Wendell Logan: Proportions." Perspectives in New Music 1970: 135-42.

38. Wright, J.R.B. "George Polgreen Bridgetower: An African Prodigy in England 1788-1799." Musical Quarterly (January 1980): 65-82.

39. "X." New Yorker 28 October 1985: 83+. On the Philadelphia production of "X (The Life and Times of Malcolm X)."

40. Yuhasz, Sister Mary Joy. "Black Composers and Their Piano Music, Part I." The American Music Teacher 19 (February/March 1970): 24+.

Books

41. Abdul, Raoul. Blacks in Classical Music: A Personal History. New York: Dodd, Mead & Co., 1977.

42. ---. Famous Black Entertainers of Today. New York: Dodd, Mead & Co., 1974.

43. Adams, Russell L. Great Negros, Past and Present. 3rd ed. Chicago: Afro-Am Publishing Co., 1969.

44. Allison, Roland. "Burleigh, Harry [Henry] T(hacker)." The New Grove Dictionary of American Music, vol. 1.

45. Ammer, Christine. Unsung: A History of Women in American Music. Westport, CT: Greenwood Press, 1980.

46. Anderson, E. Ruth, comp. Contemporary American Composers: A Biographical Dictionary. Boston: G.K. Hall, 1982.

47. Baker's Biographical Dictionary of Musicians. 6th ed. Revised edi-
    tion by Nicolas Slonimsky. New York: Schirmer Books, 1984.

48. Baker, David, Lida M. Belt, and Herman C. Hudson. The Black Composer
    Speaks. Metuchen, NJ: Scarecrow Press, 1978.

49. Banfield, Stephen. "Coleridge-Taylor, Samuel." The New Grove Dic-
    tionary of Music and Musicians. Ed. Stanley Sadie. 20 vols. London:
    Macmillan Publishers, 1980. 4:528-30.

50. Baron, John, comp. Piano Music from New Orleans, 1851-1898.   New
    York: Da Capo Press, 1980.

51. Beliague, Gerard. "Gomes, (Antonio) Carlos." The New Grove Diction-
    ary of Music and Musicians. Ed. Stanley Sadie. 20 vols. London:
    Macmillan Publishers, 1980. 7:517-518.

52. Berry, Lemuel. Biographical Dictionary of Black Musicians and Music
    Educators. (sl.1): Educational Book Publishers, 1978.

53. Bonds, Margaret. "Reminiscence." The Negro in Music and Art.   Ed.
    Lindsay Patterson. New York: Publishers Company, Inc., 1968.   190-
    193.

54. "Bridgetower, George Augustus Polgreen." The Dictionary of National
    Biography. London: Oxford University Press, 1917. 2:1231-32.

55. Brito, J. Carlos Gomes. Rio de Jeneiro, 1956.

56. Brook, Barry S. La Symphonie Française dans la séconde Moitié du
    XVIIIe Siècle. Paris: Institut de Musicologie de l'Universite de
    Paris, 1962. 3 vols. [Brooks' documented biography, 1:375-386; Cata-
    log of Works, 2:641-49; a transcription of the Symphonie Concertante
    in G, Catalog No. 10 (1782) for strings with two solo violins, 3:147-
    69).

57. ---. "Saint-Georges, Joseph Boulogne, Chevalier de." Die Musik in
    Geschichte und Gegenwart, Vol. XI (Kassel: Bärenreiter-Ver. 1963)
    Col. 1253.

58. Brown, Rae Linda. Music, Printed and Manuscript, in the James Weldon
    Johnson Memorial Collection of Negro Arts and Letters: An Annotated
    Catalog. New York: Garland Pub., 1982.

59. "Burleigh, Harry Thacker." Dictionary Catalogue of the Schomburg
    Collection. 2:1121-24. Containes an extensive list of Burleigh
    scores held by the Schomburg.

60. Carter, Madison H. An Annotated Catalogue of Composers of African
    Ancestry. New York: Vantage Press, 1986.

61. Child, Harold Hannyngton. "Coleridge-Taylor, Samuel." The Dictionary
    of National Biography: Twentieth Century 1912-21. Ed. H.W.C. Davis
    and J.R.H. Weaver. London: Oxford University Press, 1927. 122-23.

62. Christian, Marcus B. "Dede, Edmund." Dictionary of American Negro Biography. Ed. Rayford W. Logan and Michael R. Winston. New York: W.W. Norton, 1982. 168-69.

63. Claghorn, Charles Eugene. Biographical Dictionary of American Music. New York: Parker Publishing Co., 1973.

64. Cohen, Aaron I. International Encyclopedia of Women Composers. New York: R.R. Browker, 1981.

65. Coleridge-Taylor, Avril Gwendolyn. The Heritage of Samuel Coleridge-Taylor. London: Dobson, 1979.

66. Cooper, David Edwin. International Bibliography of Discographies: Classical Music and Jazz and Blues, 1962-72: A Reference Book for Record Collectors, Dealers, and Libraries. Littleton, CO: Libraries Unlimited, 1975.

67. Davis, Russell H. Blacks in Cleveland. Washington, D.C.: Associated Publishers, 1972.

68. De Lerma, Dominique-René. Bibliography of Black Music. Westport, CT: Greenwood Press, 1981.

69. ---. The Black American Musical Heritage: A Preliminary Bibliography. (n.p.): Music Library Association, 1969.

70. ---. Black Concert and Recital Music: A Provisional Repertoire List. Bloomington, IN: Afro-American Music Opportunities Association, 1975.

71. --- and Marsha J. Reisser. Black Music and Musicians in the New Grove Dictionary of American Music and the New Harvard Dictionary of Music. Chicago: Center for Black Music Research, Columbia College, 1989.

72. ---. Concert Music and Spirituals: A Selective Discography. Nashville, TN: Institute for Research in Black American Music, Fisk University, 1981.

73. ---. A Discography of Concert Music by Black Composers. Minneapolis, MN: AAMOA Press, 1973.

74. ---. "Freeman, Paul Douglas." The New Grove Dictionary of American Music. 2:167.

75. ---. A Name List of Black Composers. Minneapolis, MN: AAMOA Press, 1973.

76. ---. "Schuyler, Phillippa Duke." The New Grove Dictionary of American Music. 4:170-71.

77. Derr, Ellwood. "Saint-Georges, Joseph Boulogne, Chevalier de." The New Grove Dictionary of Music and Musicians. Ed. Stanley Sadie. 20 vols. London: Macmillan Publishers, 1980. 16:391-92.

78. Desdunes, Rodolphe. Our People and Our History. Trans. Dorothea Olga McCants. Baton Rouge, LA: State University Press, 1973. (Originally published as Nos Hommes et Notre Histoire. Montreal, 1911.)

79. Detroit Public Library. Catalog of the E. Azalia Hackley Memorial Collection of Negro Music, Dance and Drama: Detroit Public Library. Boston, MA: G.K. Hall, 1979.

80. Ewen, David. "Samuel Coleridge-Taylor 1875-1912." Composers Since 1900. New York: H.W. Wilson Co., 1969. 132-34.

81. Faurot, Albert. Concert Piano Repertoire. Metuchen, NJ: Scarecrow Press, 1973.

82. Fax, Elton C. "Burleigh, Harry T[hacker]." Dictionary of American Negro Biography. Ed. Rayford W. Logan and Michael R. Winston. New York: W.W. Norton, 1982.

83. Floyd, Samuel A. and Marsha J. Reisser. Black Music Biography: An Annotated Bibliography. White Plains, NY: Kraus International Publications, 1987.

84. Gammond, Peter. Scott Joplin and the Ragtime Era. New York, 1975.

85. "Gomes, Antônio Carlos." Encyclopedia of Latin America. Ed. Helen Delpar. New York: McGraw Hill, 1974. 252.

86. Gordon, E. Harrison. Black Classical Musicians of the Twentieth Century. New York: MSS Information Corp., 1977.

87. "Graham, Shirley." Current Biography 1946. 221-22.

88. Gray, John, comp. Blacks in Classical Music: A Bibliographical Guide to Composers, Performers, and Ensembles. Westport, CT: Greenwood Press, 1988.

89. Green, Jeffrey. Edmund Thorton Jenkins: The Life and Times of an American Black Composer, 1894-1926. Westport, CT: Greenwood Press, 1982.

90. Green, Mildred Denby. Black Women Composers: A Genesis. Boston, MA: Twayne Publishers, 1983.

91. Groves, George. "Bridgetower, George (Augustus) Polgreen." The New Grove Dictionary of Music and Musicians. Ed. Stanley Sadie. 20 vols. London: Macmillan Publishers, 1980. 3:281-82.

92. Haas, Robert B., ed. William Grant Still. Los Angeles, CA: Black Sparrow, 1972.

93. Hare, Maud Cuney. Negro Musicians and Their Music. New York: Da Capo Press, 1974. (reprint of 1936 ed.)

94. Haskin, James. Scott Joplin and the Ragtime Era. New York: 1978.

95. Hildreth. John. "Keyboard Works of Selected Black Composers." Dissertation (Ph.D.), Northwestern University, 1978.

96. Hitchcock, H. Wiley and Stanley Sadie, eds. New Grove Dictionary of American Music. 4 vols. New York: Macmillan Press, Ltd., 1986.

97. Holly, Ellistine, comp. Biographies of Black Composers. Dubuque, IA:
     Wm. C. Brown Publishers, 1990.

98. Horne, Aaron. "Orchestra Works by Black Composers: A Compilation
     from Selected Sources." Black Composers, Black Performers, and the
     Symphony Orchestra. Chicago: Center for Black Music Research, Colum-
     bia College-Chicago, 1988.

99. ---. Woodwind Music of Black Composers. Westport, CT: Greenwood
     Press, 1990.

100. Howard University Library. Dictionary Catalog of the Arthur B. Spin-
     garn Collection of Negro Authors. Boston, MA: G.K. Hall, 1970.

101. Jackson, Barbara Garvey. "Bonds, Margaret (Allison)." New Grove
     Dictionary of American Music. 1:255-56.

102. Jacobi, Hugh William. Contemporary American Composers Based at Ameri-
     can Colleges and Universities. Paradise, CA: Paradise Arts, 1975.

103. Johnson, James P. Bibliographic Guide to the Study of Afro-American
     Music. Washington, D.C.: Howard University Library, 1973.

104. Johnson, Marjorie S. "Noah Francis Ryder (1914-1964): A Study of His
     Life, Works, and Contributions to Music Education." Thesis (M.A.),
     Catholic University, 1968.

105. Jones, Velma. "The Life and Works of Mark Oakland Fax." Thesis
     (M.A.), Morgan State University, 1978.

106. Lovingood, Penman. Famous Modern Negro Musicians. 2nd ed. New York:
     Da Capo Press, 1978. (reprint of 1921 ed.)

107. Malone, M.H. "William Levi Dawson: American Music Educator." Dis-
     sertation (Ph.D.), Florida State University, 1981.

108. McBrier, Vivian. The Life and Works of R. Nathaniel Dett. Washing-
     ton, D.C.: Associated Publishers, 1977.

109. McGinty, Doris Evans. "Ryder, Noah Francis." New Grove Dictionary of
     American Music. 4:115.

110. Meadows, Eddie S. Theses and Dissertations on Black American Music.
     Beverly Hills, CA: T. Front Musical Literature, 1980.

111. Moorland-Spingarn Research Center. The Glen Carrington Collection: A
     Guide to the Books, Manuscripts, Music, and Recordings. Compiled by
     Karen L. Jefferson, assisted by Brigette M. Rouson. Washington, D.C.:
     Howard University, 1977.

112. Reed, Addison. "The Life and Work of Scott Joplin." Dissertation
     (Ph.D.), University of North Carolina, 1973.

113. Roach, Hildred. Black American Composers: Past and Present. 2 vols.
     Miami: Krieger Publishing Co., Inc., 1985.

114. Robinson, Wilhelmena S. Historical Afro-American Biographies (International Library of Afro-American Life and History). Washington, D.C.: Associated Publishers, 1976.

115. Rogers, J.A. "Carlos Gomes: First Great Operatic Composer of the New World." World's Great Men of Color. New York: Macmillan, 1972. 2:200-02.

116. Rosenberg, Deena, and Bernard Rosenberg. "Kermit Moore, Freelance Cellist." Music Makers. New York: Columbia University Press, 1979. 277-88.

117. Sadie, Stanley, ed. The New Grove Dictionary of Music and Musicians. 20 vols. London: Macmillan Publishers, 1980.

118. "Sancho, Ignatius." The Dictionary of National Biography. 17:732-33.

119. Sayers, William C. Berwick. Samuel Coleridge-Taylor, Musician: His Life and Letters. Arlington Heights, IL: Metro Books, 1969. (reprint of 1915 ed.)

120. Scobie, Edward. Black Brittainia: A History of Blacks in Britain. Chicago: Johnson Publishing Co., 1972.

121. Skowronski, JoAnn. Black Music in America: A Bibliography. Metuchen, NJ: Scarecrow Press, 1981.

122. Southern, Eileen. Biographical Dictionary of Afro-American and African Musicians. Westport, CT: Greenwood Press, 1982.

123. ---. "Burleigh, Harry [Henry] T(hacker)." New Grove Dictionary of American Music. 3:421-22.

124. ---. "Cunningham, Arthur." New Grove Dictionary of American Music. 1:555.

125. ---. "Dawson, William Levi." New Grove Dictionary of American Music. 1:590.

126. ---. "Dawson, William Levi." The New Grove Dictionary of Music and Musicians. Ed. Stanley Sadie. 20 vols. London: Macmillan Publishers, 1980. 5:286.

127. ---. The Music of Black Americans: A History. 2nd ed. New York: W.W. Norton, 1983.

128. Spady, James G., ed. William Dawson: A UMUM Tribute and a Marvelous Journey. Philadelphia, PA: Creative Artists Workshop, 1981.

129. Spencer, Jon Michael. As The Black School Sings: Black Music Collections at Black Universities and Colleges with a Union List of Book Holdings. New York: Greenwood Press, 1987.

130. Thomas, Andre Jerome. "A Study of the Selected Masses of Twentieth-Century Black Composers: Margaret Bonds, Robert Ray, George Walker, and David Baker." Dissertation (D.M.A.), University of Illinois at Urbana-Champaign, 1983.

131. Tischler, Alice. Fifteen Black American Composers: A Bibliography of Their Works. Detroit: Information Coordinators, 1981.

132. Tortolano, William. Samuel Coleridge-Taylor: Anglo-Black Composer 1875-1912. Metuchen, NJ: Scarecrow Press, 1977.

133. Trotter, James M. Music and Some Highly Musical People. Chicago: Afro-Am Press, 1969. (reprint of 1878 ed.)

134. Turner, Patricia. Afro-American Singers: An Index and Preliminary Discography of Long-Playing Recordings of Opera, Choral Music, and Song. Minneapolis, MN: Turner, 1976.

135. Uzoigwe, Joshua. "Akin Euba, An Introduction to the Life and Music of a Nigerian Composer." Thesis (M.A.), Queen's University at Belfast, Ireland, 1978.

136. White, Evelyn Davidson. Choral Music by Afro-American Composers: A Selected Annotated Bibliography. Metuchen, NJ: Scarecrow Press, 1981.

137. Williams, Ora. American Black Women in the Arts and Social Sciences. Metuchen, NJ: Scarecrow Press, 1973.

138. Wright, Josephine. Ignatius Sancho (1729-1780): An Early African Composer in England. The Collected Editions of His Music in Facsimile. New York: Garland Publishing, 1981.

About the Compiler

AARON HORNE is Professor of Music at Northeastern Illinois University as well as a lecturer with the African American Studies program at Northwestern University. Among his earlier publications is *Woodwind Music of Black Composers* (Greenwood, 1990).